# CONTEMPORARY ISSUES IN SOUTH ASIA

*Documents*

# CONTEMPORARY ISSUES IN SOUTH ASIA

*Documents*

*Editor*
Medha Bisht

Institute for Defence Studies and Analyses
New Delhi

SHIPRA

ISBN: 978-81-7541-499-0

First Published in India in 2009

*Contemporary Issues in South Asia*



*Published by*:
SHIPRA PUBLICATIONS
115-A, Vikas Marg, Shakarpur
Delhi - 110092 (India)
Ph.: 91-11-65277210, 22500954; Fax: 22458662
Email: info@shiprapublications.com
www.shiprapublications.com

# FOREWORD

South Asia is in the midst of profound socio-economic and political change. The year 2008 was a milestone in the history of South Asia as several countries held elections and democracy found roots in all of them. Elections took place during the year in Bangladesh, Bhutan, Pakistan, Nepal and Maldives. The advance of democracy in South Asia is a positive development giving rise to reasonable expectations that the people of South Asia through their democratically elected governments will be able to embark on a journey towards peace, development and prosperity.

The hope of a peaceful future, however, needs, to be tempered with the knowledge that South Asia remains vulnerable to terrorism, ethnic conflict, poverty and numerous other problems. Thus, the intensification of Taliban insurgency in Afghanistan and the intensification of ethnic conflict in Sri Lanka during the year served to remind that the journey forward will not be easy. The expansion of Taliban influence in parts of Pakistan was a matter of great concern. The terrorist attacks in Mumbai in November raised India-Pakistan tensions and reminded how fragile peace in this sub continent can be. In addition, the global economic slowdown, rise in food prices and the upsurge of terrorist activities in this sub continent were some of the major challenges faced by the people in South Asia.

One way to understand and analyse the developments in South Asia is through primary sources. The present compilation brings together a range of documents pertaining to the developments in the region during 2007 and 2008. Divided in eight sections, the book has documents on Afghanistan, Bangladesh, Bhutan, Maldives, Nepal, Pakistan, Sri Lanka and SAARC as well as BIMSTEC. Each section includes documents pertaining to that country's relations with India. The compilation also includes speeches and interviews given by the Indian leaders on relations with different countries.

It is hoped that the compilation will benefit scholars, diplomats, policy makers and students of South Asia.

The book is a collective effort of the members of the IDSA's South Asia cluster who compiled the various documents in accordance with their expertise: Mr. Vishal Chandra – Afghanistan, Dr Nihar Nayak – Nepal; Ms Sumita Kumar – Pakistan; Dr Anand Kumar – Bhutan; Dr Sreeradha Datta – Bangladesh; Dr Mayilvagagan – Sri Lanka; and Capt Alok Bansal and Ms Medha Bisht – Maldives. Special thanks to Dr Smruti Pattanaik for her valuable suggestions.

March 2009

**Arvind Gupta**
Lal Bahadur Shastri Chair, IDSA
New Delhi

# CONTENTS

## PAKISTAN



## SRI LANKA



## SAARC AND BIMSTEC

# AFGHANISTAN

# 1.

## CORRUPTION IN AFGHANISTAN[1]

*December 18, 2008*

*President Karzai at the International Anti-Corruption Day at Kabul stated that corruption in Afghanistan is a reality. He emphasized that strict judicial action against corrupt officials is the only way towards winning the trust of the people. He suggested that simplifying administrative procedures and rules and regulations and making sure that the law serves the people would help curb corruption in the government and gain the trust of the Afghan people. Emphasizing that a combined effort was needed by all sections of the society to combat the menace of corruption, he pointed out that corruption in foreign aid and manipulation of media for vested interests was another factor for the downfall of Afghan society. The President stated that coordination between foreigners and building the capacities of Afghan people was needed as an antidote to corruption and the only way to strengthen the government of Afghanistan was to strengthen laws and implement them objectively, without discrimination.*

None of the foreign countries that chant anti-corruption slogans and the slogans of high sincerity are here. Only a few of them are here. Do we have the representatives from these countries? Who is here to represent the US? Anyone from the US?

Nobody from the USA? Right. I know Ambassador Dell, he is not here. I know Ambassador Wood, he is not here.

What about the British? Anyone from Britain? We will see today. Two of them are sitting at the back but we do not know them. What about Germany? Anybody from Germany there? Good, OK. Canada? Nobody from Canada? What about France, Italy and others? Kai Eide is here. I thank Kai Eide. He has come and is sitting here. I am sure he will cooperate with us. I will discuss this issue [the absence of some countries] with the foreigners when I meet them. They are not present on an important day,

1. Speech by President Hamid Karzai on Anti Corruption Day at Kabul, December 18, 2008.

when Afghanistan holds a gathering to eliminate administrative corruption and to improve our administration. They come to us and give us lectures about it every day but they do not come here.

Not many of our own ministers, cabinet members and MPs are here. I am sure they were invited. We will see which one of the ministers is here. The esteemed Minister of Public Health is here. His ministry does a good job. The Minister of Agriculture is also here. His ministry does a good job too. The minister of Culture is here to give detailed reports to the people about today's gathering. The Minister of Public works is here. Some other brothers are also here. Chief of the Civil Service Commission is here. The esteemed Minister of women's affairs is also here. Welcome.

Anyway, as Mr. Osmani said the existence of administrative corruption in Afghanistan, in its administration, in the system, in the government, in its economy, in politics and in the media is a reality. It is an extremely annoying truth that has harmed our body and has defamed our country.

Corruption exists anywhere in the world. It even exists in very developed countries. We heard some days ago that the governor of one of the US States wanted to sell a Senate seat.

But that is not our business. It is their business. We should not use corruption in other places as excuses to justify ourselves. There is corruption in our country and it should be eliminated. It is not our business whether or not there is corruption in other countries. It cannot be an excuse for us.

Corruption in our country and government has both internal and external causes. We will speak a little bit about the external factors, but the main debate should focus on the factors that lie in our own society.

We cannot reform others unless we reform ourselves first. We cannot point the finger at foreigners and their corruption here if we can not reform ourselves.

I saw your documentary. Everything shown in the documentary is right.

I meet people from different parts of Afghanistan every day. Every day - with no exceptions - the people of Afghanistan come to me for other problems, but at the same time complain about corruption in the Afghan government and the administration.

They complain about corruption in government departments, corruption in the country's politics, in the politicians, foreign inclinations that lead to corruption among the country's politicians and corruption in the country's economy and business.

Our traders and the government should be equally blamed for corruption. It is a give-and-take deal.

We also have foreign interference and influence on our country's media and press. The Constitution of Afghanistan grants freedom to our media.

The current trend and our behavior give them freedom. My own nature as the president of Afghanistan is in favor of the freedom of the media.

But our media sources are not independent. This means there is very high foreign influence on our media. They are built with foreign money. They are unfortunately funded by foreigners. I do not mean all of them. It should be clear. I do not mean all of them. Some of them are exploited. There are many examples.

Despite all this, I have remained tolerant to help strengthen the media in our country because it is the media sources and their role in investigating and overseeing activities of the government that can help prevent the increase of corruption and that can make officials be cautious about it. We however support the media.

Corruption exists in all spheres of the government of Afghanistan. I am talking about [low-ranking] civil servants in the government of Afghanistan. I mean civil servants. I do not mean senior officials. I do not mean heads of departments, deputy ministers and others. I am talking about civil servants.

I do blame the civil servant who takes 1,000, 2,000 or 3,000 Afghanis [20, 40 or 60 dollars] as bribe. It is bad and I believe they are guilty, but I do not focus on it very much. Please pay attention to what I say dear brothers from the media. Reflect it the right way. Do not reflect it the other way round.

I blame corruption by a civil servant who receives a monthly salary of 5,000 or 6,000 Afghanis [100 to 120 dollars]. It is bad. I consider them guilty. But I do not focus on civil servants today.

Instead, we need to disclose to media cases of corruption by those who receive salaries in dollars. We have many of them in the government. We should focus on those who make high amounts of money and hold senior posts in the government of Afghanistan, but are still involved in corruption.

I have been hearing about corruption in the government of Afghanistan for a long time, but I didn't get the chance to catch anyone. But over the past one or one and half year, we have fortunately developed the capability to know about it [corruption] to some extent and to take measures.

Have these measures been sufficient and have these measures helped curb corruption in the government of Afghanistan? Not at all.

Even if we increase our efforts a thousand times higher, it will still not be enough.

Mr. Baha is here to represent the Supreme Court and the esteemed Attorney General has the most important duties in this. They enjoy my full support and the complete support of the people of Afghanistan.

Four major cases of corruption have been identified over the past two months and the perpetrators, serving in very senior government posts, have been dismissed. They included people at the level of minister, deputy minister, governor and head of department. The esteemed Chief Justice and Attorney General know about it.

We can prove to the people of Afghanistan that we are serious [in fighting corruption] only when they [those arrested on corruption charges] are taken to court and only when they are punished.

A mere dismissal of the officials is not enough. They should be legally prosecuted as well.

Mr Osmani, as you mentioned in your remarks, there are many problems in our administrative procedures, rules and regulations and laws. All this has led to corruption in the government of Afghanistan.

You have been working on this for the past two years. You spoke about the traffic department today. The continuation of your activities will undoubtedly ensure easy administrative procedures in the administration.

Corruption undoubtedly exists in any government department where you need 35 signatures and three months time to obtain driving license or registration documents for a vehicle. So, it is impossible to rule out corruption in such a department.

But the level of corruption can be low in a department where you can get things done with one or two signatures and in one or two days. It is difficult to be involved in corruption in such a department.

Simplifying administrative procedures and rules and regulations and making sure that our laws serve our people and make things easier will help curb corruption in the government and in our activities.

Developed societies have made progress by using and simplifying their laws and by removing complicated procedures. They have simplified administrative procedures and rules and regulations in their departments. This is what we should also do with our administration.

The other issue is about our politics and politicians.

A disaster Afghanistan has been suffering from for the past 30 years is the mental dependence on foreigners. Our mental captivity and our expectations of foreigners are the other problems about which I have spoken several times in the past and do not repeat it again today.

We also have problems in our economy, our practices and the lack of capability in our administration to prevent the points that you [Mr. Osmani!] mentioned. This once again depends on our laws and rules and regulations.

I know that Mr. Osmani, the Attorney General and other departments of the government have done all in their power to address the problem. I know you have been making efforts for the past three years.

Let's focus even more on our own problems, I mean the problems of our people and our Afghanistan.

The question is: Have the 30 years of war, disaster, foreign interferences and our destitution negatively affected us? The answer is unfortunately YES. Our emigration to foreign countries has also been a problem.

I have come to know now as I have said in the past, that our jihad has been very right, but our emigration has been a big mistake. Our migration abroad was an extremely big mistake. Afghanistan is still paying the price for our migration and it will have to pay the price for many more years.

Our emigration to the neighboring countries took away from us our pride and very desirable traditions and culture of self-confidence. It forced us to ask foreigners for a piece of bread. We went to refugee commissionaires and many others to ask them for help. Almost 30 or 35 percent of the people of Afghanistan took refuge outside.

The other wave of our emigration was the migration of our educated people to Europe and America, that weakened the working and intellectual capability of our society.

They have lived there for 30 years and have now grown older. Their children are there and have lived abroad all their life. They may not return.

We consider it bad, but not as bad as something that deserves punishment.

I have repeatedly faced cases of corruption and crimes in the past seven years of my government, including the past one month.

Our people, elders, scholars and tribal leaders have all been coming to me asking me to release them [criminals]. They come and ask me to release a prisoner assuring me that he will not commit the act again.

This is one of our big faults. It has happened throughout Afghanistan. People from all over Afghanistan have come to me.

People come and ask me to release terrorists and others [criminals]. If they come and ask me to release terrorists, it is of course easy for them to come and ask me to release those involved in bribery and corruption.

I hope we, as a nation, can get rid of this culture and do not mediate for the release of a criminal or corrupt person. We should instead ask for their punishment.

In one hand, we criticize corruption in the government, our media criticize and people criticize corruption, on the other hand, they [people] come and ask me to release them.

Twenty, 30, 40 or 50 people come and ask us to forget what has happened and release the person, assuring us that it will not be a problem.

They have realized the trick and know that I quickly accept what my people say.

We should start reforms from ourselves. This is our problem. This is our social problem and we should address it.

I do not say our traders or private investors should not do business and earn money. They should earn even thousands and millions of times higher than what they earn now. It is good for Afghanistan if our traders, investors and industrialists grow richer because the money will help create employment in our own country and will make our country rich. However, it is a big national crime if the traders and investors earn the money by importing outdated and low-quality medicines.

This leads to the death of our innocent people, especially in rural areas and villages, where people in the rural areas cannot read and identify the right medicines. It even happens in our cities and among our educated people.

Mr. Osmani and esteemed minister of public health! It is a very important issue and I know you are cautious about it and have been working on it for the past three or four years.

The same applies with low-quality foodstuffs. I hope our national traders, private investors and businessmen earn even more money, and I know they sometimes sell at higher prices which we still buy without complaining. But they should import high-quality goods. If not, then they should not complain.

We discuss this issue every day and in every cabinet meeting. We discuss it in every cabinet meeting.

Fuel prices fallen all over the world, falling from 150 to 40 dollars last night. But they are still the same in Afghanistan.

When prices were high, they [traders] increased the fuel prices even though they had bought fuel at a low price. Now prices have fallen, they say they bought their fuel at high prices and that is why they do not want to sell it more cheaply.

Our ministries are also not able to lower prices. I do not know why. I do not know whether it is because of corruption or their weakness or whether it is because of the inability of the government to implement its decisions.

There are many such issues in our country. We are unfortunately faced with problems of corruption in all spheres of life.

And these problems exist within the government, the National Assembly and the judiciary. We have corruption in all three branches of authority.

In the economy, we have problems in business and investment. In politics, we have problems with parties and politicians and foreign influence on them is fatal to us. We also have problems with our media sources.

This is a widespread problem in our country. The media cannot address its problems on its own. The government cannot introduce reforms in its departments on its own. Our economy sector cannot be reformed on its own. This applies to our politicians as well.

We should all make a big national decision if we rally want to live in this country, on our soil - Afghan soil.

Some days ago, I was watching a song [Dari: Ahang] on TV. I do not remember the name of the channel. We call it [the song] "baid". It was a very nice song. An Afghan refugee child - I do not know where he lives, maybe in France, Canada, America or somewhere else - sings a very good song about the country he lives in. In the song, she says it is a very beautiful place {the country she is seeking refuge in} but not her country. It is a very nice song.

Even though it is a poor country suffering from different problems, it is still our country and our soil. Those who go and live in America should try to reform America. Afghans who do not want to live here and want to live in America and Europe, will naturally not care about us very much.

We, the people who want to live on our own soil - in Kabul, Panjsher, Logar, Parwan, Gardez, Sharan, Kandahar, Bamian, Konar, Daikondi, Herat, Badghis, Fariab, Balkh, Badakhshan, Nimroz, Pamir and any other corner of Afghanistan- and if we want children to be born and brought up here, if we want to be buried here and if we want our children to grow up and live here and, we should make sure that we have a good, peaceful and prosperous land.

We should have everything. We should make sure our children and families live with confidence. All this is possible when we have laws and implement them on ourselves and only when we have laws that make our life easy. Corruption, bribery, looting, robbery and treason to this soil will never give us the opportunity to live in our soil with the hopes that we have.

With the existence of these problems, our sons will be forced to go to Iran in search of employment and be expelled from Iran in cold weather or in summer. Or our young people will go to Pakistan every day to become Taliban fighters and will be sent against us with weapons. Or their mothers and fathers will try to send their sons and children to America or Europe so they can send them back dollars to make a living.

If we want to live on our own soil, we should know that this is our home and this is our life. Every human has the right to live in comfort, peace and prosperity. This is only possible in a lawful society with a strong and prosperous government. We can build such a government and system only when we all make joint efforts. One flower does not make a spring.

Today is the day for all of us, all Afghans, to promise and to join hands with Mr Osmani so he can eliminate the roots of corruption. We, including the president, the judicial power, prosecution office and the government should stand with him to put it into practice.

What do we need to do requires a strong governance. What is strong governance? It is a government established based on laws, implements the law and a government that enjoys legitimacy and does not discriminate anyone.

Today, poor people are put in prison while powerful people are free. Even elders of our country come to ask for the release of powerful people if they are imprisoned. No one comes to ask for the release of poor people. We do not even know about the fate and imprisonment of poor people.

Thousands of people are in prison and the president is not aware whether they are in prison rightly or wrongly. The government is not aware. This is a very big problem in this land.

So this highlights the need for good governance. I explained the internal obstacles that hinder the strengthening of the government.

The internal factors include corruption and the use of personal relations to get things done. You are aware of all of it.

Unfortunately, the current government of Afghanistan and maybe the past governments too, have faced foreign obstacles. I would briefly like to speak about foreign obstacles so our foreign friends know and help us address the foreign obstacles.

One of our sisters spoke about corruption in foreign contracts. That is completely true.

The year before last, a project was implemented with foreign funding in a province of Afghanistan. The project costed 60,000 dollars. I do not remember it was last year or the year before last. It was an ordinary project. It was contracted to someone else. The foreigner in charge of the project came and gave the contractor 40,000 dollars out of 60,000 dollars and told him not to ask about the remaining 20,000 dollars and simply leave. There have been several other cases of corruption in foreign aid and in the spending of foreign aid in our country.

We have several times shared this issue with foreigners. Government officials are aware of it. We have spoken to them very openly.

The second foreign obstacle in strengthening the government is their irresponsible activities in Afghanistan.

They irresponsible entering and search of people's homes is an act against the authority of the Afghan. The government of Afghanistan can never be strengthened if foreigners are given the right to enter our homes, detain our people, or worse than that, kill or martyr our people in their homes. This destroys the government of Afghanistan instead of strengthening it.

Foreign soldiers enter a house in my country, detain people and beat them up and even kill them. They did it in Khost Province yesterday. They have entered a house and martyred the husband, wife and their child and detained some others. How can the people of Afghanistan trust their government when it cannot defend them? How can this government eliminate corruption when it cannot even prevent the killing! of its people? The irresponsible detention and imprisonment of people is also a problem and there are several other cases.

Pajhwok News Agency has published a picture today. The picture shows a child bitten by a dog belonging to foreign troops. I have the picture.

We very much thank our foreign friends for their assistance, but they will not be able to strengthen the government of Afghanistan unless they respect the government and Afghanistan's laws. This will take Afghanistan and the world to the wrong direction. The war on terror will not succeed too.

We have taken measures in the past five to six years. The last effort we made was last month. We sent a detailed list of our requests to the government of America asking them to stop entering our homes and to stop bombarding our villages and irresponsibly detaining our people. They do not have the right to do it. It is the authority of the government of Afghanistan and our laws to do it. Let us see where the process of talks reaches.

It will be very difficult to ensure good governance in Afghanistan unless we address the internal factors, the shortcomings that we have whether they are within the government or the problems in our law or whether they are our national and social problems. We will not be able to have good governance unless foreign friends respect Afghanistan's laws, Afghanistan's families and Afghan traditions.

We will not be able to strengthen the government even if we spend billions of dollars unless we stop these activities. It is not possible.

I now come to another issue that we discussed and agreed on at the Paris Conference. It is the need for coordination of assistance between Afghanistan and the international community.

I thank Mr. Kai Eide, who is the UN special envoy, for coming here. He is in touch with the international community and Afghanistan with great sincerity and friendship. I hope the international community cooperates with him in their promises of coordination and I hope they support him. We, from the Afghan government side, have given him a blank cheque.

He can come, criticize us, speak to us and tell us openly about the shortcomings in our government. He can ask me about the shortcomings and tell us that we need to address them. We accept what he says. It is our responsibility to address shortcomings wherever they exist.

We should first address our own shortcomings. Then we can tell others about their shortcomings. We support him and thank him for his friendship. I hope the international community and Afghanistan further boost their cooperation and coordination with Kai Eide.

If this happens, if we dare to take more measures inside our country, if we take fundamental measures to address our own shortcomings, we will make new progress in all fields including governance, economy, politics and media. We will be able to reach a national agreement and contract that we will not help the bad guys, but will instead make sure the government does not release them. When the government takes serious measures to address the problems Mr Osmani mentioned, we will have good achievements.

The other issue, which is important but I do not want to focus on today because we should address our own problems first, is the need for better coordination between our foreign friends. They also need to review their contracts and sub-contracts. As our sister said, it also plays a big role in corruption in Afghanistan.

The other third very important question is our governance. The only way to strengthen the government of Afghanistan is to respect it and to respect Afghanistan's laws. The people of Afghanistan and their homes should be dealt with by the government of Afghanistan under Afghanistan's laws. Foreigners should not enter our homes. They should not search our homes and should not kill or detain our people in their homes.

I am firmly committed to achieving all this. If this happens, Afghanistan will have a strong government and then this soil will be the real soil about which our 11 or 12-year-old refugee young boy sings: Paris is a beautiful place, but not my place. It is a beautiful soil, but not my soil. When we do this and when we implement laws in this beautiful soil of Afghanistan, our country will be built and corruption will be eliminated. But if we do not do it, then our life will remain bad, poor and we will continue to live in poverty and we will continue to remain dependent on others. May God save us from that condition. May God bestow on us the ability to achieve our objective which is the dream of every son of Afghanistan: A strong, rich, self-sufficient, powerful and lawful Afghanistan.

(*Source*: http://www.president.gov.af/english/statements_press_ releases/181208_presidentkarzaispeaksco.mspx)

# 2.

# BILATERAL RELATIONS WITH INDIA

## Joint Statement on the Visit of President Hamid Karzai to India

January 12, 2009

*In a joint statement by President Hamid Karzai and Prime Minister Manmohan Singh, both countries called for full compliance with bilateral, multilateral and international obligations in order to prevent terrorism in any manner originating from territories under their control. The Indian premier promised Afghanistan 2,50,000 metric tonnes of wheat in order to cope with the food crises and highlighted that subsequent to the completion of the road from Zaranj to Delaram in South-Western Afghanistan, a second major infrastructure project, the Pul-e-Khumri to Kabul transmission line and the sub-station at Chimtala in northern Afghanistan, would be handed to the Government of Afghanistan*

1. At the invitation Dr. Manmohan Singh, Prime Minister of the Republic of India, His Excellency Mr. Hamid Karzai, President of the Islamic Republic of Afghanistan, is currently on a working visit to India.
2. President Karzai's visit to India is symbolic, to express Afghanistan's solidarity with the Government and people of India in the wake of the Mumbai terrorist attack. The deplorable incident shows that terrorism is a threat to the entire humanity.
3. The leaders called for the full compliance with bilateral, multilateral and international obligations of States to prevent terrorism in any manner originating from territories under their control since terrorism emanates from the sanctuaries and training camps and the sustenance and support received by the terrorist groups.
4. While reviewing their robust, strategic partnership, the two leaders expressed satisfaction at the progress in bilateral development and reconstruction projects in all parts of Afghanistan.
5. Prime Minister Dr. Singh conveyed to President Karzai that, following the completion of the road from Zaranj to Delaram in

South-western Afghanistan, a second major infrastructure project, the Pul-e-Khumri to Kabul transmission line and the sub-station at Chimtala in Northern Afghanistan, will be handed over shortly to the Government of Afghanistan. The leaders expressed their satisfaction that the construction of the Afghan Parliament, a symbol of the common commitment of both countries to pluralism and democracy, has also begun.

6. Prime Minister Dr. Singh further conveyed that in order to help the fraternal people of Afghanistan in tiding over their current food crisis, India will gift Afghanistan 250,000 metric tonnes of wheat. The shipment will be effected immediately, as soon as the Government of Afghanistan has worked out its transportation arrangements.
7. President Karzai invited Prime Minister Dr. Singh for a State Visit to Afghanistan. The invitation was accepted with pleasure. The dates will be finalised through diplomatic channels.
8. The two leaders reaffirmed the special relationship between India and Afghanistan, to build a strong, united, and prosperous Afghanistan and to work towards peace, stability and development of the entire region.

(*Source*: http://meaindia.nic.in/)

## Terrorism—A Challenge to South Asia[1]

November 27, 2008

*President Hamid Karzai condemned the Mumbai terror attacks (November 26, 2008), stating that terrorist are a challenge to the South Asian region and Afghanistan strongly stands with India, in the fight against terror. He emphasized the need for intensified regional cooperation and coordination in order to combat terrorism.*

President Hamid Karzai has condemned unreservedly today's attacks in the Indian city of Mumbai that according to reports have claimed over a hundred innocent lives.

Reports say coordinated and multiple terrorist attacks struck the heart of Mumbai, India's commercial capital, on Wednesday night, killing dozens in machine-gun and grenade assaults on at least two five-star hotels, the city's largest train station, a movie theater and a hospital.

"Today's attacks in Mumbai once again remind us of the brutality of the terrorists and the grave threat of terrorism that the entire humanity faces. Terrorists are especially challenging the south Asia", The President said, "Afghanistan stands solidly with India."

---

1. President Karzai Strongly Condemns Mumbai Attacks, November 27, 2008.

President Karzai stressed, "A vigorous response to counter these terrorist challenges requires an even more intensified regional cooperation and coordination in all aspects."

President Karzai expressed heartfelt condolences to the families of the victims and to the people of India, saying "We share and very well understand the sorrow of the Indian nation".

(*Source*: ttp://www.president.gov.af/english/statements_press_releases/271108_prescondemnsindiaattack.mspx)

## Karzai on Assam Bomb Blasts[2]

October 30, 2008

*President, Hamid Karzai, expressed solidarity with India, strongly condemning the blasts in the Indian state of Assam (October 30, 2008). He emphasized the need to root out terrorism from the region.*

H.E. Hamid Karzai, President of Islamic Republic of Afghanistan, strongly condemned today's bomb blasts in the Indian state of Assam which killed at least 60 people and injured hundreds more, calling it an act of terror.

A series of bomb blasts ripped through northwestern State of Assam in India. According to the latest reports, at least 18 blasts shook different cities of the Indian state of Assam killing around 60 people and injuring more than 300.

Grieved by the loss of innocent lives, President Karzai once again stressed the need for rooting out terrorism in the region.

On behalf of the Afghan people, President Karzai extends his sympathies and condolences to the government and people of India and the families of victims.

(*Source*:http://www.president.gov.af/english/statements_press_ releases/301008_precondemnsindiaterorat.mspx)

## Joint Statement during State Visit of President Hamid Karzai to India

August 4, 2008

*In the India-Afghanistan Joint Statement, the Indian government pledged an additional US $ 450 million to Afghanistan. It was also announced that the road from Zaranj to Delaram – had been completed and would be handed over to the Government of Afghanistan.*

1. At the invitation of His Excellency Dr. Manmohan Singh, Prime Minister of the Republic of India, His Excellency Mr. Hamid

2. President Karzai Condemns Assam Bomb Blasts, October 30, 2008.

Karzai, President of the Islamic Republic of Afghanistan, is currently paying a State Visit to India (August 3-5, 2008).

2. During the visit, the two leaders held talks on a range of bilateral issues and regional issues.
3. India reiterated its full support to the goal of a sovereign, democratic, peaceful and prosperous Afghanistan, conducive to the peace, security and stability of the region.
4. President Karzai's visit comes at a time when there has been a resurgence of terrorism whose specter profoundly threatens our societies. The attack on the Indian Embassy in Kabul on the 7th of July was an attack on the friendship between India and Afghanistan. President Hamid Karzai's presence today conveys a befitting response to that attack. The leaders expressed their determination to fight terrorism unitedly and with all the forces at their command.
5. Prime Minister Dr. Singh conveyed to President Karzai that all of India's commitments to Afghanistan would be fully met. To this end, the Government of India pledged and additional 450 million US dollars over the 750 million US dollars announced so far to effectively meet the requirement of our ongoing and forthcoming projects.
6. Prime Minister Dr. Singh also conveyed to President Karzai that one of the important infrastructure projects in Western Afghanistan – the road from Zaranj to Delaram – is now complete and will be handed over shortly to the Government of Afghanistan. The construction of this road was a major test of our joint resolve.
7. India's efforts for the reconstruction and development of Afghanistan are also part of a larger international endeavour to help the Afghan people in forging a pluralistic and democratic society. It was agreed that a meeting of the Joint Coordination and Monitoring Bureau would be hosted by India next year.
8. The two leaders reaffirmed their common interest in developing a robust, strategic partnership, building on the foundation of the historically rich ties and suited to the dynamic of the 21st century.

(*Source*: http://meaindia.nic.in/)

## Indo-Afghan Cooperation: Opportunities and Challenges[3]

August 4, 2008

*The Indian Prime Minister in a press statement termed the attacks on the Indian embassy as an attack on the friendship between India*

3. Statements to the Press by Prime Minister of India and President of the Islamic Republic of Afghanistan in New Delhi, August 4, 2008.

*and Afghanistan. He stated that India has an abiding commitment towards Afghanistan to build a democratic, pluralistic and stable polity. Meanwhile the Afghan President emphasized the importance of strengthening cooperative mechanisms between the two countries in order to fight terrorism. He expressed gratitude over India's generous aid of USD 40 million and applauded Indian efforts in building both physical (dams, transmission line, roads) and social (education) infrastructure in Afghanistan.*

**Prime Minister of India (Dr. Manmohan Singh)**: President Karzai's visit takes place at a critical juncture for India, Afghanistan, and our region. Our discussions today were held against the backdrop of the serious threat posed by terrorism to the security and stability of Afghanistan, India and the region. As the attack on our embassy in Kabul on July 7 has tragically shown, terrorism has no barriers, and is not bound by any restraints. It was an attack on the friendship between India and Afghanistan.

We have agreed that we will not allow terrorism to stand in our way. We will fight it unitedly and with full determination. I conveyed our deep condolences on the loss of so many innocent Afghan lives in the attack on July 7, and re-affirmed to President Karzai India's abiding commitment to Afghanistan's efforts to build a democratic, pluralistic and stable polity. Such a vision is not only in keeping with our age-old association with Afghanistan, but is necessary for regional peace and stability.

I conveyed to the President that we will fulfill all our commitments to Afghanistan. For this purpose, we will allocate an additional amount of 450 million US dollars over and above the existing 750 million US dollars to meet the requirements of our ongoing and forthcoming projects.

I also informed the President that one of our important infrastructure projects in Western Afghanistan – the road from Zaranj to Delaram – is now complete. We will hand this over shortly to the Government of Afghanistan. The road is a symbol of our cooperation with Afghanistan, and a tribute to the precious Indian and Afghan lives that were lost in making this project a reality. The road has brought our two peoples closer together.

India's contribution in the reconstruction and development of Afghanistan is part of a larger international effort to help the Afghan people in forging a pluralistic and democracy society. India will be happy to host a meeting of the Joint Coordination and Monitoring Bureau, the body which oversees and harmonizes the activities of different countries in the reconstruction process in Afghanistan.

In conclusion, I would like to pay tribute to the sagacity and wise leadership of President Karzai as he leads Afghanistan through a difficult and challenging period. He represents the new face of Afghan nationalism, which draws strength from the diversity and pluralism of Afghan society. He has always stood for India-Afghan friendship. We wish President Karzai well in his noble endeavours, and all success in guiding Afghanistan through these testing times to a better future.

**President of Afghanistan (Mr. Hamid Karzai)**: Afghanistan and India indeed share in common the interests of peace and stability in the two countries, in the region, and in the larger world. And we know that together India and Afghanistan are facing the challenges of terrorism, of cold-blooded, brutal murderous activity in our two countries. And we recognize that the two countries and the world at large have no option but to be united in fighting the menace of terrorism as it affects us and as it affects the international community. I would call upon all our allies to recognize the seriousness and the brutal nature of militant radicalism as it attacks innocent lives, women, children, elderly alike wherever they can manage to attack them.

Afghanistan will stand resolutely with our friends in India in fighting the menace of terrorism; Afghanistan stands resolutely with our allies in the conduct of war against terrorism. As India has suffered immensely from this menace, Afghanistan has too. Therefore, Mr. Prime Minister, it is a moral responsibility for us - not a political activity, I would like to underline, it is a moral responsibility for us - as human beings to protect the lives of our women and children, and to prevent the loss of life caused by terrorism by defeating terrorism and by eliminating it completely, and thereby bringing security to our peoples and the world at large.

Afghanistan is very grateful to India's assistance all along. Historically we have been friends; and India has proven in particular to be a very valued ally and at the forefront of its assistance to Afghanistan in Afghanistan's effort in rebuilding itself. India has been among the best contributors of assistance to the rebuilding of Afghanistan. You have provided us help in education in a significantly important way. A thousand scholarships a year for five years; you have been building transmission lines for us; constructing dams for us; building new roads for us; and helping in all manners where India could. On behalf of the Afghan people, Mr. Prime Minister, please convey our regards and thanks to the people of India.

I am grateful for the new announcement that you have made of 450 million dollars of fresh assistance to Afghanistan. Afghanistan will value this and I am sure it will be spent correctly for the betterment of the lives of the Afghan people.

I bring you once again greetings from the Afghan people and gratitude from the Afghan people. And I assure you that Afghanistan will be a steadfast ally in the war against terrorism and Afghanistan will remember and cherish the memory of India's assistance to the rebuilding of Afghanistan at an extremely critical juncture of our history.

Of course, I must re-emphasize, as you did, that both of us will continue the journey of democracy and pluralism, values that our nations definitely enjoy and will protect.

(*Source*: http://meaindia.nic.in/)

## India on Terrorism in Afghanistan[4]

July 7, 2008

*Dr Manmohan Singh expressed his condolences towards the people affected by the attacks (July 7, 2008) on the Indian embassy. Reprimanding the attacks strongly, he stated that endeavour to help the Afghan brothers should continue with a renewed commitment.*

I am horrified to know of the death of our personnel in the dastardly terrorist attack on our Embassy in Kabul. The loss of these precious Indian and Afghan lives in the service of their country must be condemned in the strongest terms possible. Those responsible, directly or indirectly, for this terrorist attack and for making this possible are no better than the worst criminals.

I offer my deep condolences to those who have lost their loved ones and those who have suffered grievous injuries. India is with the families of those bereaved today. We will do all that we can to help them bear their loss and grief. This is our pledge.

We have lost Indians who were helping their Afghan brothers to rebuild their lives and country. That endeavour must continue with renewed commitment.

(*Source*: http://www.mea.in)

## Afghanistan-India Relations: Frameworks for Future Co-operation[5]

May 31, 2008

*In a joint seminar hosted by Center for Strategic Studies and Embassy of Kabul, Mr Pranab Mukherjee, Minister of External Affairs, India, pointed out that while Afghanistan had entered a new stage of political and social vitality, expectations were building up that the ongoing state-building process would bring a positive*

---

4. Statement by Prime Minister Dr. Manmohan Singh on the terrorist attack on the Indian Embassy in Kabul, July 7, 2008.
5. Minister of External Affairs, Shri Pranab Mukherjee's Address at the Center for Strategic Studies, Kabul on "Afghanistan-India Relations: Frameworks for Future Co-operation", May 31, 2008.

> *change in spite of the existing shortcoming of human and institutional capacities and conflicting factional interests. The Minister emphasized that the geographic location of Afghanistan provided India with exceptional opportunities and characterized Indo- Afghan relations as an enduring partnership entailing cooperation in different areas, such as security, economy, trade and culture. The Minster pointed out that India has sixty years of experience in developing modern democratic institutions, which were tuned to the traditions of the country, the needs of the people and the demands of a globalized geopolitical and geo-economic environment. He pointed out that these could be some aspects indicating the need to expand bilateral exchanges and to strengthen the bonds of friendship between both the countries.*

With great pleasure I felicitate the Center for Strategic Studies and the Embassy in Kabul of the friendly country India for holding this seminar, jointly sponsored by the Ministry of Foreign Affairs of the Islamic Republic of Afghanistan and the Ministry of External Affairs of the Republic of India. In welcoming our esteemed guests I want to express my happiness for having the opportunity to host the high-ranking Indian delegation which has come to attend the two-day seminar on "Afghanistan–India Relations: A framework for future cooperation". This seminar provides experts of both countries an occasion to discuss a range of issues of mutual interest and for us to gain access to the treasure cove of Indian experience in strengthening democracy and generating social and economic development and change.

At the outset let me highlight the intention and endeavor of the Afghan nation to develop strong bonds with the large family of democratic countries. Afghanistan has entered a new stage of political and social vitality. Approving of the Constitution, holding the presidential and parliamentary elections, and establishing an elected government by the people of Afghanistan are some of the major achievements which kindle the hope of our people for a better future after three decades of war and instability. However, we still live in a socially fragmented society, where the culture of violence prevails, where organized social forces and an active civil society are absent and institutions are inadequately equipped, where the task of reflecting and promoting policy, including foreign policy, tends to lack dynamism and a creative approach to the changing demands of reality, complicating the formulation and consensual pursuance of national interests. Simultaneously expectations run high, that the ongoing state-building process will bring a change for the better, in spite of the shortcoming of human and institutional capacities and conflicting factional interests. These circumstances demand to seek solutions by trying to bridge the gap between the inadequate reality and aspirations. Certainly we all are aware that foreign policy in a country that is in a state of transition has certain of its own characteristics. On the one hand it faces the continuation of the past, the residual structures, values, beliefs and a host of skewed power relationships inherited from the past. On the other hand it is influenced by a dynamic present, the evolving social structures and values that are new but not yet fully established as determining forces.

The foreign policy of Afghanistan is formulated in line with the requirements of cooperation with the international community in the war against terrorism. We believe in the principle of collective security and defending it against actual and perceived potential threats. We want the strengthening of regional security in the context of a global security order. In this spirit we want to encourage multilateralism in the broadest possible sense.

The geographic location of Afghanistan provides our country with exceptional opportunities to enable and promote regional cooperation to the advantage of all countries concerned. So far we have not succeeded in fully utilizing our potential. The volume of trade between the countries of the region is far less than with countries outside the region. Even our cultural and educational exchanges are not well designed and organized. And unfortunately our political relations are still influenced by old rivalries and suspicions.

The need to accelerate regional cooperation endows us and our neighbours with the responsibility to consistently base our policies on the principles of peaceful coexistence, non-interference and respect for national sovereignty.

In pursuit of a foreign policy based on the principles of friendship and cooperation Afghanistan maintains productive political and economic cooperation with the Republic of India. In this context I reconfirm the statement I made during a visit to India some time ago, addressing the Indian Council of World Affairs, where I characterized Afghanistan's relations with India as an enduring partnership entailing cooperation in different areas, such as security, economy, trade and culture. And I am convinced; this list can be expanded and filled with substance to our mutual benefit.

Since 2001 Afghanistan has made considerable progress economically. Our growth rate reached 13% in 2007. And, we expect to keep a 10% economic growth in the following years. The ground has also been paved for foreign investment. Banking facilities are available. Our investment regulations allow 100% ownership and transfer of profits abroad. In order to provide facilities for investment the Afghanistan Investment Support Agency (AISA) has been established and is working successfully. And the experience of the last years has shown that investors are rewarded by a very high rate of return.

In search for investment opportunities it appears that our mineral resources are of growing interest. In the energy sector both production and transmission of electricity and other energy transmissions, have a tremendous scope for sustainable development in South Asia. These fields as well as many others, for instance in the agricultural sector, food production and processing, live stock holding and dairy farming could create a large number of jobs and provide alternative livelihoods. Additionally such developments would ease Afghanistan's trade balance. We would like to see Indian entrepreneurs and institutions come forward in these areas and let us partake of their vast experience.

In developing the relationship between Afghanistan and India we can build on traditions of long standing, rooted deeply in history and culture. More recently, after the fall of Taliban, the people of India consistently stand by the people and Government of Afghanistan. India is one of the major participants in the reconstruction process of our country in various fields. Most of the Indian assistance has been delivered through the Afghan government channels, setting an example for many other donors. We are hopeful that the forthcoming Paris Conference will convince the international community to follow suit to a growing degree for the efficiency of spending support for the Afghanistan government leadership. Donated rebuilding projects by India through the Afghanistan governmental channels proved efficient. India also was helpful in having Afghanistan admitted to SAARC, opening new opportunities and challenges for the integration of our country into the vibrant developmental network of this region.

India has sixty years of experience in developing modern democratic institutions, tuned to the traditions of the country, the needs of the people and the demands of a globalized geopolitical and geo-economic environment. India's UNITY IN DIVERSITY is not only a slogan, it is practiced reality. Ethnic, linguistic, cultural, religious, geographic, political, social and economic diversity have posed challenges to this great country. But the solutions found have added to the strength of the democratic system and institutions.

The lessons learnt in this process should be analyzed for our own purposes. How does India deal with threats to democracy.

These are just some aspects indicating the need to expand our exchanges and to strengthen the bonds of friendship. Strengthening of the Afghanistan Indian relations is a main pillar of stability and common prosperity in the region. However, this seminar also gives me an opportunity to thank the people and government of India for their generous and wholehearted support to Afghanistan during the last more that six years. It has empowered us to deal with the legacies of the past with the confidence we need. I am confident India shares our desire to deepen the relations. In this spirit I wish seminar lively and useful deliberations.

(*Source*: http://www.mfa.gov.af/Documents/Ministerspeeches/Afghanistan-India%20Joint%20Seminar.pdf)

## Memorandum of Understanding between the Government of the Republic of India and the Government of the Islamic Republic of Afghanistan for setting up of the India-Afghanistan Foundation

April 3, 2007

*MoU signed between Afghanistan and New Delhi mentions the establishment of an India-Afghanistan Foundation, with the prime objective of fostering educational, cultural, scientific and technical cooperation. The source of finance would be a Trust Fund, which would be primarily financed by Afghanistan and India. The focal points of cooperation recognized between the two countries are: education and culture, agricultural research, science and technology, health, technical training, development studies, women's studies and area studies.*

The Government of India and Islamic Republic of Afghanistan

Desiring to promote mutual understanding and cooperation between the peoples of India and Afghanistan by a wider sharing of knowledge and professional talents through academic and technical exchanges and contacts,have agreed to conclude this Memorandum of Understanding for the setting up of the India-Afghanistan Foundation (hereinafter called the Foundation).

**Article I**

There shall be established a Foundation, to be known as the India-Afghanistan Foundation, with the objective of fostering educational, cultural, scientific and technical cooperation between Afghanistan and India. This Foundation shall function under the terms of the present Memorandum and shall implement a programme aimed at achieving the above-mentioned goals.

**Article II**

The Foundation shall be financed through revenues from a Trust Fund. This Trust Fund shall be set up principally through grants made available by Government of Afghanistan and the Government of India. It may, however, also accept contributions from other agencies, both public and private.

**Article III**

The revenues from the Trust Fund, within the conditions and limitations here in after set forth, shall be used by the Foundation for the purpose of:

(1) Financing higher studies, research and other educational activities andin service training for citizens of Afghanistan at institutions of learning located in India, and vice versa.
(2) Financing visits and exchanges between India and Afghanistan of scholars, poets, writers, journalists, artists, and of teachers, instructors, professors and other professionals both in the general field of education and in the fields of agriculture, public health, science and technology, and such other fields as may be mutually agreed upon by the two Governments.
(3) Financing other related programmes and activities such as seminars, symposia, colloquia, workshops, etc. on subjects of common interests.
(4) Extending financial support to non-Governmental organizations, both in Afghanistan and in India, whose work helps achieve the objectives of the Foundation.
(5) Contributing towards the publication of standard works in the field of Afghanistan's history and culture.
(6) Encouraging the translation of standard works of Afghanistan's literature into Indian languages and vice-versa and arranging for their publication.
(7) Adopting any other measures, which may be considered necessary for the fulfillment of the objectives of the Foundation.

**Article IV**

The following shall be the thrust areas for the activities to be carried out by the Foundation: i) Education and culture; ii) Agricultural Research; iii) Science and technology; iv) Health; v) Technical training; vi) Developmental Studies; vii) Women's Studies; and viii) Area Studies.

**Article V**

In furtherance of the aforementioned purposes, the Foundation may, subject to the provisions of the present memorandum, exercise all the powers necessary for carrying out the purposes of the present memorandum including the following:

A) Receive funds;
B) Open and operate bank accounts in the name of the Foundation;
C) Disburse funds and make grants and advances of funds, including payment for transportation, tuition, maintenance and other expenses incidental thereto;

D) Plan, adapt, carry out programmes in accordance with the purposes of the present Memorandum;

E) Recommend/nominate to the Universities/Colleges in India, and in institutions run by the government of India, trainees, professors, research scholars, teachers and professionals resident in Afghanistan for various programmes/courses in India, and vice versa;

F) Provide for periodic audit of the accounts of the foundation by auditors selected by GOA and GOI.

**Article VI**

All commitments, obligations and expenditure incurred by the Foundation shall be made pursuant to an annual budget to be approved by the GOA and the GOI.

**Article VII**

The management and direction of the affairs of the Foundation shall be vested in a Board of Directors consisting of 10 Directors (hereinafter designated as "the Board"). The Ambassador of India to Afghanistan and the Ambassador of Afghanistan to India shall be the Co-Chairpersons of the Board. The GOA and the GOI shall each nominate four other members of the Board. Respective Embassy officials designated by the concerned Ambassadors shall act jointly as Secretaries of the Foundation.

**Article VIII**

The Board shall adopt such by-laws and appoint such Committees, as it shall deem necessary for the conduct of the affairs of the Foundation.

**Article IX**

A report on the activities of the Foundation shall be prepared annually by the Board and presented to the GOI and the GOA.

**Article X**

The Co-Chairpersons of the Board shall be responsible for the direction and supervision of the Board's programmes and activities in accordance with the Board's resolutions and directives and the provisions of this memorandum.

**Article XI**

Meetings of the Board shall be held twice a year alternately in Kabul and New Delhi.

**Article XII**

Wherever, in the present Memorandum, the terms the GOI and the GOA are used, it shall be understood to mean the Foreign Secretary of Ministry of External Affairs of Government of India and the Deputy Foreign Minister (Political Affairs) of the Ministry of Foreign Affairs of Government of Afghanistan.

**Article XIII**

The present Memorandum may be amended by the exchange of diplomatic notes between the GOI and the GOA.

**Article XIV**

The GOI and the GOA shall make every effort to facilitate the exchange of persons and programmes provided for in this Memorandum and to resolve problems, which may arise in the operation thereof through bilateral discussions.

**Article XV**

The present Memorandum will come into force upon the date of signature. IN WITNESS WHEREOF, the undersigned, being duly authorised thereto by their respective Governments, have signed the present Memorandum of Understanding.

DONE at New Delhi on 3rd April 2007 in two originals each in Hindi, Dari and English languages, all texts being equally authentic. In case of any divergence in interpretation, the English text shall prevail.

(*Source*: http://meakabul.nic.in/bl/2007/04/03bl01.pdf)

# 3.

# BILATERAL RELATIONS WITH IRAN

## Cooperation Agreements between Iran and Afghanistan[1]

October 21, 2008

*President Ahmadinejad visited Kabul in October 2008. The two countries signed a number of agreements including, road building, fighting against drug smuggling, anti-terrorism campaign as well as scientific and research cooperation in the field of mining.*

Six bilateral cooperation agreements were signed here on Tuesday by the visiting President of Iran Mahmoud Ahmadinejad and his Afghan counterpart Hamid Karzai.

The documents were inked in the fields of road building, fighting against drugs smuggling and anti-terrorism campaign as well as scientific and research cooperation in the field of mining.

The two presidents attended a joint press conference after the document signing ceremony.

President Ahmadinejad arrived in Afghanistan Tuesday morning on the first leg of his three-nation tour of Central Asia which would later take him to Turkmenistan and Kyrgyzstan.

His visit to Afghanistan is the second made by an Iranian president after his predecessor Mohammad Khatami's visit to the country in August 2002.

(*Source*: http://www.president.ir/en/?P=1&M=0&y=2007&m=8&c= 37&c=37)

## Negotiating with Afghanistan Taliban: An Iranian View[2]

October 19, 2008

*Foreign Minister of Iran, Manouchehr Mottaki, in a joint press statement with Bernard Membe, discouraged foreign forces from entering into a dialogue with the Afghanistan Taliban.*

---

1. Cooperation Agreements between Iran and Afghanistan, October 21, 2008.
2. Iranian Foreign Minister warns certain States concerning talks with Afghanistan Taliban, October 19, 2008.

Foreign Minister Manouchehr Mottaki warned foreign forces present in Afghanistan on Sunday against incurring another defeat by entering into talks with Taliban forces.

'One who plants wind, will harvest storm, ' Mottaki told certain European states that have entered into negotiations with Taliban.

He made the remarks during a joint press conference with his Tanzanian counterpart Bernard Membe who is currently in Iran.

'Afghanistan has become more unsafe today than it was seven years ago when the foreign troops arrived in the country, ' Mottaki said.

He stressed that everyone has now admitted failure of the strategies adopted by foreign forces in Afghanistan.

'Terrorism and extremism know no geographic border and will reach Europe and the West sooner or later,' Mottaki said stressing that no one could ever claim success in containing terrorism or extremism.

The minister added that the most important job to be done by West 'is to make an honest diagnosis about its policies in Afghanistan'.

Mottaki advised Western powers to be careful about the consequences of the ongoing regional developments in order not to repeat the same old mistakes.

Foreign Minister Manouchehr Mottaki announced on Sunday that Tehran will host first Iran-Africa joint session in early 2009.

The session which is to be attended by senior African officials, will open a new chapter in the two sides' relations, Mottaki added.

He referred to Tanzania as an important African country and chairperson of African Union.

The Iranian Foreign Minister voiced Tehran's readiness to help settle the existing problems facing the African nations and establish peace and stability in that continent.

(*Source*: http://www.mfa.gov.ir/cms/cms/Tehran/en/index.html)

# 4.

# BILATERAL RELATIONS WITH PAKISTAN

## Joint Declaration between the Islamic Republic of Afghanistan and the Islamic Republic of Pakistan on Directions of Bilateral Cooperation

January 6, 2009

*Afghanistan and Pakistan recognized that militancy, extremism and terrorism were common threats to both countries as well as to the region and the world at large and pledged to further develop a joint comprehensive strategy for combating terrorism and strengthening bilateral cooperation by the Ministries of Foreign Affairs of Afghanistan and Pakistan. The countries also decided to develop bilateral programs and projects for the exploitation of mineral resources and other fields in their respective countries and promote bilateral trade on preferential terms thus working expeditiously towards full implementation of the South Asia Free Trade Agreement (SAFTA) and Economic Cooperation Organization Trade Agreement (ECOTA). Regional and international cooperation also emerged as the major theme, whereby countries agreed to cooperate closely at regional and international forums, including the United Nations (UN), the Organization of Islamic Conference (OIC), Economic Cooperation Organization (ECO) and South Asian Association for Regional Cooperation (SAARC).*

The Islamic Republic of Afghanistan and the Islamic Republic of Pakistan, *Recalling* their historical, cultural and religious bonds; *Firmly believing* on the need to open a new visionary chapter in their bilateral relations to further strengthen the overall good neighborly relations and mutual cooperation between the two countries, as well as to enhance regional cooperation and world peace;

Stressing *on mutual respect for each other's sovereignty, independence and territorial integrity as well as on the principle of non-interference in each other's internal affairs according to the United Nations Charter, Kabul Declaration on Good-Neighborly Relations as well as Ankara and Istanbul Declarations;*

Affirming *their deep commitment for working resolutely towards making the South Asia an abode of stability, peace, prosperity and moderation;*

Recognizing *that militancy, extremism and terrorism are common threats to both countries as well as to the region and the world at large;*

Encouraging *the vital role of moderate, progressive and democratic forces;* Reaffirming *their deep commitment to completely eliminate the scourge of militancy, extremism and terrorism in all their forms and manifestations, including entities promoting them;*

Reaffirming *their sincere commitment to develop closer bilateral relations and to pursue forward-looking policies in all fields, in this spirit, and with a view to create sound foundations for deepening bilateral cooperation in all fields, the two countries hereby agree as follows:*

1. To maintain frequent exchange of high level visits and contacts and to strengthen the exchange of visits and communications between the governmental departments, parliaments, armed forces, security agencies and non-governmental organizations of the two countries with a view to enhance mutual understanding and friendship in all fields.
2. To remain fully supportive of the Joint Peace Jirga process.
3. To remain fully engaged with other frameworks of cooperation between the two countries.
4. To further develop a joint comprehensive strategy for combating terrorism and strengthening bilateral cooperation by the Ministries of Foreign Affairs of Afghanistan and Pakistan.
5. To closely cooperate with each other as well as with the international community to counter and completely eliminate the menaces of militancy, extremism and terrorism from the region.
6. To cooperate closely for the complete eradication of narcotics drugs and psychotropic substances, including their production, consumption and trafficking from the region.
7. To make full use of their historical, political and geographical advantages as well as the region's rich resources in order to promote bilateral and regional cooperation in all fields, especially in the realms of economy, trade, transit, investment, agriculture, education and technology.
8. To take urgent steps to improve connectivity through quantitative and qualitative improvement in infrastructure, especially improving and adding road and rail links and building transportation, transit and communication corridors connecting the entire region.
9. To collaborate closely in developing energy corridors in the region via Afghanistan, including building oil and gas pipelines and electricity networks.

10. To develop bilateral programs and projects for the exploitation of mineral resources and other fields in their respective countries. In this context, they express their readiness to seek assistance from third parties on the basis of mutual interest and agreement.
11. To promote bilateral trade on preferential terms and working expeditiously towards full implementation of the South Asia Free Trade Agreement (SAFTA) and Economic Cooperation Organization Trade Agreement (ECOTA).
12. To encourage cultural as well as people -to-people exchanges and contacts, especially between the academia, think tanks, media and civil society of the two countries.
13. To cooperate closely in regional and international forums, including the United Nations (UN), the Organization of Islamic Conference (OIC), Economic Cooperation Organization (ECO) and South Asian Association for Regional Cooperation (SAARC).

(*Source*: http://www.mfa.gov.af/detail.asp?Lang=e&Cat=1&ContID=917)

## Afghanistan and Pakistan Emphasise Shared Concerns[3]

October 22, 2008

*The Foreign Ministers discussed a wide range of important subjects pertaining to bilateral cooperation, regional and global issues of mutual interest and concern. In the spirit of celebrating the new beginning to the Afghanistan and Pakistan bilateral relations, the two Foreign Ministers exchanged views and highlighted the enormous potential of the region to become the abode of peace, moderation and prosperity for the two countries and the entire region. Pakistan shared a draft declaration on directions of bilateral cooperation which he stated would be finalized soon. Both sides agreed to comprehensively upgrade their bilateral relations and hold regular strategic dialogues at the level of Foreign Ministers.*

On the invitation of H.E. Makhdoom Shah Mahmood Qureshi, Minister of Foreign Affairs of the Islamic Republic of Pakistan, H.E. Dr. Rangin Dadfar Spanta, Minister of Foreign Affairs of the Islamic Republic of Afghanistan paid an official visit to Islamabad on October 22nd, 2008. During the visit, the Foreign Minister of Afghanistan held talks with his counterpart as well as the President, Speaker of the National Assembly and the National Security Advisor of Pakistan.

The visit took place in light of the understanding reached between Prime Minister Yousaf Raza Gilani and President Hamid Karzai during

---

3. Joint Press Release between Afghanistan and Pakistan,October 22, 2008.

their fruitful meeting in Colombo on 3rd August 2008, in which the two Foreign Ministers were mandated to prepare a framework of constructive engagement across the board.

The talks were very constructive and took place in warm and cordial atmosphere characteristic of the brotherly relations between the two countries.

In the talks, the Foreign Ministers discussed a wide range of important subjects pertaining to bilateral cooperation, regional and global issues of mutual interest and concern.

In the spirit of a new beginning to the Afghanistan and Pakistan bilateral relations, the two Foreign Ministers exchanged views on the ways to articulate a new vision for their bilateral relations as well as for the region. They highlighted the enormous potential of the region to become the adobe of peace, moderation and prosperity for the two countries and the entire region. Pakistan shared a draft Declaration on Directions of Bilateral Cooperation which will be finalized soon.

The two Foreign Ministers emphasized that extremism and terrorism posed a common threat to the two countries as well as to the regional and international peace. They agreed to collaborate closely to eliminate the scourge of extremism, militancy and terrorism. In this context, there will be regular contacts on political; military; security and intelligence tracks.

Both sides agreed to comprehensively upgrade their bilateral relations and to hold regularly a Strategic Dialogue at the level of Foreign Ministers. The Foreign Ministers will oversee the work of a Specialized Commission in all disciplines notably, political, security and economic sectors.

The two Foreign Ministers noted with satisfaction the convening of Jirga Gai in Islamabad on October 27-28, 2008. They also expressed satisfaction at the preparatory work for the holding of 7th Joint Economic Commission (JEC) in Kabul in the second half of November 2008 and the 3rd Regional Economic Cooperation Conference on Afghanistan (RECCA) in January 2009, in Islamabad.

Responding to the serious concern expressed on the abduction of Ambassador-designate of Afghanistan to Pakistan, Mr. Abdul Khaleq Farahi, the Foreign Minister Shah Mahmood Qureshi expressed deep anguish at the unfortunate abduction of the Ambassador-designate and assured H.E. Dr. Rangin Dadfar Spanta that the Government of Pakistan will leave no stone unturned for the safe and early recovery of the Ambassador-designate.

On behalf of H.E. President Hamid Karzai, Dr. Rangin Dadfar Spanta extended a warm and cordial invitation to President Zardari to visit Afghanistan in the near future. The Foreign Minister of Pakistan also accepted the invitation by the Foreign Minister of Afghanistan to visit Kabul at his earliest convenience.

(*Source*: http://www.mfa.gov.af/detail.asp?Lang=e&Cat=1&ContID=866)

# 5.

# BILATERAL RELATIONS WITH UNITED STATES OF AMERICA

## War in Afghanistan: Updating Counterinsurgency Approaches, Congressional Research Service, 2009[1]

Counterinsurgency approaches, by definition, require continual adaptation to the local environment. One set of COIN military strategy questions in Afghanistan concerns population security, and in particular, how best to balance the need to maintain a dispersed footprint, living among the population, given the antipathy of some parts of that population toward any foreign presence. In Afghanistan, this dilemma has been particularly evident in some isolated mountain valleys. One option is to sustain an international troop presence, coupled with development and governance assistance, aiming to win over the local population eventually. An alternative – diametrically opposed both theoretically and practically – is to accept that "population security" may not work identically in every context, to withdraw the antagonizing foreign force presence in some locations, and to sacrifice some measure of security against insurgents for a different kind of stability – an absence of discord between foreign forces and the local population. Another set of options concerns possible adjustments to the use of kinetic air operations in Afghanistan. The year 2008 witnessed sharp criticism from GIRoA and UNAMA of civilian casualties caused by air strikes. Such incidents have the potential to sharply discourage popular support for the government, essential to the success of any counterinsurgency. In late 2008, ISAF updated its Tactical Directive, carefully articulating rules for the use of fires. The year 2009 may prove a good test of the impact on civilian casualties of the 2008 Directive, and of a larger international forces presence that may allow some reduction in the use of kinetic air power.

1. Catherine Dale, "War in Afghanistan: Strategy, Military operations and issues for Congress", Congressional Research Service, January 2009.

A further set of options concerns the balance of effort between Special Operations Forces (SOF) and conventional forces. Some experts have argued that the military effort in Afghanistan would benefit from boosting the role of SOF vis-à-vis conventional forces. In Afghanistan, SOF play the lead role in targeting insurgent leaders, and proponents argue that increasing SOF troop strength might lead to more targeting successes. Other experts counter that successful SOF efforts rely on international conventional forces and the ANSF, both to provide information about a battle space in advance, and to "hold" that battle space after kinetic operations. That collaborative partnership, they argue, is essential to the success of overall COIN efforts, and therefore, the utility of unilateral increases in SOF deployments for the overall COIN mission would be limited.

Experts generally agree that the development of the Afghan National Security Forces is essential to the future security and stability of Afghanistan[2]. In late 2008, GIRoA, backed by the support of the international community, decided to increase the target end strength of the Afghan National Army (ANA). Further major policy issues include the size of the total ANSF, the mix of forces within it, the focus of effort of those forces, the timeline for developing those forces, and funding further ANSF development.

Practitioners underscore that ANSF development is highly dynamic. As Afghan National Police (ANP) capabilities grow, the ANP may increasingly assume responsibility for some domestic missions now performed by the Afghan National Army (ANA). As total ANSF numbers and capabilities grow, Afghan forces may increasingly assume responsibility from international security forces. And when – as expected – the security challenges from the insurgency diminish, the ANSF may shift from COIN to more traditional peacetime foci, including external defense for the ANA, and civilian law enforcement for the ANP.

One critical issue is funding the development and sustainment of the ANSF. Senior Afghan and international officials estimate that it will cost approximately $3.5 billion per year to increase ANSF force structure, and then $2.2 billion per year to sustain it. Unlike Iraq, whose oil revenues

---

2. See General James L. Jones, USMC (ret), Ambassador Thomas R. Pickering, *Afghanistan Study Group Report: Revitalizing our Efforts, Rethinking our Strategies,* Center for the Study of the Presidency, January 30, 2008, p. 23. The authors argued for an enhanced international effort: "The U.S. and its NATO partners also need to focus more efforts and resources on training and standing up the Afghan National Army and recruiting, training, and providing adequate pay and equipment to the Afghan National Police so they can maintain security in an area once coalition forces depart."

have funded an increasing share of the costs of growing and sustaining the Iraqi Security Forces in recent years, Afghanistan has few natural resources and little economic activity, other than poppy production, that could generate significant revenue in the near future. GIRoA, which contributed $320 million to the ANSF in 2008, is not a realistic source of ANSF funding in the near term.[3] International support, and particularly U.S. support, is expected to bear the near-term burden of developing the ANSF, until it reaches its current end strength targets.

Growing the ANA to 134,000 – or more – raises the twin questions of funding and sustainability.

It is expected that the currently planned ANA growth will be funded by the international community; the United States is currently the leading contributor. If GIRoA wanted to sustain the force beyond that time frame, theoretical options would include continued U.S. and international support, or Afghan assumption of some level of financial responsibility. Alternatives could include demobilizing some part of the force – if GIRoA had the ability to do so – or, hypothetically, making part of the force available to serve in multi-lateral peace operations, in which case the international community might bear some of its costs.

For the future, one option, in the absence of GIRoA ability to shoulder the burden, would be sustained international support, a responsibility likely to fall to the U.S. Government, based on current patterns. The policy question for the U.S. Government, in turn, would concern whether national interests support sustaining that sizable commitment – and if so, at what levels, and for how long.

In the absence of either Afghan or international funding sources, one option would be demobilizing some part of the Afghan forces. A conclusive defeat of insurgent forces might increase the plausibility of such an approach, by reducing the requirement for ANSF numbers for the COIN fight. One challenge could prove to be limited ability on the part of the Afghan civilian leadership to direct the security ministries to decrease their forces.

One additional option, with some cost implications, would be a future role for Afghanistan as net exporter of security, providing trained, interoperable ANSF to serve in UN peace operations or other multi-national coalition efforts around the world. Minister of Defense Wardak suggested this possibility by noting, "One day we will pay our debt by fighting shoulder to shoulder with you," words that might apply abroad as well as at home.[4] Playing such roles might help GIRoA. secure some international

3. MG Robert Cone, Interview, Kabul, Afghanistan, November 2008.
4. Minister of Defense of Afghanistan Abdul Rahim Wardak, Interview, Kabul, Afghanistan, November 2008.

support for maintaining its force. A further policy issue concerning the ANSF is force modernization – including the likely future requirements the ANSF will face, and the steps the ANSF might begin taking now, in terms of training and procurement, to prepare to meet those future requirements. While army and police commanders on the ground are fully focused on the current fight, Minister of Defense Wardak has argued in favor of beginning to build a mix of forces that would also be appropriate to the post- COIN environment. One implication for the U.S. Government is the impact GIRoA force modernization decisions may have on foreign military sales requests.

One final consideration concerning the development of the ANSF, is the nature of emerging civil military relationships within the Government of Afghanistan. Some civil-military experts caution that there is an inherent danger, when a state's army is by far its most competent, effective organization that civilian control of the military may erode. In late 2008, some Afghan officials, including Minister of Defense Wardak, have pointed to a tendency on the part of President Karzai to ask the ANA to play non-military roles – for example, guarding civilian prisons – when civilian personnel are unavailable. U.S. military officials have noted that they spend significant time with senior Afghan security officials, mentoring them on the role of security forces in a democracy.[5] By the end of 2008, a near-consensus had emerged among practitioners and observers that the challenges Afghanistan faces could not be successfully addressed without a "regional" approach.

Policy options might include various avenues for influencing the behavior of neighboring states, particularly Pakistan and Iran, in order to shape the security climate in Afghanistan. Some but not all commentators argue, in addition, that because Pakistan and India tend to make use of Afghanistan as a pawn in their own long-simmering conflict, successful "regional" initiatives concerning Afghanistan must also take into account the Pakistan-India relationship. Some commentators also suggest that Iraq is germane as a major security preoccupation for Iran, whose behavior in Afghanistan may be affected by developments across its opposite border. While the exhortation to consider the broader region has widespread support, no consensus on regional strategy has emerged – to date; experts have put forward a very wide range of specific policy prescriptions, some of them mutually contradictory. The U.S. Government may wish to address both strategic and operational policy options concerning Pakistan's role vis-à-vis Afghanistan.

---

5. MG Robert Cone, Interview, Kabul, Afghanistan, November 2008.

At the strategic level, a central question concerns the most effective ways to encourage Pakistani action against those supporting and fomenting the Afghanistan insurgency. One group of experts urges assistance efforts to support governance and development in "the impoverished areas that have become breeding grounds for militants", in particular along the border, in order to diminish the generation of, and support for, insurgents[6].

Several other groups of experts particularly emphasize the importance of the U.S.-Pakistani milto- mil relationship, as a tool for shaping Pakistani actions. Some argue that the key is to continue to build Pakistani capabilities and to shape their orientation by strengthening current initiatives – for example, by boosting U.S. efforts to train the Pakistan Army Special Forces for counterterrorism operations, expanding Pakistani participation in military exchange programs, and fostering closer mil-to-mil coordination along the Afghanistan-Pakistan border.[7] Others agree that mil-to-mil initiatives are key but urge making the provision of the benefits they offer conditional on stronger Pakistani support along the border with Afghanistan.[8] Some experts, in contrast, argue that the close U.S.-Pakistan mil-to-mil relationship is part of the problem, as it may tend to diminish Pakistani civilian control over its military. Therefore, one regional expert writes, "the United States must relinquish, not strengthen, the privileged relationship between the United States and the Pakistani military[9]."

---

6. Christopher D. Kolenda, "How to Win in Afghanistan," *Weekly Standard*, October 13, 2008. Colonel Christopher Kolenda recently commanded a U.S. Army battalion in Afghanistan along the border with Pakistan.
7. See Thomas Lynch, "Afghan Dilemmas: Staying Power," *The American Interest,* vol. 3, no.5 (May/June 2008), p. 36. U.S. Army Colonel Thomas Lynch has served in Afghanistan.
8. Barnett R. Rubin, "Afghan Dilemmas: Defining Commitments," *The American Interest,* vol. 3, no.5 (May/June 2008), p.49. He adds that the United States "must instead support civilian control over the government and military alike, even by parties that oppose U.S. objectives openly (rather than covertly, like the military)."
9. See the replies to questions for the record, submitted by Secretary of State nominee Hillary Clinton to the Senate Foreign Relations Committee (SFRC), for her January 13, 2009, confirmation hearing, available at http://www.foreignpolicy.com/files/KerryClintonQFRs.pdf. Under Secretary of Defense for Policy Michèle Flournoy, in replies to questions for the record submitted for her own confirmation hearing, with the Senate Armed Services Committee on January 15, 2009, echoed the same premise, stating: "The U.S. must have an integrated strategy to promote development and prevent terrorism across the Afghanistan-Pakistan border region." See replies to questions for the record, submitted by Under Secretary of Defense for Policy nominee to the Senate Armed Services Committee (SASC), for her

Another set of experts argues that efforts to shape Pakistani actions vis-à-vis Afghanistan are likely to be successful only as part of a broader approach to Pakistan's concerns and its role in the region. Key issues, in this broader perspective, might include Pakistan's role as a nuclear power, and its tendentious relationship with nuclear-armed neighbor India – in particular their rival claims to the disputed territory of Kashmir. Policy options might include, for example, more robust U.S. unilateral, or multilateral, diplomatic efforts to help India and Pakistan forge a stable, sustainable relationship.

The Obama Administration has indicated initial support for a Pakistan policy that includes both increasing non-military aid, and conditioning the provision of mil-to-mil assistance on Pakistani actions such as "...clos[ing] down training camps, evict[ing] foreign fighters, and prevent[ing] the Taliban and al Qaeda from using Pakistan as a sanctuary."[10]

Meanwhile, at the operational level, a key question is whether to continue U.S. cross-border attacks while strategic-level dialogue and other attempts to exercise leverage are underway. Continued cross-border attacks might lead to political blow-back in Pakistan, but they might also persuade Pakistani officials to take more decisive steps to end support to insurgents. Options, therefore, might include either accelerating or decreasing the use of cross-border attacks. Options might also include seeking additional avenues for strengthening tactical-level cross-border coordination, including increasing the frequency or scope of regular coordination meetings, establishing further border coordination centers, and improving the ease of tactical-level coordination in actions against insurgent targets.

Practitioners and observers recognize Iran's dual track role in Afghanistan – providing both humanitarian and lethal aid. The key issue in U.S. Afghanistan policy debates is how best to leverage concerns that Iran shares with the rest of the international community – including regional security and the impact of the narcotics trade – to shape Iranian choices. Options include a more concerted diplomatic outreach to Tehran, by the United States and/or other members of the international community, designed to build on shared regional concerns. Some experts suggest that Tehran may be more likely to respond positively to outreach efforts by the Obama Administration, than to those by its predecessor. Another option – not mutually exclusive – is robust countering of any Iranian efforts to provide lethal aid to insurgents in Afghanistan.

---

January 15, 2009, confirmation hearing, available at http://armedservices.senate.gov/statemnt/2009/January/Flournoy%2001-15-09.pdf.

10. See Vikram J. Singh and Nathaniel C. Fick, "Surging Statecraft to Save Afghanistan", *Small Wars Journal*, October 2, 2008.

Despite the existence of broadly agreed counternarcotics (CN) strategies, and some recent declines in cultivation, many practitioners see little likelihood of significant further CN progress until GIRoA takes major further strides in establishing the rule of law, including both building a formal judicial system and encouraging a pervasive law-based culture. Some observers have further suggested that there may be inherent contradictions between CN and COIN efforts, since a key premise of COIN is fostering popular support for the government, while some CN initiatives may alienate parts of the population, at least temporarily.

One near term option is for GIRoA and ISAF to take full advantage of the October 2008 NATO decision expanding the interpretation of the CN role ISAF may play, to include targeting drug facilities when a connection with the insurgency can be shown. Focused diplomatic efforts might prove useful in persuading some Allies to fully embrace this broader interpretation.

A further option might be more assiduously cultivating the cooperation of community as well as provincial leaders in CN efforts, including strengthening the system of incentives available to those who lend their support. The Afghanistan Social Outreach Program, designed to foster and focus ground-up capacity-building, might naturally complement any such outreach efforts.

Most NATO observers suggest that "Afghanistan" is a critical test for the Alliance, including its ability to conduct major out-of-area missions, and its relevance to 21st century security challenges, and many have argued that failure in Afghanistan could spell the end of the Alliance.

The issue of the role of NATO in Afghanistan is likely to gain prominence on the world stage in early 2009, amidst preparations for NATO's 60th anniversary summit, scheduled for April 2009. In January 2008, the Afghanistan Study Group argued, "A failure of the NATO mission in Afghanistan would also damage the future prospects of the organization itself."[11] For a number of practitioners, that line of thinking implies an imperative to make sure that the Alliance is successful in Afghanistan – which is not quite the same thing, logically, as making sure that Afghanistan itself succeeds. Key policy considerations include what it would take for the outcome in Afghanistan to be considered a "NATO success", and what if any differences that might entail from a strict pursuit of security, good governance and development for Afghanistan.

---

11. See for example General James L. Jones, USMC (ret), Ambassador Thomas R. Pickering, *Afghanistan Study Group Report: Revitalizing our Efforts, Rethinking our Strategies,* Center for the Study of the Presidency, January 30, 2008, p. 17.

In some circumstances, U.S. policy-makers might wish to weigh the imperative of accomplishing the mission against the imperative to support NATO as an institution.

Some observers suggest that the growing presence of U.S. forces, and possibly a stronger U.S. role in ISAF command and control, may lead to the perception that any progress in Afghanistan is due to U.S. rather than NATO efforts. In that vein, the Afghanistan Study Group argued, "Burden sharing among NATO allies is critical to the mission in terms of both available resources and public perceptions – an increasingly unilateral mission will be politically vulnerable in Afghanistan, the U.S., and NATO."[12] Options for countering such perceptions, if so desired, might include maintaining U.S. battle space-owning units under ISAF command; using diplomatic channels to forge stronger consensus on the nature and stakes of the fight in Afghanistan; and soliciting non-military forms of assistance from those countries unwilling or unable to provide large ground force contingents for the counterinsurgency fight.

A number of key practitioners and observers have supported "reconciliation" outreach initiatives, to insurgent leaders and/or their foot soldiers, as one avenue toward final settlement of the conflict in Afghanistan. Senior U.S. military officials in Afghanistan underscore that questions concerning to whom to reach out, at what time, with what offers, and with what end state in view, are policy matters for GIRoA decision. Any "reconciliation" efforts would likely have a direct bearing on security efforts in Afghanistan, because they concern the formal adversary – the insurgents – in the fight.

Some experts have argued that leadership-level reconciliation initiatives risk institutionalizing formal political roles in the future Government of Afghanistan for known "bad guys". Such inclusion, they suggest, might alienate parts of the Afghan population who suffered repression under the Taliban regime. Worse, such alienated constituencies might take up arms to protest such brokered deals. Institutionalizing leading roles for former Taliban or other insurgent leaders might also, it is suggested, push the orientation of the Government of Afghanistan in more repressive directions.

U.S. Government policy considerations might include determining the U.S. preferred outcome of any such talks, and exercising diplomacy to influence the form and content of any such initiatives. From an operational perspective, U.S. deliberations might include assessing how different

12. General James L. Jones, USMC (ret), Ambassador Thomas R. Pickering, *Afghanistan Study Group Report: Revitalizing our Efforts, Rethinking our Strategies,* Center for the Study of the Presidency, January 30, 2008, p. 17.

military strategies might contribute to bringing Taliban leaders to the negotiations table in a frame of mind conducive to agreeing to conditions acceptable to GIRoA. For example, Taliban leaders might be compelled to come to terms by even more aggressive targeting, or by more strident efforts to cut off the funding support they receive from the narcotics trade.

For the longer term, defense practitioners and analysts are likely to continue to seek lessons from U.S. military prosecution of the wars in Afghanistan and Iraq to apply to future U.S. force shaping and sizing. Such conclusions, and they way they are applied, are likely to have a profound impact on how the Military Services fulfill their responsibilities, in accordance with Title 10, U.S. Code, to organize, man, train and equip military forces. Critical policy considerations for DoD are likely to include the capabilities required to successfully prosecute complex contingency operations like those in Afghanistan and Iraq, the likelihood that the United States will engage in similar complex contingencies in the future, and the relative importance of such skills compared to more traditional military capabilities.

The publication of Department of Defense Directive 3000.07 on "Irregular Warfare", in December 2008, which stated that "IW is as strategically important as traditional warfare," reflected and helped institutionalize a growing DoD emphasis on complex contingency capabilities.[13]

Should this school of thought continue to hold sway, options might include further increasing the end strength of the ground forces, and raising the profile of the mission to train and advise foreign security forces. In a resource-constrained environment, any such choices would like entail tradeoffs with other DoD capability areas.

Years of operational experience in Afghanistan, like those in Iraq, have helped fuel debates about appropriately balancing military and civilian capabilities in the U.S. Government, and effectively integrating those capabilities with each other.

A key short-term policy consideration is the U.S. Government response to the appeal from U.S. Embassy Kabul for further civilian resources –

---

13. Department of Defense, "Irregular Warfare (IW)", DoDD 3000.07, December 1, 2008. The Directive defined IW this way: "A violent struggle among state and non-state actors for legitimacy and influence over the relevant population(s). Irregular warfare favors indirect and asymmetric approaches, though it may employ the full range of military and other capacities, in order to erode an adversary's power, influence, and will." It noted that "IW can include a variety of steady-state and surge DoD activities and operations: counter-terrorism, unconventional warfare; foreign internal defense; counterinsurgency; and stability operations that, in the context of IW, involve establishing or reestablishing order in a fragile state."

personnel and ready funds – to support capacity building efforts in Afghanistan. One constraint may be the availability of trained civilian personnel with the appropriate expertise, ready to deploy. Another constraint may be the availability of funds – in particular, civilian funding streams relatively free of bureaucratic red tape that allow quick execution.

Some U.S. commanders on the ground, while generally welcoming the prospect of civilian expertise, caution that such an initiative would be most valuable if it carefully recruits people with relevant expertise. Simply "throwing bodies at the problem," they caution, would not be helpful. Some add that it would also be important to ensure that additional civilian personnel are included in clear civilian chains of command, to ensure unity of effort among their various activities.

Some outside experts, in turn, caution against any infusion of civilian personnel that might detract from GIRoA efforts to govern their own country. One regional expert, arguing that the U.S. Government should not increase its involvement in the Afghan government or economy, has written: "The more responsibility we take in Afghanistan, the more we undermine the credibility and responsibility of the Afghan government and encourage it to act irresponsibly."[14] Another expert has urged, "Rather than sending in thousands of civilians, the shift in emphasis could be to training Afghans to do the jobs themselves."[15] U.S. Embassy appeals for a "civilian surge" are predicated on precisely that advisory approach.

Key policy considerations for the longer-term, suggested by U.S. experience in Afghanistan, might include whether the U.S. government requires increased civilian capacity to meet possible future complex contingency requirements, and if so, what capabilities would be required, and how might they best be cultivated and organized. A related consideration concerns the implications of any enhancement of U.S. government civilian capacity for military requirements – whether, for example, increased civilian capacity might decrease the missions military forces should be prepared to accomplish. And finally, regardless of the balance in numbers and capabilities between military and civilian personnel, a further policy consideration is how best to effectively integrate military and civilian complex contingency efforts, in both planning and execution.

---

14. Rory Stewart, "How to Save Afghanistan," *Time,* July 17, 2008.
15. Clare Lockhart, "Learning from Experience," *Slate,* November 5, 2008.

## "Troops Surge" in Afghanistan[16]

December 22, 2008

*The U.S. decision to increase the troops by 20,000 to 30,000 in Afghanistan was discussed between the two countries. Karzai urged the American government that Afghan government had to be consulted regarding the stationing of the new troops, the conduct of military operations and the role of Afghan National Army in the operations. Meanwhile Adm. Mullen, US Army Chief of Staff, briefed President Karzai that the new troops would be sent to areas with more security threats, particularly in areas along the Durand Line to help stop militants' infiltration to Afghanistan and to help strengthen and equip Afghan National Army. He emphasized that winning people's support is the key to defeating terrorism in Afghanistan.*

President Karzai discussed, bilateral relations between Afghanistan and the US, current developments in the region, US military assistance to Afghanistan and the war on terror at a meeting with Adm. Mike Mullen, the chairman of the Joint Chiefs of Staff of the US military.

President Karzai asked Adm. Mullen for details on the US deployment of additional 20,000 to 30,000 troops to Afghanistan, urging that the US had to consult with the Afghan government as to where the new troops needed to be stationed, the conduct of military operations and the role of Afghan National Army in the operations.

Adm. Mullen told President Karzai that the new troops would be sent to areas with more security threats, particularly in areas along the Durand Line to help stop militants' infiltration to Afghanistan and to help strengthen and equip Afghan National Army.

President Karzai stressed that US troops needed to be extra careful in behaving the Afghan villagers and civilians and that it was necessary to win people's hearts minds through cooperation with Afghan Police and Army. "American troops need to avoid uncoordinated house searches and baseless detention of people. Winning people's support is the key to defeating terrorism in Afghanistan", added the President.

President Karzai also grieved over the recent incident in Khost and demanded that a broader probe be launched into it, to which Adm. Mullen agreed and pledged that the results would be reported to the President.

(*Source*: http://www.president.gov.af/english/news)

---

16. President Karzai Discusses "Troops Surge" with Adm. Mike Mullen, Chairman of the Joint Chiefs of Staff of the U.S. Military, December 22, 2008.

## Strategic Partnership Dialogue between Afghanistan and the United States of America[17]

September 25, 2008

*The United States delegation expressed regret over the loss of innocent civilian lives incurred during security operations and strongly condemned, along with the UN Secretary General, the murder of two UN doctors and multiple Afghan civilians during the UN's humanitarian efforts to vaccinate Afghan children in southern Afghanistan. In the Security Working Group, the two sides reaffirmed their commitment to pursue a comprehensive security strategy to address Afghanistan's security challenges and threats. The U.S. side welcomed the agreement to expand the Afghan National Army (ANA) to 134,000 personnel. Meanwhile, the Independent Election Commission of Afghanistan, briefed the Governance Working Group on Afghanistan's preparations for the 2009 Presidential and Provincial Council elections. The United States delegation also hailed the recent steps taken by the Government of Afghanistan to place operations and maintenance of public infrastructure on a sound cost-recovery basis. The United States pledged to support both of these efforts by sharing high quality technical expertise. The Afghanistan Compact and the Afghanistan National Development Strategy were recognized as useful frameworks to foster Afghanistan's reconstruction and revitalization. The Afghan side also spoke of the importance of U.S. support toward the restructured and reformed Counter Narcotics Trust Fund (CNTF).*

Senior representatives of the Governments of the United States of America and the Islamic Republic of Afghanistan met in Washington DC today for the third round of the United States-Afghanistan Strategic Partnership dialogue. President Bush and President Karzai created and signed into effect the Strategic Partnership in May 2005 to enhance the long-term security, democracy and prosperity of Afghanistan, as well as to support U.S. national interests. Today's meeting again underscores the commitment of the United States and Afghanistan to carrying forward a shared vision through senior-level dialogue to further improve bilateral coordination and cooperation to address near- and long-term challenges.

The United States delegation expressed regret over the loss of any innocent civilian lives incurred during security operations. In response to concerns expressed by the Government of Afghanistan, the United States

17. Afghanistan-United States Strategic Partnership Dialogue Joint Statement, September 25, 2008.

is conducting a senior level review and assessment of the August 22 Shindand operation. In addition, both sides recognize the need for establishing a mutually agreed-upon a framework and mechanism to minimize civilian casualties and to maintain the strong support of the Afghan people in fighting terrorism. The United States reiterated during discussions that it takes every precaution to avoid harming any Afghan civilian during military operations and drew a sharp contrast to the Taliban and Al Qaida and their deliberate campaigns of intimidation and terror on the Afghan populace. The United States especially condemned, along with the UN Secretary General, the recent murder of two UN doctors and multiple Afghan civilians during the UN's humanitarian efforts to vaccinate Afghan children in southern Afghanistan.

In the Security Working Group, the two sides reaffirmed their commitment to pursue a comprehensive security strategy to address Afghanistan's security challenges and threats. By commending the growing professionalism and sacrifices of the Afghan National Security Forces, they reiterated their determination for the Afghan National Security Forces to progressively assume the leading role in defending the sovereignty and territorial integrity of Afghanistan and protecting the lives of Afghan citizens. The U.S. side welcomed the recent agreement to expand the Afghan National Army (ANA) to 134,000 personnel. This agreement will allow the ANA to move closer to our shared goal of a well equipped and fully capable force. The Afghan National Police (ANP) also continues to strengthen its capabilities, with the Focused District Development Program serving as the cornerstone of these efforts. Hence, in order to support Afghanistan's Ministry of Defense and Ministry of Interior visions, both sides agreed that the assistance of the international community is essential to realizing the improving capabilities of both ANA and ANP. The ANA, ANP and the International Security Assistance Force (ISAF) are playing central roles in voter registration security and are working to ensure that Afghan voters are able to exercise their rights fully, freely and in a secure environment. The two sides recognized the successes of the United States-Afghan Defense Parliamentary Exchange Program and the Agri-Business Development Teams and continue to look for ways to expand cooperation in these areas.

Both sides emphasized the important roles of regional countries, particularly in confronting transnational terrorism, extremism, organized crime and narcotics trafficking.

In the Governance Working Group, both sides emphasized the fundamental role of respecting and institutionalizing principles of good governance and human rights. The Independent Election Commission of Afghanistan briefed the Governance Working Group in detail on Afghanistan's preparations for the 2009 Presidential and Provincial Council elections. The Afghan side expressed its gratitude for the significant funding and expertise provided by the United States to support this process, including assistance to the Independent Electoral Commission and a number of non-governmental organizations helping Afghan citizens to prepare for this upcoming election. The delegation of the Government of Afghanistan emphasized the transformation in sub-national governance, built around the Independent Directorate of Local Governance (IDLG). The two parties agreed on the importance of improving the ability of governors to connect to and serve their constituents. The United States, noting the milestone represented by this second round of democratic elections, pledged funding and technical expertise to support this outreach program.

The Governance Working Group welcomed Afghanistan's recent legal and institutional measures to establish the High Office of Oversight and Anti-Corruption, including special units in the Office of the Attorney General and in the Supreme Court, to intensify and oversee efforts aimed at eliminating corruption through preventative, educational and enforcement measures. Both sides committed themselves to seek more progress on corruption over the next year, and to help ensure concrete results – including successful prosecutions where appropriate – the U.S. side agreed to assist the above-mentioned entities in their efforts to secure the necessary resources and means to carry out their respective mandates. We look forward to Afghanistan's next step in establishing anti-corruption tribunals in the Supreme Court.

In the Prosperity Working Group, both sides expressed concern over increased food insecurity in Afghanistan and pledged to take appropriate actions to resolve this problem. They also acknowledged the enormous needs facing victims of drought, returnees, and internally displaced persons. Private sector-led economic growth as a stability and confidence-building measure, beginning with passage and implementation of a package of pro-competitive, transparent commercial and investment laws and regulations designed to attract investors and to create new jobs was deemed essential for Afghanistan. The two delegations highlighted the importance of promoting a number of key infrastructure projects as prioritized by the Afghanistan National Development Strategy (ANDS), such as irrigation, agriculture, roads, and power. The delegations noted positively the progress toward electricity sector agreements between Afghanistan and its neighbors. The United States pledged to continue to support efforts to build both bilateral and regional linkages in electricity, and to explore such linkages in transportation and communications.

Both sides also supported concrete steps to expedite and increase Afghanistan's trade with neighbors in the region, eliminate obstacles to commerce, and focus on preparations to implement the Reconstruction

Opportunity Zone (ROZ) legislation now under consideration by the U.S. Congress. This type of economic strategy is key to fighting terror and narco-trafficking by creating jobs, promoting sustainable development, and drawing investment to targeted areas and the border regions of Afghanistan. Transit trade and Reconstruction Opportunity Zones will be discussed in more detail in the October 8, 2008, U.S.-Afghanistan Trade and Investment Framework Agreement talks in Kabul.

The two delegations discussed the importance of strengthening fiscal sustainability, including the challenge of increasing domestic revenue. The Afghan side is considering a number of steps to ensure that all revenues are duly collected and properly transferred to the Ministry of Finance for recording and allocation. The United States delegation welcomes recent steps taken by the Government of Afghanistan to place operations and maintenance of public infrastructure on a sound cost-recovery basis. These include commercializing the management of key public services such as electrical power in Kabul and the provision of urban water to several major municipalities, as well as the establishment of a Road Maintenance Unit within the Ministry of Public Works. The United States pledges to support both of these efforts by sharing high quality technical expertise.

Both sides recognize the importance of the Afghanistan Compact and the Afghanistan National Development Strategy as useful frameworks to foster Afghanistan's reconstruction and revitalization.

Both delegations in the Counter-Narcotics Working Group welcomed the success achieved this year in reducing poppy cultivation by 19 percent from 2007. This reversed the trend of record poppy growth over the past two years and expanded the number of poppy-free provinces from 13 to 18 of Afghanistan's 34 provinces. During the same period, Nangarhar province went from being Afghanistan's number two poppy-producing province to achieving poppy-free status. These developments are inspiring confidence that the Government of Afghanistan's broad-based counter-narcotics strategy of incentives and disincentives, with the support of the United States and the international community, is working in areas that enjoy relative security and stability. However, connections among narcotics, terrorism, organized crime and corruption are undeniable and the drug problem remains a pressing concern, particularly in the insecure south and southwest regions where seven provinces accounted for 98 percent of total opium production this year. The Government of Afghanistan and its international partners are collaborating on an effort to target more intensively these areas to reduce opium production.

The two delegations endorsed the Afghan Government's plan for Helmand province to further improve security and governance in that province, and consequently make sustainable progress in eliminating poppy cultivation. The United States will expand the Drug Enforcement

Administration's operations in Afghanistan and continue to build the Afghan Counter Narcotics Police's capacity. The two sides will work together and will focus on creating an intensified mix of disincentives and incentives for further reductions in opium poppy cultivation and trafficking, including expanded alternative development programs and improving market access infrastructure to support the growing of alternative crops. The Afghan side also spoke of the importance of U.S. support toward the restructured and reformed Counter Narcotics Trust Fund (CNTF). The Government of Afghanistan is committed to carrying out a more robust counter-narcotics campaign for the coming year, including poppy elimination and eradication; strengthening the justice sector; enhancing public information and education; taking vigorous anti-corruption measures, and arresting and prosecuting high-value drug kingpin targets.

Based on this Strategic Partnership Joint Statement, the United States and Afghanistan hereby recommit themselves to shared efforts towards Afghanistan's commitment to join the family of nations as a secure, prosperous, progressive and democratic nation.

(*Source*: http://www.mfa.gov.af/detail.asp?Lang=e&Cat=1&ContID=850)

# 6.

# INTERNATIONAL DOCUMENTS

## Afghanistan and its Neighbours: Opportunities for Regional Cooperation[1]

December 14, 2008

*Discussions of the Informal Ministries Meeting of Afghanistan and its Neighbours at Paris focused on three broad agenda items: Afghanistan and the region; counter-narcotics and counter-terrorism and regional economic cooperation. The participants stressed that both the region and Afghanistan benefited from strengthening regional cooperation .The countries recognized that there can be no stability, security and prosperity in Afghanistan without regional cooperation and expressed their support for existing initiatives to reinforce cooperation between Afghanistan and its neighbors. The countries also pledged full support to the work of the United Nations Assistance Mission in Afghanistan and the Special Representatives of the UN Secretary General Ambassador Kai Eide, in implementing his coordination mandate.*

The Government of the Islamic Republic of Afghanistan and its neighbors, together with representatives of India, the United States, Russia, Germany, the United Kingdom, the high representative for ESDP and the EU Commissioner for external relations met today in La Celle Saint-Cloud. At the invitation of the French presidency of the Council of the European Union, of the Special Representative of the UN Secretary General for Afghanistan to reaffirm their commitment to enhancing regional cooperation and to constructive bilateral relationships based on the principles of non interference in each others internal affairs, mutual respect, sovereignty and territorial integrity, friendly relations, cooperation, as enshrined in the 2002 Kabul Declaration on Good Neighborly relations.

---

1. Declaration of the Informal Ministers Meeting of Afghanistan and its Neighbours in Paris, December 14, 2008.

Participants expressed their strongest solidarity to the Indian authorities and the Indian people after the heinous acts of terrorism committed in Mumbai on November 26th.

Discussions focused on three broad agenda items: Afghanistan and the region. Counter-narcotics and counter-terrorism, regional economic cooperation.

In this context, participants stressed that both the region and Afghanistan stand to benefit from strengthening regional cooperation. They

- agreed that there can be on long-term security and peace in the region without a stable, secure, prosperous and democratic Afghanistan. They pledged their full support to the government of Afghanistan in its efforts to achieving this goal;
- Underlined the regional character of terrorism and the need for visible firm and coordinated action against terrorist groups;
- Recognized that there can be no stability, security and prosperity in Afghanistan without regional cooperation. They expressed their support for existing initiatives to reinforce cooperation between Afghanistan and its neighbors. They committed to the effective implementation of these initiatives;
- Agreed to work more closely to strengthen border security as a key component of counter-narcotic and counter-terrorism while facilitating the legal movement of goods and people across borders, by establishing necessary trade agreements and harmonizing customs practice and regulations. In this context they welcomed proposals to develop people exchanges, for example in the framework of the Afghanistan-Pakistan Jirga Process;
- Agreed that better water management is necessary in order top stimulate economic growth and agricultural production and that this issue must be addressed fairly be all states of the region;
- Pledged full support to the work of the United Nations Assistance Mission in Afghanistan and the special Representatives of the UN Secretary General Ambassador Kai Eide, in implementing his coordination mandate. Including with regard to regional cooperation;
- Agreed on:
- an expert meeting in Brussels on regional cooperation in preparation for the Islamabad meeting of the REEC planned for early 2009;
- a follow-up informal ministerial meeting to be held in the region in 2009.

(*Source*: http://www.mfa.gov.af/detail.asp?Lang=e&Cat=1&ContID=909)

## Joint Statement of Afghanistan-Pakistan-Turkey

December 8, 2008

*Afghanistan, Pakistan and Turkey affirmed that the trilateral process would promote economic and trade cooperation between Afghanistan, Pakistan and Turkey and that the three countries would work to promote regional/ trans-regional development. The countries identified certain areas of cooperation including military training, enhanced security cooperation, energy projects, and transport corridors to name a few.*

His Excellency Hamid Karzai the President of the Islamic Republic of Afghanistan, Asif Ali Zardari, the President of the Islamic Republic of Pakistan, visited Istanbul on 5 December 2008 at the invitation of His Excellency Abdullah Gul, the President of the Republic of Turkey.

The three presidents, together with His Excellency Recep Tayyip Erdogan, Prime Minister of the Republic of Turkey, held cordial and fruitful talks on regional and international issues, and expressed their political will to expand and strengthen the scope of their cooperation within the framework of the trilateral Ankara Process, initiated on 30 April 2007.

During the meeting, Presidents Karzai and Zardari, mindful of the common future shared by their people, the commonality of interest of their countries, expressed satisfaction on increasing contacts and continuing cooperation in all areas between the two brotherly countries and their respective democratically elected governments, and committed themselves to continue their bilateral, political dialogue in a structured and comprehensive way.

The three Presidents:

Reiterated their pledge to cooperate towards promoting security, stability, peace, and economic development in the region, with reference to the Ankara Declaration of 30 April 2007, the Joint Press Release of the Joint Working Group of 6 July 2007 and the Joint Declaration of 30 October 2008;

Reaffirmed the need to respect, preserve and support unity, territorial integrity and sovereignty of all countries in the region as well as the need to uphold principles of nonintervention and noninterference in the internal affairs of other States; Expressed their determination to strengthen trilateral cooperation to confront the scourge of terrorism in all its forms and manifestations in an effective manner. They welcomed the decision of the Ministers of Foreign Affair of Afghanistan and Pakistan to develop a joint comprehensive strategy for combating terrorism and strengthening bilateral cooperation;

Reiterated their full support and confidence to the peace Jirga and the Jirgagai as authentic, traditional and key processes for dialogue and enhanced cooperation between the two countries, and the promotion of peace in the region;

Expressed their support for the ongoing comprehensive process of constructive engagement between Afghanistan and Pakistan including security and counterterrorism as well as initiatives taken by both sides to promote future perspectives for common development and regional and trans regional economic/trade cooperation including joint projects between Afghanistan and

Pakistan in the energy, minerals, agriculture, manufacturing and other sectors, as well as to enhance physical connectivity, including road/rail links and communication links;

Welcoming the kind offer of Pakistan to host the next Regional Economic Cooperation Conference in Islamabad, expressed their appreciation for the progress achieved in the seventh meeting of the Afghanistan and Pakistan Joint Economic Commission, held in Kabul on 25 and 26 November 2008, including deliberations on trade, economic coordination, transit trade, Pakistan's assistance for reconstruction in Afghanistan, health, education and cooperation between businessmen of the two counties;

Mindful that security peace and development are interlinked and bearing in mind that sustainable development depends on fostering diversified local productive capacity, especially by motivating the private sector and increasing trade and investment, and that socioeconomic development is essential to bringing lasting stability, aware of the challenges posed by the global financial crisis;

Affirmed that the trilateral process would promote economic and trade cooperation between Afghanistan, Pakistan and Turkey and that the three countries will work to promote regional/trans regional development cooperation and noted in this context the importance of the role played by the public and private sector companies and corporations;

Approved as a framework of cooperation the attached recommendations finalized by the Joint Working Group during its meeting on 4 December 2008, including:

Continuation of structured and comprehensive dialogue at different levels:

- continuation of structured and comprehensive dialogue at different levels;
- trilateral military cooperation, including military training;
- enhanced security cooperation in counterterrorism and counter narcotics;

- energy projects;
- transport corridors;
- stablishment of organized industrial zones in Afghanistan and Pakistan, utilizing complementarities wherever possible;
- various socio-economic projects on education, health and vocational training;

Expressed their support for the Istanbul Forum mechanism comprising the apex organizations of the private sectors of the three countries, and their valuable work in tandem with the trilateral process, as well as welcoming the convening of the Forum session on 4 December, 2008.

The Presidents of the Islamic Republic of Afghanistan and the Islamic Republic of Pakistan expressed gratitude for the initiative of Turkey for hosting the Second Summit Meeting and agreed to hold further meetings in 2009."

(*Source*: http://www.mfa.gov.af/detail.asp?Lang=e&Cat=1&ContID=905)

## An Afghan View on the Non-Aligned Movement[2]

July 30, 2008

*Afghan Foreign Minister Rangin Dadfar Spanta at the 15th Ministerial Conference of the Non-Aligned Movement in Tehran stated that the legacies of colonization had been compounded by the emergence of new threats and challenges. He insisted on the importance of peaceful and diplomatic settlement of all bilateral and international disputes. Lauding the democratic developments in Afghanistan, the Minister pointed out that Afghanistan had an elected President, a National Assembly, a new constitution, expanding interactions with the international community, emerging national security forces, a growing national economy and thriving civil and private sectors. He pointed out that the greatest challenge the country faced was terrorism.*

It gives me a great pleasure to address the 15th Ministerial Conference of the Non-Aligned Movement. From the outset, allow me to extend my cordial thanks and appreciation to the people and the Government of the Islamic Republic of Iran for hosting this meeting and for the excellent preparation and organization of the Conference and the warm hospitality extended to Afghan delegation.

---

2. Statement of Afghan Foreign Minister Dr. Rangin Dadfar Spanta at the 15th Ministerial Conference of the Non-Aligned Movement in Tehran, July 30, 2008.

We are also profoundly appreciative of the contribution made by the Republic of Cuba for the accomplishments and successes of the initiatives undertaken during their Chairmanship.

Since the inception of the fraternity of the Non-Aligned Movement, there have been remarkable progresses in attaining the founding principles, ideals and purposes of the Movement. The end of formal colonization, growing central role of the UN on the international stage and emergence and consolidation of new norms and principles of international law have created a conducive environment for all members of the family of nations to contribute to building a peaceful, prosperous and just world. The tireless efforts, firm determination and unity of the Non-Aligned Movement played a crucial role in overcoming those forces that were reluctant to accept an equitable world order.

Despite our proud achievements, there remain formidable obstacles in establishing an international system based on sovereignty, shared responsibility and justice. The end of formal colonization has not been accompanied by the legacies of colonization. International institutions, including the UN still reflect the balance of power rather than the equality of their members. Many parts of the world still suffer from the imposed demarcation of their territories by colonial powers.

The legacies of colonization have been compounded by emergence of new threats and challenges. The international community, particularly many of us faces the threats of terrorism, climate change, environmental degradation, organized crimes, poverty, food insecurity, underdevelopment, proliferation of weapons of mass destructions, culturally-oriented racism, Islamophobia, religious intolerance and hatred and growing inequality between and among nations.

Fortunately our Movement is well-placed to assist its members to deal with both types of threats and challenges and utilize the opportunities that our globalizing world has to offer. The Plan of Action on the Non-Aligned Movement is an important tool at our disposal to strengthen the Movement's role and capability in promoting and safeguarding our collective interests and objectives. In order to maintain the relevance and vitality of our Movement, it is imperative that we continue to engage proactively and confidently with issues concerning the Movement. We should not shy away from confronting the issues that may involve ourselves.

Palestine continues to suffer from the unjust treatment that was imposed upon the region. Afghanistan reiterates its call for the full implementation of the UN resolutions on the just settlement of Arab- Israeli conflicts. In this context, we accord full support to all regional and international efforts in creating a peaceful Middle East for all its nations. Afghanistan is also pleased to see recent positive steps and progresses in Iraq, Lebanon and Islamic Republic of Iran's nuclear issue. We insist on the importance of peaceful and diplomatic settlement of all bilateral and international disputes.

Afghanistan is continuing its arduous journey towards re-joining the family of nations as a stable, independent, progressive and democratic nation after emerging from three decades of conflicts. Since the collapse of the Taliban's regime, we have taken important steps towards realizing this objective. Thanks to the determination of the Afghan people and Government and the support of the international community, we have laid down the foundations of our state institutions.

Afghanistan now has an elected President, a National Assembly, a new constitution, expanding interactions with the international community, emerging national security forces, a growing national economy and thriving civil and private sectors.

Rebuilding our country has been accompanied by confronting the legacies of wars, emergence of new challenges and the resurgence of some of the old ones. Unfortunately, Afghanistan is being confronted by the most dangerous types of terrorism. Whereas there are terrorist acts that are prompted by a pervert interpretation of religious texts and doctrines, we also suffer from the utilization of terrorism as an instrument of foreign and security policy of the sponsoring entities.

Afghanistan and Pakistan not only are bounded by a common border but we also share many common characteristics such as language, religion, history and culture. The manifestation of such a friendship was displayed by Pakistan's generous reception of millions of Afghan refugees during our struggle against the invading Red army. We sincerely hope that all entities in the Islamic Republic of Pakistan join hands in the fight against terrorism in all its forms and manifestations for the wellbeing of our two brotherly nations.

We remain confident of your continuing support and engagement with Afghanistan and I can reassure you of our full commitment and firm conviction to the ideals and principles of the Non-Aligned Movement.

(*Source*: http://www.mfa.gov.af/detail.asp?Lang=e&Cat=1&ContID=785)

## United Nations Security Council Resolution 1817

June 11, 2008

**Adopted by the Security Council**
**at its 5907th meeting, on 11 June 2008**

*The Security Council,*

*Recalling* its previous resolutions on Afghanistan, in particular its resolutions 1659 (2006), 1776 (2007) and 1806 (2008), and the statement of its President on 17 June 2003 (S/PRST/2003/7),

*Recalling* its resolutions 1267 (1999) and 1735 (2006), and *reiterating* its support for international efforts to combat terrorism in accordance with international law, including the Charter of the United Nations,

*Reaffirming* its strong commitment to the sovereignty, independence, territorial integrity and national unity of Afghanistan,

*Reaffirming* its continued support for the Government and people of Afghanistan as they rebuild their country, strengthen the foundations of sustainable peace and constitutional democracy and assume their rightful place in the community of nations,

*Noting* with concern the existing links between international security, terrorism and transnational organized crime, money-laundering, trafficking in illicit drugs and illegal arms, and in this regard *emphasizing* the need to enhance coordination of efforts on national, subregional, regional and international levels in order to strengthen a global response to this serious challenge,

*Reiterating* its concern about the security situation in Afghanistan, in particular the continued violent and terrorist activities by the Taliban, Al-Qaida, illegal armed groups, criminals and those involved in the narcotics trade, and the links between illicit drugs trafficking and terrorism, and *Calling upon* the Afghan Government, with the assistance of the international community, including the International Security Assistance Force and Operation Enduring Freedom coalition, in accordance with their respective designated responsibilities as they evolve, to continue to address the threat to the security and stability of Afghanistan posed by the Taliban, Al-Qaida, illegally armed groups, criminals and those involved in the narcotics trade,

*Welcoming* the ongoing efforts of the Government of Afghanistan in the fight against narcotic drugs and also welcoming the efforts of neighbouring countries to address the impact on the region of the production of illicit drugs in Afghanistan, including through interdiction activities, and encouraging the international and regional organizations to enhance their role in the fight against illicit trafficking in narcotics and precursors, Paying homage to the sacrifice of members of the security forces of Afghanistan and its neighbouring countries in the fight against drug traffickers,

*Reiterating* its support for the fight against illicit production and trafficking of drugs from and chemical precursors to Afghanistan, in neighbouring countries, countries on trafficking routes, drug destination countries and precursors producing countries, encouraging increased cooperation between those countries to strengthen anti-narcotics controls to curb the drug flow, including through border management cooperation, and expressing its support for the Paris Pact Initiative, for the outcome of the Second Ministerial Conference organized in Moscow in June 2006, and for the meeting organized in Kabul in October 2007 in the framework of the Paris Pact Initiative; Stressing the need for Member States to take measures, with the support of relevant international actors to combat the laundering of proceeds of criminal activity, corruption and illicit trafficking in narcotics and precursors in line with the outcome of the Moscow Conference,

*Recalling* that achieving a sustained and significant reduction in the production and trafficking of narcotics with a view to eliminating the narcotics industry has been identified as a cross-cutting priority by the "Afghanistan Compact" adopted in London in 2006, which provides the framework for the partnership between the Afghan Government and the international community, as well as the Government of Afghanistan's National Drug Control Strategy,

*Stressing* the importance of a comprehensive approach to address the drug problem of Afghanistan, which, to be effective has to be integrated into the wider context of efforts carried out in the three areas of Security, Governance, Rule of Law and Human Rights, and Economic and Social Development, stressing that the development of alternative livelihood programmes is of key importance in the success of the efforts in counter-narcotics in Afghanistan, and reiterating that extensive efforts have also to be made to reduce the demand of drugs globally in order to contribute to the sustainability of the elimination of illicit cultivation in Afghanistan,

*Expressing* utmost concern at the increase of illegal smuggling, for illicit use, to and within Afghanistan of chemical precursors needed to produce heroin, in particular acetic anhydride, and also hydrochloric acid and acetone, linked to the high level of opium cultivation, production and trafficking, and noting that most of the opium produced in Afghanistan is now processed in the country,

*Recalling* the Political Declaration adopted by the General Assembly at its twentieth special session, in which Member States decided to establish the year 2008 as a target date for States to eliminate or significantly reduce, inter alia, the diversion of precursors, and recognizing that action against the world drug problem is a common and shared responsibility requiring an integrated and balanced approach in full conformity with the purposes and principles of the Charter of the United Nations and international law,

*Acknowledging* the role of the Commission on Narcotic Drugs of the Economic and Social Council as the central policymaking and coordinating body within the United Nations system on international drug control issues, and *welcoming* its intention to consider the issue of precursors control as one of the central questions to be discussed during the high-level segment of the fifty-second session of the Commission on Narcotic Drugs,

*Acknowledging* the mandate and the leading role played by the International Narcotics Control Board (INCB), as an independent treaty body, in the implementation of the United Nations international drug control conventions and the international control of precursors,

*Stressing* the central role played by the United Nations Office on Drugs and Crime (UNODC) in assisting Member States, notably by providing technical assistance, in the fight against illicit drugs,

1. *Expresses* utmost concern at the high level of opium cultivation, production and trafficking, which involves in particular the diversion of chemical precursors, and stresses once again the serious harm that it causes to the security, development and governance of Afghanistan as well as to the region and internationally, and to the success of the international efforts;
2. *Calls upon* all Member States to increase international and regional cooperation in order to counter the illicit production and trafficking of drugs in Afghanistan, including by strengthening the monitoring of the international trade in chemical precursors, notably but not limited to acetic anhydride, and to prevent attempts to divert the substances from licit international trade for illicit use in Afghanistan;
3. *Invites* all Member States, in particular chemical precursors producing countries, Afghanistan, neighbouring countries, and all countries on the trafficking routes to increase their cooperation with the INCB, notably by fully complying with the provisions of article 12 of United Nations Convention against Illicit Traffic in Narcotic Drugs and Psychotropic Substances, 1988, in order to eliminate loopholes utilized by criminal organizations to divert chemical precursors from licit international trade;
4. *Urges* exporting States to ensure the systematic notification of all exports of relevant chemical precursors, upon request from importing States, in accordance with provisions of the 1988 Convention, and encourages importing States to request the systematic notification of such exports; also urges the Governments that have not yet done so to register with and utilize the online system for the exchange of pre-export notifications (PEN Online);
5. *Calls upon* States that have not done so to consider ratifying or acceding to, and State parties to implement fully the multilateral treaties whose aim is to fight against the illicit trafficking of narcotic drugs, notably the United Nations Single Convention on Narcotic Drugs, 1961, as amended by the Protocol of 25 March 1972 and the United Nations Convention against Illicit Traffic in Narcotic Drugs and Psychotropic Substances, 1988, underlines the importance for all States parties to these treaties to implement them fully, and stresses that nothing in this resolution will impose on State parties new obligations with regard to these treaties;

6. *Expresses* its continued support to the commitment and efforts of Afghanistan to achieve a sustained and significant reduction in the production and trafficking of narcotics with a view to complete elimination, *Expresses also* its support to the Afghan National Drug Control Strategy and calls on the Afghan Government, with the assistance of the international community, to accelerate its implementation, as discussed at the seventh meeting of the Joint Coordinating and Monitoring Board (JCMB) held in Tokyo in February 2008, and *Calls for* additional international support for the priorities identified in that Strategy;
7. *Calls upon* all Member States, in particular chemical precursors producing countries, Afghanistan, neighbouring countries and all countries on the trafficking routes to adopt adequate national legislation, consistent with the requirements of relevant international conventions to which they are parties, where it has not yet been done, and to strengthen their national capacities in the areas of
   (i) regulation and monitoring of manufacture and trade of chemical precursors, with a view to controlling the final destination of such chemicals and (ii) specialized enforcement operations against the diversion of precursors, including for their detection and disposal in Afghanistan and the region, and for strengthening border controls;
8. *Invites* the international community to provide financial and technical assistance and support, in building national capacity in the fields referred to in paragraph 7, to Afghanistan and, where appropriate and upon request, neighbouring countries, including through voluntary contributions to UNODC; *stresses* in particular the importance of training and equipping law enforcement agencies, including border police and customs officers, so as to allow them to deal efficiently with such tasks as detection, scanning, stockpiling, transportation and destruction of chemical precursors; and *encourages* Afghanistan and its neighbours to make full use of such assistance;
9. *Reiterates* its support for the Paris Pact Initiative aimed at facilitating counter-narcotics cooperation and coordination among countries seriously affected by the trafficking of narcotic drugs produced in Afghanistan, for the outcome of the Second Ministerial Conference organized in Moscow in June 2006 (S/2006/598), in cooperation with UNODC, and for other international and/or regional relevant initiatives, such as Project Cohesion, and calls upon Paris Pact partners to further promote international and regional initiatives;

10. *Welcomes* the launch, under the guidance of UNODC and the Project Cohesion Task Force, of the Targeted Anti-Trafficking Regional Communication, Expertise and Training (TARCET) initiative, targeting precursors used in the manufacture of heroin in Afghanistan, and urges the Paris Pact partners to cooperate closely in a view to achieve its successful implementation;
11. *Recognizes* the legitimate need of industry to have access to precursors and its important role in preventing the diversion of precursors, and *encourages* all Member States, in particular producing countries, Afghanistan and its neighbours to develop partnerships with the private sector so as to prevent the diversion of precursors;
12. *Looks forward* to the outcome of the international conference in support of Afghanistan, which will be held in Paris on 12 June 2008, and encourages the participants to the Conference to make concrete proposals on the ways to address the problem of diversion of chemical precursors for illicit use, in the wider framework of the discussions on the strengthening of counter-narcotics activities in the Afghanistan National Development Strategy and National Drug Control Strategy;
13. *Encourages* Member States to submit to the Committee established pursuant to resolution 1267 (1999) for inclusion on the Consolidated List names of individuals and entities participating in the financing or support of acts or activities of Al-Qaida, Usama bin Laden and the Taliban, and other individuals, groups, undertakings and entities associated with them, using proceeds derived from the illicit cultivation, production, and trafficking of narcotic drugs produced in Afghanistan and their precursors, in order to give full effect to the relevant provisions of resolution 1735 (2006);
14. *Requests* the Secretary-General to include, as appropriate, in his regular reports to the Security Council and the General Assembly on the situation in Afghanistan, in close consultation with UNODC and INCB, observations and recommendations on the fight against drug production and trafficking, notably on the issue of the illicit traffic of chemical precursors to and within Afghanistan;
15. *Invites* the Commission on Narcotic Drugs to consider, in accordance with its mandate, ways to strengthen regional and international cooperation to prevent the diversion and smuggling of chemical precursors to and within Afghanistan, and further opportunities for Member States to support the Afghan Government in developing capacities to tackle precursors and trafficking;
16. *Decides* to remain seized of the matter.

## An Appraisal on Developments in Afghanistan[3]

April 3, 2008

*President Hamid Karzai underlined the role that the external powers along with NATO had played in Afghanistan. Citing that over thousands schools and hundred health clinics have been built; he stated that Afghanistan could be an effective economic land bridge in the Asian region. He asserted that efforts should be focused on training, equipping and expanding the Afghan security forces.*

Six and half years ago, Afghanistan presented the world with a crucial set of questions, the answer to which is continuing to define not just the future of Afghanistan but also the security of the world at large. Would the world decide to act together to address the threat of international terrorism? And would the Afghan people finally get a chance to decide their own destiny, become a stable, democratic prosperous country that will never again become a safe haven for international terrorism. Six and half years ago, the people of Afghanistan and the international community led by the United States joined hands to liberate Afghanistan from the grip of international terrorism and to begin the journey of rebuilding a nation from a past of violence, destruction and terror. We have come a long way in this shared journey. Today, I am here not just to discuss the way forward in Afghanistan, but also to express the gratitude of the Afghan people for the invaluable role that NATO, individual member states and other countries from around the world have played over the past years.

In a few short years, as a result of partnership between Afghanistan and the international community, we were able to create a new, democratic constitution, embracing the freedom of speech and equal rights for women; voted in the first-ever democratic elections for the president and brought an elected parliament. Today close to five million Afghan refugees have come home, one of the largest return movements in history.

Thousands of schools have been built, welcoming over six million boys and girls, the highest in our history. Hundreds of health clinics have been established boosting our basic health coverage from a depressing 9 percent six years ago to over 85 percent today. Access to diagnostic and curative services has increased from almost none in 2002 to more than forty percent today. We have built 4,000 km of paved roads, over the past six years, more than ever existed in Afghanistan. Our rapid economic growth, with a double digit growth rate almost every year, has resulted in

---

3. Statement by Mr. Hamid Karzai President of the Islamic Republic of Afghanistan, Afghanistan Contributor's Meeting, NATO Summit, April 3, 2008.

higher income and better living conditions for our people. With a developing road network and a state-of-the-art communication infrastructure, Afghanistan is better poised to serve as an economic land-bridge in our region.

The creation of the Afghan National Army and police represents a guarantee of future stability for our country. While the Afghan National Army has received early attention and as such its abilities have increased, we are placing a stronger emphasis on support to building the capabilities of our national police.

All these and much more that I did not mention today would not have been possible without your help.

I hasten to point out that our achievements must not distract us from the enormity of the tasks that are still at hand.

I find this summit a great opportunity to share with you my expectations and concerns about the way forward.

Among the challenges, terrorism is by far the most menacing, particularly with a view to the growing regional dimensions of the threat. Today, the terrorism thathas affected Afghanistan for years is also presenting a challenge to the stability of Pakistan and requires a stronger military and political response from all of us.

I reiterate Afghanistan's commitment to a strong regional and international cooperation in the fight against terrorism and our readiness to play a full part. Asan integral element of this cooperation, NATO must remain strong, united and flexible to adjust to the evolving need of the campaign.

In the political context, we believe that those members of the Taliban willing to return to Afghanistan to lead more rewarding, civilian lives under our constitution, must be allowed to do so. We must also work more vigorously to retain and promote the active support of local communities who, in reality, are at the frontline of our war against terrorism. In this regard, the issue of civilian casualties as a result of counter-terrorism operations remains a serious concern for the Afghan people. I thank General Dan McNeil for his constructive engagement with us on the issue and I hope that NATO members will take every possible measure to prevent civilian casualties.

The Afghan nation has a genuine desire to stand on its own feet, and not to be a burden on your shoulders longer than necessary. In our effort to assume greater responsibility in meeting our security challenges, I call for the strengthening of efforts aimed at training, equipping and expanding the Afghan security forces.

Thankfully, with your help, today we are at a stage where we can begin the long desired process of Afghan-i-zation. As a concrete step in this direction, I am pleased to announce that the Afghan forces are prepared to take responsibility for the security of Kabul and we are currently working with NATO to implement this decision by August this year. I am confident that in the future, with the increased capabilities of our security forces, we will gradually assume responsibility in other parts of the country as well.

In our on-going efforts for government reform, in 2007 I established the Independent Directorate for Local Governance and tasked it to vigorously review and address the cumbersome system of provincial and district administrations in the country.

Recognizing the key importance of a credible and functioning administration at these levels, the new department has streamlined the process of senior appointments to local government jobs.

The restoration of Afghan judiciary from a shattered, discredited institution in the past, to a functional and credible system, capable of dispensing justice and putting an end to impunity, has been one of our hardest tasks. We have come a long-distance in this effort and, thankfully, today tangible results are visible. Continued efforts, matched by your continued support in this field will be needed for a much longer time to come.

On corruption, we are fully aware that our progress is affected by the betrayal of public trust by some functionaries of the state, or the faulty mechanisms of aid delivery. I appointed a commission last year, led by the Chief Justice, to identify the sources and causes of corruption and draw up an anti-corruption action plan after a year of hard work, the commission has completed a very detailed study which was presented to me two weeks ago. We will soon decide on the effective implementation of the Commission's recommendations.

Allow me to turn for a moment to the menace of narcotics, another of Afghanistan's serious challenges and one that has a close relationship with terrorism. It is troubling that, despite the significant reduction in poppy growing provinces, the total poppy harvest in 2007 moved upwards.

Our objective for 2008 is to further increase the number of poppy free provinces, and to reduce the poppy growing fields by at least 25 percent. The fight against poppy cultivation will only be successful through increased security, better governance and more importantly alternative livelihood. This calls for a greater role by the international community to step in and help the Afghan government more vigorously. What remains to be addressed is the strong and diffused network of drug trade in the region and beyond that is sustaining the drug economy in Afghanistan.

While the challenges in the governance area are mostly for the Afghans to address, and we will address them; we need your support in further strengthening the development agenda. We Afghans are very grateful for your generous assistance in the reconstruction of our country, but it is clear that we must use your hard earned tax-payers' money better and more efficiently. It is time aid effectiveness became a central concern for all of us.

In two months, at the initiative of President Nicolas Sarkozi, a donor conference on Afghanistan will be held in Paris. I would like that conference to be an opportunity for the Afghan Government and our partners from the international community to emphasize the correlation between security and development, and to revisit the question of whether the scale of the development programme for Afghanistan is commensurate to the challenges facing the country.

I also emphasise the critical role of the United Nations in coordinating the positions of the international community, and maintaining strong partnership with the Afghan Government. In this context, I welcome the appointment of the new special representative of the Secretary General of the UN, Mr Kai Eide. My government and I are looking forward to working closely with him.

Today, at this important summit, I am asking you to recommit, fully and unreservedly, to the goal of supporting Afghanistan to achieve stability and prosperity. Thanks to your support, a remarkable transformation is already afoot in Afghanistan. Our nation is liberated from decades of oppression, violence and interference and moving to realize its long-suppressed potential for development. It is not easy for me to describe what it really means when a nation gets an opportunity to take its destiny in its own hands! Suffice to imagine a thriving moment, bursting with hope and anxiety, in a struggle between the gift of freedom and a deep sense of responsibility to protect it.

Thanks to the sacrifices of your men and women, and to the continued determination of our own people, that moment in Afghanistan is today.

(*Source*: http://www.fco.gov.uk/en/fco-in-action/uk-in-afghanistan/afghanistan-news-archive/afg-newsfile-karzaiNATOsummitBuc).

## United Nations Security Council Resolution 1806

March 20, 2008

**Adopted by the Security Council at its 5857th meeting**

*The Security Council,*

*Recalling* its previous resolutions on Afghanistan, in particular its resolution 1746 (2007) extending through 23 March 2008 the mandate of the United Nations Assistance Mission in Afghanistan (UNAMA) as established by resolution 1662 (2006), and *recalling also* its resolution 1659 (2006) endorsing the Afghanistan Compact,

*Reaffirming* its strong commitment to the sovereignty, independence, territorial integrity and national unity of Afghanistan,

*Reaffirming* its continued support for the Government and people of Afghanistan as they rebuild their country, strengthen the foundations of sustainable peace and constitutional democracy and assume their rightful place in the community of nations,

*Reaffirming* in this context its support for the implementation, under the ownership of the Afghan people, of the Afghanistan Compact, of the Afghanistan National Development Strategy (ANDS) and of the National Drugs Control Strategy, and *noting* that sustained and coordinated efforts by all relevant actors are required to consolidate progress made towards their implementation and to overcome continuing challenges,

*Recalling* that the Afghanistan Compact is based on a partnership between the Afghan Government and the international community, based on the desire of the parties for Afghanistan to progressively assume responsibility for its own development and security, and with a central and impartial coordinating role for the United Nations,

*Stressing* the central and impartial role that the United Nations continues to play in promoting peace and stability in Afghanistan by leading the efforts of the international community, including, jointly with the Government of Afghanistan, the coordination and monitoring of efforts in implementing the Afghanistan Compact, and *expressing* its appreciation and strong support for the ongoing efforts of the Secretary-General, his Special Representative for Afghanistan and the women and men of UNAMA,

*Recognizing* once again the interconnected nature of the challenges in Afghanistan, *reaffirming* that sustainable progress on security, governance and development, as well as the cross-cutting issue of counter-narcotics is mutually reinforcing and *welcoming* the continuing efforts of the Afghan Government and the international community to address these challenges through a comprehensive approach,

*Stressing* the importance of a comprehensive approach in addressing the challenges in Afghanistan and *noting*, in this context, the synergies in the objectives of UNAMA and of the International Security Assistance Force (ISAF), and *stressing* the need for strengthened cooperation, coordination and mutual support, taking due account of their respective designated responsibilities,

*Reiterating* its concern about the security situation in Afghanistan, in particular the increased violent and terrorist activities by the Taliban, Al-Qaida, illegally armed groups, criminals and those involved in the narcotics trade, and the increasingly strong links between terrorism activities and illicit drugs, resulting in threats to the local population, including children, national security forces and international military and civilian personnel,

*Stressing* the importance of ensuring safe and unhindered access of humanitarian workers, including United Nations staff and associated personnel,

*Expressing also* its concern over the harmful consequences of violent and terrorist activities by the Taliban, Al-Qaida and other extremist groups on the capacity of the Afghan Government to guarantee the rule of law, to provide security and basic services to the Afghan people, and to ensure the improvement and protection of their human rights and fundamental freedoms,

*Recalling* the importance of the Kabul Declaration of 22 December 2002 on Good-Neighbourly Relations (Kabul Declaration) (S/2002/1416), *looking forward* to the Third Regional Economic Cooperation Conference on Afghanistan to be held in Islamabad, and *stressing* the crucial importance of advancing regional cooperation as an effective means to promote security, governance and development in Afghanistan,

*Welcoming* the holding of the Afghan-Pakistani Peace Jirga in Kabul on August 2007 and the collective determination expressed at the Jirga to bring sustainable peace to the region, including by addressing the terrorist threat, and *expressing its support* for the relevant follow-up processes,

*Recalling* its resolutions 1265 (1999), 1296 (2000), 1674 (2006), 1738 (2006) on the protection of civilians in armed conflict, its resolution 1325 (2000) on women and peace and security, and its resolution 1612 (2005) on children and armed conflict, and *taking note with appreciation* of the 7th report of the Secretary-General (S/2007/757) on Children and Armed Conflict of 21 December 2007,

1. *Welcomes* the report of the Secretary-General of 6 March 2008 (S/2008/159);
2. *Expresses its appreciation* for the United Nations long-term commitment to work with the Government and the people of Afghanistan;
3. *Decides* to extend the mandate of UNAMA, as defined in its resolutions 1662 (2006) and 1746 (2007), until 23 March 2009;
4. *Decides* further that UNAMA and the Special Representative of the Secretary-General, within their mandate and guided by the principle of reinforcing Afghan ownership and leadership, will lead the international civilian efforts to, inter alia:
   (a) promote, as co-chair of the Joint Coordination and Monitoring Board (JCMB), more coherent support by the international community to the Afghan Government and the adherence to the principles of aid effectiveness enumerated in the Afghanistan Compact, including through mobilization of resources, coordination of the assistance provided by international donors and organizations, and direction of the contributions of United Nations agencies, funds and programmes, in particular for counter-narcotics, reconstruction and development activities;

(b) strengthen the cooperation with ISAF at all levels and throughout the country, in accordance with their existing mandates, in order to improve civil-military coordination, to facilitate the timely exchange of information and to ensure coherence between the activities of national and international security forces and of civilian actors in support of an Afghan-led development and stabilization process, including through engagement with provincial reconstruction teams and engagement with non-governmental organizations;

(c) through a strengthened and expanded presence throughout the country, provide political outreach, promote at the local level the implementation of the Compact, of the ANDS and of the National Drugs Control Strategy, and facilitate inclusion in and understanding of the Government's policies;

(d) provide good offices to support, if requested by the Afghan Government, the implementation of Afghan-led reconciliation programmes, within the framework of the Afghan Constitution and with full respect of the implementation of measures introduced by the Security Council in its resolution 1267 (1999) and other relevant resolutions of the Council;

(e) support efforts, including through the Independent Directorate for Local Governance, to improve governance and the rule of law and to combat corruption, in particular at subnational level, and to promote development initiatives at the local level with a view to helping bring the benefits of peace and deliver services in a timely and sustainable manner;

(f) play a central coordinating role to facilitate the delivery of humanitarian assistance in accordance with humanitarian principles and with a view to building the capacity of the Afghan Government, including by providing effective support to national and local authorities in assisting and protecting internally displaced persons and to creating conditions conducive to the voluntary, safe, dignified and sustainable return of refugees and internally displaced persons;

(g) continue, with the support of the Office of the United Nations High Commissioner for Human Rights, to cooperate with the Afghan Independent Human Rights Commission (AIHRC), to cooperate also with relevant international and local non-governmental organizations, to monitor the situation of civilians, to coordinate efforts to ensure their protection and to assist in the full implementation of the fundamental freedoms and human rights provisions of the Afghan Constitution and international treaties to which Afghanistan is a state party, in particular those regarding the full enjoyment by women of their human rights;

(h) support, at the request of the Afghan authorities, the electoral process, in particular through the Afghan Independent Electoral Commission (AIEC), by providing technical assistance, coordinating other international donors, agencies and organizations providing assistance and channelling existing and additional funds earmarked to support the process;

(i) support regional cooperation to work towards a stable and prosperous Afghanistan;

5. *Calls upon* all Afghan and international parties to coordinate with UNAMA in the implementation of its mandate and in efforts to promote the security and freedom of movement of United Nations and associated personnel throughout the country;
6. *Stresses* the importance of strengthening and expanding the presence of UNAMA and other United Nations agencies, funds and programmes in the provinces, and *encourages* the Secretary-General to pursue current efforts to finalize the necessary arrangements to address the security issues associated with such strengthening and expansion;
7. *Calls* on the Afghan Government, and the international community and international organizations, to implement the Afghanistan Compact and its annexes in full, and *stresses* in this context the importance of meeting the benchmarks and timelines of the Compact for progress on security, governance, rule of law and human rights, and economic and social development, as well as the cross-cutting issue of counter-narcotics;
8. *Reaffirms* the central role played by the JCMB in coordinating, facilitating and monitoring the implementation of the Compact, *stresses* the need to strengthen its authority and capacity to, inter alia, measure progress towards the benchmarks outlined in the Afghanistan Compact and facilitate the coordination of international assistance in support of the ANDS, and *calls upon* all relevant actors to cooperate with the JCMB in this regard, including by reporting assistance programmes to the Afghan Government's aid coordination unit and to the JCMB;
9. *Welcomes* the progress made by the Afghan Government in the finalization of the ANDS, *looks forward* to its launch, and *stresses* the importance, in this context, of adequate resource mobilization, including through the fulfilment of the pledges made at the London Conference, possible new pledges and increased assistance to the core budget;

10. *Notes* with interest the intention, expressed by JCMB members at the Political Directors Meeting on Afghanistan held in Tokyo on 5 February 2008, to prepare an international conference to review progress on the implementation of the Afghanistan Compact, *welcomes* the offer of France to host such conference in Paris in June 2008, and *requests* the Secretary-General to report to the Security Council on its outcome and to include in this report, if necessary, further recommendations concerning UNAMA's mandate;
11. *Calls upon* the Afghan Government, with the assistance of the international community, including the International Security Assistance Force and Operation Enduring Freedom coalition, in accordance with their respective designated responsibilities as they evolve, to continue to address the threat to the security and stability of Afghanistan posed by the Taliban, Al-Qaida, illegally armed groups, criminals and those involved in the narcotics trade;
12. *Condemns* in the strongest terms all attacks, including Improvised Explosive Device (IED) attacks, suicide attacks and abductions, targeting civilians and Afghan and international forces and their deleterious effect on the stabilization, reconstruction and development efforts in Afghanistan, and *condemns further* the use by the Taliban and other extremist groups of civilians as human shields;
13. *Reiterates* its concern about all civilian casualties, *calls* for compliance with international humanitarian and human rights law and for all appropriate steps to be taken to ensure the protection of civilians, and *recognizes* in this context the robust efforts taken by ISAF and other international forces to minimize the risk of civilian casualties, notably the continuous review of tactics and procedures and the conduct of after-action reviews in cooperation with the Afghan Government in cases where civilian casualties have reportedly occurred;
14. *Expresses its strong concern* about the recruitment and use of children by Taliban forces in Afghanistan as well as the killing and maiming of children as a result of the conflict, *reiterates its strong condemnation* of the recruitment and use of child soldiers in violation of applicable international law and all other violations and abuses committed against children in situations of armed conflict, and *stresses* the importance of implementing Security Council resolution 1612 (2005); in this context, *requests* the Secretary-General to strengthen the child protection component of UNAMA, in particular through the appointment of child protection advisers;

15. *Stresses* the importance of increasing, in a comprehensive framework, the functionality, professionalism and accountability of the Afghan security sector through training, mentoring and empowerment efforts, in order to accelerate progress towards the goal of self-sufficient and ethnically balanced Afghan security forces providing security and ensuring the rule of law throughout the country;
16. *Welcomes* in this context the continued progress in the development of the Afghan National Army and its improved ability to plan and undertake operations, and *encourages* sustained training efforts, including through the Operational Mentoring and Liaison Teams (OMLTs), and advise in developing a sustainable defence planning process as well as assistance in defence reform initiatives;
17. *Calls* for further efforts to enhance the capabilities of the Afghan National Police in order to reinforce the authority of the Afghan Government throughout the country, *welcomes* the increasing role played by the International Police Coordination Board in policy setting and coordination, and *stresses* the importance, in this context, of the contribution of the European Union through its police mission (EUPOL Afghanistan);
18. *Calls* for further progress in the implementation by the Afghan Government, with support from the international community, of the programme of disbandment of illegal armed groups (DIAG);
19. *Expresses* its concern at the serious harm that increasing opium cultivation, production and trafficking causes to the security, development and governance of Afghanistan as well as to the region and internationally; *calls on* the Afghan Government, with the assistance of the international community, to accelerate the implementation of the National Drug Control Strategy as discussed at the JCMB meeting held in Tokyo in February 2008, in particular at the local level, and to mainstream counter-narcotics throughout national programmes; *encourages* additional international support for the four priorities identified in that Strategy, including through contributions to the Counter Narcotics Trust Fund;
20. *Calls upon* States to strengthen international and regional cooperation to counter the threat to the international community posed by the illicit production and trafficking of drugs originated in Afghanistan, including through border management cooperation in drug control and cooperation for the fight against the illicit trafficking in drugs and precursors and against money-laundering linked to such trafficking, taking into account the outcome of the Second Ministerial Conference on Drug Trafficking Routes from Afghanistan organized by the Government of the Russian

Federation in cooperation with the United Nations Office on Drugs and Crime held in Moscow from 26 to 28 June 2006 (S/2006/598), within the framework of the Paris Pact initiative;

21. *Welcomes* the adoption by the Afghan authorities, in accordance with the outcome of the Rome Conference on the Rule of Law in Afghanistan, of the National Justice Programme launched at the JCMB meeting held in Tokyo in February 2008, and *stresses* the importance of its full and timely implementation by all the relevant actors in order to accelerate the establishment of a fair and transparent justice system, strengthen the rule of law throughout the country and eliminate impunity;
22. *Stresses* in this context the importance of further progress in the reconstruction and reform of the prison sector in Afghanistan, in order to improve the respect for the rule of law and human rights therein;
23. *Notes with concern* the effects of widespread corruption on security, good governance, counter-narcotics efforts and economic development, and *calls on* the Afghan Government, with the assistance of the international community, to vigorously lead the fight against corruption and to enhance its efforts to establish a more effective, accountable and transparent administration;
24. *Encourages* all Afghan institutions, including the executive and legislative branches, to work in a spirit of cooperation, *calls on* the Afghan Government to pursue continued legislative and public administration reform in order to ensure good governance, full representation and accountability at both national and subnational levels, *stresses* the need for further international efforts to provide technical assistance in this area, and *recalls* the role of the Senior Appointments Panel in accordance with the Afghanistan Compact;
25. *Encourages* the international community to assist the Government of Afghanistan in making capacity-building and human resources development a cross-cutting priority;
26. *Notes* the leading role that the Afghan institutions will play in the organization of the next elections, *encourages* the Afghan Government, with support from the international community, to accelerate the planning and preparation of such elections, *stresses the need* to establish a permanent Civil Voter Registry (CVR) in accordance with the Afghanistan Compact, and *emphasizes* the importance of free, fair, inclusive and transparent elections in order to sustain the democratic progress of the country;
27. *Calls for* full respect for human rights and fundamental freedoms and international humanitarian law throughout Afghanistan, *notes with concern* the increasing restrictions on freedom of media,

*commends* the AIHRC for its courageous efforts to monitor respect for human rights in Afghanistan as well as to foster and protect these rights and to promote the emergence of a pluralistic civil society, and *stresses* the importance of full cooperation with the AIHRC by all relevant actors;

28. *Recognizes* the significant progress achieved on gender equality in Afghanistan in recent years, *strongly condemns* continuing forms of discrimination and violence against women and girls, *stresses* the importance of implementing Security Council resolution 1325 (2000), and *requests* the Secretary-General to continue to include in its reports to the Security Council relevant information on the process of integration of women into the political, economic and social life of Afghanistan;
29. *Calls for* enhanced efforts to ensure the full implementation of the Action Plan on Peace, Justice and Reconciliation in accordance with the Afghanistan Compact, without prejudice to the implementation of measures introduced by the Security Council in its resolution 1267 (1999) of 15 October 1999 and other relevant resolutions of the Security Council;
30. *Welcomes* the cooperation of the Afghan Government and UNAMA with the Security Council Committee established pursuant to resolution 1267 (1999) with the implementation of resolution 1735 (2006), including by identifying individuals and entities participating in the financing or support of acts or activities of Al-Qaida and the Taliban using proceeds derived from illicit cultivation, production and trafficking of narcotic drugs and their precursors, and *encourages* the continuation of such cooperation;
31. *Welcomes* ongoing efforts by the Government of Afghanistan and its neighbouring and regional partners to foster trust and cooperation with each other, including recent cooperation initiatives developed by regional organizations, and *stresses* the importance of increasing cooperation between Afghanistan and the partners against the Taliban, Al-Qaida and other extremist groups, in promoting peace and prosperity in Afghanistan and in fostering cooperation in the economic and development sectors as a means to achieve the full integration of Afghanistan into regional dynamics and the global economy;
32. *Calls for* strengthening the process of regional economic cooperation, including measures to facilitate regional trade, to increase foreign investments and to develop infrastructure, noting Afghanistan's historic role as a land bridge in Asia;
33. *Recognizes* the importance of voluntary, safe, orderly return and sustainable reintegration of the remaining Afghan refugees for the

stability of the country and the region, and *calls for* continued and enhanced international assistance in this regard;

34. *Requests* the Secretary-General to report to the Council every six months on developments in Afghanistan, in addition to the report requested in paragraph 10 of this resolution;
35. *Decides* to remain actively seized of the matter.

## An Afghan View on the Security Policy[4]

October 2, 2007

*The Afghanistan National Security Advisor, Mr. Zalmai Rassul, spoke of the challenges confronting the country specifically in the South and East. He appreciated the role played by the NATO, Afghan National Security Forces and pointed out that fighting terrorism is the key responsibility of Afghanistan. He also commented upon on the state of education, which he stated was being adversely affected by the conflict. He highlighted the need for a counter narcotics and eradication programme and underlined the need for oversight mechanisms to fight corruption.*

Thank you for your kind invitation to participate in this 43rd meeting. Before I begin my short remarks, I want to extend the gratitude of the Afghan people for your commitment and sacrifices to improving the lives of all Afghans and for welcoming my country into the civilized community of democratic nations. It is that welcome to democracy that we embraced five years ago, and ever since, have devoted our daily efforts to attain. Yes indeed, a democratic, peaceful and prosperous Afghanistan would contribute much in furthering democracy and peace throughout the Greater Middle East. Let me briefly outline some key areas we are diligently working on and some challenges we are committed to overcome.

Some of you here today have personally experienced the transition from a totalitarian regime to a democratic government and can certainly attest that striving to live and breathe democracy is hard work indeed. It takes security, good governance and prosperity - all three need to be moving in the right direction, and any one area that falls short can dramatically and negatively affect the other two. So, how is Afghanistan faring on its path to democracy and as a contributor to regional stability?

### SECURITY

The security situation in the South and East remains a challenge to all of us - Afghans, NATO, the U.S. and our Coalition allies. The resurgence of

4. Speech by Afghan National Security Advisor, Mr Zalmai Rassul, at the 43rd Munich Conference on Security Policy, October 2, 2007.

Talibans and influx of foreign fighters is a great cause of concern. With a safe sanctuary across the border the Talibans are able to rearm, recruit, regroup and reorganise at will. Almost 4,000 lives were lost last year, including Afghan, international, civilian and military. Our enemies have successfully adopted the hideous tactics of suicide bombings, IEDs and assassination. Last year we witnessed a 6-fold increase in suicide attacks, a 3-fold increase in direct attacks against Afghan and Coalition forces, and a doubling of the number of IED attacks. But with the help of our coalition friends and NATO, the Afghan National Security Forces continue to be better manned, better equipped, better trained, and increasingly able to conduct operations on their own. The recent arrival of hundreds of tactical vehicles and weapons will greatly assist our efforts as we continue to grow more capable and confident army and police leaders. After all it is our responsibility to be the front line of the fight against terrorism.

We recently welcomed General Dan McNeil back to Afghanistan as the commander of 35,000 NATO and Coalition forces from 37 nations. We also welcomed his words that indicated his primary mission will be to facilitate the reconstruction of Afghanistan so that the Afghan people will enjoy their hopes and dreams. Isn't that what democracy is all about? Yes, full victory in Afghanistan will take more than the military success that we will certainly see this year from NATO and Coalition warriors - it will take more reconstruction and development, a good system of governance and something we are hoping for - working partnership with Pakistan in addressing the issue of sanctuary and cross-border activities of the terrorists.

In that vein, let me thank my Pakistani colleague here today on their recent establishment of a Commission to address the joint Loyal Peace Jirgas agreed to by both our Presidents last fall in Washington. A key ingredient to improved border security; these Jirgas will empower the border region's traditional leadership against extremist elements. We look forward to positive results and a significant decrease in insurgent attacks from our eastern and southern borders. We have always believed that the full cooperation of Pakistan with Afghanistan and our allies is critical for defeating the terrorist threat and realizing the regional stability of the Greater Middle East.

Another area of security that impacts our forward progress toward democracy is the threat to our schools, our teachers, and our young students. Five years ago, there were only one million Afghan children attending school - today, there are over six million, and most encouraging, more than two million of those are girls - as you know, forbidden from education under the Taliban. But of the 9,000 schools in my country today, nearly 200 were burned or destroyed last year and 400 more closed by threats or intimidation, driving 130,000 students from their classrooms. Instinctively, the Afghan people have taken to creating "defence committees" with the help of local elders, clerics and ordinary citizens to stop this impediment to progress and democratic reform.

## GOVERNANCE

Again, many of you here know that rebuilding a nation takes time, determination and great patience. Five years on since Bonn, and just one year since the Afghan Compact in London, Afghanistan has made great strides toward democratic governance, but we still have serious challenges and a very long ways to go. Still, in just five years since emerging from rubble, we have a strong Constitution, a popularly elected President, an elected and increasingly engaged Parliament, and an appointed Chief Justice and Supreme Court. All three branches of government are striving to communicate better, function better, and govern better in the interests of the nation and its people. We are developing better practices, employing improved technology, and striving to employ the most professional and ethical citizens for government service. Our serious challenges to effective governance remain the illegal drug trade and corruption.

Most of you have read that opium production in my country increased by 49% last year and represents almost 90% of the world's illegal opium output. While most districts and localities do not grow opium and it involves only 4% of cultivable areas, its illegal economy represents almost a third of Afghanistan's total economic activity. We desperately need more effective counter-narcotics and eradication programs that provide viable incentives and development - since eradication without aid merely supports the Taliban. This challenge also underlines the importance of increased efforts to strengthen and reform key governance institutions such as the police, to help rebuild trust in government.

Corruption is poisoning our efforts to build a capable and credible system of governance. Eliminating corruption is the most important issue for building confidence of the people and the people have vigorously made their views known that they support our efforts. Our new Attorney General has already taken initiatives to identify, arrest and prosecute corrupt officials and our government will continue to get better in this regard. In order to eliminate corruption entirely, it is important to direct more funds to projects that not only improve our economy, but also increase government revenues - such as power plants, roads and initiatives in the agricultural sector.

## PROSPERITY

Economic prosperity for the Afghan people is critical for our successful journey to democracy and regional stability. While the average Afghan continues to do better every year, there is still a long way to go. 74% of Afghans say that living conditions today are better than under the Taliban.

Per-capita income has doubled in the last three years and the inflation rate of 48% in 2002 is down to just 9% today. While our economy is growing, it is still not sufficient to generate the large numbers of jobs necessary to substantially reduce poverty or overcome widespread popular disaffection. So, while we have come far these past five years with the tremendous help of the international community, we are standing at a crossroads in 2007 between continuing to move forward along the democratic path with rejuvenated economic development efforts, or letting our opportunities for success slip from our grasp. The recent commitment from the United States for an additional 2 billion dollars for reconstruction will go a long way to moving us further along that path.

Although landlocked, Afghanistan is privileged to share common borders with six other nations and is striving to become a viable contributor to regional stability, not a detractor. It is therefore critical for regional stability that our joint and sustained approach to security issues with all our neighbours be successful. But it is clear to me that ultimately, it will be the success of Pakistan and Afghanistan, acting as strong, stable and prosperous neighbours that will contribute the most to the security and stability of our region.

Yes, democracy is very hard work but we know it is worth it. The will of the Afghan people to move forward with our transition remains strong and steadfast. With dedicated leadership in Kabul and sustained help from our international friends, I believe 2007 will see Afghanistan making great strides to improve security, governance and prosperity on our path to democracy and regional stability.

(*Source*: http://www.securityconference.de/konferenzen/rede.php?menu_2007=&menu_konferenzen=&sprache=en&id=191&)

## Joint Statement by the Foreign Ministers of the G-8 and the Foreign Ministers of Afghanistan and Pakistan on the "G-8 Afghanistan-Pakistan Initiative", Potsdam

May 30, 2007

*A joint statement by G-8, Pakistan and Afghanistan, reinforced the core values of the Afghanistan Compact, 2006, stating that promotion of freedom, democracy, rule of law, human rights, economic growth and opportunity would be the core priorities. The linkage between terrorism, organized crime and drug trafficking was highlighted. Pakistan and Afghanistan resolved to cooperate on specific issue relating to security, refugees, economic development etc.*

1. The Foreign Ministers of the G8, Afghanistan and Pakistan came together today to reiterate their strong commitment to security, stability and lasting peace in Afghanistan and the region. They recalled the commitments made in the Afghanistan Compact in January 2006. Continued support of the international community to the region is a vital element in the global fight against terrorism and for the promotion of freedom, democracy, rule of law, human rights, and economic growth and opportunity.
2. They underlined their common interest in working together to promote peace, security and development in the region and stressed the need for the international community to support this objective.
3. In this context, the Foreign Ministers of the G8 recalled the Kabul Declaration of Good Neighbourly Relations of 22 December 2002 and their statement of 23 June 2005. They commended the joint Peace and Security Jirgas (gatherings) between Afghanistan and Pakistan as well as the commitments Afghanistan and Pakistan have taken on in the "Ankara Declaration" on 30 April 2007 to enhance their cooperation and combine their efforts to enhance the security and prosperity of their peoples. They also appreciated the Government of Pakistan's offer to host the next meeting of the Regional Economic Cooperation Conference on Afghanistan (RECCA).
4. The Foreign Ministers of the G8, Afghanistan and Pakistan reinforced their commitment in the fight against all dimensions of terrorism and stressed the vital importance of security for long-term reconstruction and development in the region and in Afghanistan in particular. They further committed to continue supporting moderation, fighting all forms of extremism and terrorism, including its financial, training and ideological centers through mutually agreed and coordinated action.
5. They highlighted the connection in the region between terrorism, drug-trafficking, and organized crime, and emphasized their determination for concerted efforts by all concerned parties to combat these menaces.
6. The Foreign Ministers of Afghanistan and Pakistan renewed their Governments' commitment to strengthen cooperation and dialogue between their countries and governments at all levels, in particular in the field of security, refugee issues, economic development and increased contacts between civil societies.
7. The members of the G8 commit themselves to work closely with the Governments of Afghanistan and Pakistan in support of their endeavour through concrete projects and targeted assistance in various fields.

8. The Foreign Ministers of the G8 highlighted the importance of practical cooperation between Afghanistan and Pakistan in matters of security concerns they share as neighbours.
9. They reiterated the importance of long-term and sustainable development and towards that end of joint initiatives in the economic field, reconstruction, agriculture, enhanced regional trade with appropriate import and export controls and transport links between Afghanistan and Pakistan as well as to other neighbouring countries, in particular those in Central and South Asia. They underlined the importance of engaging and developing the private sector, including through financial and technological assistance, to help build a vibrant local economy and the necessary infrastructure.
10. They commended the UNHCR and the governments of Afghanistan and Pakistan for their important work towards a repatriation of Afghan refugees from Pakistan. They stressed the commitment of the G8 to helping with arrangements towards enhancing the sustainability of return and pledged to further assist and complement already ongoing efforts in particular by helping to improve conditions for returnees in Afghanistan and in refugee-impacted areas in Pakistan.
11. Likewise they highlighted the importance of promoting increased contacts between civil societies as a further confidence building measure between Afghanistan and Pakistan and offered to support stronger interaction between political representatives, parliamentarians, the media, universities, as well as contacts in the field of sports and civil society at large.
12. They underlined that the G8 will build on and work with existing UN, regional and bilateral mechanisms to support Afghanistan and Pakistan and that as a follow-up to the initiative concrete projects will be identified and further pursued by the G8 in close consultation and in agreement with Afghanistan and Pakistan. To this effect, an expert meeting is to be convened at an early date with the task of specifying the projects in detail. A final list of projects is to be evaluated and endorsed at a meeting in Berlin in autumn.

(*Source:* www.auswaertigesamt.de/diplo/en/Aussenpolitik/InternatOrgane/G8/Downloads/070530-JointStatement.pdf)

# Memorandum of Understanding between the Government of the Islamic Republic of Afghanistan and the Government of the Republic of India and the United Nations Development Programme on Co-operation in the Field of Capacity Development in Public Administration

January 23, 2007

*A trilateral Memorandum of Understanding (MoU) signed between India, Afghanistan and United Nations Development Project (UNDP) emphasized on a cooperative framework on public sector capacity development in Afghanistan. The cooperation revolves around facilitating job capacity development in Afghan civil service.*

**PREAMBLE**

The Government of the Islamic Republic of Afghanistan through its Independent Administrative Reform and Civil Service Commission, the Government of the Republic of India through its Ministry of External Affairs, and the United Nations Development Programme through its country office in Kabul (hereinafter referred to in the singular as a "Party" and jointly as the "Parties");

**DESIROUS** of facilitating capacity development within the public administration in

Afghanistan, through collaborative activities under the overall framework outlined in the UNDP South-South Cooperation project and the Capacity for Afghan Public

Service project focusing on public sector capacity development have agreed as follows:

**ARTICLE 1**

The competent authorities responsible for the implementation of this Memorandum of Understanding (hereinafter referred to as "this MoU", shall be —-

(a) In the case of the Government of the Islamic Republic of Afghanistan, the Independent Administrative Reform and Civil Service Commission (hereinafter referred to as "GOA").
(b) In the case of the Government of the Republic of India, the Ministry of External. Affairs, through the Embassy of India in Kabul (hereinafter referred to as "GOI"); and
(c) In the case of the United Nations Development Programme, its country office in Kabul (hereinafter referred to as "UNDP").

### ARTICLE 2

1. The Parties shall co-operate in the field of capacity development, in public administration in accordance with the applicable domestic law in force in the respective countries in which the activities are undertaken.

### ARTICLE 3

1. The co-operation under this MoU shall be towards the GOI and the UNDP supporting the capacity development of the Afghan public service. For this purpose the GOI would provide officers from the civil services in India to undertake coaching and advisory support in selected Ministries and other agencies of the Government of Afghanistan.

More specifically, the objectives of the MoU would be implemented through the following measures:

(a) The GoI will provide up to 30 coaches to support the Capacity for Afghan Public Service and South - South Cooperation Project being implemented by the GOA to facilitate on the job capacity development in the Afghan civil service;

(b) The coaches to be so provided being engaged under a contract between the GOA and the coach as per a model contract placed at Annexure I.

(c) The GOI will contribute an amount of US $ 3000 per month for each of the coaches which will be inclusive of a fee equal to five percent (5%) towards UNDP's General Management Support (GMS). UNDP will pay the remaining dues in respect of coaches from its resources and resources mobilized from other sources. GoA will make the payments to the coaches through UNDP.

(d) The GOI will contribute funds to the UNDP as per the schedule of payments in Annexure II for which, a third-party cost-sharing agreement will be signed between GOI and UNDP. UNDP would use the GOI contribution to defray part of the monthly remuneration to the coaches engaged under the terms of this MoU.

(e) The UNDP will pay the costs of travel and other allowances as per the terms of their respective contracts to the coaches engaged under this MoU.

(f) The GOI will arrange to obtain a list of officers from the civil services in India who are willing to work as coaches with different Ministries and other agencies of the GOA and will provide details of the background and experience of such officials to the GOA.

(g) A Capacity Development Secretariat within the IARCSC with support from UNDP and the agreement of the concerned Government Institution will arrange to make a selection from out of the names forwarded to them and after carrying out the necessary selection, through a process of reviewing the curriculum vitae and carrying out interviews where considered necessary, will inform the GOI of the selection so made.

(h) The GOI will arrange for the selected official to be suitably released from his/her current assignment to join his/her assignment with the IARCSC as early as practically feasible and in any case within a period of 30 days from the date of his/her selection being informed to the GOI and to be able to complete the term of their appointments.

2. The specific responsibilities of the three parties will be as spelt out in Annexure III

## ARTICLE 4

(1) For the effective implementation of this MoU, each Party shall designate a person to act as coordinator, who shall be responsible for the arrangement and implementation of co-operation under this MoU.

(2) The designated coordinators shall, in writing, agree on a detailed work plan for the implementation of this MoU, which would comprise a pilot phase and a main phase.

(3) The progress on activities carried out under this MoU shall be monitored through meetings of the designated coordinators every three months at an agreed venue.

## ARTICLE 5

(1) A Party may for reasons of security, public order or public health suspend temporarily, either in whole or in part, the implementation of this MoU. The suspension shall take effect 30 days after written notification of the suspension to the other Party.

(2) The suspending Party may terminate the suspension by way of written notice to the other Party. The termination of suspension shall take effect 30 days after the notification.

## ARTICLE 6

(1) This MoU may be amended by mutual consent of the Parties through an Exchange of Notes between the Parties.

(2) An amendment shall not affect any rights and obligations arising from this MoU before the effective date of the amendment unless the Parties agree otherwise in the Exchange of Notes.

## ARTICLE 7

Any dispute between the Parties arising out of the interpretation or implementation of the provisions of this MoU shall be settled amicably through consultation and negotiation between the Parties.

**ARTICLE 8**

(1) This MoU shall come into force on the date of signature thereof by all three Parties.

(2) This MoU shall remain in force initially for a period of eighteen months.

Thereafter, it shall be renewed for further periods as may be agreed between the parties.

(3) The termination of this MoU shall not in any way affect the validity and completion of any activities undertaken in terms of this MoU before the date of termination, which shall he carried out until due discharge by performance.

**IN WITNESS WHEREOF**, the undersigned, being duly authorized, have signed and sealed this MoU in three originals each in the Hindi, Dari and English languages, all texts being equally authentic. If any conflict arises between the three texts, the English text shall prevail.

(*Source*: http://meakabul.nic.in/bl/2007/01/23bl01.pdf)

# BANGLADESH

# 7.

# INTERNAL DEVELOPMENT

## Election Manifesto of Bangladesh Awami League

A Charter for Change

Bangladesh achieved its independence thirty eight years ago through the supreme sacrifices of thirty lakh Bengalis, three crore displaced people and half a million abused and tortured women. Today, the country stands at the crossroad of history. After a seven year period of misrule and emergency, there is going to be a free, fair and peaceful election to parliament on 29 December 2008

Bangladesh Awami League is proud of its glorious leadership in the liberation war and its upholding of the core principles of nationalism, democracy, secularism, and an equitable society free from exploitation. It may be recalled that the architect of our independence, the greatest Bengali of all time, Bangabandhu Sheikh Mujibur Rahman, was the founder of our Party. Under the bold leadership of Bangabandhu, difficult but successful steps were initiated to reconstruct the war-devastated country and to build a prosperous Bangladesh. But all of a sudden the dastardly assassination of the Father of the Nation, members of his family, and some colleagues on 15th August 1975, and the subsequent killing of four national leaders inside the Dhaka Central Jail on 3rd November, 1975 transformed Bangladesh into a country of military rule and autocratic governance.

The military government and the political parties formed in the cantonment in the aftermath of this change destroyed the spirit of the freedom struggle and the promise of a secular, democratic, equitable and prosperous Bangladesh. The rape of the democratic constitution, rehabilitation of war criminals and religious fanatics, criminalization of politics and promotion of militancy, institutionalization of corruption, and the sway of black money and muscle power overtook the post-Bangabandhu governments.

The people of Bangladesh were, however, only temporarily defeated but not vanquished and the heroic struggle of the people and the martyrdom of many resulted, after 21 long years, in the formation of a government by the daughter of Bangabandhu, Sheikh Hasina through the power of the ballot exercised on 12th June 1996.

**Achievements of Bangladesh Awami League (1996-2001)**

A glorious chapter replete with successes was written during the five year rule of Awami League from 1996-2001. In only five years, Bangladesh attained self sufficiency in food production. Prices remained within the purchasing capacity of the people. Inflation came down to 1.59 percent. Meanwhile, the growth rate of the economy increased to 6.2 percent. The treaty on the water sharing of the river Ganges, the peace accord in Chittagong Hill Tracts, recognition of 21st February as international mother language day, election to the UN Security Council, sub-regional cooperation through the formation of D-8, BIMSTEC and the Association for Asian Parliamentarian for Peace (AAPP) bestowed on Bangladesh a new position of prestige and importance in the global arena.

Various initiatives taken for alleviation of poverty resulted in the reduction of poverty from an annual average of .50 to 1.50 percent, while the human poverty indicator came down from 41.6 percent to 32 percent. Achieving growth of 56 percentage points in the UN Human Development Index (HDI) in five years was a record. Increase of literacy rate to 65 percent, formulation of an education policy and the removal of session backlogs in educational institutions were significant achievements in the educational front. Incredible success was also achieved in the electricity and power, and transport and communication sectors. In only five years, production of 1,800 megawatt of electricity raising the total output to 4300 megawatt, increase in gas production and exploration, completion of the Jamuna Bridge; construction of 62,000 kilometers of paved and unpaved roads and building of 19,000 bridges and culverts vastly improved the country's overall infrastructure. Internal savings increased from 14.7 percent of national income to 18 percent over the five year period and the rate of investment increased from 20 percent to 23.1 percent. During the Awami League rule, 1 lakh 22 thousand small and medium size industries were established. Millions of job opportunities for the unemployed were created through facilitating private investment. One community clinic for every six thousand people was established at government initiative. Withdrawal of taxes and duties on medical equipment encouraged setting up of clinics and hospitals in the private sector. By abolishing monopoly in the mobile telephone sector and making mobile phones available to everyone at low prices and increasing access to information technology by reducing import duties, the Awami League government made it possible for Bangladesh to enter the digital age.

Rule of law and establishment of human rights were ensured by repealing the infamous indemnity ordinance, bringing to trial the killers of Bangabandhu and the four national leaders and by establishing the Law Commission. The Public Administration Reform Commission (PARC) was formed to establish good governance in the country. A progressive women's development policy was also formulated. In the parliament, the Prime Minister's Question hour was introduced and the Parliamentary Committees were activated and strengthened by appointing members as chairmen of parliamentary committees replacing the ministers. Necessary laws were passed to decentralize power through establishing a four tier local government system. Various steps were taken to bring back the spirit of the Liberation War and the glory of freedom movement and a regeneration of Bengali culture. During the five year rule of Awami League, the country had effectively turned around and transformed itself into a land of immense possibilities. The Awami League's five year rule will go down in the annals of history as nothing short of a golden period.

## Corruption and Misgovernance of BNP-Jamat Alliance Government

### Bangladesh in a Critical State

The five-year misrule of the BNP-Jamat alliance government did away with all the promises generated by the Awami League government. The situation in Bangladesh became grim both politically and economically. There was a phenomenal rise of terrorism.An assassination attempt was made on the Leader of the Opposition Sheikh Hasina on 21st August, 2004 ostensibly under government tutelage that resulted in the murder of 24 party leaders and workers, including a women leader Mrs. Ivy Rahman. BNP-Jamat Alliance and its criminal cronies killed 21,000 leaderss and workers of the Awami League including former Finance Minister and Member of Parliament, SAMS Kibria; labour leader and Member of Parliament, Ahsanullah Master; Advocate Monzurul Imam and Momtazuddin. Hundreds of thousands of Awami League supporters and members of the minority community became victims of political vengeance of the BNP-Jamat alliance. Criminal syndicates were organized under the patronage of the infamous Hawa Bhaban combine. Thousands of women and girls became victims of rape. Teachers, students, journalists, intellectuals, women and children, businessmen – no groups of people could escape the clutches of the fascist forces. People's lives became absolutely insecure. With support from the government, extreme communal militancy was born and serial grenade and bomb attacks and murders turned Bangladesh into a haven of extremist terrorism. Meanwhile, extra-judicial killings became a norm, and the rule of law disappeared. Bangladesh was then being described as a failed state.

During the five year rule of the BNP-Jamat alliance, prices of food and other essential commodities rose beyond the reach of the common people. Commodity prices increased by 100 to 200 percent. Inflation increased from 1.59 during Awami League rule to over 10 percent during the BNP-Jamat alliance government. On the other hand, the average growth rate of 5.6 percent achieved during the Awami League rule declined to 5.1

percent. Though the population increased by more than one crore, food production decreased to 2 crore 61 lakh tons from the 2 crore 68 lakh tons annually produced during Awami League rule.

Poverty levels again increased to 45 percent and the population planning stagnated. Income disparity between the poor and the rich increased. During the last seven years, an additional one crore twenty lakh people slipped below the poverty line. Both domestic and foreign investment decreased. Though BNP-Jamat combine came to power on the slogan of jihad against corruption, criminalisation and corruption became the policy of the government. Under the leadership of the son of the Prime Minister, criminal godfathers became extremely influential. The Hawa Bhaban became a parallel centre of state power and the source of all corruption and militancy.

The incredibly high levels of corruption and misuse of power by the Ministers of the BNP-Jamaat alliance; the members of Parliament and the leaders and workers of the alliance as well as a very politicised administration drove Bangladesh to the top of the list of the world's most corrupt nations, where it remained for five successive years.

Governmental corruption, inefficiency and mismanagement led to failure in development. The power crisis became unbearable but the government failed to add a single megawatt of electricity to the national power grid during its entire five year term. In the power sector alone, Taka twenty thousand crore was misused or stolen. Due to the extreme shortfall in the production of power, education and agricultural sectors faced an acute crisis. When farmers took to the streets demanding uninterrupted power supply at Kansat, some twenty of them were shot and killed.

An all-pervasive stagnation prevailed in the education, health, communication and women's development sectors. The alliance government politicized the administration, police, armed forces, judiciary, universities, public service commission, and all other government and many non-governmental organizations. Hundreds of civil, military and police officers were dismissed from service or given forced retirement. At the same time, irregular appointments and promotion were given to corrupt and inefficient personnel who were party loyalists. Leakage of public service examination question papers became a norm to facilitate recruitment of party cadres.

The constitution was amended and the retirement age of the judges of the appellate division of the Supreme Court was extended by two years with the ultimate objective of appointing a party loyalist who would then serve as the Chief Advisor of the Caretaker government. By appointing inefficient and corrupt people as judges, the prestige of the judiciary and its status as a bastion of fairness and justice were destroyed. BNP-Jamaat alliance government made the Parliament ineffective and destroyed all democratic institutions. The opposition members of Parliament were not allowed to speak, the permanent committees ceased to function effectively, and democratic practices were trampled under brute majority enjoyed by the then government.

The Election Commission was turned into a loyalist organ and election engineering was resorted to so that the BNP-Jamaat alliance could win the election due in January 2007, and permanently enjoy power. Disregarding the constitution and the judgment of the Supreme Court, a voters list was prepared which added12.3 million fake voters. Three hundred party loyalists were appointed as Upazilla election officers. Stealing of people's voting rights and election engineering were taken to such a level that the whole electoral process lost its credibility.

**Caretaker Regime (October 2006-November 2008)**

The BNP-Jamaat alliance government faced strong resistance from the public while trying to transfer power to loyalists. At the very end of their rule, they killed 70 leaders and workers of Awami League throughout the country. In its effort to come back to power, the BNP-Jamaat combine began implementing its blue print. Violating constitutional provisions Begum Zia's puppet President lajuddin Ahmed formed a Caretaker government appointing himself as Chief Advisor. Chief Adviser Iajuddin could never rise above party interests and four of his Advisers resigned in protest against his indecision and duplicity. He failed to create conditions for a free and fair election and faced people's resistance. At a critical juncture, on 11 January 2007, Emergency was declared in the country. Prof Iajuddin admitted his guilt and resigned from the position of Chief Advisor. With popular support, a new Caretaker government was formed under the leadership of Dr. Fakhruddin Ahmed with behind the scene support of the armed forces. Under the Emergency political activities were banned for an indefinite period.

Meanwhile, the tenure of the present Caretaker government has crossed nearly two years. The government has been ruling the country with various limitations, weaknesses, lapses as well as some successes. This government has separated the judiciary from the executive, reformed the Election Commission, Public Service Commission, Anti-Corruption Commission etc. Another positive step taken by this government was the preparation of a voters' list with photograph. Our armed forces have earned people's admiration for accomplishing this task with great efficiency. The caretaker government has also reformed the electoral laws and procedure.

The forthcoming parliamentary elections have created an opportunity for the re-establishment of democracy and inspired hopes for rapid socio-economic development mainly by providing good governance and people's participation. In this context Bangladesh Awami League declares its election manifesto with the promise of change by making our dear motherland a country free from hunger and poverty, illiteracy, corruption and militancy. We believe that the right to vote and the right to food hold the key to the alleviation of poverty.

## Our Promise, Work Programme and Declaration

### Awami League's Vision 2021

Awami League is committed to freeing Bangladesh from its current state of crisis and building a country whose citizens are able to live prosperous and happy lives. The year 2021 will mark the golden jubilee of Bangladesh's independence, while the year 2020 will be the hundredth anniversary of the birth of the Father of the Nation, Bangabandhu Sheikh Mujibur Rahman. We envision a democratic system where people choose their government freely and get services from it without hassle, enjoy freedom from fear and intolerance, live with dignity; where every citizen is assured of social justice, environmental protection, human rights and equal opportunities; and where the rule of law and good governance flourish. We envision a liberal, progressive and democratic welfare state. Simultaneously we envision a Bangladesh which by 2020/2021, will be a middle income country where poverty will be drastically reduced; where our citizens will be able to meet every basic need and where development will be on fast track, with ever-increasing rates of growth. Towards that goal, Bangladesh Awami League will frame a strategy paper, at the core of which will be the promise of change. This strategy paper will contain both mid-term and long term plans.

Bangladesh Awami League is placing before the nation the following set of election promises, work schedule and declaration in the light of its Vision 2021, and in the context of problems the country is facing as well as the existing global financial crisis. This election manifesto has been prepared keeping in mind the 31-point election reform program of 15th July 2005, the 23-point common minimum program of 14 Party Alliance on 22nd November, 2005 and the experience and realities of the past seven years. Considering the existing politico-socio-economic crisis, five subjects have been given priority:

### Five Priority Issues

**1.** In the Face of Global Financial Crisis, Maintenance of Economic Stability And Control Over Commodity Price Hike

(*i*) *Commodity Price Hike:* Measures will be taken to reduce the unbearable burden of price hike and keep it in tune with the purchasing power of the people. After giving the highest priority to the production of domestic commodities, arrangements will be made for timely import to ensure food security. A multi-prong drive will be made to control prices along with monitoring the market. Hoarding and profiteering syndicates will be eliminated. Extortion will be stopped. An institution for commodity price control and consumer protection will be set up. Above all, price reduction and stability will be achieved by bringing equilibrium between demand and supply of commodities.

(*ii*) *Global Financial Crisis*: It is necessary to urgently form a task force which will devise a policy to save Bangladesh from global meltdown, develop a comprehensive information center, continually monitor national and global situations and provide prompt advice to help take necessary decisions. Necessary steps would be taken for investment promotion, energy security, retaining and enhancing domestic demand, safeguarding value of money, assisting exports and continuing export of manpower.

**2. Effective Action against Corruption:** Multi-pronged measures to fight corruption will be put into place. Powerful people will have to submit wealth statement annually. Strict measures will be taken to eliminate bribe, extortion, rent seeking and corruption. Strong measures will be taken against those having unearned and black money, against loan defaulters, tender manipulators, and users of muscle power in every stage of state and society. State or private monopoly will be broken up. Discretionary power of officials will be curtailed. To establish peoples' right, citizens' charter will be introduced in every department. Opportunities for corruption will be eliminated or minimized through widespread computerization.

**3. Power and Energy:**

(*i*) A comprehensive long term policy on electricity and energy will be adopted. Economic usage of oil, gas, coal, hydro power, wind power and solar energy will be ensured. Big and small power generation stations, coal extraction, and oil and gas exploration will be given priority. Under a three year crash program quick implementation of ongoing and under consideration power generation stations, import of electricity from neighboring countries, arranging 100/150 megawatt gas turbine projects on urgent basis, and the reactivation of the past AL initiatives for constructing 10, 20 and 30 megawatt power stations will be undertaken. A schedule for repair, maintenance and overhauling or salvaging of old power stations will be made to increase and stabilize power production. Supply of gas and LPG will be increased. The Rooppur Nuclear Power Project will be implemented.

In the next three years or by 2011 power production will be increased to 5000 megawatt and by 2013 it will be further increased to 7000 megawatt.

(*ii*) Priority will be given to exploration and exploitation of oil and new gas fields. Arrangements will be made to supply gas in the north and western regions of the country. Supply of gas and LPG will be significantly increased.

(*iii*) A Coal Policy will be formulated safeguarding national interest. Special initiatives will be taken to ensure economic use of the coal available so far and also to develop coal-based power plants. Priorities will be given to the exploration and exploitation of new coal fields and other mineral resources.

**4. Elimination of Poverty and Inequity:** The following strategy and aims will be followed for socio-economic development.

(*i*) The main strategy of poverty reduction will center on bringing vibrancy in agriculture and rural life. Social safety net will be extended for the ultra-poor. By 2013 poverty level and proportion of ultra-poor will be brought down to 25% and 15% respectively. At present there are 65 million poor people in the country. This number will be reduced to 45 million by 2013 and will further come down to 22 million in 2021. In order to achieve this objective, among other steps will be the revival of previously adopted projects such as "one house, one farm", rural housing, ideal village and returning homes. The number of recipients of old age allowance and destitute women allowance would, at the least, be doubled. Employment Banks will encourage young entrepreneurs by supplying necessary capital. Revision of the just formulated PRSP will be undertaken after a thorough evaluation within six months of assuming office.

(*ii*) *Employment guidelines*: A comprehensive employment guideline will be formulated aiming at poverty reduction, solving unemployment problem and making citizens' lives meaningful. The core components of the guidelines will be: a. creating employment opportunities in rural economy b. providing credit and training for self-employment c. creating employment opportunities for wage-labour in industries d. promoting sub-contracting arrangements between big and small & medium scale industries and e. providing special training arrangements for facilitating export of labour. The number of unemployed people in the country, estimated at 28 million, will be reduced to 24 million by 2013 and will be further reduced to 15 million by 2021.

**5. Establishment of Good Governance:**

(*i*) Terrorism and religious extremism will be controlled with iron hand. Trial of war criminals will be arranged.

(*ii*) Genuine independence and impartiality of the judiciary will be ensured. Extrajudicial killings will be stopped. The judgment of the Bangabandhu murder case will be made effective and the retrial of jail killings will be held. Trial of real criminals responsible for the grenade attack of the 21st August, 2004 through proper investigation will be arranged. Rule of law will be established, The Human Rights Commission will be strengthened and made effective, and an Ombudsman will be appointed. Human rights will be strictly enforced.

(*iii*) The on-going reform programme of the Election Commission and electoral system will continue. The Parliament will be made effective and the government will be made accountable for all its activities. Wealth statement and source of income of the Prime Minister, members of cabinet, Parliament members and of their family members will be made public every year. Except for some specific subjects related to the security of the state, Parliament members will be allowed to express differing opinions.

(*iv*) Use of religion and communalism in politics will be banned. Security and rights of religious and ethnic minorities will be ensured. Courtesy and tolerance will be inculcated in the political culture of the country. Militancy and extortion will be banned. Awami League will take initiative to formulate a consensual and unanimous charter of political behavior.

(*v*) Opportunities will be created for the expatriate Bangladeshis to take part in national reconstruction and their right to franchise will be ensured. Special initiatives will be taken to attract expatriate's remittance in productive investment. A consultancy network will be developed to fruitfully use expatriate's talents.

(*vi*) Administration will be free from politicization and will be pro-people. Efficiency, seniority and merit will be the basis of appointment and promotion in public service. Administrative reform, right to information and e-governance will be introduced. A permanent Pay Commission will be set up for civil servants.

(*vii*) In order to provide security to every citizen of the country, police and other law and order enforcing agencies will be kept above political influence. These forces will be modernized to meet the demands of the time. Necessary steps will be taken to increase their remuneration and other welfare facilities including accommodation.

(*viii*) Rangpur will be made a new administrative division.

**Other Important Programs**

**6. Local Government:** Union, Upazilla and District Councils will be strengthened through decentralization of power. District Councils will be transformed into centres for implementation of programmes on education and health and all other development plans, and programmes, and for maintenance of law and order Every union will be made the headquarter for development and administration of the area and be developed as a planned rural township. And every Upazilla headquarter will be developed as an industrial growth centre and a planned township. The power and sphere of responsibility of City Corporation and municipalities will be enhanced; the standard and quality of civic facilities will be improved.

**7. Agriculture And Rural Development:**

(*i*) Our main aim is to ensure "food for all" by taking all possible measures and to make Bangladesh self-sufficient in food by 2013. Subsidy for agricultural inputs will be enhanced and availability of inputs will be made easier. The amount of agricultural loan will be increased and the lending procedure simplified. Incentives will be provided for development of rural warehousing. Fair price for all crops and agricultural products will be ensured. Efforts will be made to attain self-sufficiency in the production of fish, milk, egg, livestock and salt. Efforts will be directed to exporting surplus products after meeting domestic requirement.

(*ii*) Loan for share croppers will be made available, employment facilities for farm labourer will be created and they will be brought under rural rationing system.

(*iii*) Appropriate measures to face the challenges of globalization will be taken, including developing commercial agriculture, use of genetic engineering methods and development of nonagricultural sector in villages. In order to increase agricultural production, special emphasis will be placed on modernization of agriculture, innovation of technology and expansion of facilities for research in agriculture.

(*iv*) Village development will include provision of urban facilities and distribution of Khas land among landless farmers. Efforts will be taken to ensure that lease of khas ponds/haors is given to genuine fishermen. All land records will be computerized and a land reform commission will be formed to ensure increased production and social justice in the distribution of land and water bodies.

(*v*) Measures will be taken to reclaim land in the coastal areas.

**8. Environment and Water Resources:** An integrated policy and plan will be formulated to protect the country from the adverse effects of global warming; to create pollution free environment and to save water resources. Projects will be undertaken for river dredging, water conservation, flood control, prevention of river erosion and protection of forestry. Attempts will also be made for restoring and maintaining ecological balance. Initiatives will be taken to implement the Ganges· barrage project to expand irrigation facilities, prevent salinity and to solve the problem of scarcity of sweet water in the Sundarban region.

Effective regional and international co-operation will be sought for environmental protection and development of water resources. Modern scientific methods will be adopted to prevent water and air pollution and in the disposal of waste.

**9. Commerce and Industry:**

(*i*) Short, medium and long term plans will be made and implemented for poverty reduction, efficient management for quick industrialization that can provide employment, speedy expansion of stock market, maintenance of law & order and discipline, elimination of bribe and corruption and administrative difficulties, avoidance of political influence, creation of an investment friendly environment and a competitive market system, adoption of innovative technology, and provision of infrastructural facilities that are able to attract entrepreneurs and expand domestic market.

(*ii*) In order to encourage investment by local and foreign entrepreneurs and expatriate Bangladeshis, the ONE-STOP facility will be made effective by simplifying legal and procedural formalities. Measures will be put in place to protect indigenous industries.

(*iii*) Development of IT industry, strengthening of RMG and textile sectors and expansion of food processing, pharmaceuticals, leather, chemical products, toys, jewelry and furniture industries will be given priority. Special initiative will be taken for alternative use of jute and to make jute industry viable. Small and handicraft industries and agro-based industry will be encouraged and will be given all cooperation in the expansion of markets at home and abroad. Expansion in tourism sector, increase in labor export, and investment of remittance received from expatriate Bangladeshis in productive sectors will be ensured.

(*iv*) Assistance will be provided for expansion of small, medium and cottage industries. Special incentives will be given to weavers, blacksmiths and clay potters. Weaving industry will be given protection and silk, benarasi and jamdani villages will be set up.

**10. Human Resources Development**

(*i*) *Education and Science*: In order to ensure human resources development, the highest budgetary allocation will be given to education, science and information technology sectors. An education policy meeting the needs of the time will be framed keeping these in view. Net enrollment at primary level will be increased to 100% by 2011 and by 2017 the country will be rid of the curse of illiteracy. Improvement in the quality of education, depoliticisation of educational institutions, and ensuring a higher salary scale for teachers will be ensured. A permanent Pay Commission and a separate Service Commission will be instituted for teachers. Education up to graduation level will be provided free of cost in phases.

(*ii*) In order to encourage female education the opportunity for free education along with scholarship will continue.

(*iii*) Educational institutions will be rid of terrorism and session backlogs. Science and technology education will be especially encouraged. Madrasa education will be reoriented to develop productive skills and knowledge for the real world. Scope of science education and research will be expanded. Particular care will be taken in cases of disadvantaged pupils.

(*iv*) More government secondary schools will be set up in the capital in phases. The govt. secondary schools located at every district headquarter will be developed and expanded and government. secondary schools will be established at every Upzilla headquarter in phases.

(*v*) *Information and communication technology*: The potentials of ICT sector will be realized. Software industry and IT services will be developed by providing all possible assistance to talented young people and interested entrepreneurs. This measure will increase export and promote employment opportunities. Our vision is to make Bangladesh digital in 2021. IT education will be made compulsory at secondary level by 2013 and at primary level by 2021. The task force on ICT that was established during the Awami League rule but rendered ineffective by the BNP-Jamat Alliance will be reactivated. High-tech park, software technology park, ICT incubator and computer villages will be set up at suitable locations in the country.

(*vi*) *Welfare of the disabled*: The Disabled Welfare Act passed by Awami League in 2000 will be updated and implemented. Special steps will be taken to facilitate education, employment, movement and communication of the disabled and to enhance their social dignity.

**11. Health and Family Welfare:**

(*i*) In order to ensure health facilities to every citizen of the country, the health policy of the erstwhile Awami League government will be reevaluated and adjusted according to the demands of the time. In the light of this policy, 18000 community clinics, established during Awami League rule, will be commissioned. Nutrition to children and mothers' welfare will be ensured. The Population Policy will be updated. And accordingly birth control and reproductive health care will be ensured.

(*ii*) The arsenic problem will be tackled and measures will be taken to supply pure drinking water for all by 2011 and to provide sanitation facility in every house by 2013.

(*iii*) An appropriate pharmaceutical policy to bring self- sufficiency in the production of medicines of international standard and to promote their export will be formulated. Concurrently, effective measures will be taken for education in traditional medicine and improvement of the quality of traditional medicine.

**12. Empowerment of Women and Child Welfare:** In order to ensure women's empowerment and equality in rights and opportunities, the Women Development Policy formulated by Awami League in 1997 will be revived. The number of reserved seats for women by direct election in the Parliament will be increased to 100. Necessary measures will be taken for appointment of women in senior posts in the administration and in all spheres of employment. Strictest legal measures will be taken to stop oppression of women. Discriminatory laws against the interest of women will be rectified.

**13. Welfare of Children and the Juvenile:** Child labor will be gradually abolished in all sectors. Use of children in political and other activities through coercion or enticement will be prohibited. In keeping with the UN convention on children's rights, adequate measures will be taken for developing their physical and mental capacity and for their nutrition and entertainment.

**14. Youth and Employment:**

(*i*) A comprehensive employment policy will be developed setting targets for employment enshrining *i.* agricultural employment, *ii.* Off-farm activities in rural areas, *iii.* Self-employment and income generating activities, *iv.* Urban service employment, *v.* wage employment in industry, *vi.* Employment in infra-structure development, vii. Employment abroad and necessary training for it and viii. Employment of youth and students.

(*ii*) An employment guarantee scheme will gradually be made effective to provide 100 days employment to one youth per family. All citizens able to work will be registered. A project will be undertaken for young men and women with HSC degrees for appointment in the "national service" for two years.

**15. Communication and Infrastructure**

I. Appropriate policy and project implementation will be undertaken in transport, road building, housing, and port development and construction sectors. An extensive road network in each district will connect villages, unions, upazillas and the district headquarter.

II. Appropriate measures will be taken to construct the Padma and Karnaphuli bridge/tunnel, Dhaka-Chittagong four- lane express way, and expansion and modernization of the railway.

III. Rail and road connection with neighboring countries under the Asian Rail and Highways schemes will be established.

IV. Dredging of every big and small river will be undertaken and measures will be taken to maintain their navigability throughout the year. River routs will be improved and river transportation system will be modernized to facilitate safe and cost effective transportation of cargo and passengers.

V. Construction of deep sea ports and modernization of Chittagong and Mongla ports and opening them up to all of Asia will be taken up.

VI. Bangladesh Biman will be restructured to enable it to operate on commercial & profitable basis. Aviation services in the private sector will be encouraged. Modern airports of international standard will be constructed to facilitate air transportation linking Bangladesh with the world.

VII. Telecommunication facilities will be extended upto rural villages. All Upazilas will be brought under internet communication system in the next five years.

VIII. Railway will be given importance and new rail lines will be installed as it maintains communication link with the capital and provides cheaper transportation.

Underground railway, mono or circular rail and navigable river route around Dhaka will be constructed to the solve the public transportation problem and traffic jam in the capital.

**16. Labor Policy:**

(*i*) National labour policy will be reevaluated and corrected. Discrepancy in wages between male and female workers will be removed. National minimum wage will be refixed and a permanent wage board will be formed. To meet international demand, tradewise training will be given to produce and export skilled manpower. As per ILO convention, the right to trade union will be granted.

(*ii*) Rationing system will be introduced for all labourers including garment worker, ultra poor and rural landless farm labourer, as special consideration.

**17. Freedom Struggle and Freedom Fighters:**

(*i*) Continuous efforts will be made for the realization of the dream and commitment of liberation war. Dignity and status of the freedom fighters, who are the greatest sons of the nation, will be restored. And in state recognition of their contribution to the nation, steps will be taken to increase their alliance, particularly of the distressed freedom fighters. Arrangements will be made to provide then old-age subsistence allowance and free health care service. Quota in jobs and educational institutions for the children of freedom fighters will continue. As honourable citizens, the freedom fighters will be given the privilege of travel by rail, bus, and river free of cost.

(*ii*) Construction of the Victory Monument in the Suhrawardy Udyan will be completed according to the original plan. Special work programme will be undertaken all over the country to preserve the memory of the war of liberation and to portray its real history. All over the country, slain field and mass graves of the Liberation War period will be identified, the names and identities of the martyrs will be collected and memorials in their honour will be built.

**18. Religious Minorities, Disadvantaged People and Under-developed Areas**

(*i*) Terrorism, discriminatory treatment and human rights violations against religious and ethnic minorities and indigenous people must come to an end permanently. Security of their life, wealth and honor will be guaranteed. Their entitlement to equal opportunity in all spheres of state and social life will be ensured. Special measures will be taken to secure their original ownership on land, water bodies, and their age-old rights on forest areas. In addition, a land commission will be formed. All laws and other arrangements discriminatory to minorities, indigenous people and ethnic groups will be repealed. Special privileges will be made available in educational institutions for religious minorities and indigenous people. Such special privileges will also apply for their employment.

(*ii*) The 1997 Chittagong Hill Tract Peace Accord will be fully implemented. More efforts will be directed toward the development of underdeveloped tribal areas, and special programmes on priority basis will be taken to secure their rights and to preserve their language, literature, culture, and unique lifestyles.

**19. Freedom of mass media and information**

(1) The freedom of all types of mass media and flow of information will be ensured. Initiatives will be taken for community radio services, besides national radio network.

(2) Investigation and trial of assassination of all journalists will be made expeditiously and the real criminals will be given exemplary punishment. Persecution and intimidation of journalists will be stopped. All false cases against them will be withdrawn.

(3) Discrimination in distribution of advertisements on partisan consideration shall be discontinued, and development of the newspaper as an industry will be aided.

**20. Defence**

(1) Bangladesh Awami League will keep the armed forces above all controversies with a view to building it up as a patriotic, brave, efficient and invincible force. The defence system will be improved for the security of the people and the country. A National Defence Policy will be formulated.

(2) The principle of competence, merit, fitness and seniority will be strictly followed for recruitment, appointment and promotion. Autonomy, as consistent with the Constitution, will be granted in matters of internal discipline, administration and management. Welfare oriented projects will be undertaken for the members of the defence forces.

(3) Steps will be taken so that our defence and the police forces can participate more widely in the U. N. Peace-keeping Force and make further contribution to international peace.

**21. Culture and Sports**

(1) The State will provide necessary assistance for preservation of the secular and democratic tradition of Bengali culture as well as further improvement of Bengali language and literature, music, arts and all branches of creative works and fine arts.

The International Mother Language Institute Project undertaken by the Awami League Government earlier (1996-2001) will be reactivated.

(2) Creation of social awareness, scientific and liberal outlook will be emphasized with a view to resisting communalism and narrow mindedness.

(3) Laws repugnant to Quran and Sunnah shall not be made. Due respect will be shown to the principles and values of all religions.

(4) Sports: Sports arena and organizations shall be depoliticized. Improvement of management, training and facilities shall be made for enhancing the standards of sports to international levels. Sports and exercise for physical and mental development of the children, the adolescent and the young shall be made compulsory for all education institutions.

**22. Government and NGO:** The non-government organizations shall be free to manage themselves in accordance with their own internal rules subject to compliance with the laws of the country. The NGOs shall not take part in politics. Transparency and accountability of their income/ receipts and expenditures shall have to be ensured.

**23. Foreign Policy**

(*a*) Bangladesh will take an active role in the preservation of world peace. An independent foreign policy will be pursued in adherence to the principles of "Friendship with all and malice towards none." Friendly relationship will be maintained with India, Nepal, Bhutan and Myanmar, our neighboring countries, in the context of further strengthening cooperation with all. Regional and sub-regional cooperation will be further strengthened including relationship with the member countries of SAARC, BIMSTEC and D-8.

(*b*) Development cooperation will be deepened and expanded with the developed countries including USA, European Union, Japan and Canada. Friendly relations will be strengthened with Russia, China and the member states of ASEAN.

(*c*) Initiatives will be taken for enhancing and deepening relationship with Australia and the Pacific countries.

(*d*) Fraternal relationship with the countries of the Middle East including Saudi Arabia, Egypt, Palestine, United Arab Emirates and Kuwait as well as Turkey, Malaysia and Indonesia will be maintained. Solidarity with the Muslim Ummah and economic cooperation within the framework of OIC will be enhanced. Steps will be taken for establishing fruitful relationship with the countries of Africa and South America.

(*e*) A South Asian Task Force will be formed for meeting the challenge of terrorism and militancy.

The image and prestige of Bangladesh will be retrieved and improved in the international arena.

## Call to the People of Bangladesh

Dear countrymen,

You are aware that the activities of the past governments have now placed our dear motherland in a critical state. The people do not wish to return to the days of poor governance of the kind they have seen under the

BNP-Jamaat Alliance. The people want a country free of terrorism and corruption; they want a just and progressive society. They want to see Bangladesh move towards steady development and good governance.

Bangladesh Awami League, therefore, wants not only a mere change of power. We are determined to salvage the country from its present critical state and to transform it into a land of real democracy with rule of law, having food security, rapid development and peaceful existence. With this end in view we are presenting our long term vision for the nation as well as an implementable five year work plan with specific targets and strategies.

We believe that the invaluable experience that Bangladesh Awami League gained in administering the country (during the 1996-2001 term) can be utilized with great efficiency, honesty and commitment to take the country forward.

We dedicate our Vision-2021 to the young generation, who are enrolled as voters this year for the first time, with the aim of building a bright future for them. In order to prepare ourselves to face the challenges of globalization in this 21st century, we want to utilize the immense potentials of our new generation of voters. We have formulated our Election Manifesto and work programme for them. We believe the successful implementation of this work programme and Vision-2021 depends on our young generations' active participation and involvement in the process.

By implementing this Manifesto with the collective efforts of the entire nation, we will present a bright and successful future to the new generation. We call upon them to participate in this great endeavour of national reconstruction and build a bright future for themselves and as well as successive generations.

Dear Countrymen

If Awami League is voted to rule the country, we will bring back peace and trust in your life by reducing the price of daily essentials.

We call upon you to forget past differences and disputes and, in the spirit of our glorious struggle for freedom, work unitedly in this fight for change. Let us put a permanent end to persecution, deprivation, inequity, and mis-governance. Let us construct a just and democratic society and build a happy, prosperous, golden Bengal.

We seek the help and blessings of the Almighty in our endeavours.

Joy Bangla.

Joy Bangabandhu.

Long live Bangladesh.

**ANNEXURE**

The vision of Awami League for resolution of crisis and a prosperous future (Vision 2021)

**Bangladesh as we want to see in 2021**

1. Caretaker Government, Democracy & Effective Parliament *Democracy and strong democratic institutions will be established for holding reliable election at regular intervals, accountability of government and effective Parliament. All necessary steps will be taken for making Parliament effective.

2. Political framework, Decentralization of Power & People's Participation

*Local government will be given due importance with a view to effecting radical change of the political system. The local government institutions will play a critical role in development programmes. Self-reliant local self-government institutions will be established at upazila and zila levels to this end.

3. Good governance through establishing Rule of Law and avoiding Political Partisanship

*Human rights will be established on a strong footing with a view to ensuring rule of law. Independence of the judiciary will be ensured and the Institutions of the State and Administration will be freed from partisan influence. The basis of appointment and promotion will be merit, efficiency, seniority, honesty and loyalty to the Republic; political connection will have no relevance.

4. Transformation of political culture

*Terrorism, corruption and use of religion for politics will be stopped. Steps appropriate to the time will be taken to establish democratic principles in the political parties, transparency of political funding, civility and tolerance.

5. A society free from corruption

*The institutions of the State will be made more effective along with the independent and strong Anti-corruption Commission for curbing corruption. Social resistance to corruption will be promoted along side legal steps. All possible steps will be taken to stop corruption such as Charter of Citizens' Rights, Right to Information, Computerization of Official Documents, and Decentralization of Power.

6. Empowerment and Equal Rights for Women

*The Women's Policy of 1997 will be revived for ensuring equal right and access for women to the state and social space; laws which discriminate against women will be amended; and 100 seats will be reserved for women for direct election.

7. Economic Development & Initiative

a. Meeting basic needs: With a view to providing food, clothing, shelter, education and health care to the citizens in accordance with Article 15 of the Constitution, gross domestic product will be raised to 8% by 2013 and 10% by 2021 which will be sustained thereafter.

b. Population and labour force: Population in 2021 is estimated at 165 million, and labour force at 105 million. Programmes will be taken up for employment of 85% of the work force.

c. Alleviation of poverty: We aim not at reduction of poverty, but removal of poverty, to which end we shall try to achieve the Millennium Goals declared by UN by 2015, and by 2017 latest. Beginning in 2021, poverty will be reduced to 15% from 45% now progressively. Poverty will rise from 45 million now to 65 million in 2021, and then fall to 25 million in 2021. Sustainable safety net will be established for the extreme poor until poverty is removed.

d. Food & nutrition: Food deficit will be removed and self-reliance in food production achieved by 2012, which will enable us to meet the nutrition needs of 85% of the population.

e. Health Care: By 2021, minimum daily intake of 2122 kilo calories of food, elimination of contagious disease, primary health care and sanitation for all will be ensured. Average longevity will be increased to seventy years, and efforts will be made for the reduction of child and maternal mortality.

f. Education: Enrolment at the primary level will be increased to 100 percent net by 2010. Elimination of illiteracy by 2014, improvement in the quality of education, creation of a generation educated in science and technology, make degree level education free by 2013 and ensuring higher salary for teachers are the other educational goals.

g. Industry: A strong foundation for industrialization will be established by 2021. Contribution of the industrial sector to national GDP will be doubled. Primacy will be given to agro and labour intensive industries and the highest emphasis will be given to information technology sector. The investment policy will be geared to implementing a strategy attracting both domestic and foreign investment.

h. Energy Security: An energy policy will be adopted tapping all sources of traditional and non-traditional energy to ensure accelerated rate of economic development and industrialization. A three year crash programme will be taken up to meet the existing crisis. By 2015, electricity production will be increased to 8000 megawatt. By 2021, demand for electricity is projected to increase to 20,000 megawatt. We will take all possible actions aiming at enhancing our generation capacity. To increase gas production, regular survey of gas resources and work on well development will be undertaken. To meet energy demand, efforts will be undertaken for regional energy security through mutual cooperation in addition to exploring internal sources.

i. Infrastructural Development: Road, rail, river and air transport and telecommunication systems will be expanded. Construction of bridge, tunnel for Padma and Karnaphuli rivers, connecting Bangladesh with Asian

Highway and Asian Railway, improvement of port facilities, building of a deep sea port to open up Bangladesh ports to countries of Asia will be implemented. In Dhaka, construction of metro tunnel, elevated rail and circular rail to remove traffic jams and to solve public transport problems will be studied forthwith in order to undertake a feasible project. The project will then be implemented on a priority basis

j. Housing: By 2015, housing for all will be ensured. In every union and upazila, 'growth center' centric village housing and in towns housing with modern amenities will be implemented.

k. Environment: All measures will be taken to protect Bangladesh—including planned migration abroad— from the adverse effects of climate change and global warming. Facing natural calamities, planned reduction of air pollution, prevention of industry and transport related air pollution and disposal of waste in scientific manner will be ensured. Steps will be taken to make Bangladesh an ecologically attractive place through retention of forests and water bodies and prevention of river erosion.

l. Water Resources: Bangladesh Awami League will take the initiative to formulate a comprehensive regional water policy along with India, Nepal and Bhutan for regional water security. In addition, in keeping with a comprehensive water police, articulated earlier by Bangladesh Awami League, measures will be taken for development of our water resources and their rational use.

**8. Bangladesh in the Global Arena**

(*a*) Achievments of liberation: Multi-pronged measures will be taken to uphold the glorious history and the fruits of liberation, to energize the new generation with the spirit of liberation struggle, patriotism and love for humanity. Highest priority will be given to development of innovative spirit of the younger generations and opportunity will be provided for them to participate in nation building activities.

(*b*) Culture: Measures will be taken to remove obstacles in the development of Bengali culture, literature, art, music and sport and to provide all opportunities by the state to enable the younger generations to attain international standards and to contribute to the nation.

(c) Foreign Policy: In international affairs Bangladesh will follow the policy of 'friendship towards all and malice towards none'.

**Proposed Milestones**

- 2010: 100 percent net student enrolment at primary level.
- 2011: Supply of pure drinking water for the entire population.
- 2012: Self-sufficiency in food.
- 2013: Each house brought under hygienic sanitation.
- 2013: Attain 8 percent annual growth rate; this will be increased to 10 percent in 2017 and sustained.

- 2013: Bangladesh generates 7000 megawatt of electricity which will be further increased to 8000 megawatt in 2015. Steps will be taken to increase power generation capacity assuming that the demand for power will reach the level of 20000 megawatt in 2021.
- 2013: Free tuition up to degree level.
- 2014: Bangladesh attains full literacy.
- 2015: Living accommodation for the entire population.
- 2021: Contribution of agriculture, industry and service sector to GDP will stand at 15, 40 and 45 respectively in place of 22, 28 and 50 percent as at present.
- 2021: Unemployment reduced to 15 percent from the present rate of 40 percent.
- 2021: Labor in agriculture comes down to 30 % from 48% at present.
- 2021: Labor in industry is 25% from 16% and in service 45% from 36% at present.
- 2021: Poverty rate comes down to 15% from 45% at present.
- 2021: Bangladesh known as a country of educated people with skills in information technology.
- 2021: 85% of the population have standard nutritional food.
- 2021: Poor people ensured a minimum of 2122 kilo calories of food.
- 2021: All kinds of contagious diseases eliminated.
- 2021: Longevity increases to 70 years.
- 2021: Infant mortality comes down to 15 from 54 per thousand at present
- 2021: Maternal death rate reduced to 1.5% from 3.8%.
- 2021: Use of birth control methods increased to 80%

(*Source*: http://www.albd.org/autoalbd/index2.php?option=com_ content&task= view&id=367&pop=1&page=0&Itemid=1)

## A Synoptic View of Internal Developments in Bangladesh[1]

September 20, 2008

*Dr Fakhruddin Ahmed, highlighted some key actions taken by the caretaker government of Bangladesh. Emphasizing on oversight mechanisms such as the Election Commission, Anti-Corruption Commission and separation of judiciary and the executive, he assured that the preparations are being made in the country for the conduct of free and fair elections.*

---

1. Address to the Nation by Chief Adviser Dr. Fakhruddin Ahmed, Dhaka, September 20, 2008.

We have been running the government for nearly 20 months. Immediately after taking over the responsibility of the government, I had announced that our desired aim is to transfer power to a political government through a free, fair, neutral and credible election. We have not deviated even slightly from that objective.

For this, the foremost requirement was to bring important institutional and structural reforms in the country. As part of this, we have reconstituted the Election Commission and established it as a neutral commission. The Anti-Corruption Commission has been reconstituted and made it stronger and effective. To ensure rule of law in the country, we have separated judiciary from the executive in November last year.

The Election Commission is responsible for holding the elections. The duty of the government is to extend cooperation to the commission in holding the polls and creating a level playing election field i,e to create equal opportunity for all. Indeed, right from the beginning the government has been working for creating such an atmosphere in the election-field

The subject of my today's speech is not to describe the tasks that the government has accomplished; rather it is for seeking your cooperation in completing properly the future tasks. I would like to say, with the blessings of Allah, support of people and sincere cooperation from the political parties, we have reached such a position today that henceforth, there is no scope for doubt or confusion about the election. A credible election is on the threshold of our doors. It is my firm belief that we have been certainly moving forward to the path of creating such an environment that an election must be held with the participation of all political parties, Inshallah. With this end in view, we held series of dialogues with the political parties. We have discussed with the leaders of two major parties. The two leaders have already declared their willingness to participate in the polls. In my address to the nation in May last, I had declared that parliamentary election will be held on any day in the third week of December. Today, I want to inform the nation that after taking decision the Election Commission told me that parliamentary elections will be held on December 18 this year. The Election Commission has also decided to hold upazila elections in two phases on December 24 and 28 next. The Election Commission will announce detailed schedules of the elections in an appropriate time.

The Election Commission has decided to hold parliamentary election first showing honour to the requests from the majority of political parties and to avert any kind of hindrance or conflict in this journey towards transition to democracy. At the same time, keeping in mind the spontaneous desire of common people about the local government polls, upazila polls will be held immediately after the parliamentary elections. In the greater national interest the desired goal of all will be achieved through this plan.

For holding of a free, fair and acceptable election, a flawless voter list is a major element. In the past, many a controversies were created about the voters list. The Election Commission with the assistance of the members of the Armed Forces has completed the preparation the draft voter list with photographs of more than eight crore voters in only 11 months. At the same time, a database has been made to prepare the national identity cards. National identity cards are also being issued. It is rare in the world history of creating the electronic database of so many numbers of voters in such a short span of time. This work is a major achievement for our government as well for all the countrymen.

In the meantime, elections to four city corporations and nine municipalities have been held in a very peaceful atmosphere. In those elections, the turnout of voters was at record high rate — from the lowest 75 percent to the highest 92 percent. In a jubilant and festive mood, without any untoward incident, voters exercised their franchise without fear and had chosen their municipalities' representatives.

I believe, elections will be held in a free, fair and lively environment. In this contest, the question of relaxation or even withdrawal of emergency has been raised. I want to make it very clear in unequivocal terms that the government would not hesitate and would not retreat to do whatever would be required to hold a transparent and fair election.

Our pledge and determination shall be reflected in light of the national expectation. The relevant provisions of Emergency Power Rules (EPRs) will be relaxed or repealed in an appropriate time so that candidates could take necessary preparations and could conduct their electioneering easily; elections could be held with free and spontaneous participation of all in a vibrant environment. The Emergency Rules were relaxed during the just concluded City Corporations and municipalities' polls. In light of this experience, the government is also considering relaxation of other provisions of the EPRs. I can assure you that no rules of the Emergency Act would be a barrier to election activities. However, nobody would certainly desire that law and order would so be disrupted in the pre- or during polls period making the holding of the fair elections impossible or reflection of the people's verdict in the results of the polls would be impossible or distorted. If anybody would like to create such a situation, the government would definitely tackle it with an iron hand in the greater national interest and that would have to be done for the sake of the fair elections and for the interest of transition to democracy.

We have all started our journey towards the process of handing over power to the government through a free election. Standard principle and cooperation of all are, therefore, most essential today. The political parties have to take a lead in this matter. The government has neither any hostile relationship with the political parties nor any clash of interests or objects.

A corruption-free environment has to be created with collective endeavour of all, including political parties, where no prominence of black money, muscle power and evils will exist. Selfishness and immorality must be defeated to the goodwill and principle. We have to keep in mind that the objective of all political parties and the government is same; the pathway is also one and, therefore, compromise, fellow feelings and tolerance are inevitable. There might be political differences, but such discord must not tear-down us.

We like to see such a democratic environment in the country where there will be no chaos and confrontation and where petty personal or party interest may not ruin the national interests. We dream of such a Bangladesh that will be totally free from hunger, poverty, illiteracy and conflicts. We have to continue our united thrust to establish a real democracy in our beloved motherland Bangladesh and to attain a desired goal by accelerating its economic prosperity.

After the forthcoming national elections, a democratically elected government will run the country. It is expected that after the national election, all political parties will work together to establish a congenial and stable atmosphere in the country and the nation will come out from the vicious circle of violence and corruption. The next government will not only continue but also expedite the process that has been initiated by the present government in the forms of anti-corruption drives, lodging cases and starting trial procedures. The next government will further strengthen the institutional reform process that has been initiated by the present government. The nation expects that the next government will be sincere in dispensation of state functioning. It is our earnest hope that the political parties will come forward to materialise such expectations of the people. All have to reach in a consensus on basic national issues shunning all negative and destructive politics. The nation does not want to see anarchic situation anymore.

On this holy month of Ramadan, let us exchange mutually our good wishes. Let us we wish well-being of all. Let us take a pledge together that we shall prove before the world that we are a democratic, peace-loving and forward-looking nation. We will attain our goal of holding a free, fair, neutral and acceptable election as per schedule. We shall not allow deteriorating law and order in the country. We must shun conflict and confrontation. We shall totally proscribe corruption.

We never claim that all activities of the caretaker government are above criticism. Recently, some criticisms were heard on the course of anti-corruption drives. But there was a priority in our all endeavours towards a dream of holding of a free, fair and credible national election and to build up a political understanding towards that goal. In this process, there may be some ebb in certain reforms initiatives. But the national politics has reached the doorsteps of a cordial understanding. In future, good governance will pulsate with new life through our spontaneous inventiveness attuned to this spirit. It is my earnest belief that the political ambiance will no longer be marked by doubt and taken an opposite direction.

The 2008 election will be the new milestone of our democracy, good governance, transparency and accountability. We shall join the march of attaining overall development of the country's progress and prosperity with new inspiration.

(*Source*: http://www.cao.gov.bd/ca_address/sep20addr08_eng.html)

## A Synoptic View of Internal Developments in Bangladesh[2]

May 12, 2008

*Dr Fakhruddin Ahmed, Chief Advisor of the Caretaker Government, in his National Address, spoke on the political transition in Bangladesh. Some of the points flagged off in the address were: the timing of elections, which as announced, was be held on the third week of December. Dr Ahmed stated that formal dialogue with the political parties would commence from May 22, 2008 and efforts would be directed towards formulating the National Charter. Initiating anti-corruption oversight mechanisms was also a key focal point in Dr Ahmed's speech.*

I appear before you today at a critical juncture of the national life. We took over the responsibility of the government on January 12, 2007 in the backdrop of inevitable changes. We are near to the threshold of the final phase of our desired political transition today on the basis of the reform programmes of about 16 months.

After assuming the responsibility, the main objective of the caretaker government was to conduct holding of a free, fair and neutral election acceptable to all. It aims at ushering a new healthy and democratic post election political trend. To achieve this goal, we required a flawless voter list and creation of a congenial environment to hold the election. You know, the preparation of a flawless voter list was the common demand of all political parties. To achieve this, we immediately accomplished the task of reconstituting the Election Commission and consequently the Election Commission engaged itself in preparing a flawless voter list. Registration of almost 6.5 crore voters have already been completed. For this, I sincerely congratulate the Election Commission, Armed Forces,

---

2. Address to the Nation by the Chief Adviser of the Non-Party Caretaker Government, Dr. Fakhruddin Ahmed, May 12, 2008.

field administration, and all development partners. Simultaneously, I also express my gratitude to the countrymen for extending all assistance and support the effort by making successful this historic activities.

To create environment to hold a free, fair and proper and meaningful election acceptable to all, one of the major conditions is to clampdown on black money and use of muscle power, establish rule of law and carry out anti-corruption drives, improvement of law and order and above all, make effective and dynamic the state-run institutions. You know, our government is working uncompromisingly to achieve these goals and has already been successful to a great extent in creating a election- friendly environment. In this context, on behalf of the government, I would like to make a clear announcement about the date of the next Jatiya Sangsad election. The election would be held on any day in the third week of December next. The Election Commission will make announcement of the specific date and election schedule as per rule.

I hope all questions, suspicions and speculations centering election will come to an end after it. The sun-rise of the new-year after December next, will greet a newly elected people representative government in office. And it will be made possible by the democracy-loving people of Bangladesh, its supportive political parties, concerned government and non-government organizations and the people of the right thinking civil society.

We have almost reached now the final phase of the election process. Our aim is to establish a proper sustainable democratic process in the country by holding a free, fair and acceptable election as per the earlier announced roadmap. It is true that the achievement of this goal is not possible by the caretaker government alone. It requires an indifferent national unity. In the light of this reality, steps have been taken to initiate a dialogue on the basis of proposals made by various political parties and professional organizations. We held pre-dialogue discussion staggering over 22 days before starting the main dialogue. Five advisers of the government completed the pre-dialogue discussions working relentlessly.and trying to intensively understand the views of the parties. I firmly believe, by holding the pre-dialogue discussion, we have been able to send the message of our earnest desire in building the foundation of respect and trust in political parties. The five advisers of the government have prepared the dialogue document and presented their views to me containing the main objective of the dialogue, its procedure, and different action programmes that may be taken. In this context, I would like to announce that we would sit in formal dialogue with political parties starting from May 22. Letters will be sent from tomorrow from my office to various political parties inviting them to join the dialogue.

I firmly believe, in this historic dialogue we will be able to reach consensus on all important national issues. It will reflect the hopes and aspirations of all political parties, groups, professions and the people of the country at large. It cannot be denied that the national consensus to be reached in this way needs to be given a moral compulsion and permanent shape. In the light of this, a 'national charter' needs to be adopted through concerted discussion of the government, political parties, representatives of all groups and professions. A proper and fair electoral framework will be established through this national charter. It will help launch a healthy and stable democratic process in the country.

I have already mentioned that the government has accomplished various programmes aimed at making the election meaningful. It is at the final stage of the process to promulgate soon the Election Commission proposed amended electoral law, rules and regulations. We hope that the political parties will spontaneously come forward to take steps towards reform spontaneously keeping inconformity with the electoral law, rules and regulations. I firmly believe that the political parties would remain committed to playing an effective supportive role to the steps taken by the government. The nation expects that the entire election process would be free from black money, muscle power, administrative biases, nomination trade and excessive expenses for poll campaigns. Also it is expected that the political parties would reach a consensus through dialogue to create an election-friendly environment with improved law and order situation.

The Election Commission has already expressed its decisions to hold polls in city corporations and some municipalities before the national elections. Besides, polls at upazila levels are also in their work plan. It's a demand of the time to hold polls at upazila, pourasabha and city corporations as part of strengthening local government institutes aimed at people's welfare. The government, in this context, would provide all out support and cooperation based on the needs and demands from the election commission. However, the elections at local levels would not create any obstacle to attain our prime target— to hold national elections. We would remain uncompromising in regards to national elections. We would just expect that the polls at the local levels would able to create a positive flow towards greater national elections.

Our all endeavours would turn into despair unless a healthy and stable democracy is introduced. To that end, our first task is to reach consensus on all issues towards qualitative improvement of politics. In this context, we expect a successful implementation of voluntary internal reforms of all political parties. The nation today wants to see a successful implementation of cherished reforms for the creation of a trend of democratic attitudes within political parties, as well as to make inroads for honest, worthy and dynamic leadership. Side by side, the people also expect a reflection of mutual respects among political parties for each other as well as cordial and effective relationship among them. I do hope that all would realize the urgency of reaching consensus to introduce and spearhead the motto of a healthy and stable democratic system in all party and state activities.

It is very urgent to reach a consensus before elections to make the parliament effective even after the elections. Different proposals have already been discussed in this context. It must be ensured that none would reject election results, nor they boycott parliament. I would hope that this thing would be discussed in dialogue with special importance. The obligations to be realized by all to continue and proceed further the institutional and legal reforms done by the caretaker government that include separation of judiciary, election commission and anti-corruption commission.

All know, the culture of 'lackey politics' is one of the major sources of 'evil politics'. Whatever good intentions gave birth to front organizations, the ground reality of today is that most of these organizations are now plunged into an ill culture of lackey politics that is void of ideology. It has become imperative to rescue politics from such trends, put it on track and resume a health trend through qualitative changes in politics. We have to realize these important issues through dialogues and find clear solutions to those as well.

The present world is very competitive and fast moving. All political and administrative activities should be complementary to economic development to keep pace with the world economy. Every day and every hour is very important to keep economic wheels moving on. So, we have to reach consensus that we would shun all forms of destructive and negative politics. Hartal, blockade and violent agitation would be buried forever. The nation doesn't want to see any form of anarchic political activities in future.

Here, I want to raise another issue for considerations. To make power permanent, the tendency of politicization in different public institutions including administration has been expanded severely in the past. Sadly I am to say that the ill culture of such politicization is not at all good for the nation in any sense. Running administration based on efficiency and merit is a clear reflection of a successful regime. All political leadership has to think it deeply. I hope that an effective solution would be sort out from dialogues to this effect and consensus would also be established.

You know, the serious degradation of rule of law was the main reason for creating unbridled anarchic situation before January 11 of 2007. Our government has been playing an uncompromising role to establish the rule of law. The supports from all of you and your deep respect to rule of law have together made it possible to establish an improved law and order situation in the country. I would like to extend my heartfelt thanks to all political parties, professional organizations, civil society and others for it.

You all will agree that the people might not be fully informed about the grim picture of corruption unless our government would have conducted the anti-corruption drive. Corruption is the main enemy to national progress and development. We have to come out of the vicious circle of corruption at any cost. We all must unite to build a corruption free society. I hope, all political leaders and people of all walks of life would make proposals so that all avenues for corruption get closed in the future.

From the political point of view, the lack of balance is the main weakness of power structure. Too much centralized power is not helpful at all for a stable and responsible governance. Preparing specific proposals and forging of consensus regarding what kind of power re-structuring among the highest constitutional posts can play positive role for political stability can be one of the major achievements of dialogue. I hope, all parties, would lead the nation towards desired goals through utilization of their talents and creativity.

There is no doubt that the nation wholeheartedly expects the overall stability of the post-election government. Balance of power, rule of law, healthy politics, effective parliament, accountable administration are the components of a stable ruling system. An infrastructure or guideline is essential for containing these components. Such an infrastructure or guideline will keep the nation united in the national interests. There might have differences in political philosophy or ideology, but there must have the system that such differences can in no way hamper stability. I appeal to all political parties, professional organizations and the people- let's develop such infrastructure or guideline for ensuring stability for the next governments where political, economic and administrative stability would always be upheld. The valuable proposals of all of you and consensus on these matters are now the expectation of the nation.

We expect that the political parties would take part in the upcoming dialogue in an open mind. I can assure that the government has no pre-fixed agenda. Nor even it has hostility against anyone. Rather it has an open mind for understanding. The political parties would make their opinion in open mind about the actions in resolving all problems in political arena, their possible solutions and work plans. They will make constructive proposals for bringing qualitative improvement in political structure. I declare lifting of ban on indoor politics throughout the country from tomorrow to make room for taking preparation for the elections to be held in December next and also easing participation of all political parties in this process. Necessary directives in this matter are being made from the government.

For conducting election publicity, it is necessary to ensure free movement of political activists, their unhindered participation in holding meetings and making other means of publicity. The EC has formulated an election code of conduct through discussion with the political parties, and the commission is determined to implement it fully. Considering all relevant matters, the government will take steps to suspend or relax certain provisions of emergency rules and its regulations at an appropriate time for creating an atmosphere for holding election. The government is firmly determined to do everything that is required for making the election meaningful and fruitful.

The record production of three main staple foods — Boro, wheat and potato — for the first time in the country's history, is the latest example that we can achieve any success through an integrated and united effort. We have proved, through the bumper production of crops, that we can do many things if there are good wishes and initiatives.

For this great success, I, on behalf of the government and the people, convey my sincere gratitude and appreciation to the farmer community. I congratulate all concerned including various ministries, field level administration and the army who played their due role for achieving the success. I hope, the trend of new reawakening would be continued during the upcoming Aman season. The government is firmly committed to provide all kinds of cooperation to the farm sector and the farmers.

The dialogue in one sense is a trust-based initiative. There may be disputes, rivalry and competition within us. But in eventual judgment, these are not our main features. The nation expects from us a healthy and stable transition. We will have to overcome all narrowness, vengeance and mistrust in proceeding towards that end.

I know, we have the courage to discard these challenges. This is the time to express our determination. We don't have any scope to go backward. All the hearts of 150 million people of our beloved motherland developed an irresistible dream in view of the reality of the time. This dream is for a political and economic transition and to stand before the comity of the world with a national identity, flourished with the spirit of self-confidence.

We think the role of common masses in the process of electoral and political reforms is to be most crucial. We don't want to go back to the situation which had witnessed violent political conflicts. We want a qualitative and meaningful change in the governance and political structures. The people will have to take the responsibility to ensure that the political parties are run according to the law and the constitution in a democratic atmosphere. You will also have to ensure that honest, competent, patriotic, meritorious and efficient candidates dedicated to public welfare are elected to represent the people in parliament.

We will have to keep in mind that the key to build an enlightened future for society and state lies with the people or voters. I will hope, all voters of the country will perform this duty accurately on the day of the election. Allah willing, we will definitely succeed in installing an honest, patriotic, transparent and really accountable government through the accurate exercise of our voting rights.

The next election is also opening up a golden horizon for politicians who intend to unveil the door of a golden future for the motherland. I hope, the honest, competent and enthusiastic politicians will also properly take this advantage.

At this transition point of the history, I would like to express my hope that we will be able to remove the apparent differences of our opinions or thoughts through cordial discussions and exchange of opinions since our goal is the same. Definitely, we will have to instill in the soil of this country the democracy and democratic system, values and rules and regulations. And it will have to be done for a permanent period. We will have to ensure this sustainable system to announce our democratic entity with pride in the world stage defying all odds or barriers.

Before conclusion, I would like to reiterate some points of my today's statement.

1. The election for the ninth parliament will be held in the third week of December this year.
2. We will start the formal dialogue with the political parties of the country from May 22.
3. The ban on indoor politics across the country will be lifted tomorrow.
4. According to the necessity, we will suspend or relax the relevant sections of the emergency rules and regulations at appropriate time to create a favourable atmosphere for the election and ease the poll campaigns.
5. Efforts will be made to formulate "National Charter" on the basis of consensus on relevant matters prior to the polls so qualitative changes are ensured in government and political systems after the election.

The responsibility of making the dialogue a success lies with all of us. To say in one word, there is no scope for failure in this regard. In terms of aspirations, the nation is united today. Here lies our main strength. The successful eventuality of the journey we started on January 11, 2007 is at our doorstep. We will definitely reach our aspired goal with our united efforts.

The present caretaker government will no more be in office at the end of this year but it will leave behind a sustainable democratic system based on a firm foundation. We extremely hope that the hopes and aspirations of the struggling people of Bangladesh will get a real shape through this foundation.

(*Source*: http://www.cao.gov.bd/ca_address/index.htm)

## A Synoptic View of Internal Developments in Bangladesh[3]

January 21, 2007

*In his address to the nation, Chief Adviser Dr. Fakhruddin Ahmed, emphasized the caretaker government's sensitivity towards holding fair and free elections and called upon various political parties to cooperate with each other in order to achieve the same. He also touched upon combating imminent challenges in Bangladesh, like corrupt practices, need for an independent judiciary and terrorism amongst many others.*

The solemn responsibility of the Chief Adviser of the Non-Party Caretaker government has been placed on me at this critical juncture of Bangladesh's history. I ask for the blessings of the Almighty, and the sincere good wishes, fullest support and cooperation of my fellow citizens in properly discharging this difficult responsibility.

I must begin by recalling with great respect the courageous individuals, the valiant freedom fighters and the heroic martyrs-by whose supreme sacrifice, extraordinary contributions, dedication and hard work our dear motherland was established as an independent, sovereign and democratic state. I remember also the leaders of our nation, who have guided our country and provided inspiration as we continue to move along the path of progress and prosperity.

It is by pledging our allegiance to the sacred Constitution of Bangladesh that I and my council of advisers have assumed the responsibility of running the government at this critical moment, with the objective of ensuring peace, happiness, prosperity, and the overall security of our nation and society. You all are aware under what circumstances we had to take this difficult responsibility. I am sure that my countrymen will agree with me that none of us would have wished for this path. But the difficult reality remains that our dear motherland finds itself in the midst of a serious crisis. The greatest challenges today are to maintain political and social stability as well as to uphold and strengthen our democracy by holding free and fair polls which ensure every citizen's right to vote. We also face the challenge of keeping the wheels of progress and prosperity of our country fully operational. We must face all these challenges with strong determination. We must strive to make our future brighter, more enlightened and vibrant. To achieve these objectives I urge my countrymen to demonstrate patience, tolerance and patriotism.

---

3. Address to the Nation by the Chief Adviser of the Non-Party Caretaker Government Dr. Fakhruddin Ahmed,January 21, 2007.

Why do I now make this appeal to you and why are these tasks incumbent on my government? Looking back on the experience of the Bangladeshi people over the past 36 years, we must ask ourselves if we have achieved the happiness, peace and prosperity that we all desire ? Why have we not achieved the achievable? The answers to these questions bring to light the distressing picture of a nation plagued by rampant corruption, mired in the dominance of individual and group interests over the national interest, beset by unscrupulous competition for power, wealth and influence, stuck ever deeper in the cult of personality, and preyed upon by the indiscriminate use of black money and muscle power to achieve narrow interests. Despite repeated calls for caution from the honest and sincere segments of our society, their message has not been heeded Hence the time has now come when we must work together to pursue the goal of establishing a solid foundation for our country. For our efforts to succeed, it is essential for us to unite as a nation and work together with a common sense of patriotism.

You all know that a general election was scheduled for 22nd January 2007, to hand over power to an Elected Government through a universally recognized democratic process. But the controversy, uncertainty and lawlessness that emerged around the elections not only endangered economic advancement, social cohesion and security but also threatened the very democratic core of our country.

Destructive and subversive activities, violent and hostile attitudes harbored by opposing political parties, and the absence of a conducive environment for free and fair polls not only made holding the scheduled elections impossible, but also imperiled the very heart of our democratic system. I believe that the dedicated and patriotic political leaders and workers, the civil society and people from all walks of life want an end to this situation. We must therefore work together to end this situation once and for all.

Bangladeshi people from all strata want a free, fair, peaceful and neutral election as per constitutional provisions and with the participation of all political parties. Achieving this is the central goal of our government.

Any general election becomes meaningless if the essential rules and regulations of the election are not followed. Therefore, the most important responsibility of the present government is to create a transparent, peaceful and congenial atmosphere for conducting a truly democratic election. It is therefore the responsibility of this government to undertake the necessary electoral reforms to ensure a free, fair and universally acceptable election with participation from all parties as soon as possible. We must outline a clear program and then formulate and implement a specific plan to achieve these goals. Our efforts must be concentrated to ensure the success of our endeavor, for in this task we cannot afford to fail. The nation cannot bear to stumble again and return to the unstable and intolerable situation of the recent past.

It is one of the principal pre-conditions of our democratic state to have a neutral, robust and independent Election Commission. Though unpleasant to acknowledge, it is nevertheless true that the activities of the Election Commission were not above question even in the past. The present Election Commission has become especially controversial, and the reconstitution of the Election Commission has therefore become imperative. In order to hold a free, fair and credible election, it is equally important to prepare and publish an accurate and flawless voter list. Necessary and effective steps will be taken in this regard. Appropriate measures will also be taken to ensure compliance with the electoral code of conduct and to monitor electoral expenditures. You are aware that there have been calls for voter identity cards and transparent ballot boxes from various quarters. Steps will be taken in regards to these issues following detailed analysis and planning.

While it is necessary to fulfill these conditions to ensure the holding of a free, fair and credible election, it is also important for the political parties to nominate honest and qualified candidates to ensure a meaningful and universally acceptable process. Today, the Bangladeshi people demand it, and the hour demands it.

There is no denying that we cannot attain real democracy without emancipating ourselves from the vicious cycles of corruption and terrorism in the country. Therefore, we are committed to freeing the election from corruption and muscle-power. Effective programs will be undertaken to reform the overall poll process so that black money and muscle-power cannot obstruct free and fair elections and cannot alter the true reflection of the people's will. In particular, appropriate measures will he taken to take detailed accounts of the earnings and assets of all candidates and to ensure the validity of such disclosures. We must banish the use of muscle power and black money from the election scene. I hope that all political parties will join us and provide full cooperation in this regard and will reflect these ideals in the political culture, including the nomination process.

Maintaining law and order is the principal precondition for a peaceful and acceptable election as well as for the continued development of the country. We have been working relentlessly to further improve the law and order situation, to ensure the safety and security of people's lives and property, and to restore peace and stability to the country. As part of this effort, joint drives and combined operations by the armed forces, police, BDR, RAB and other law-enforcement agencies have been launched. Stern legal action is being taken against the so-called 'godfathers', identified criminals, terrorists, extortionists and anti-social elements. Strong measures are being taken against those who resorted to hurling bombs in the name of religion, and against all extremist activities, illegal weapons and smuggling. My firm belief is that the law and order situation has improved as a result of all these steps. These drives and activities will therefore be intensified further.

You are aware that our remarkable armed forces, known for their patriotism and for their great spirit of sacrifice, and acclaimed in the national and international arena for the professionalism, is assisting the civil administration in maintaining law and order. I believe that it will be possible for the law-enforcement agencies to maintain social stability and a peaceful environment with your continued, active and sincere cooperation. I want to make it very clear that all concerned have been instructed so that no innocent citizen is unnecessarily harassed or victimized.

You all are aware that the present emergency has been declared in the face of a political crisis. It has no contradiction with the people's expectation. As a result, we remain vigilant in upholding the basic rights of the people, including human rights and freedom of the press and mass media.

Now let me turn to a few other relevant matters. We must ensure that the country's administration is non-partisan and neutral, without which holding a neutral general election or establishing a fair democratic system is not possible. Government officials should always remember that the political parties are not their masters. They must remain neutral in their work for the Republic, for they are the servants of the people. They must remain free from the undesirable influence of party politics.

The judiciary shall be independent and neutral. You have seen that the present caretaker government has taken a bold and momentous step to separate the judiciary from the executive within a short span of time. This step will be regarded as a milestone in the history of the country's judiciary. People from all walks of life, including lawyers and civil society, have appreciated this measure. We want the judiciary to uphold its dignity. Let the rule of law and justice be established on a firm footing.

You have seen that rampant corruption and plundering of the nation's wealth by some dishonest individuals have left the country's economy, society and politics polluted, shattered and backward. The country's image and standing has been tarnished around the globe. This situation cannot be allowed to continue.

The people of the country want stern measures against the corrupt persons. We will launch a firm and systematic campaign soon to curb corruption. The Anti-corruption Commission and other government organizations concerned will be restructured and reinvigorated. These organizations will be restored and will be kept free from all forms of outside influence.

You are aware of the sufferings of the people of all spheres due to the power crisis and its negative impact on trade, commerce, agriculture and industries. The increasing power demand and the deficit in its supply, the corruption in power distribution and general mismanagement have not only curtailed the prospects of industries and production but also jeopardized everyday life. We must overcome this situation quickly. As you know, large expenses and a long time is required to set up new power stations. We cannot expect increases in power generation overnight. But the country will incur further economic loss if proper measures for increasing power generation are not taken right now. Steps will be taken immediately to curb corruption and increase power supply through fair management.

The price-hike of essentials has made the life of the people, particularly the low-income group, miserable. Increasing the supply of various items can have a positive impact on the price level. If the market is allowed to function normally, then the regular supply of essentials will determine the prices of commodities fairly, which will protect the interests of both producers and consumers. Mismanagement of the ports, extortion in the transportation of goods and the control of markets by some unscrupulous traders and other distorting activities disrupt the supply of commodities and create a negative impact on the prices of essentials. Stringent measures will be taken against such practices.

An atmosphere of mutual respect and tolerance, coupled with a free-thinking and fraternal attitude, are essential to establish a proper democratic system and to allow for the participation of different parties in the elections. There is a need to allow for forward thinking debate on specific issues without becoming emotionally-charged, unreasonable, or narrow-minded. The nation must be freed from the ills of social and religious-based divisions and we must keep our communal harmony intact. We must work together to create a society that fulfills the promise that the 'head is held high where heart is free from fear'*. It is my firm belief that our active media and objective journalists will undoubtedly help in guiding the nation in the right direction. Our vigilant society will always remain active and alert to protect and uphold the national conscience and ideals.

As a nation, we believe in peace and harmony, in respect for human rights and in democratic values. We have traditionally maintained a friendly attitude towards all countries, specially our neighbors. We are determined to continue our campaign against international extremism and terrorism. Our activities in this field are guided by internationally recognized principles and values both at home and abroad. We are determined to follow and strengthen the principles enshrined in the Charter of the United Nations. We want to progress along the path of democracy while

---

* A famous quote from Rabindranath Tagore, Bengali poet and recipient of the 1913 Nobel Prize in Literature.

maintaining regional co-operation and upholding good relations with all countries based on mutual respect.

I want to make it absolutely clear that we are determined to hand over power to an elected government at the earliest instance by arranging free, fair and acceptable general elections. But to achieve this objective the sincere and whole-hearted cooperation of the people is essential, as is the active support of the political parties. The involvement of all relevant institutions and organizations is also important. The support of all friendly democratic countries and international agencies will help make the election acceptable at home and enhance Bangladesh's image abroad.

We will devote all our strength to achieving these goals, as we surely will with your blessings, support, and sincere cooperation, and by the grace of Almighty Allah. We have liberated our dear motherland through innumerable sacrifices and through the loss of so many precious lives. The blood of millions of martyrs has blended with the soil of our nation. We must prove the truth that their sacrifices were not in vain. And as we must think of our debt to the martyrs of independence, so too must we remember that we are accountable to future generations.

Let Bangladesh live forever and keep its head high in the world, as it has throughout its glorious history. Let us all work together to take our beloved Bangladesh on the path of rapid progress in order to achieve its enormous potential. Leaving behind petty personal interests, let us be imbued with a strong sense of patriotism. Let us help future generations by building the Bangladesh of their dreams.

It is my and my colleague's firm belief that we shall be able to reach these cherished goals, insha-Allah, through the active and collective cooperation of all. We will build Bangladesh, a country of unlimited potential, with a firm commitment to its march along the path of democracy. We will build a happy, prosperous and self-reliant Bangladesh-a dream nurtured since the birth of our nation. We can and will be successful in building a modern, strong and democratic Bangladesh.

(*Source*: http://www.cao.gov.bd/ca_address/index.htm)

# 8.

# BILATERAL RELATIONS WITH INDIA

## Joint Press Conference by Foreign Secretaries of India and Bangladesh after annual Foreign Office Consultations in New Delhi

July 17, 2008

*In a joint press conference by India and Bangladesh, Foreign Secretary Shiv Shankar Menon, spoke about the shared cultural heritage and historical bond between the two countries. He spoke on many issues of common interest including trade and commerce relations, political relations, common security issues and water issues amongst many others. Foreign Secretary of Bangladesh Mr. Md Tohid Hossain, meanwhile emphasized on the Technical Committee, which he considered was an important subject to be addressed, in order to resolve the issue of embankment, protection of rivers, which had been harming people on both sides of the border.*

**Foreign Secretary of India (Shri Shivshankar Menon)**

Good afternoon, ladies and gentlemen. Thank you for coming. I am very happy to welcome Foreign Secretary of Bangladesh and his delegation to India for the annual Foreign Office Consultations between our two countries.

We have had very friendly, open, cordial and substantive discussion on our relationship this morning. We have covered all aspects of our relations. For us in India, as I informed the Foreign Secretary, relations with Bangladesh are a matter of the highest priority. We share a common cultural heritage and historical bonds. As a close and friendly neighbour we stand committed to strengthening our relationship with Bangladesh. We had a very good discussion today where we discussed our trade and economic relations, our political relations, common security issues, water issues and the other aspects where we would like to carry our relationship forward.

It has been a productive year for our relationship. In the last April we started the Maitri Express between Kolkata and Dhaka. We have also had the visit of the Chief of Army Staff of Bangladesh. Our Army Chief will be visiting Bangladesh soon. The Home Secretary will also be going to Bangladesh in the near future. Last year, our External Affairs Minister visited Bangladesh twice; and we tried to help Bangladesh to the extent that we could when she was hit by a series of natural disasters.

Today, we also discussed issues about connectivity between our two countries. From our point of view I think the discussions were very useful and have led to much greater understanding of each other's concerns and interests. We are convinced that our security is interlinked, and that terrorism will have to be tackled resolutely.

We both exchanged views on how to deal with some of the humanitarian aspects, water resources issues for instance; and we are trying to enhance cooperation in agriculture and in science and technology. I am confident that this round of Foreign Office Consultations helped build trust and understanding between our two countries, and we look forward to continuing this process.

**Foreign Secretary of Bangladesh (Mr. Md. Touhid Hossain):**

I would first like to thank all of you for being here to cover the present round of Foreign Office Consultations between India and Bangladesh

I know that for the media, both in Bangladesh and in India, there is a very keen interest to follow how the relations between our two countries are evolving. This is natural and this is also welcome for I believe that the media in both our countries can play a major positive role in creating the conditions that may help both our countries to remain on a positive trajectory to improve and strengthen their relations.

I thank Foreign Secretary Menon for inviting me over to Delhi for this round of Foreign Office Consultations between our two countries despite his extremely busy schedule and other important preoccupations. I am delighted to come here in response to his invitation; and we have had, as he has mentioned, very useful and constructive discussions on the entire range of issues in which we have shared interests.

The Foreign Secretary has indicated to you broadly the issues that we discussed. I can only add to what he has said by saying that we did not shy away from discussing all issues which we considered important for the present and the future of the robust, friendly relations between Bangladesh and India.

Our discussions have been candid, comprehensive and forward-looking. I have every reason to believe that ours has been a useful round of discussions which would enable us to continue to work constructively in the days and years ahead to enrich our already close bilateral relationship. I have invited Mr. Menon to visit Bangladesh at a time that he finds convenient to carry forward the useful discussions that we have had in Delhi.

I would like to mention here one small thing which is that on the water issue we have agreed that the Technical Committee should sit very quickly to resolve one small issue that can be resolve quickly which is the embankment protection of the rivers which has been harming the people on both sides of our border. We hope that very soon they will sit and resolve this issue.

Thank you.

Question: This is addressed to both Foreign Secretaries. Recently in all the terror attacks that have taken place in India, fingers have pointed towards the HuJI which is supposed to have its base in Bangladesh. Was this discussed in the meeting between the two Foreign Secretaries?

Foreign Secretary of India: We discussed the issue of terrorism and how we both need to face it together. The details, of course, are dealt with in other fora. We have other places where we discuss these things, the Home Secretaries' talks and so on. And we look forward to working together against terrorism.

Foreign Secretary of Bangladesh: I fully agree with what he has said. I just have to add one thing that we think this is a global problem. We have a mechanism for cooperation in this sector and we will continue to do that.

Question: What is the status of BIPA?

Foreign Secretary of Bangladesh: This is in an advanced stage of finalization and we believe that in the near future we will be able to do something on that.

Foreign Secretary of India: I will ditto that.

(*Source*: http://meaindia.nic.in/)

## Bangladesh and West Bengal: Cultural Linkages[1]

June 30, 2008

*Minister of External Affairs, Pranab Mukherjee, in his inaugural address at South Asian Free Media Association, spoke at length about the Bengal- Bangladesh relations. While emphasizing on building trust and mutual confidence, he pointed out that the focal point of interaction between the two sides was people to people contact and promotion of trade and commerce. Touching upon the many developments witnessed by both sides, he lauded the commencement of Kolkata-Dhaka Passenger Train Service. The Indian Foreign Minister also highlighted the significant role of*

1. Inaugural Address by Shri Pranab Mukherjee, Minister for External Affairs at South Asian Free Media Association (SAFMA) Conference of Journalists from Bangladesh and West Bengal, June 30, 2008.

> *SAARC in facilitating cooperation, through initiation of SAARC Development Fund, which, he underlined would be the umbrella financial institution for all SAARC development projects. Intra regional connectivity was another subject, spoken in length and the linkages enabling land-locked member states to have access to sea via other SAARC states was in particular highlighted.*

It gives me immense pleasure to be present here today on the occasion of the inauguration of the South Asian Free Media Association (SAFMA) Conference of Journalists from Bangladesh and West Bengal. The event organized by the SAFMA's India Chapter gives an opportunity to the media from both sides to promote mutual understanding and cooperation between the two countries. SAFMA has also played an important role in addressing the constraints and concerns of media, and look for solutions while pursuing its endeavour to foster peace, stability and cooperation in South Asia. I have been given to speak on West Bengal-Bangladesh interaction on building trust and mutual confidence, a theme well-timed and opportune.

With Bangladesh, India shares not only enduring feelings of civilizational, fraternal, linguistic and cultural ties but also a common history of struggle and liberation. These close bonds are logically manifested in the common historical legacy and friendship which West Bengal shares with Bangladesh. It is, therefore, but natural that people from both sides of the border have aspirations to enhance connectivity for promoting trade, people to people contact and interaction.

Relations between India and Bangladesh especially over the last few years have seen much dynamism and closer interaction in all spheres. Building trust and mutual confidence in our relations is the acknowledgement of issues in our relations and to address them comprehensively with an open mind. Understanding can only be built on this determination to address issues of concern to both countries. Last year, I visited Bangladesh twice in February and in December and held frank discussions with leaders of Bangladesh on the entire gamut of our bilateral relations. Governments of both countries are committed to try and resolve all issues in our relations with a mutually constructive approach.

The commencement of Kolkata-Dhaka Passenger Train Service in April fulfilled a long standing aspiration of the people of both countries to enhance connectivity. This comes as a welcome development to the people of West Bengal to enhance their fraternal links with Bangladesh. Equally important is the connectivity of ideas, minds and hearts. Recently, for the first time a delegation of Indian War Veterans of the 1971 war visited Bangladesh to participate in the Independence Day celebrations. A delegation from Muktijodhas from Bangladesh now visits Kolkata annually to participate in the Vijay Divas celebrations.

It is also in this spirit of engagement that India has made several unilateral gestures in the recent past to Bangladesh. These gestures are precisely to build trust and mutual confidence in each other. They include allowing Bangladesh to export eight million pieces of readymade garments to India duty-free, lifting the ban on FDI from Bangladesh, providing duty-free access starting January this year. We are also undertaking several initiatives to improve the trade infrastructure including Land Customs Stations, Road, Rail and riverine routes which would help to facilitate trade.

India has provided Bangladesh aid and assistance to help it overcome the damage caused by some of the worst natural disasters last year. These included cash assistance of US $ 10 million, supply of food aid consisting of essential items including rice and milk powder of a total value of nearly 100 crores is underway. In the aftermath of the cyclone in November 2007, India sent an emergency relief package of essential commodities and announced waiver of a ban of rice to Bangladesh for an additional 5 lakh tonnes of rice. We are also in the process of rehabilitating 11 severely cyclone affected villages. Needless to add, our hand of friendship always remains extended.

One of the important vehicles for creation of trust and mutual cooperation between India and Bangladesh is through the means of regional cooperation of SAARC. Following its inception 22 years ago, the geographic contours of SAARC have also changed. Afghanistan is the newest and eighth member of SAARC. SAARC has transformed from declaratory to implementation with the establishment of the SAARC Development Fund (SDF), the Project Office of the South Asian University (SAU), incorporation of services in the on-going negotiations in SAFTA and implementation of key projects in areas of tele-medicine, tele-education, solar rural electrification, rain water harvesting and seed testing laboratories.

SAARC is strengthening intra-regional connectivity through up-gradation of physical linkages that were identified at the 1st meeting of SAARC Transport Ministers in New Delhi in August 2007. These linkages would enable land-locked member states of SAARC to have access to sea via other SAARC member states. Discussions are on going for agreements for seamless travel between SAARC member states, on motor vehicles by rail etc.

Conscious of the adverse impact of climate change, SAARC adopted a Draft Declaration on Climate Change at the 29th Council of Ministers following up with a ministerial meeting hosted at Dhaka. As SAARC evolves further, strengthening its core mechanisms and engaging the outside world through observers and project-based cooperation, the vision of its founding fathers for a vibrant, dynamic regional economic entity is being realized. An area of concern for both countries is to combat the growing menace of extremism and terrorism in the region. Closer cooperation on security issues for building trust is the need of the hour. We should move to address such issues without rancour and with the understanding that both our countries will benefit in the long run. Keeping in mind that development can never take place in an atmosphere of insecurity, SAARC is also cooperating on an agreement to enable security agencies of SAARC member states, strengthen their cooperation to counter terrorism and bring criminals to book.

In the globalized world of today, it is important for both countries to enhance connectivity, linkages and boost our trade which would bring prosperity to the region. Initiatives like transit for Indian goods via Bangladesh can generate synergy and mutual dependence. Closer engagement has emerged as the key to build mutual confidence between countries and I see no reason why our two countries cannot go the way numerous countries have done with India. In this the private sector of both countries has an important role to play.

In any civil society, journalists have a very important role in forming public opinion. All of you can contribute to highlight the issues as also the vast avenues of close cooperation which exists between our countries. I also assure you of our government's help in removing problems and difficulties that may be identified during your discussions. I convey my best wishes for the success of this SAFMA conference and hope it would help in disseminating information on issues and initiatives in the region which can promote understanding and bring people of both countries closer.

(*Source*: http: //www. meaindia.nic.in)

## Creating a South Asian Community: India-Bangladesh Relations[2]

June 27, 2007

*Foreign Secretary, Shiv Shankar Menon, touched upon the key idea of South Asian Community. He talked at length about the economic opportunities, which could be exercised by the South Asian countries and the political challenges which need to be mitigated by the respective countries at the domestic level. While stating that South Asian countries are linked not only through their shared past but also their future, he provided a vision of South Asian Community envisioning a region which witnesses a smooth flow of goods,*

2. Speech by Shri Shivshankar Menon, Foreign Secretary at the Bangladesh Enterprise Institute, "Creating a South Asian Community: India-Bangladesh Relations", June 27, 2007.

*services, people, technologies, knowledge, capital, culture and ideas in the region. Citing that though intra South Asia trade had come down to 6.0 percent, where it was 34 percent in 1948, he highlighted the spectacular growth rate witnessed by the region within the past three years. Some of the major challenges posed to the region; he asserted was the growing threat of terrorism and political transition being experienced by various countries. Touching upon Indo-Bangladesh relations, he complimented the rise of exports from Bangladesh to India and emphasised the significance of enhancing connectivity.*

## The Idea

The idea of a South Asian community has a long history. It was partly an instinctive reaction to our history in the late nineteenth and the first half of the twentieth century. More than that, it recognizes that historically our periods of prosperity and well-being have come when the subcontinent was connected to itself and to the rest of the world. Our best times economically, politically and culturally, have been when we worked together and were linked together. It was then that we managed to realize our potential. This was the impulse that led Bangladesh to suggest the formation of SAARC and to host its first summit.

Given the situation we found ourselves in, it was natural that thinking South Asians would envisage such a community as a means to free our people from poverty, enabling each of our citizens to lead a life of dignity, free from hunger and illiteracy.

The objective basis for such a community exists. In comparison to other sub-regions in the world, our subcontinent probably has more affinities and common historical experience than most.

That is why Prime Minister Manmohan Singh has said that we need to work for a South Asian Community where borders have ceased to matter, and where there is an unhindered flow of goods and peoples, culture and ideas. We believe that the destiny of the people of South Asia is interlinked. It is not just our past that links us, but our future too.

Our leaders have endorsed the vision of a South Asian community formally at successive SAARC summits since 1998. At the fourteenth summit in New Delhi this April they envisioned a South Asian community where there was a smooth flow of goods, services, peoples, technologies, knowledge, capital, culture and ideas in the region.

## The Present Opportunity

Unfortunately, our real progress towards this goal has been uneven and limited by the intervention of political factors. In 1948 over 34% of our trade was within the Indian sub-continent. Today it is less than 6%. This is the lowest amongst all the regions in the world, except perhaps for sub-Saharan Africa. SAFTA and other measures which would have enabled us to break out of the patterns of the recent past are only now being operationalised, and even then not by all of us. The list of future steps remains long.

Fortunately there is recognition within the region today of an opportunity to break out of the sterile patterns of some of our relationships in South Asia, and to put in place the building blocks of a true South Asian community.

This opportunity arises because of changes in India, changes in our neighbours, and a relatively benign international environment. South Asia is today one of the fastest growing regions of the world.

India has seen sustained economic development, with about 6% growth over the last twenty-five years, accelerating in the last three years to over 8%. The resulting changes in the structure and competences of the Indian economy, and the scale and pace of changes in India, have meant that we in the subcontinent have complementarities that never existed before. The potential to work together for mutual economic benefit is greater than ever before.

We believe that India's economic growth offers unique opportunities to our neighbours, who can become stakeholders in this expanding economy. Some of our neighbours have been quick to recognise the benefits of cooperation. The India-Sri Lanka FTA, which became operational in 2000, quadrupled bilateral trade in six years, (from US$ 658 million in 2000 to US$ 2.3 billion in 2006), with Sri Lankan exports growing much faster than India's and thus redressing the balance of trade somewhat. The FTA attracted Indian investment to Sri Lanka, made Indians the largest source of tourism income, and converted Sri Lankan Airlines into the largest foreign airline operating in India, with 90 flights a week! That FTA would not have been possible without the changes in the Indian economy after 1991, and that opportunity is available to India's other neighbours.

India's preferential trade agreements with neighbours do not seek reciprocity and recognize asymmetry. At the recent SAARC Summit Prime Minister Manmohan Singh announced that SAARC LDCs like Bangladesh will enjoy zero-duty access to the Indian market by the end of this year. We will also prune our sensitive list of items considerably. We are well on course to implement these commitments.

Secondly, our neighbours have seen sustained economic growth and change, despite some difficult political situations. I do not have to tell you about the changes in Bangladesh and your own remarkable economic performance. High growth rates in the region are an opportunity to advance together through trade, open borders and economic cooperation, to bring about shared prosperity between India and her neighbors. Between us economics is no longer a zero-sum game.

The rate at which trade in South Asia has grown recently, (and the extent of the unofficial trade), suggest that the potential complementarities created by recent changes are still far from being tapped. Some estimates say that while official two-way India-Bangladesh trade in 2005-6 was US$ 1.83 billion, informal trade may be twice as much again.

Interestingly technological changes such as the internet and satellite TV have also meant that today there is increased exposure and interaction among the peoples of our countries, breaking down stereotypes and building popular support for cooperative relationships.

Finally the international environment is also conducive. The post Cold War world that we are in today is one where globalization and other trends have led to a degree of unprecedented inter-dependence between the major powers, where they are therefore engaged in both competition and cooperation simultaneously. A new international balance of power is evolving and there is a window of opportunity which can be helpful to our quest for development.

The SAARC Summit in April proved some of these proposi-tions. It was easily the least contentious and smoothest summit that we have seen, and was productive and practical. Afghanistan became a formal member, decisions were taken on establishing a South Asian University and a South Asia Food Bank, and the regional multi-modal transport study was approved. We are now working on concrete projects for implementation by SAARC in energy, food, environment and water (including flood control).

It therefore seems that a combination of factors has created a window of opportunity for us to remake our relationships in the subcontinent.

## Challenges

This is not to say that there are no obstacles to our realizing the vision of a South Asian community. If the opportunities are economic, the challenges that come to mind immediately are primarily political. Terrorism is one such. A South Asian community can hardly be realized if terrorist violence and the politics of hate and confrontation continue in our subcontinent.

Common threats, like fundamentalism and terrorism, which recognise no boundaries, must be confronted together. India is ready to work with together with her neighbours in this quest. We must confront such obstacles with our united efforts.

Political transitions also pose a challenge. Many of us are in the midst of political and socio-economic change. It is for each of our countries to choose its own political path. But these choices also have broader consequences and effects. India will not interfere in the internal affairs of her neighbours, believing that decisions on their own future are best taken by the people of these countries themselves through free, fair and democratic political processes. We are close neighbours with shared destinies. It is natural, therefore, that India sees a peaceful, democratic and prospering neighbour-hood as being in our own interest. Security, democracy and economic development are the best answers to common threats like fundamentalism and terrorism and the political misuse of religion.

The vision of a South Asian community must include as an essential component the idea of a South Asia free from violence and disputes, at peace with itself, free to concentrate on its primary tasks of abolishing poverty, improving the life of its people as well as seeking common prosperity.

### The Way Forward

The successful outcome of the 14th SAARC Summit in New Delhi in April this year is an encouraging sign that our countries recognise the value of mutual cooperation. To realize the vision of a South Asian community several steps could be taken in tandem.

We need to work on improving physical and economic connectivity and our connectivity of the mind. Dismantling barriers will enable not only cross-border investment flows and transfer of technology, but also facilitate market access to a wide range of small and middle-sized businesses that may not be able to enter developed markets. In our case, Bangladeshi handicrafts, ethnic clothing, Jamdani sarees, marine, poultry and dairy products, fruits and vegetables could then be easily exported to India.

Then there needs to be a freer flow of people across the region to build upon the cultural and civilizational affinities that we enjoy.

There is also a need to work together to deal with the challenges of terrorism and other threats to the life, peace and security of all our peoples. No country can pretend that one man's terrorist is another's freedom fighter. No government can pretend that what happens across the border is not going to hurt it.

Be it poverty, be it disease, be it natural disasters, or future challenges such as energy security, food security, water or climate change, the destiny of South Asia is inter-linked and we must learn to work together to deal with these challenges.

### India-Bangladesh Relations

A few words on India-Bangladesh relations. We see better relations between India and Bangladesh as integral to a South Asian community. After all it was Bangladesh's vision, which put forward the idea of SAARC.

A peaceful, stable, democratic, secular and prosperous Bangladesh is in India's own national interest. Our unique relations are based on shared history, culture, traditions and common language and literature. India attaches the utmost importance to strengthening our friendly and cooperative ties with Bangladesh. I also wish to reiterate that India fully respects Bangladesh's independence and sovereignty. The people of Bangladesh and their political parties should resolve outstanding issues through discussions and dialogue among themselves, rather than through external intervention or pressure.

It is natural for close neighbours to have problems. Intimacy is not always easy. In the last few days, during our foreign office consultations and in meetings with your leaders, we have sought to review the entire gamut of our relationship, the positive and the complicated, and sought mutually satisfactory solutions or ways forward together. We have discussed issues such as security, our land boundary, the rivers that join us and other emotive issues. We have also looked at the complementarities that creates our opportunity.

I see positive trends in our relations with Bangladesh and am confident that these will become stronger in the coming years. Our commonalities far outweigh our differences. About half a million Bangladeshis visited India legally last year. Visitors between us always return with a profound impression of inherent goodwill. Businessmen from both countries are increasingly discovering that it is most convenient to procure goods and services from each other, rather than from more distant sources. I am particularly pleased by the sharp increase in Bangladesh's exports to India in the last two years.

Bangladesh's geographical location and its common border with a number of Indian States offer considerable opportunities. Over 80% of our bilateral trade is currently routed through Benapole-Petropole. We hope to diversify, opening additional routes and Land Customs Stations. We hope that the Kolkata-Dhaka passenger train can commence operations soon and will be the precursor for a comprehensive network of bus, train and ferry links. We can also cooperate to revive our waterways, which once carried so many of our goods. India is willing to improve air connectivity by establishing daily air services to our metropolitan cities, Delhi, Mumbai, Chennai, Bangalore, Hyderabad and Kolkata, and to 18 other destinations across India.

The possibility of Bangladesh exploiting its strategic geographic location to position itself as a transportation hub for South Asia, South East Asia and China, by upgrading roads, railways and ports, has been articulated by prominent Bangladeshis, such as Nobel Laureate Mohammad Yunus and Prof. Rehman Sobhan, among others. Better connectivity can include linking national power grids, gas pipelines, and telecommunications, to overcome shortages in certain areas and create synergy.

India is prepared to work with friends in Bangladesh to take our bilateral relations to an irreversible higher trajectory and to strengthen cooperation in all spheres. We have revived existing mechanisms for bilateral dialogue and hope to intensify these exchanges. We look forward to identifying solutions to outstanding issues through friendly negotiations and to ensuring that the people of our countries can enjoy the fruits of vigorous interaction and buoyant linkages.

**Conclusion**

To conclude, I am optimistic about our future. Prime Minister Manmohan Singh has said that, every Indian wants to live in a neighbourhood of peace, stability and prosperity. People in our neighbouring countries share the same aspirations. The common aspirations of our peoples provide the basis on which we can work together to usher in an era of peace and prosperity for our peoples. Let us remake our relations and remake our future.

(*Source*: http://meaindia.nic)

## Indo-Bangladesh Dialogue on Media and Culture[3]

March 8, 2007

*Dr Iftekhar Ahmed Chowdhury, Advisor to the Caretaker Government, at the Indo-Bangladesh Dialogue on Media and Culture, stated that a key change of mindsets was needed for rectifying the wrongs of the past. Highlighting the positive contribution made by the armed forces of both the countries, he specifically talked about the constructive role media could possibly play between the two countries. Dr Chowdhury also talked at length on prospects of cultural diplomacy between the two countries. Bangladeshi culture could play a positive role in educating and enriching both sides. Dr Ahmed considered this to be a key element in facilitating mutual understanding between the two countries.*

I am delighted to be able to participate in this track-two process. This method of engaging the non-governmental levels of our two countries, Bangladesh and India, to create an appropriate matrix on which official relationship can be built is a concept whose time has surely come. Indeed, I believe, the situation is appropriate for both tracks, the governmental

3. Speech by Dr. Iftekhar Ahmed Chowdhury, Adviser to the Caretaker Government, Ministry of Foreign Affairs, on Indo-Bangladesh Dialogue on Media and Culture organized by CPD, March 8, 2007.

and non-governmental, to run concurrently, feeding into each other, ultimately serving what is our common interest.

Let me declare unequivocally that it is the intention of the current Caretaker Government to accord high priority to cultivating close relationship with all our neighbors, including India. We sincerely believe that in South Asia, together we are strong and a power to reckon with in the global arena. Conversely, if we are separate, we are weak. There used to be a tendency in our part of the world to perceive the regional pre-eminent actor as an entity that must be countered with by building a web of extra-regional linkages. No longer. Bangladesh is keen to extend the hands of friendship to all countries of the region, big and small, with the confidence that with the dawning of this new era of regional cooperation, it will be warmly grasped. I am aware that there have been times when misunderstandings have clouded the commonality of our values and the similarities of our culture. There must now be a sea change in our mind-set without which, in a world rapidly forging ahead in myriad ways, South Asia will lag behind.

Bangladesh and India share borders, cultural affinities, common historical experience and values that do us proud. We warmly recall the memories of the occasions that had linked our destinies, just like the liberation war in Bangladesh and the creation of SAARC. It is our intention to use these linkages to build a harmonious relationship between us at present. For future we will continue to mark this relationship with cordiality and cooperation.

Ideas that have taken roots in South Asia, our intellectual resources, have made a huge contribution towards advancing global civilization. Some of these have emanated from the soil of Bangladesh. We have taught the world, and this we can say with a modicum of pride that simplest concepts can often effect the profoundest changes. Take micro credit and non-formal education of women for instance. Our Armed Forces from both Asian countries contribute a preponderant component of the UN Peace Keeping operations. They render yeoman's service in stabilizing the strife torn world beyond our shores. Through our policies at home and abroad, we have given globalization a human face.

So let these be the bedrock values of our South Asian home. Let us coexist and cooperate among ourselves. Let us optimize our potentials. And let us deepen and strengthen the bonds that tie us all. India among us is most blessed in terms of size, population and resources. A special responsibility therefore would naturally devolve on her. I have every confidence that she will not shy away from it, and as she grows, she will help us grow with her.

These would entail awarding some special privileges or preferences to those less endowed in trade and other spheres. Such overtures would engender the spirit of greater understanding. It is rare that in relations between nations unilateral gestures are not reciprocated. In other words, one good turn would surely beget another.

At times, of course, there will be differences among us. There will be hiccups in this relationship and pitfalls in the journey to our goals. But we are resolved to overcome all of those and arrive at our destination together in friendship, peace and harmony.

The media has a special responsibility on this score. In South Asia they are an asset that has helped render our societies so intensely pluralist. It is experience culled from observing the operation of South Asian media that led Amartya Sen to famously conclude that a free press and famine are incompatible. Indeed, historically, the media, in erstwhile Bengal in the 19th Century had a major role in sustaining the efflorescence of the "renaissance," that rebirth and revolution in the mindset brought about by the "bhadralok" of Calcutta.

The "bhadralok" were a part of the Weberian status group distinguishable by the way they dressed, spoke, behaved and argued. They challenged the existing mores of their culture and religions by their protestant spirit, refusing to accept without question what they were taught at the feet of the guru. They employed Socratic dialecticism to arrive at their extrapolations. They would agree with Aristotle's retort; " amicus Plato sed magis amica veritas; dear is Plato, but dearer still is the truth!" In many ways, the Bangladeshi media wears the same mantle, speaking for the urges of the "bhadralok" in our contemporary times, upholding their values, acting as the "conscience" of the masses, as a watchdog of the principles that we have always cherished and which have made us nations great.

Therefore, it is obvious that we must create conditions for both our media, to cooperate in the promotion of a common cultural ethos, at the same time, celebrating the distinctiveness and variety that lends it added richness.

In order to be able to do so, the following steps are well worth considering:

- Ensuring free and unimpeded flow of information between our countries.
  Up grading of infrastructural facilities especially in the ICT sector.
- Promoting networking and syndication arrangements between the press and media of both countries.
- Increasing the frequency of contacts and visits by the media people both at the governmental and private level.
- Facilitating travel for the press, media people and the journalists.
- Increasing usage should be considered of video and tele-conferencing facilities for interactive sessions among the press and the media people.

- Increasing awards, grants and fellowships for facilitating visits by media people.
- Encouraging private sector to fund and promote interaction by the media people between the two countries.
- Periodical publication through joint initiatives of supplements, articles, publications on issues of mutual interest such as on poverty, trade and environment.
- Encouraging resident correspondents in both countries for facilitating objective reporting.
- Encouraging positive coverage and presentation of perspective of both the sides in reports by the print and the electronic media.
- Facilitating the increased usage of radio considering its spread, coverage and economy.

The wealth of our culture extends to areas of literature, drama, music, poetry and the performing arts. I am pleased to note young and promising Bangladeshi artistes have availed of this opportunity to learn at Indian centers of excellence such as the Delhi National School of Drama, Sriram Bharatiya Kala Kendra, National Film Institute at Pune and Shantiniketan. Grants and scholarships to facilitate these needs to be increased.

Within the context of SAARC, we have agreed on the elements of an Agenda for Culture. Festivals under its auspices have been organized. The spontaneity and success of these events should encourage us to organize similar ones dedicated to music and culture in our two countries. Competitions in Nazrul and Tagore songs for young and talented artistes from Bangladesh and India could be held alternately in the two countries.

It is felt that a 'Bangladesh Cultural Center ', if established in India could contribute much to the promotion of the Bangladeshi culture. This center can also cater to other educational aspects. It could have a library where Bangladeshi books would be available. A theater hall could be established where Bangladeshi films and documentaries of high quality and standard could be screened.

Another issue that merits serious consideration is increased translation of literary works from India and Bangladesh from Hindi to Bengali and vice versa. They will greatly facilitate mutual understanding and increase popularity of these litterateurs in both countries. Bangladesh and India could jointly embark on a project of anthology of poems, short stories and dramas selected from both the countries.

Our cultural heritage consisting of archaeological sites, historical monuments and relics provides an opportunity for increased people to people contact through Cultural Tourism. Introduction of package tours at reduced rates by the National Tourism Organizations to heritage sites will help.

Our region is a treasure trove of folklores that has been passed on from one generation to another. Each region prides in a distinctive type of folk dance and music. In the realm of dance, the forms and expressions are often symbolic and elemental in nature: to name a few- Kathak, Khasi, Jaintia, Manipuri, Kuchipudi and Bharatnattyam create permanent impressions in our minds because of their expressive nature. In the realm of song, there would be ghazal, bhajan, Lalongeeti and baul songs. Both India and Bangladesh has been home to great exponents of classical music. Through Audio-Visual Exchanges and live performances of cultural programs we can assist in building bridges of goodwill and understanding, and create bonds that will sustain.

Allow me to conclude by wishing this track two process every success. I have full confidence that it will help rekindle the torch of hope that will light the path of our march to our goals. Let the flow of ideas from events such as this enlighten us. As the mighty Rabindranath Tagore, a supreme symbol of our common heritage, had said; "

" Where the mind is without fear and the head is held high;Where knowledge is free. Where the world has not been broken up into fragments by narrow domestic walls;......... Into that heaven of freedom, my father, let my country - or rather, paraphrasing him, our countries, awake !

(*Source*: http://www.mofa.gov.bd/Adviser_speech.htm)

# BHUTAN

# 9.

## BILATERAL RELATIONS WITH INDIA

### Indo-Bhutan Hydro-Power Cooperation[1]

July 28, 2008

*On his visit to Thimpu, Minister of External Affairs, Mr Pranab Mukherjee, signed an agreement on the implementation of Punatsangchhu-I Hydro Electric Project. The project will be funded by the Government of India with 40% grant and 60% loan with an interest of 10%. The project envisages installed capacity of 1095 MW (6x182.50 MW) with annual average energy generation of 5377.45 GWH. The construction of the project is expected to commence in 2008 and completed by 2014.*

Bhutan and India today signed a landmark agreement on the implementation of the Punatsangchhu-I Hydro Electric Project. The agreement was signed at Gyelyong Tshokhang, Thimphu by Mr. Pranab Mukherjee, External Affairs Minister, on behalf of the Government of the Republic of India and Lyonpo Khandu Wangchuk, Foreign Minister on behalf of the Royal Government of Bhutan.

The Punatsangchhu-I project is a run-of-the-river scheme on the Punatsangchhu river located between 8.5 KM and 18.5 downstream of Wangdue Phodrang Bridge. The project will be funded by the Government of India with 40% grant and 60% loan an interest of 10%. The estimated capital cost of the project as per the DPR is Nu. 38,148.10 million (December 2006 price level). The project envisages installed capacity of 1095 MW (6x182.50 MW) with annual average energy generation of 5377.45 GWH. The project will have 137 m high concrete gravity dam, 4 intakes, 4 underground de-silting chambers, 7.50 Km long (10.3 m diameter) headrace tunnel and 2 vertical pressure shafts and an underground powerhouse. A new provision that would enable both Governments to benefit from Carbon Emission Revenue has also been introduced.

---

1. Joint Press Release on the Agreement between the Government of Republic of India and the Royal Government of Bhutan regarding the Punatsangchhu-I Hydro-Electric Project, July 28, 2008.

In accordance with the agreement, a Punatsangchhu Hydroelectric Project Authority will be set up for the construction of the project. The construction of the project is expected to commence in 2008 and complete by 2014. Pre-construction activities of the project have already started.

A Memorandum of Understanding (MoU) for the preparation of the Detailed Project Report (DPR) of the Punatsangchhu-I was signed between the two Governments on 15th September 2003. Accordingly the DPR was prepared by WAPCOS (India) Limited, a Government of India Undertaking and approved by both Governments in 2007.

In July 2006, an agreement on cooperation in the field of hydroelectric power was signed between the two Governments. Under this agreement, both countries have set out to achieve, inter alia, the export of a minimum of 5,000 MW of hydropower from Bhutan to India from 2020.

Cooperation between Bhutan and India has been highly successful and to the mutual benefit of both countries. Three hydroelectric power projects have already been commissioned in Bhutan with Indian assistance, namely, Chukha (336 MW), Kurichhu (60 MW) and Tala (1020 MW). Surplus power generated from the hydropower projects is exported to India.

Punatsangchhu-I will be the largest hydro power project to be undertaken in Bhutan in partnership with the Government of India and is yet another milestone in India-Bhutan cooperation in the field of hydropower.

(*Source*: http://www.meaindia.nic.in)

## GOI Press Release on the National Council Elections in Bhutan: On successful conduct of first ever elections to National Council in Bhutan

January 1, 2008

*Government of India congratulated the Royal Government of Bhutan for the successful conduct of the National Council elections. While the Election Commission of India had deputed three election observers to witness the polling for National Council elections its security agencies have also been cooperating with their Bhutanese counterparts in maintaining law and order in the border areas.*

1. Government of India congratulates the Royal Government of Bhutan for the successful conduct of the first ever elections for National Council (Upper House) of Bhutan that were held on December 31, 2007 for 15 Dzongkhags.

2. This is indeed a great moment in Bhutan's history and an important step in Bhutan's transition into a new system of governance. India is committed to extending full support in the establishment of institutions required for the consolidation of Democratic Constitutional Monarchy in Bhutan.

3. India and Bhutan share uniquely warm and cordial relations. These relations are characterized by close consultations, maturity, complete trust and mutual understanding and are based on the foundation of shared interests and mutually beneficial cooperation. They are an exemplary model of good-neighbourly relations.

4. India has been privileged to share its resources and experience with Bhutan during its period of transition to a democratic constitutional monarchy, and has reiterated its commitment to provide all possible assistance within its resources to the Royal Government of Bhutan. India is assisting Bhutan by supplying EVMs and deepening linkages between the Election Commissions of both the countries in conduct of elections. The Election Commission of India had deputed three election observers who witnessed the polling for National Council elections in Bhutan. Indian security agencies have been cooperating with their Bhutanese counterparts in maintaining law and order in the border areas.

5. Elections for the remaining five Dzongkhags will be held on January 29, 2008.

(*Source*: http:www.mea.nic.in)

## Press Release of 29th March 2007 on Government of India's (GOI) Assistance for Ninth Five Year Plan of Bhutan (2002-2008)

March 29, 2007

*The press release states that the Union Cabinet agreed to a total package of Rs. 2610.14 crore for the Ninth Five Year Plan to Bhutan. The key elements of the Ninth Five Year Plan include development subsidy, refunds and subsidies and project bases assistance.*

The Union Cabinet today gave its approval to continue the Indian assistance under 'Aid to Bhutan' Non-Plan budget of MEA towards Bhutan's extended Ninth Plan (July 2002 – June 2008). The GOI package for the Ninth Plan comprises of :

- Development Subsidy
- GOI Project Tied Assistance
- Refunds and Subsidies

The package would be total Rs. 2610.14 crore. This decision will result in continued strengthening of India-Bhutan relations based on our strategic and economic interests in an area of high geo-political sensitivity. It will support to the new King of Bhutan, and Bhutan's transition to a Constitutional democracy. It will also generate the opportunities of Indian companies to participate in major projects and strengthen goodwill for India in Bhutan by fulfilling our existing commitments.

(*Source*: http://www.meaindia.nic.in)

## India-Bhutan Friendship Treaty

March 5, 2007

*The Government of India and the Kingdom of Bhutan, signed the India-Bhutan Friendship Treaty in March 2007. While both countries agreed to refrain from allowing the use of their territory from anti-national activities against each other, free trade and commerce was identified as one of the primary areas of cooperation.*

The Government of the Republic of India and the Government of the Kingdom of Bhutan:

Reaffirming their respect for each other's independence, sovereignty and territorial integrity;

Recalling the historical relations that have existed between our two countries;

Recognizing with deep satisfaction the manner in which these relations have evolved and matured over the years into a model of good neighbourly relations;

Being fully committed to further strengthening this enduring and mutually beneficial relationship based on genuine goodwill and friendship, shared interests, and close understanding and cooperation;

Desiring to clearly reflect this exemplary relationship as it stands today;

And having decided, through mutual consent, to update the 1949 Treaty relating to the promotion of, and fostering the relations of friendship and neighbourliness between India and Bhutan;

Have agreed as follows:

**Article 1**

There shall be perpetual peace and friendship between India and Bhutan.

**Article 2**

In keeping with the abiding ties of close friendship and cooperation betweenBhutan and India, the Government of the Kingdom of Bhutan and the Government of the Republic of India shall cooperate closely with each other on issues relating to their national interests. Neither Government shall allow the use of its territory for activities harmful to the national security and interest of the other.

The Government of Bhutan and the Government of India agree to continue to consolidate and expand their economic cooperation for mutual and long term benefit.

**Article 3**

There shall, as heretofore, be free trade and commerce between the territories of the Government of Bhutan and the Government of India.

Both the Governments shall provide full cooperation and assistance to each other in the matter of trade and commerce.

**Article 4**

The Government of India agrees that the Government of Bhutan shall be free to import, from or through India into Bhutan, whatever arms, ammunition, machinery, warlike material or stores as may be required or desired for the strength and welfare of Bhutan, and that this arrangement shall hold good for all time as long as the Government of India is satisfied that the intentions of the Government of Bhutan are friendly and that there is no danger to India from such importations. The Government of Bhutan agrees that there shall be no export of such arms, ammunition and materials outside Bhutan either by the Government of Bhutan or by private individuals.

**Article 5**

The Government of Bhutan and the Government of India agree that Bhutanese subjects residing in Indian territories shall have equal justice with Indian subjects, and that Indian subjects residing in Bhutan shall have equal justice with the subjects of the Government of Bhutan.

**Article 6**

The extradition of persons wanted by either state for crimes and for unlawful activities affecting their security shall be in keeping with the extradition agreements between the two countries.

**Article 7**

The Government of Bhutan and the Government of India agree to promote cultural exchanges and cooperation between the two countries. These shall be extended to such areas as education, health, sports, science and technology.

**Article 8**

The Government of Bhutan and the Government of India agree to continue to consolidate and expand their economic cooperation for mutual and long Term benefit.

**Article 9**

Any differences and disputes arising in the interpretation and application of this Treaty shall be settled bilaterally by negotiations in a spirit of trust and understanding in consonance with the historically close ties of friendship and mutually beneficial cooperation that form the bedrock of Bhutan-India relations.

**Article 10**

This Treaty shall come into force upon the exchange of Instruments of Ratification by the two Governments which shall take place in Thimphu within onemonth of the signing of this Treaty. The Treaty shall continue in force in perpetuity unless terminated or modified by mutual consent.

In witness whereof, the undersigned being duly authorized thereto by their respective Governments, have signed this Treaty.

Done at New Delhi on the Eighth Day of February Two Thousand and Seven, in two originals each in Hindi, Dzongkha and English languages, each text being equally authentic. However, in case of difference, the English text shall prevail.

(*Source*: *www.indianembassythimphu.bt/India-Bhutan%20Friendship%20Treaty.pdf*)

## Indo-Bhutan Cooperation[2]

January 28, 2007

*During his visit to India, Prime Minister of Bhutan J.Y Thinley, identified areas of mutual interest-hydro power- being one of them. While GOI decided to provide a standby credit facility of Rs 400 crore, it also announced its commitment to support the Tenth Five Year Plan in Bhutan. Bhutan intends to export 10,000 MW of power to India by 2020.*

The Prime Minister of Bhutan, His Excellency Lyonchen Jigmi Y. Thinley, is on a State visit to India from July 14-17, 2008. He is accompanied by Mrs. Thinley and a high-level delegation that includes H.E. Lyonpo Khandu Wangchuck, Minister for Economic Affairs, H.E. Lyonpo Ugyen Tshering, Minister for Foreign Affairs, H.E. Lyonpo Wangdi Norbu, Finance Minister, and other senior officials from the Royal Government of Bhutan. This is his first visit outside the country, after being elected Prime Minister of the first democratically elected Government in Bhutan.

Bhutanese Prime Minister called on President and Vice President and met Chairperson UPA, leader of the opposition, EAM, Home Minister, Minister for Power, Health Minister, Minister for Tourism and Culture and Deputy Chairman, Planning Commission. He also met NSA and Foreign Secretary. Ministers accompanying the Prime Minister have also held extremely useful meetings with their counterparts in diverse areas of mutual interest and cooperation. All meetings were held in an extremely friendly, warm and cordial atmosphere, reflecting the spirit of, trust, cooperation and mutual understanding that marks our bilateral relations. The visit has provided a useful opportunity to continue the tradition of highest level exchanges and further the initiatives annnounced during Prime Minister visit to Bhutan in May 2008. Areas of mutual interest discussed

---

2. Briefing Points by Official Spokesperson on the visit of the Prime Minister of Bhutan, January 8, 2007.

during the visit included our exemplary cooperation in the hydropower sector and India's economic engagement in Bhutan's development programmes during its 10th Five year Plan period.

The main outcomes of the discussions include:

(1) GoI has decided to revitalize the standby credit facility for Bhutan enhancing the amount to Rs 400 Crores. The credit would be drawn on favorable terms by RGoB, as and when necessary, to ensure stability of its currency reserves and to meet its obligations. An agreement to this effect will be finalized shortly.

(2) GoI reiterated its commitment to assist RGoB in its socio-economic development programmes and reaffirmed its full support to Bhutan's 10th Five Year Plan(FYP). GoI has committed to double its 10th FYP assistance over the revised outlay assistance in the 9th Plan period. Project-tied assistance of the GoI would be implemented as per the existing implementation mechanism. Small development projects in rural areas will be implemented according to mutually agreed modalities. Actual assistance would be determined by implementation of agreed programmes and priorities.

(3) GoI is committed to enhancing its development assistance and cooperation. To this end, GoI and RGoB will undertake mid-term reviews on a rolling basis, of the plan to enhance the allocation of resources as required. Experts from both sided would examine and work on identify sectors of cooperation based on RGoB's priorities. These would include the establishment of a medical college in Bhutan and capacity building in health sector, education, rural development and agriculture. These projects would be taken up for execution with assistance from GoI outside Bhutan's 10th Five Year Plan.

(4) GoI is committed to developing 10000 MW of hydropower in Bhutan for export to India by the year 2020. This would be done through direct assistance and in collaboration with indian public sector undertakings. In the course of developing hydropower projects, GoI will also undertake capacity building and skill enhancement by establishing specialised Industrial Training Institutes in Bhutan, to generate employment opportunities for the local population.

(5) GoI is committed to developing the human resource within Bhutan including through various scholarship schemes such as the Nehru-Wangchuck scholarship. In addition it is committed to developing infrastructure within Bhutan including roads and a rail line from Hashimara to Phuentsholing.

(6) GoI has exempted Bhutan from the ban on export of essential commodities. GoI also agreed to positively consider RGoB's request for removal of export duty on the supply of industrial raw material including coal and steel billets to Bhutan.

(*Source*: http://www.meaindia.nic.in)

# 10.

## RESETTLEMENT OF BHUTANESE REFUGEES[1]

### Refugees in Goldhap Camp in Eastern Nepal

January 7, 2009

*The United Nations High Commissioner for Refugees (UNHCR) has announced that more than 8,000 refugees from Bhutan left their camps in Nepal for resettlement in third countries in 2008, with the vast majority of them going to the United States.*

Nearly 7,550 of the refugees have gone to the US, which announced that it would resettle 60,000 refugees and even more if needed. The rest of them have resettled in Australia, New Zealand, Canada, Netherlands, Norway and Denmark.

"We are pleased to see so many refugees starting their lives afresh after living in difficult conditions in the camps for the last 18 years and to learn that those resettled are adapting well in their new country," said Daisy Dell, UNHCR Representative in Nepal.

The programme to resettle Bhutanese refugees living in Nepal, one of UNHCR's largest and most promising resettlement programmes, began in November 2007. Since then more than half of the 60,000-strong refugee population have already expressed their interest for resettlement.

Currently, there are some 103,000 refugees from Bhutan living in seven camps in eastern Nepal, with some having been in exile for as long as 18 years. Some 16,000-18,000 of them are expected to leave Nepal in 2009.

UNHCR noted that, while it continues to assist with resettlement efforts, it will also continue to advocate for the option of voluntary repatriation to Bhutan for those refugees who wish to do so.

(*Source*: http://www.un.org/apps/news/story.asp?NewsID= 29483&Cr= nepal&Cr1=refugee)

1. Number of Bhutanese Refugees Resettled from Nepal Last Year tops 8,000 – UN, January 7, 2009.

# MALDIVES

# 11.

# BILATERAL RELATIONS WITH INDIA

## Joint Statement on the State Visit of President of Maldives to India

December 25, 2008

*In his state visit to India, Mr Mohamed Nasheed, President of the Republic of Maldives identified a range of areas for enhancing investment cooperation, including information technology, higher education, fisheries, transport, tourism and infrastructure. The two sides also expressed their commitment to enhance their defence and security relations based on shared maritime threats and other security concerns. India also expressed appreciation to the Maldives for its support to India's candidature for a permanent seat in the expanded Security Council and to the non permanent member seat of the UN Security Council for the year 2011-2012. A bilateral agreement was signed, whereby India agreed to extend a standby credit facility of US$100 million to Maldives.An Air Services Agreement was also signed between the two countries.*

1. His Excellency Mr Mohamed Nasheed, the President of the Republic of Maldives paid a State Visit to India from 23 to 25 December 2008 at the invitation of Smt. Pratibha Devisingh Patil, President of the Republic of India. He was accompanied by his wife Mrs. Laila Ali and a high-level delegation, including businessmen. This was His Excellency President Mohamed Nasheed's first visit to India after assuming the office of the President of the Republic of Maldives in November 2008.

2. His Excellency President Mohamed Nasheed called on President Smt. Pratibha Devisingh Patil, who also hosted a banquet in his honour. The Vice President of India Shri Mohammed Hamid Ansari, the External Affairs Minister Shri Pranab Mukherjee, the Chairperson of the United Progressive Alliance Smt. Sonia Gandhi and the Leader of Opposition Shri L. K. Advani called on H.E. President Nasheed. His Excellency President Mohamed Nasheed and Prime Minister Dr. Manmohan Singh held official level discussions.

3. The bilateral discussions were held in an atmosphere of friendship, warmth and close understanding. The two sides recalled the historic and traditionally close and friendly relations and expressed complete satisfaction at the excellent state of bilateral relations. They reaffirmed the importance attached by both countries to further strengthen bilateral cooperation in a wide range of areas.

4. The two sides agreed to work together for the further enhancement of their multifaceted relationship based on shared democratic values, commitment to economic development and social welfare, mutual understanding and cooperation and shared views on major international issues. The Indian side welcomed the establishment of the first multi-party democracy in the Maldives and the smooth transition of power.

5. The two sides discussed a wide range of issues of bilateral interest covering defence and security, trade and investment, health, tourism, information and communications technology, science and technology, transportation and air services, higher education, non-conventional energy, fisheries, culture, education and training. The leaders also exchanged views on regional and international issues of mutual interest.

6. The following agreements were signed during the visit:

(*i*) Agreement on extending a Standby Credit Facility of US$100 million to Maldives

(*ii*) Air Services Agreement

7. The two sides noted that there was great potential to increase trade and investment between the two countries. In this connection, they agreed to revive the Sub Group on Trade under the India-Maldives Joint Commission to recommend ways and means to enhance trade and investment. The two sides noted that the Joint Commission has proved to be a useful mechanism in giving direction to enhance India-Maldives cooperation in diverse areas.

8. The two sides identified a range of areas for enhancing investment cooperation, including information technology, higher education, fisheries, transport, tourism and infrastructure. They also agreed to expedite the construction of the Faculty of Hospitality and Tourism Studies, being set up in Male through Indian assistance.

9. The two sides welcomed the signing of the new MOU on the Indira Gandhi Memorial Hospital in Male in September 2008 and agreed to convene the Joint Committee envisaged under the MOU. The hospital stands as a shining symbol of India-Maldives cooperation in the health sector and both sides agreed to explore ways of strengthening health care services in Maldives, including through capacity building.

10. The two sides expressed their commitment to enhance their defence and security relations based on shared maritime threats and other security concerns. They expressed their satisfaction at the on-going DOSTI

exercises between the Coast guards of both countries. They also agreed to strengthen cooperation in other areas as well, including police training. They agreed that drug transit and control are important issues, which require joint efforts of the two countries for effective prevention.

11. The two sides stressed that terrorism constitutes one of the gravest threats to international peace and security. They strongly condemned terrorism in all its forms and manifestations, and stressed that there can be no justification, whatsoever, for any acts of terrorism. The Maldives side condemned the recent terrorist attacks in Mumbai and expressed its deep sympathies for the affected people. The two sides emphasised the need for concerted and coordinated action by the international community both at regional and international levels to realise the objective of preventing, combating and eradicating terrorism in all its forms and manifestations.

12. His Excellency President Mohamed Nasheed addressed a meeting of Indian and Maldivian businessmen and industrialists organised jointly by Association of Chambers of Commerce and Industry (ASSOCHAM), the Federation of Indian Chambers of Commerce and Industry (FICCI) and the Confederation of Indian Industry (CII). He presented the economic policy and the privatisation programmes of the Government and invited the Indian entrepreneurs to participate in these programmes.

13. Both sides welcomed the signing in September 2008 of the MOU to set up the India-Maldives Foundation to foster India-Maldives relations through the enhancement of economic, scientific, educational, technical, and cultural cooperation between India and Maldives and the promotion of greater understanding between the peoples of the two countries.

14. The Maldives side conveyed its appreciation to India for the scholarships provided by the latter for short term and long term training as well as scholarships for higher education and professional courses for its nationals in various institutes and universities in India. The Indian side agreed to conduct a professional course for Maldivian diplomats in the Foreign Service Institute in New Delhi in 2009.

15. The Indian side thanked Maldives for its support to various Indian candidatures in international organisations. In particular, India expressed appreciation to the Maldives side for its support to India's candidature for a permanent seat in the expanded Security Council and for its candidature to the non permanent member seat of the UN Security Council for the year 2011-2012. Maldives also thanked India for its supports for its candidature to the non-permanent seat of U.N Security Council for the year 2019-20. The two sides agree on the need for a comprehensive reform of the international financial and economic architecture and improved global economic governance to ensure that the adverse impact of the ongoing global financial crisis, especially on developing countries, is minimised.

16. Both leaders expressed satisfaction with the outcome of the State Visit and concluded that it had contributed positively to the strengthening of the existing friendly ties between the two countries.

17. The President of Republic of Maldives invited the President of India and the Prime Minister to pay a visit to the Maldives. The invitations were accepted.

18. His Excellency Mr Mohamed Nasheed, President of the Republic of Maldives expressed deep gratitude to President Smt. Pratibha Devisingh Patil and Prime Minister Dr. Manmohan Singh for the kind reception and warm hospitality extended to him and his delegation.

(*Source*: http://meaindia.nic.in/searchhome.htm)

## India Welcomes Democracy in Maldives[1]

October 29, 2008

*The External Affairs Minister, Mr Pranab Mukherjee lauded the Presidential elections in Maldives. The Minister stated that the elections were a step forward towards strengthening of bilateral relations between the two countries.*

We welcome the election of His Excellency Mr Mohamed Nasheed as the new President of the Republic of Maldives. This is an important milestone in the history of Maldives and marks the ushering in of a new era in democracy and political reform. We express our appreciation at the free and fair nature of the elections wherein the people of Maldives turned up in large numbers and made their choice.

India and Maldives have traditionally enjoyed excellent bonds of friendship and cooperation. We are confident that the new democratically elected government will strengthen these links and build on the close and multi-faceted engagement between the two countries.

(*Source*: http://meaindia.nic.in/searchhome.htm)

## India-Maldives Cooperation[2]

September 18, 2008

*In a press release by the Government of India, prospective areas of cooperation between Maldives and India were highlighted. The release states that India and Maldives have traditionally enjoyed close and friendly relations given the historical, ethnic and cultural*

1. Statement by EAM on Presidential Elections in Maldives, October 29, 2008.
2. Visit of the Foreign Minister of the Republic of Maldives to India, September 18, 2008.

*ties. It states that the Indira Gandhi Memorial Hospital, set up in 1995 with Indian assistance, symbolizes the essence of India-Maldives cooperation. The MOU on the establishment of the India-Maldives Foundation, which was renewed in the visit, envisages Indian aid of Rs. 2 crores.*

H.E. Mr. Abdulla Shahid, Minister of Foreign Affairs of the Republic of Maldives shall be paying an Official Visit to India between 19-20 September, 2008. During his visit, Mr. Shahid will meet the External Affairs Minister, who will also host a dinner in his honour. Two MOUs are expected to be signed including the MOU concerning Manpower Requirements of Indira Gandhi Memorial Hospital (IGMH), Male and the MOU for the establishment of the India-Maldives Foundation.

India and Maldives have traditionally enjoyed closed and friendly relations given the historical, ethnic and cultural ties. Over the years, this relationship has blossomed into a multi-faceted one encompassing a range of areas. India is committed to enhancing these ties and assisting Maldives in its various developmental efforts. India welcomes the ratification of the new Constitution in August and holding of the first multi-party Presidential elections in Maldives in October, 2008.

India is engaged in the development of infrastructural facilities in Maldives through its technical and economic assistance programmes. The Indira Gandhi Memorial Hospital, Male, set up in 1995 with Indian assistance, symbolizes the essence of India- Maldives cooperation. The MOUs will continue the close links between India and the hospital and meet much of Maldives manpower and training needs in the areas of health and medicine. The MOU on the establishment of the India-Maldives Foundation envisages corpus of Rs. 2 crores. This corpus will be used by the two countries to undertake a range of activities with a view to bring the peoples of the two countries closer. India is also assisting in setting up of the Faculty of Hospitality and Tourism Studies in Maldives. After its completion, the Faculty is expected to substantially meet Maldives requirements in the important area of tourism.

(*Source*: http://meaindia.nic.in/searchhome.htm)

# 12.

# BILATERAL RELATIONS WITH CHINA

## Maldives-China Development Cooperation[1]

June 25, 2008

*On the visit of Ms. Gao Yuanyuan to Maldives, Mr. Abdul Azeez Yoosuf expressed gratitude to China for its sustained assistance to the Maldives. Ms. Gao YuanYuan in turn confirmed that China would continue to provide assistance to the development of the Maldives. Ms. Gao Yuanyuan also conveyed that the Chinese government would assist the Maldives in conducting a technical research program to identify key developmental areas requiring support. China is one of the key countries lending developmental support to the Maldives.*

The Director General of the Department of Aid to Foreign Countries of the Chinese Ministry of Commerce, Ms. Gao Yuanyuan has met with the Maldives' Ambassador at Large, H.E. Mr. Abdul Azeez Yoosuf. The meeting was held in January, 2008 morning at the Ministry of Foreign Affairs.

Ms. Gao Yuanyuan's visit to the Maldives is symbolic of the growing relationship between China and the Maldives, and is a follow-up to the official visits previously paid by the President of the Republic of Maldives, H.E. Mr. Maumoon Abdul Gayoom, and the Minister of Foreign Affairs, H.E. Mr. Abdulla Shahid to the President of the People's Republic of China, H.E. Mr. Hu Jintao in China. These meetings resulted in the further consolidation of diplomatic ties between the two nations, and reaffirmed the support of the Chinese government to the developmental needs of the Maldives.

The Chinese Delegation's visit to the Maldives represents a timely and speedy response from the Chinese Government to the requests made by the Government of the Maldives, and has helped further strengthen the

1. High-Level Chinese Delegation Visits the Maldives, 25 June, 2008.

relations between the countries. H.E Mr. Abdul Azeez Yoosuf expressed gratitude on behalf of the Maldives to the Government of China for its sustained assistance to the Maldives, and Ms. Gao YuanYuan in turn confirmed that China will continue to provide assistance to the development of the Maldives. Ms. Gao Yuanyuan also conveyed that the Chinese government will assist the Maldives in conducting a technical research program to identify key developmental areas requiring support.

The Maldives has long shared a strong history of friendly relations with China, receiving its first assistance grant from the Chinese government as early as in 1981. Since then, relations have progressively strengthened and China is now one of the key countries lending developmental support to the Maldives.

Ms. Gao Yuanyuan is the head of the Chinese Delegation to the Maldives, and she is accompanied by officials from the Ministry of Commerce, Ms. Zhan Haiyan, the Director General Assistant, Mr. Li Hai and the Deputy Architect General, Mr. Chen Zheglun of Northeast Architectural Design and Research Institute. The Chinese Delegation also includes Engineers, Mr. Wang Zhije, Ms. Liu Yinghhiu, Ms. Li Piye and the Interpreter to the delegation is Ms. Zhao Xin.

(*Source*: http://www.foreign.gov.mv/v2/news.php?news=3008&page=3)

## Maldives-China Bilateral Relations[2]

May 26, 2008

*The Minister of Foreign Affairs, Mr. Abdulla Shahid and the Minister of Foreign Affairs of China Mr. Yeng Jiachi discussed ways of advancing the existing bilateral relations between the Maldives and China. While the Foreign Minister expressed gratitude to the Chinese Government for its continued support to the socio-economic development of the Maldives; the two Ministers emphasized on future development cooperation programmes. In particular China's expressed its readiness towards the development of human resources in the Maldives.*

The Minister of Foreign Affairs H. E. Mr. Abdulla Shahid and the Minister of Foreign Affairs of China Mr. Yeng Jiachi have discussed ways of advancing the existing bilateral relations between the Maldives and China. These discussions took place at the Chinese Foreign Ministry in Beijing today.

2. Maldives and China Discuss Further Strengthening of Bilateral Relations, May 26, 2008.

During the meeting, the two Ministers highlighted the close historical relations between the two countries and discussed promotion of relations in future endeavours. In his remarks, Minister Shahid highlighted the Maldives' commitment to the 'One China Policy' and noted the extensive programmes conducted between the two countries in the pursuit of consolidated bilateral relations. The Foreign Minister also expressed gratitude to the Chinese Government for its continued support to the socio-economic development of the Maldives and the two Ministers discussed future development cooperation programmes.

Foreign Minister Yeng thanked Minister Shahid for undertaking the visit to Beijing and expressed gratitude and warm appreciation for the close ties the Maldives share with China and reiterated China's continued support to the socio-economic development of the Maldives. In particular Minister Yeng noted China's readiness to the development of human resources in the Maldives. Foreign Minister Yeng also thanked the Maldivian Government for the contribution to the victims of the Earthquake in Sichuan Province two weeks ago and highly noted the Maldivian medical students in Dalian for their commendable voluntary initiatives in organizing blood donation programmes for the victims.

Discussions were also held on issues of common concern to both countries including global climate change and its impact on small island nation such as the Maldives, international security and the growing trade between the two countries. Foreign Minister Shahid also briefed Minister Yeng on the progress of the Reform Agenda and the constitution drafting process.

Today's meeting was attended by the Deputy Minister of Foreign Affairs H. E. Mr. Abdullah Hameed, Maldives Ambassador to China H. E. Mr. Ahmed Latheef, Director at the Ministry of Foreign Affairs Ms. Fathimath Inaya and Director at the Department of External Resources Ms. Aishath Azeema.

(*Source*: http://www.foreign.gov.mv/v2/news.php?news=2679&page=2)

## On the Occasion of the Opening of Maldivian Embassy in China[3]

May 26, 2008

*The Foreign Minister of Maldives, Mr. Abdulla Shahid, on the occasion of the opening of the Embassy of Maldives in China stated that despite disparity in terms of the size of geographical territory,*

3. Statement by Mr. Abdulla Shahid, Minister of Foreign Affairs on the Occasion of the Opening of the Embassy of Maldives in China, May 26, 2008.

*population, and geo-strategic importance, both countries shared commonality of purpose on various issues of international importance. He emphasized that both countries set a good example of strong state-to-state relationship between big and small nations based on equality, sincerity, cooperation and harmonious coexistence. The Maldivian Minister supported One China Policy, and emphasized that the People's Republic of China is the legitimate and rightful representative of the aspirations of all Chinese people. He stated that business and leisure are two areas symbolizing growing people to people contact between the countries.*

It gives me great pleasure to be here today at the official opening of the Embassy of the Republic of Maldives in China. I am delighted to see so many friends and colleagues in the room including distinguished representatives of the Chinese Ministry of Foreign Affairs, Ambassadors from many friendly countries including our neighbours in SAARC, the Honorary Consuls of the Maldives in Shanghai and Hong Kong, former Chinese Ambassadors to the Maldives.

On this happy occasion I would like to extend my congratulations to His Excellency President Maumoon Abdul Gayoom as well the government and people of the Maldives on this positive and important step we have taken in extending the Maldives' diplomatic outreach.

I would like to take a moment to reflect, with great sadness and sorrow, on the devastation and human misery wreaked by the catastrophic earthquake in Sichuan province exactly two weeks ago to this day. At this time of great national sorrow in China, I wish to reiterate our sincere sympathies and condolences to the government and people of China as well as members of the bereaved families. In spite of the immense magnitude of this tragedy, I am greatly humbled by the resilience and indomitable spirit of the brave people of China to persevere in the face of all difficulties. I salute the Chinese people for the spirit of fellowship and brotherhood they have shown to their fellow countrymen in their hour of need. Let me also make a humble donation on behalf of the Government and people of the Maldives to help our Chinese brothers and sisters rebuild their lives. While this donation is small in comparison to the scale of the disaster, it is more a token and symbol of the Maldives' friendship with China and goes to show that the prayers and well-wishes of all Maldivians are with our fellow Chinese brethren in their hour of need. I would also like to take this opportunity to proudly note the efforts of the Maldivian students in Dalian Medical University to assist the victims of the tragic earthquake, by raising funds and donating blood.

The event that we celebrate tonight is an extremely important one as it signifies another solid link in the chain of friendship that binds the Maldives and China since times ancient. While we would be marking the

36th anniversary of formal diplomatic relations between our two countries this year, I am proud to note that this relationship has deeper historical roots that go back to at least the middle ages. Historical archives clearly note Chinese merchant fleets visiting the Maldives during the Ming Dynasty in the fifteenth century. In fact, much remains to be understood from the chronicles of the great Chinese mariner Zheng He who wrote early authoritative accounts of the geography and anthropology of the Maldives. Historiography also indicates that King Yusuf of the Maldives had, on three separate occasions, sent Maldivian emissaries to China in the early fifteenth century. I am therefore pleased that as the Embassy begins its important work, it will be able to build on already strong bilateral relations between the Maldives and China.

To an outsider, the Maldives and China may seem like very different countries with little in common. Yet in spite of the immense disparities in the sizes of our geographical territory, population, and geo-strategic importance, the Maldives and China enjoy great commonality of purpose. As President Hu Jintao said, during the visit of President Gayoom in 2006, Maldives-China relations "set a good example of strong state-to-state relationship between big and small nations based on equality, sincerity, cooperation and harmonious coexistence." Indeed, since the establishment of formal diplomatic relations in 1972, our relationship with China has continued to expand in virtually every sphere of life. This is most evident in the ever-increasing people-to-people contact between our two countries. In recent years, the number of Maldivians traveling to China for purposes of business and leisure is on the increase. Similarly, China has become one of the strongest and most important emerging markets for Maldivian tourism, with the number of Chinese tourists visiting the Maldives last year at an all time record of nearly 36,000.

The Maldives and China also share a common vision of how to approach the many challenges facing the world today. Indeed both our countries are firmly committed to international peace and prosperity through mutual recourse to the fundamental principles of sovereignty and the norms of international law. We remain, in this regard, firmly committed to the One China Policy, and believe that the People's Republic of China is the legitimate and rightful representative of the aspirations of all Chinese people. We would therefore continue, without exception, to express our strong reservations at any attempt to undermine this most important of principles. The Maldives congratulates the Chinese government for its impressive preparations for this year's Summer Olympiad and unequivocally condemns the regrettable attempts made by certain naysayers to disrupt or politicize the games. We believe that the games provide an apolitical forum through which sportsmanship and camaraderie contribute to global peace and greater friendship among nations.

Our relationship with China is also characterized by great generosity. China's contribution to the socio-economic development of the Maldives is immense. Over the course of the years, China has generously provided assistance towards developing vital areas such as housing and infrastructure development. We also note, with no small measure of gratitude, the immense moral and material support the Chinese government rendered to the Maldives following the Asian Tsunami of 2004. As Foreign Minister, I acknowledge the beautiful building, constructed with Chinese assistance, currently housing the Maldives Ministry of Foreign Affairs. On behalf of a grateful nation, I extend our sincere gratitude and thanks for China's spirit of generosity.

Nearly four years ago, the Maldives' presence on the international stage was limited. With just three diplomatic missions, our global reach did not go very far. Today, with the opening of this mission, we are represented internationally by 12 separate missions spread across 3 continents – a significant contrast from the status quo nearly four years ago. It is my duty, in this regard, to commend the unyielding efforts of President Maumoon Abdul Gayoom to project the image of the Maldives globally. Indeed President Gayoom's vision to expand our international horizons is greatly responsible for the establishment of this mission.

The fact also remains that this mission would not have been established without the support and assistance of the Chinese government. I thank the Government of China, especially Foreign Minister Yang Jie Chi and his staff at the Chinese Ministry of Foreign Affairs for their unwavering support in this endeavor. I am also grateful for the services rendered by our Honorary Consuls in Hong Kong and Shanghai, Mr Bob Harilela and Professor Guisheng Yang, respectively, for their invaluable work as advocates of strong relations between the Maldives and China.

I take great comfort and pride in the fact that the conduct of this Embassy has been entrusted with His Excellency Mr. Ahmed Latheef. Ambassador Latheef is a distinguished public servant, veteran diplomat and, to the great dismay of his opponents, an accomplished table tennis player, who, I am certain, will do much towards furthering Maldives-China relations. I also wish to use this opportunity to thank staff members of the Embassy as well as my own staff in the Ministry of Foreign Affairs for their support in realising this mission.

The opening of a bilateral embassy has obvious practical implications and benefits. An embassy provides a permanent gateway between two countries and peoples, allowing them to increase interaction, cooperation and understanding. Aside from these practical considerations, it is clear that the opening of a new embassy is also symbolically important. It is a concrete and practical demonstration of one country's commitment to another – a clear and resonant declaration of the importance that the Maldives attaches to its relations with China and to furthering those relations in a mutually advantageous manner.

Before I conclude, I would like to say to our Chinese friends that Maldives and China will always remain close allies and their peoples true friends. We shall march together on our journey to achieve greater progress and prosperity for our peoples and to create a harmonious world.

(*Source*: *http://www.foreign.gov.mv/v2/speech.php?speech=42&page=1)*

# 13.

## INTERNATIONAL DOCUMENTS

### Towards a Low Carbon Economy[1]

December 11, 2008

*Mr. Ahmed Naseem, Minister of State for Foreign Affairs Maldives at the Third Sustainability Summit, drew attention to the rapid economic growth in region, which he said was leading to a host of environmental problems. He emphasized that the balance between economic growth and environmental sustainability could only be achieved by fulfilling the commitments undertaken by countries towards the Millennium Development Goals. He brought to notice Goals 7 and 8 of the MDGs, which he urged were roadmaps for environmental sustainability and a global partnership for development. He also highlighted the UN Human Rights Resolution, which was undertaken by the United Nations to link human rights with climate change. He stated that renewable energy resources-solar, tidal, and wind energy, and the consolidation of a centralized energy system, were of paramount importance to the country.*

Let me begin by extending my sincere thanks to Development Alternatives and Confederation of Indian Industry for organizing this important Summit, and also for giving me the opportunity to speak at this important event.

We meet in the wake of a sequence of multi-faceted crises that have thrown our world into a state of turmoil. With the global food and fuel crises, we are also faced with a financial crisis of colossal weight that has borne down on every nation, irrespective of its size or wealth. A far more serious crisis looming on the horizon and one that would have more dire and long-lasting implications for the sustainable development of peoples across a wide spectrum of backgrounds is the effect of climate change and resulting impacts to life as we know it.

---

1. Statement by H.E. Mr. Ahmed Naseem, Minister of State for Foreign Affairs of the Republic of Maldives at the Third Sustainability Summit: Asia 2008, at the plenary session titled 'Towards a Low Carbon Economy', New Delhi, India, December 11, 2008.

South Asia is home to one fifth of humanity and 40 percent of the world's poor. It is also one of the fastest growing regions in the world. The rapid economic growth currently being experienced by the region is inevitably contributing to a host of environmental problems. As the pace of urbanisation accelerates and industrial development expands, pressures are put on the available limited natural resources in the countries of the region. Even in small countries such as my own, rapid urbanisation is causing the depletion of forest areas and other resources such as fresh water, and polluting the air through the increasing consumption of fossil fuels for the generation of electricity, motor vehicles and sea transport. This is just one example from the smallest country in the entire region of South Asia, a country with a negligible carbon foot-print in global terms. However, this is a scenario that can be replicated in varying proportions, in most countries of the region and the rest of the developing world.

What the recent crises have clearly demonstrated is that without fundamental improvements in our current system, we cannot maintain the present momentum of unparalleled growth. No doubt, the highly interdependent world we live in today is faced with the paradoxical challenge of increasing economic growth while ensuring environmental sustainability. In this crucial balancing act, countries of the region need not only the mutual support of each other, but also the support of the international community and its various actors, including the global business network and the global civil society. Together, they have a strategic role to play, if not a fundamental one in ensuring that we do not fail the dreams and aspirations of our children and the generations to come!

We have to stand firm in our belief that achieving unprecedented rates of economic growth at the expense of our environment is both unsustainable and unethical. I wish to re-iterate, in this regard, UN Secretary General Ban-Ki-Moon's call at the recent International Conference on Financing for Development held in Doha, for a new sharpened focus in the fight against climate change; to seize this challenge and make it part of the solution to the current economic decline.

Indeed, this reveals a new paradigm shift in climate change debates, where the ethos now is to embrace new economic directions and new technologies centred on the preservation of our fragile and inter-connected ecosystem. While the Maldives, as a Small Island Developing State, applaud such magnanimous steps in the search for innovative paths to sustainability, we would also like to remind the international community that these objectives can only be fulfilled by their strengthened commitment to the Millennium Development Goals. More specifically by ensuring that Goals 7 and 8 of the MDGs, that urge for environmental sustainability and a global partnership for development are honoured.

As world leaders gather in Poznan, we have an opportune moment to harmonise our efforts in the spirit of solidarity, to overcome and re-orient our future priorities in a manner that awards greater justice to the wider world.

We now know well that global climate change is not just an environmental theory postulated in isolation by a handful of environmental scientists, but indeed, it is a real crisis, essentially rooted in the very survival of humankind.

The Maldives' has early on, acknowledged the potential threats of a change in global climatic patterns on a small low-lying island country such as ours. It is this realisation that prompted the government to lead a global initiative to bring the human rights aspect of climate change implications to the attention of the world. Thanks to the understanding of the international community, we now have the Human Dimension of Global Climate Change as a UN Human Rights Resolution. This highlights the immediate and far-reaching adverse effects of climate change for survival of vulnerable peoples.

It is truly unfortunate that those at the front lines of the battle against climate change are often the world's poorest and most vulnerable populations. We, therefore, feel it imperative that the future course of action, to be taken up at Copenhagen next year, will be one that takes into account the collective voice of all developing countries, and that which promotes a long-term vision for a transformed financial landscape. The eventual outcome, we hope, will result in an equitable successor to the Kyoto Protocol, to accelerate the transition to a low-carbon economy. This will require a consolidated effort of the global community, in ensuring that green technologies and ideas are made accessible to all developing regions, particularly those that are most vulnerable, in an effective manner.

In order to achieve this, we need to realign policies; especially with regards to intellectual property rights and the use of patents that greatly restrict necessary technology transfer- as evident in the AIDS epidemic in the African continent where millions are deprived of much needed life-sustaining medicines and technology.

It is time for changed behaviours- in the way we live our lives, in the way we do business, and in the way we work as a unified global community.

The vast socio-economic gains the Maldives has made over the past decades are constantly being been threatened by rising global temperatures and the acidification caused by greenhouse gases. The economic and environmental vulnerability of the Maldives therefore makes it highly exposed to external shocks. This, together with our expected graduation from the UNs list of LDCs by 2011, has forced us to search for innovative approaches to attract investments in sustainable development.

Maldives is a highly dispersed country; with a population distributed widely across 200 islands stretching over 800 km. Unlike land-bound countries, our key form of travel is sea transport. As a result, the cost of delivering vital goods and services to our people in an equitable manner has been a major challenge. As part of our aim to enhance connectivity across the islands, plans are already underway to establish an extensive transport system that will achieve this objective. To further this goal, seven regional growth centres will also be established across the archipelago.

At the same time, the Maldives is embarking on a bold programme, to explore alternative energy sources to overcome current inefficiencies in energy supply. The Maldives has no conventional energy source; 98% of its energy needs are met by the import of fossil fuels. If our long-term aim is to be sustainable, the utilisation of renewable energy resources-namely solar, tidal, and wind energy, and the consolidation of a centralised energy system, is of paramount importance.

At present, our energy system is prone to high levels of wastage and inefficiency as each individual island has their own generator. The Vulnerability and Poverty Assessment of 2005 noted marked disparities in access to electricity between different islands. In today's world where communication and the use of electricity are so intricately related to our propensity to progress, such disparities in access to basic electricity are a worrying concern for the Maldives. The Assessment also highlights that businesses in the manufacturing sector and tourism sector spend at least an equivalent of five to seven percent of their total fixed assets on the purchase of generators. Such wastefulness can be minimized through a strong centralized framework for energy distribution.

Therefore, we call on the international community to lend us your expertise and assistance in paving the way to a sustainable future.

We believe the development and installation of wind, solar, diesel hybrid energy systems on consolidated grids, serving groups of islands in close proximity, would enable us to achieve a sustainable, cost-effective and low-maintenance alternative to the existing stand-alone diesel generators, currently used for power generation. In 2005, a private sector initiative launched the first pilot hybrid energy system project in the Maldives. The success of this has encouraged its expansion to three more islands. The benefits of such green technologies such as the low operational costs and high energy efficiency, coupled with the positive impact on the ecosystem, greatly offsets its disadvantage of relatively high initial investment costs.

It is not only in the area of electricity generation that we can bring about drastic change in the reduction of carbon emission in the Maldives. Inter-island transportation and, to a lesser extent, land transportation are equally important areas that can greatly benefit from such consolidated approaches to energy conservation.

Together with our development partners, the Maldives has also engaged an initiative, the National Adaptatation Programme of Action (NAPA) that works to formulate climate resilient policies. Our experience in the Asian Tsunami of 2004 serves as a constant reminder of our acute vulnerability to the forces of nature. In this regard, we have achieved an important milestone in the successful development of the island, Dhuvaaafaru that is built in the norms of a safe-island concept.

The new democratically elected Government in the Maldives firmly believes in opening up of such ventures for Foreign Direct Investment in order to ensure that our goals of more equitable and sustainable development for our people are fully realised.

The Maldives is well on its way to achieving its Millennium Development Goals, yet if we continue to stay silent on this issue, global warming and its compound effects will push backwards our hard-earned achievements in this respect. As such, we welcome the new dynamism in current climate change debates- a fact clearly seen by the today's plenary session and also the UNEP's World Environment Day theme on moving towards a low carbon economy.

I wish this conference every success! I also once again thank the organisers for their leadership, in taking such timely steps in the right direction towards a more sustainable path to development.

(*Source*: http://www.foreign.gov.mv/v2/speech.php)

## OHCHR Welcomes Democratic Reforms in Maldives[2]

### August 24, 2008

*United Nations Office of the High Commissioner for Human Rights (OHCHR) lauded ratification of the new Constitution of the Maldives. It highlighted Maldives accession to various human rights instruments like the International Covenant on Civil and Political Rights, the International Covenant on Economic, Social and Cultural Rights. It urged the government to take necessary steps to incorporate international human rights obligations into the domestic normative framework.*

United Nations Office of the High Commissioner for Human Rights (OHCHR) has welcomed the ratification of the new Constitution of the Maldives.

2. OHCHR Welcomes New Directions of Reform, August 24, 2008.

In a letter by H.E. Ms. Kyung-wha Kang to the Minister of Foreign Affairs H.E. Mr. Abdulla Shahid, the OHCHR noted the consultative and transparent process that was adopted in the drafting of the new Constitution. The letter further elaborated that the new Constitution reflected the democratic aspirations of the people of Maldives and the commitment of the Government to its human rights obligations. Ms. Kang further welcomed the entrenchment of the independence of the judiciary and the introduction of a non-discrimination clause, which stressed the constitutional rights and freedoms guaranteed to apply to everyone under the jurisdiction of the State.

Continuing her letter, the Acting High Commissioner also conveyed hope that supplementary progressive measures will be adopted by the Maldives to ensure that the country fully incorporates its international human rights obligations into the domestic normative framework.

Ms. Kang concluded her letter by expressing her Office's gratitude to the Government "for its open collaboration with the UN human rights mechanisms and the continuous support it [continued] to extend to the Human Rights Adviser and the United Nations Country Team in the Maldives. She also conveyed that the "OHCHR would continue to collaborate closely with the Government to further promote and protect human rights."

Over the past three years, the Maldives has acceded to numerous human rights instruments. These include the International Covenant on Civil and Political Rights, the International Covenant on Economic, Social and Cultural Rights. The Government continues to take strident steps to fully implement its international human rights obligations. The Maldives is also a strong advocate of a powerful Human Rights Council and has practiced a policy of open dialogue and engagement with the OHCHR.

(*Source*: http://www.foreign.gov.mv/v2/news.php?news=2826&page =14)

# NEPAL

# 14.

# BILATERAL RELATIONS WITH INDIA

## Joint Press Statement on Official Visit of Mr. Pranab Mukherjee, Minister of External Affairs of India to Nepal

November 26, 2008

*The Minister of External Affairs of India Mr. Pranab Mukherjee paid an official visit to Nepal at the invitation of Mr. Upendra Yadav, Minister for Foreign Affairs of Nepal. The Minister of External Affairs of India noted that this was the first high level visit from India to Nepal after the elections to the Constituent Assembly of Nepal and expressed India's continued support to Nepal in its transition to multiparty democracy. The Ministers reviewed implementation of actionable points in the Joint Press Statement and agreed to review Nepal's requirements from time to time. Mr. Mukherjee expressed over the business environment in Nepal affecting existing Indian investments and joint ventures. Both the Ministers discussed steps to promote cooperation in the hydro-power sector with a view to work towards realization of Government of Nepal's target of generating 10000 MW over the next 10 years,*

1. The Minister of External Affairs of India His Excellency Mr. Pranab Mukherjee paid an official visit to Nepal from November 24-26, 2008 at the invitation of Hon. Mr. Upendra Yadav, Minister for Foreign Affairs of Nepal.

2. During his visit, the Minister of External Affairs of India called on Rt. Hon. Dr. Ram Baran Yadav, the President of Nepal, Rt. Hon. Mr. Parmananda Jha, the Vice President of Nepal, and Rt. Hon. Mr. Pushpa Kamal Dahal 'Prachanda', the Prime Minister of Nepal. The Minister of External Affairs of India also called on the Rt. Hon. Chairman of the Constituent Assembly, Mr. Subas Chandra Nembang and held an interactive session with leaders of parties in the Constituent Assembly. During his visit, the Minister of External Affairs of India held official talks with the Minister for Foreign Affairs of Nepal on all issues of mutual interest. The Minister for Foreign Affairs of Nepal hosted a dinner in honor of the Minister of External Affairs of India. The Minister of External

Affairs of India undertook an aerial overview of the Kosi area and also visited Birgunj.

3. The Minister for Foreign Affairs of Nepal extended a warm welcome to the Minister of External Affairs of India. The two Foreign Ministers shared views on aspects of the bilateral relationship, which is characterized by close, cordial and extensive interactions at the government as well as at the people to people levels. They expressed their commitment to further consolidate the relationship in future.

4. The Minister of External Affairs of India noted that this was the first high level visit from India to Nepal after the elections to the Constituent Assembly of Nepal and expressed India's continued support to Nepal in its transition to multiparty democracy.

5. The two Foreign Ministers recalled the official visit by the Rt. Hon. Prime Minister of Nepal Mr. Pushpa Kamal Dahal 'Prachanda' to India in September 2008 as well as the bilateral meeting between the two Prime Ministers earlier this month on the margins of the BIMSTEC Summit in New Delhi. The two Foreign Ministers also noted with satisfaction that this was their fifth meeting after the assumption of office by a new government in Nepal in August 2008. They recognized that bilateral interactions at high levels have imparted new dynamism to the relationship between the two countries in tune with the changing realities of the time as well as the wishes and aspirations of the peoples of both countries.

6. The Ministers reviewed implementation of actionable points in the Joint Press Statement on the official visit of the Rt. Hon. Prime Minister of Nepal to India from September 14-18, 2008. It was noted with satisfaction that several decisions had been implemented, such as:

(*i*) Meeting of Home Secretaries of the two countries in New Delhi on October 31-November 1, 2008 which agreed on further steps to enhance cooperation in dealing with cross-border crimes and addressing shared security concerns.

(*ii*) The Joint Committee on Water Resources at the level of Water Resources Secretaries of the two countries met in Kathmandu from 29 September- 1 October 2008 and reviewed all aspects of bilateral cooperation in the field of water resources in a forward looking and mutually beneficial framework.

(*iii*) The Inter-Governmental Committee (IGC) at the level of Commerce Secretaries met in Delhi on 19-20 October 2008 and discussed steps to bolster and develop bilateral trade and to conclude the revision of the Treaty of Trade at the earliest.

7. It was acknowledged that the recent high-level meetings of existing bilateral mechanisms have reactivated bilateral relations in key areas. The two Foreign Ministers stressed the need to continue this process and implement relevant decisions taken at these meetings.

8. Both Ministers discussed steps to promote cooperation in the hydro-power sector. With a view to work towards realisation of Government of Nepal's target of generating 10000 MW over the next 10 years, both Ministers agreed that existing and future projects in this area should be pursued expeditiously.

9. The two Ministers reviewed ongoing works to rehabilitate the breached portion of the Kosi embankment and stressed the need to expedite work so that it is concluded by March 2009.

10. The Nepalese side appreciated the removal of ban on the export of some essential commodities to Nepal by the Government of India. The two sides agreed to review Nepal's requirements from time to time. While taking note of the removal of some of the barriers to trade, both Ministers agreed to hold regular discussions to further facilitate bilateral trade between the two countries.

11. The Minister of External Affairs of India pointed out that concerns remain about the business environment in Nepal affecting existing Indian investments and joint ventures. He requested that these issues be addressed urgently and effectively. The Nepalese side reiterated the commitment of the Government of Nepal to take necessary measures for the promotion of an investor-friendly business environment to encourage Indian public and private sector investments in Nepal.

12. The two Ministers discussed issues relating to management of the open border between the two countries. It was agreed that necessary steps would be taken to have effective institutional and other mechanisms to address cross-border crimes and shared security concerns based on agreements reached at the recent Home Secretary level talks.

13. The two Ministers noted that Joint Technical Committee on the boundary had completed scientific strip mapping of about 98% of Nepal-India border and agreed to take further necessary steps for signature of the agreed strip maps at an early date. They also directed the officials concerned to expeditiously resolve the outstanding issues relating to the boundary.

14. The Nepalese side expressed its sincere appreciation to the Government and people of India for the generous assistance that India has been providing over the years in various fields of development activities in Nepal. In continuation of this process, both sides would study the feasibility of railway projects in Nepal. The Nepalese side appreciated Government of India's support for Terai Roads Project. It was decided that necessary preparatory work for undertaking this project would be expedited.

15. The Indian side reiterated the commitment of the Government of India to continue assisting the Government and people of Nepal in its democratic transition and economic development.

16. The External Affairs Minister of India handed over a formal invitation from the President of India Smt. Pratibha Devisingh Patil to Rt.

Hon. President of Nepal Dr. Ram Baran Yadav to visit India at an early, mutually convenient date.

(*Source*: http://meaindia.nic.in/)

## Indo-Nepal Economic Cooperation[1]

October 21, 2008

*India-Nepal Inter Governmental Committee on Trade, Transit and Cooperation to Control Unauthorized Trade agreed to work towards further strengthening of economic ties and to help generate employment opportunities and enhance industrialization in Nepal. Reiterating India's commitment to continue to provide preferential access to Nepalese goods and products to the Indian market, Nepal was urged towards creating an investor-friendly and enabling business environment with a view to attract Indian investments. Both sides also agreed to conclude Bilateral Investment Promotion and Protection Agreement, Motor Vehicles Agreement and revised Double Taxation Avoidance Agreement.*

India-Nepal Inter Governmental Committee on Trade, Transit and Cooperation to Control Unauthorized Trade, met in New Delhi on 19-20 October, 2008. G.K. Pillai, Commerce Secretary, and Purushottam Ojha, Secretary, Ministry of Commerce & Supplies, Government of Nepal, led the respective delegations. The two sides have agreed to work towards further strengthening of economic ties between the two countries and to help generate employment opportunities and enhance industrialization in Nepal. Reiterating India's commitment to continue to provide preferential access to Nepalese goods and products to the Indian market, Pillai urged Nepal to work towards creating an investor-friendly and enabling business environment with a view to attract Indian investments. Towards this end, both sides agreed to conclude Bilateral Investment Promotion and Protection Agreement, Motor Vehicles Agreement and revised Double Taxation Avoidance Agreement at an early date.

India also agreed to support a project for technical capacity building of Nepalese labs so that they can conform to Indian standards and certification requirements, in respect to major products of their export interest. India also agreed to exempt Nepal from export restrictions up to 10000 ton of wheat and 15000 Ton of non-basmati rice. Both sides made considerable progress on the modification and revision of the India-Nepal Treaty of Trade so as to make it a more effective instrument of bilateral trade between the two countries. The two sides will again meet at Joint

1. India, Nepal to Strengthen Economic Ties, October 21, 2008.

Secretary level within three months to finalize the modifications. The meeting took place as a follow up to the decision taken during the visit of the Prime Minister of Nepal to India in September, 2008.

The visiting Nepalese Secretary for Commerce & Supplies also called on the Minister of State for Commerce and Power Jairam Ramesh.

(*Source*: www.commerce.nic.in/PressRelease/pressrelease)

## Joint Press Statement on Official Visit of Mr. Pushpa Kamal Dahal 'Prachanda', Prime Minister of Nepal to India

September 17, 2008

*In the joint press statement issued on the conclusion of the official visit of Nepalese Prime Minister to India, the two Prime Ministers underlined the importance of smooth political transition in Nepal. Both sides have agreed to enhance cooperation in handling cross-border crime and security concerns and it has been suggested that Home Secretaries would be responsible for implementing the decision. Economic development and infrastructural projects including road, rail and hydel-power projects were also discussed in detail. The Government of India has agreed to implement the Naumure Hydro-electric Project on Rapti River. The two sides agreed to review, adjust and update the 1950 treaty of peace and friendship between the two countries.*

1. The Rt. Hon'ble Pushpa Kamal Dahal 'Prachanda', Prime Minister of Nepal, is on an official visit to India from September 14-18, 2008 at the invitation of H.E. Dr. Manmohan Singh, Prime Minister of India. The Prime Minister of Nepal is accompanied by Hon'ble Mr. Upendra Yadav, Minister for Foreign Affairs, Hon'ble Mr. Krishna Bahadur Mahara, Minister for Information and Communication, Hon'ble Mr. Bishnu Prasad Poudel, Minister for Water Resources and Hon'ble Mr. Rajendra Mahato, Minister for Commerce and Supplies. The delegation includes four members of the Constituent Assembly, senior officials of the Government of Nepal, a business delegation and a delegation of media representatives.

2. During his visit, the Prime Minister of Nepal called on H.E. Smt. Pratibha Devisingh Patil, the President of India, and on H.E. Shri Mohammad Hamid Ansari, the Vice President of India. The Prime Minister of Nepal had a meeting with the Prime Minister of India, which was followed by delegation level talks, led by the two Prime Ministers, on issues of mutual interest and concern. The Prime Minister of India hosted a banquet in honour of the Prime Minister of Nepal. Shri Pranab Mukherjee, Minister of External Affairs, Prof. Saif-u-Din-Soz, Minister of Water Resources and Shri L.K. Advani, Leader of Opposition in the Lok Sabha called on the Prime Minister of Nepal. The Prime Minister of Nepal had a

meeting with Smt. Sonia Gandhi, Chairperson of the United Progressive Alliance (UPA) and the President of Indian National Congress. The Prime Minister of Nepal also visited Rajghat and paid homage to the memory of Mahatma Gandhi. An interaction with the Indian business community was jointly hosted by ASSOCHAM, CII and FICCI in honour of the visiting dignitary. During his stay in India, the Prime Minister is visiting Bangalore from September 17-18,2008.

3. The Prime Minister of India extended a warm welcome to the Prime Minister of Nepal as the first Prime Minister of Federal Democratic Republic of Nepal. The two Prime Ministers expressed satisfaction at the age-old close, cordial and extensive relationships existing between Nepal and India. Both Prime Ministers expressed their support and cooperation to further consolidate the relationship in the days ahead.

4. The talks were held in an atmosphere of utmost cordiality and warmth. They shared their views and assessment of the situation. The two Prime Ministers acclaimed the importance of peaceful, political, democratic transformation of historic significance in Nepal.

5. The Prime Minister of Nepal appreciated the positive support extended by the people and Government of India throughout the peaceful political democratic transformation in the country.

6. The Government of India expressed full support to the peaceful, political, democratic transition in Nepal.

7. Both leaders recognized the historic changes that have taken place in Nepal with the elections to the Constituent Assembly and the declaration of the Federal Democratic Republic of Nepal according to the wishes of the people of Nepal.

8. The Prime Minister of Nepal stressed that following the Constituent Assembly elections, bringing the peace process to a logical conclusion, writing a new Constitution and accelerating the pace of economic development are the main priorities of the Government of Nepal in the days ahead.

9. The two sides felt the need to inject new dynamism into the relations between the two countries for a forward looking change in tune with the realities of the time as well as the wishes and aspirations of the people of both the countries.

10. Both sides agreed to reactivate the existing bilateral mechanisms in the evolving context.

11. Both sides noted that the multi-faceted and deep-rooted relationships between the two countries needed further consolidation and expansion in a forward-looking manner to better reflect the current realities. It was in this broader context that the two Prime Ministers agreed to review, adjust and update the 1950 Treaty of Peace and Friendship and other agreements, while giving due recognition to the special features of the bilateral relationship. A High-Level Committee at the level of Foreign Secretaries will be set up for this purpose.

12. The Nepalese side informed that Government of Nepal will take further necessary measures for the promotion of investor friendly, enabling business environment to encourage Indian public and private sector investments in Nepal.

13. Both sides agreed to enhance cooperation in handling cross-border crime and security concerns. Home Secretaries will meet soon to implement this decision.

14. Government of India will continue to assist the Government and people of Nepal in its peaceful, democratic transition; its economic development and reconstruction. The areas of assistance would include infrastructure, human resource development, health and education.

15. Both sides expressed concern over the large-scale damage caused by the breach of embankment by the river in the Kosi barrage area and decided to launch relief and rehabilitation measures for the victims and the reconstruction of the damaged infrastructure, and other measures as per the agreements, immediately, and take up preventive measures to avoid the recurrence of such events in the long term. They decided to take up preventive measures for the Gandak and other barrages under existing bilateral arrangements. Likewise, the two sides also discussed the problem of inundation in the border areas between Nepal and India and agreed to take up necessary work for its effective prevention on the basis of bilateral consultation.

16. Government of India will provide Rs. 20 crores as immediate flood relief to the people in Nepal. Government of India will also rebuild the segments of the East-West Highway, damaged in the recent Kosi floods.

17. Both sides agreed that Government of India will set up a camp office in Biratnagar for facilitating movement of Nepali vehicular traffic through Bihar for improved access to other parts of Nepal till the Highway is repaired.

18. A three-tier mechanism at the level of Ministerial, Secretary and technical levels will be established to rationalize and raise the efficacy of the existing bilateral mechanisms in order to push forward discussions on the development of water resources in a comprehensive manner, including hydro-power generation, irrigation, flood control and other water related cooperation. The Secretaries will meet in two weeks.

19. The two Prime Ministers directed the Inter-Governmental Committee (IGC) at the level of Commerce Secretaries to meet in one month to initiate a comprehensive review of the existing trade and transit arrangements with a view to promoting industrialization in Nepal, expanding complementarities of bilateral trade on a sustainable basis and removing the barriers to trade.

20. Both sides agreed to further enhance the pace of economic development between the two countries by extending support for the preparation and execution of mega projects, including infrastructure

development such as road, rail and hydel-power projects. As a gesture of goodwill of the Government and people of India, Government of India agreed to implement the Naumure Hydro-electric Project on Rapti river.

21. In view of the shortages felt in Nepal for the essential commodities, Government of India will remove bans on the export of rice, wheat, maize, sugar and sucrose for quantities agreed with Nepal. Government of India will also provide a credit of up to Rs. 150 crores to Government of Nepal for the next three months to ensure uninterrupted POL supplies to Nepal.

22. The Prime Minister of Nepal extended an invitation to the Prime Minister of India to pay an official visit to Nepal at an early date. The Prime Minister of India accepted it with pleasure. The date of the visit will be decided through the diplomatic channel.

(*Source*: http://meaindia.nic.in/)

## Nepal's Political Transformation and India-Nepal Relations[2]

*Mr Shyam Saran, speaking on the Indo-Nepal relations, welcomed the political transformation in Nepal and said that India was prepared to strengthen economic ties with Nepal. He stated that Nepal has the potential to become the richest state in South Asia, with an exorbitant hydro-potential of 85,000 MW. He stressed the importance of Nepal as a prospective health, tourism and education center.*

Mr. Chairman, distinguished guests from both India and Nepal, friends, ladies and gentlemen. It is honour for me to be invited to give the keynote address at this political segment of the Indo-Nepal Seminar. It is appropriate that Patna is the venue for this seminar, since the region of Bihar has long-standing historical, cultural, religious, ethnic and kinship ties with Nepal. Even in contemporary times, several leaders of Nepal's democratic movement made Bihar their home and several generations of Nepali friends have graduated from Bihar's educational institutions. Thus, there is an easy familiarity which the people of Bihar enjoy with the people of Nepal and being from Bihar myself, I was deeply conscious of this valuable asset when I served as India's Ambassador to Nepal a few years back. It is against this backdrop that we gather here today to look at the dramatic political events that have recently taken place in Nepal and consider how we can take forward the already close and friendly relations between our two countries in the context of Nepal's political transformation.

2. Keynote Address by Shri Shyam Saran, Special Envoy to the Prime Minister, on Nepal's Political Transformation and Future of India-Nepal Relations, April 26, 2008, Patna.

Let me begin by saying that the people of Nepal deserve to be congratulated for having carried out a remarkably successful electoral exercise to re-establish democracy in their country. The political parties, irrespective of gains and losses they registered in the recent elections, also deserve to be commended. Against all odds and I must say, against the cynical expectations of most observers, they maintained the Seven-Party alliance as a united political and democratic force. They also worked together to keep the peace process on track! This is no mean achievement. This record encourages us to believe that in confronting the many ensuing challenges of political reform and restructuring, economic reconstructions and economic reform and in consolidating a truly inclusive and responsive democracy, Nepal's newly elected political leadership will not be found wanting. India is proud to have been a modest part of this historic transformation in a friendly neighbouring country and stands ready to assist in whatever manner it is called upon to assist the continuing process of political and economic transformation in Nepal.

Several people in India have asked whether the government was not caught by surprise by the election results and whether these do not constitute a setback for India's Nepal policy. I am surprised by these comments, not because we were not surprised at the results but because people seem to think that our surprise was an unpleasant one. There seems to be an assumption that the Indian Government had a preferred electoral outcome and put its bets, much like a punter, on different horses. Let me make it clear. Throughout the peace process in Nepal, India has not played favourites with this or that political party. Our stand has been that it is for the people of Nepal to deliver, through free and fair elections, their verdict on who should govern them and in what manner. Our approach has been to engage with all key political actors in Nepal, with whom we have managed to establish, in my opinion, a relationship of trust and confidence. We are, therefore, comfortable with whatever, political permutation or combination which emerges from the exercise of democratic rights by the people of Nepal. This approach gives us the confidence that we can do business with the new political dispensation in Nepal.

It is my view that Nepal is in the midst of a major political transformation because of certain underlying factors. The country is witnessing a generational transition. If India has more that 50% of its population under 25, Nepal has an even higher percentage. This new, vibrant and young Nepal has a mindset very different from those representing an earlier generation. Their outlook is different, their aspirations are different. They are also exposed to what is happening in the world around them. After all, many of them have migrated in search of jobs and livelihood to neighbouring India and to many other countries beyond. They come back to Nepal with a very different perspective. No political structure will be enduring unless it is in tune with this generational change.

The new Nepal is also a very diverse Nepal. Even the more limited democracy of the 90s opening the space for the reassertion of ethnic identities and cultural particularities and a growing demand for a more inclusive and egalitarian political structure. These trends became much stronger as part of the *Jan Andolan*, in particular, with respect to the Madhesi and other ethnic groups in the Terai. The Nepal of the future will be a more diverse, more complex but also a more culturally enriching and enriched society. A plural democracy like India has learnt to celebrate its diversity and counts this as one of the pillars of its democracy. It is my hope that Nepal will do so, too, because only a more inclusive, a more accommodative approach is required for a stable and enduring democracy.

The economic challenge will be a daunting one. But I for one, have always believed that Nepal has the prospect for becoming the richest nation in South Asia. It has both tangible and intangible assets. Its hydro-power resources are estimated at over 85,000 MW of which only a miniscale percentage has been utilized. Even a modest utilization of these resources and the sale of power to energy-hungry India could quickly transform Nepal's economic prospects.

There are other assets. Nepal, with its natural beauty and pleasant climatic conditions can be transformed into a Health Centre as well as an Education Centre for our entire region. This has the added advantage of also helping meet the educational and health requirements of a growing Nepal's population.

Tourism, of course, is already Nepal's forte. However, the entire mid-hills region of the country could be home to several potential Simlas, Mussoories and Ranikhets, catering to several thousand tourists from the hot plains of India. All you need is good, cross border highways and why not, rail connections.

I hope that finally Nepal and its people will look upon India as an opportunity; you are not India-locked as you think. You are India-open - open to an India that is economically dynamic, a vast and growing market and a source of skills and technology that is not always so easy to access. Yet, you have an open border with India. You have free access to our market. Please make use of it, and we could establish a very mutually rewarding economic partnership between our two countries.

Let me conclude by welcoming our Nepali guests. Many are familiar faces. Many of you are close friends. I take this opportunity to congratulate you on your remarkable success and tell you that the transformation of Nepal is as much a reason for celebration in India as it is in Nepal.

(*Source*: http://meaindia.nic.in/)

# 15.

## BILATERAL RELATIONS WITH CHINA

### Nepal-China Bilateral Relations[1]

*On December 3 ,2008, official talks between Nepal and China were held at the level of Foreign Ministers'. The Foreign Minister of Nepal briefed the Chinese Foreign Minister about the current developments in Nepal and the peace process. The Nepalese side lauded the economic achievements that China has made over the years and requested for Chinese cooperation in enabling Nepal to derive due benefits from bilateral partnerships and joint undertakings. On bilateral trade, both sides emphasized the need for promoting sustainable trade, thereby enhancing mutually beneficial trading relationship through promotion of Nepalese exports to China. Nepalese side highlighted the advantages of better connectivity by all means of transport including railways to promote linkages between Nepal and China. The Nepalese Foreign Minister also appreciated the China's endeaveur for providing scholarships as well as human resource training opportunities in China. Both sides agreed to promote tourism between the two countries through various initiatives and appropriate measures.*

Official talks between Nepal and China were held today at the level of Foreign Minister at Shital Niwas. The Chinese delegation led by Foreign Minister H. E. Mr Yang Jiechi consisted of the Chinese Ambassador to Nepal H.E. Mr Qiu Guohong as well as Senior Officials of the Ministry of the Foreign Affairs of the People's Republic of China. The Nepalese delegation led by Minister for Foreign Affairs of Nepal Hon. Mr Upendra Yadav comprised Advisor Mr Shyamananda Suman, Foreign Secretary Mr Gyan Chandra Acharya as well as other Senior Officials of the Government of Nepal.

Welcoming the Foreign Minister of China the Foreign Minister of Nepal highlighted the importance of such a high level visit from China after the declaration of Republic in Nepal.

---

1. Bilateral Relations with China, December 3, 2008.

During the talks, both the Foreign Ministers agreed to enhance and upgrade bilateral relationship to a new height with the expansion and consolidation of mutual interaction in diverse fields. They also agreed that regular exchange of visits at high levels will contribute towards enhancing mutual understanding and goodwill between the two countries.

The Foreign Minister of Nepal briefed the Chinese Foreign Minister about the current developments in Nepal and the peace process. He also expressed his thanks to the people and the Government of China for their valuable support during Nepal's transition and peace process. They agreed to enhance and broaden the areas of cooperation in the days ahead. The Nepalese side lauded the economic achievements that China has made over the years and requested for Chinese cooperation in enabling Nepal to derive due benefits from bilateral partnerships and joint undertakings.

They also reviewed the projects being undertaken with the assistance of China such as Syafrubesi-Rasuwagadi Road, National Ayurveda Research and Training Centre and National Trust for Nature Conservation as well as other important projects. They also discussed about future projects for their detailed technical study and prioritization.

On bilateral trade, both sides emphasized the need for promoting sustainable trade, thereby enhancing mutually beneficial trading relationship through promotion of Nepalese exports to China. In this context, they also agreed to consider Comprehensive Trade Agreement between the two countries. Both sides noted with satisfaction the Chinese investment in Nepal in diverse areas and also decided to further promote such investments to contribute towards strengthening economic ties between the two countries.

Both sides also discussed about the establishment of Special Economic Zones (SEZ) and Dry Ports in border areas. They also agreed to make the best use of the existing geographical advantage to expand relations between Nepal and Tibet and promote border trade between the two countries through more facilitating measures. While expressing their appreciation for growing business to business and people to people relations between the two countries both sides agreed to promote and encourage them for mutual benefit in the days to come.

Nepalese side highlighted the advantages of better connectivity by all means of transport including railways to promote linkages between Nepal and China. The Nepalese Foreign Minister also appreciated the Government of China for providing scholarships as well as human resource training opportunities in China. Both sides agreed to promote tourism between the two countries through various initiatives and appropriate measures.

Both sides directed the bilateral consultation mechanism to hold regular meetings to review all aspects of bilateral cooperation, explore new areas of cooperation and prepare long-term measures and a vision paper to promote bilateral relationship between the two countries. They also discussed other issues of mutual interest.

The two Foreign Ministers reviewed regional and international issues of mutual concern and agreed to cooperate in the international forums for promoting their common interests. The Chinese side appreciated the reaffirmation of Nepal's 'One China Policy' and its principled stand of not allowing its territories to be used against China.

The Chinese Foreign Minister extended invitation to the Nepalese Foreign Minister to pay an Official visit to China at a mutually convenient time. On the occasion, the Government of the People's Republic of China agreed to provide the Government of Nepal with a grant of RMB 100 million (Renminbi Yuan one Hundred Million only) equivalent to Nepalese Rs. 1.2 billion approximately. To this effect, an Agreement on Economic and Technical Cooperation between the Government of Nepal and the Government of the People's Republic of China was also signed by the Foreign Ministers of the two countries. According to the Agreement the grant is to be used for projects to be discussed and decided upon by the two Governments of Nepal and China.

(*Source*: http://www.mofa.gov.np/uploads/news/20081203155520.doc)

# 16.

## INTERNATIONAL DOCUMENTS

### Nepal: Prospects for Socio-Economic Development[1]

*In his first address at the 63rd Session of the United Nations General Assembly, Prime Minister Pushpa Kamal Dahal, highlighted the positive developments in Nepal, stating that Nepal has been successful in getting together a Constituent Assembly which is inclusive and symbolic of a new beginning in Nepal. He stated that poverty reduction and pro poor governance policies are the national priorities of Nepal. He highlighted the urgency to take policy initiatives on climate change so that vulnerabilities could be minimized. Hydro-power is one sector, the Prime Minister stated that could be harnessed for Nepal's development and that Nepal would be open to investments in hydro-power projects. He also expressed concern over the lack of progress being made on the trading framework of Doha Development Agenda, which, he argued, should consider the interests of LDCs.*

It is indeed a historic opportunity for me to address this august Assembly as the first Prime Minister of Nepal of the newest republic of the world. As I stand here in front of the global leadership, I think of the long struggle that I and my party waged with single mindedness for the liberation of the common man from the clutches of the age-old suppression, deprivation, marginalization and outright negligence of the then existing polity. My fellow countrymen and women, toiling in the mountains and valleys, working day and night in the low lands and the urban areas and yet unable to ensure even the simple necessities of life for his or her family had a hope and expectation that one day they would lead a decent life with equal rights and opportunities and be recognized as respectful citizens of the country. We are at this significant turning point in the political history of Nepal. And I and my party are proud to be the leading force of that positive historical change. Today I see a great hope in the glinting eyes of the dalit

1. Address by Mr. Pushpa Kamal Dahal 'Prachanda', Prime Minister of Nepal, to the General Debate of the Sixty-Third Session of the United Nations General Assembly New York, September 26, 2008.

boy from the far west, downtrodden women from the indigenous nationality in the east, homeless Tharu girl and landless Madhesi and other peasants from the hills living under the thatched roofs. I intend to lead them with conviction and sincerity towards a new journey of sustainable peace and equitable progress in a modern Nepal. I have therefore the honor and great privilege of bringing with me the greetings and best wishes of the people and Government of that new Federal Democratic Republic of Nepal to this august Assembly.

Following the Comprehensive Peace Agreement in November 2006 after a decade-long armed struggle, we began our peace process and eventually held elections to the Constituent Assembly in April this year. People have overwhelmingly voted for my party and made us the single largest political party in the Assembly with great hope and expectations. At its first meeting, the Constituent Assembly declared Nepal a Federal Democratic Republic formally ending the 240-year old monarchy and creating a new opportunity to transform the old feudalistic state into an inclusive and federated 'new Nepal'. This was in keeping with the long-standing aspirations of the Nepalese people. They voted in favour of change and transformation that my own party had fought for so many years. After the historic political transformations, our agenda now is to bring about equally historic socio-economic transformation of the country. Today I must inform you with all humility that our Constituent Assembly is the most inclusive representative body in which all marginalized, oppressed ethnic communities, indigenous nationalities, dalits, disadvantaged and the people from the backward regions and communities are its members which will herald a new beginning in the country. This may very well be an example of representativeness to the world in the first decade of the twenty first century.

The Government is committed to restore law and order, provide immediate relief to the people affected by the conflict, fight against the cancerous growth of corruption and start an economic recovery package focusing on pro-poor growth, infrastructure development and public-private partnership. The government will build an effective partnership with the international community in creating an atmosphere for unleashing a new socio-economic transformation that the Nepalese people are waiting for so long.

Nepal's peace process is unique in its characteristics and is based on multiparty democracy, inclusiveness, accommodation, dialogue, and the recognition of the people as the ultimate arbiter. It is the outcome of our own creative disposition towards peace and we feel that it can also serve as a reference model for peace elsewhere.

We appreciate the United Nation's continued support to the peace process, especially in monitoring the management of arms and personnel through the United Nations Mission in Nepal (UNMIN). The UN Mission has undertaken its mandated tasks well. I also take this opportunity to thank our neighbors, friends, and donors for their continued support in favor of the peace process and the institutionalization of democracy in Nepal. I am confident they would do so for unleashing its development potentials also as per the wish of the Nepalese people.

As we proceed ahead along the peace process within the country, new problems in the form of global food crisis, rising oil prices and imminent dangers from climate change stare us in the face. These challenges also undermine our achievement of the Millennium Development Goals (MDGs). There will be no success in achieving MDGs without ensuring them in the LDCs. Solemn pledges were made in the 2000 Millennium Declaration and in the 2002 World Conference on Financing for Development held in Monterrey. Many of these commitments are yet to be fulfilled and achievement of the Millennium Development Goals remains elusive to most of the world's poor people.

The United Nations agenda today has to tackle these development challenges and many other issues such as religious extremism and terrorism, proliferation of nuclear weapons and weapons of mass destruction, transnational crimes such as drugs, human trafficking and money-laundering, continuing conflicts within and among states, and gross violations of human rights, genocide, war crimes and crimes against humanity. It is more than obvious that many of these global problems require global solutions. Together we can rise to the occasion and adopt a vision and strategy that the founders of the United Nations Organization charted in the purposes and principles of the Charter of the Organization. Multilateralism, not unilateralism is the answer to these problems.

The least developed countries like Nepal are faced with special predicament in their development efforts. We are trapped in a vicious circle of poverty. For many historical reasons, we have low economic growth, low productivity, underdeveloped industries and traditional agriculture. Because of the low level of social indicators and less opportunities, conflict and crisis continue to be prevalent in these countries. Today, the growing gap between the rich and the poor within the country as well as between the nations is a sure sign of a looming disaster. It is also inhuman and unjust that such a high level of inequality is still so common in this age of human achievements, abundance and progress. Equally important is the fact that islands of prosperity in the sea of poverty is not sustainable and certainly not in the enlightened self-interest of even the developed countries themselves, as it breeds resentment, fuels conflict and undermines their own progress in the long run. It also goes against the fundamental spirit of the United Nations. Because of the peculiar nature of the LDCs and their high level of vulnerabilities, I strongly urge that the issues of LDCs should be looked at by the United Nations separately and with special and focused programs. They should be ensured dedicated support and cooperation if we want to make our world just and inclusive that the United Nations so proudly espouses.

We are not only least developed but also land-locked. That is a double disadvantage in our efforts to fulfill developmental aspirations. In fact, we feel further marginalized due to the overwhelming impact of the downside of globalization and the high cost of doing trade. We want full implementation of the respective global compacts, the Brussels Program of Action for the Least Developed Countries and the Almaty Program of Action for the Landlocked Developing Countries. In particular, I would like to highlight the need in the part of our developed country partners to fulfill the commitment and pledges in allocating certain percentage of their GNP to these countries and in making available trade concessions, debt relief and other capacity building measures in accordance with these compacts. On our part, I would like to commit that Nepal will fulfill its pledge to own its development programs in accordance with its national priorities including on poverty reduction and pro-poor governance policies.

We need to protect our people from the rising vulnerabilities of climate change. For example, in my own country Nepal, the melting of glaciers and shifting weather patterns, are threatening the life support systems, undermining the sustainability of agriculture and inducing extreme climate-induced disasters such as frequent floods and landslides. The Himalayan range provides life supporting water downstream for more than a billion people. The Mt. Everest, as the roof of the world, and the Himalayan range need to be protected and utilized properly to contribute to the humanity as a whole. So I strongly appeal to the international community to extend all necessary support and cooperation to protect and promote its pristine environment. We need to create a regime of common but differentiated responsibilities, in which the developed countries will lift the burden of adaptation in the vulnerable countries, such as the least developed countries and small islands. The world will stand to benefit in addressing the climate change if we are able to harness the tremendous potentials of Nepal's hydro-power as it is a renewable and clean source of energy. For this, Nepal is ready to invite and encourage investment in its hydro-power projects.

I am pleased that the UN Regional Centre for Peace Disarmament in Asia and the Pacific has been now operational from Kathmandu twenty years after it was established by this august Assembly. I thank all the members, countries from the region and the Secretary General and the officials of the Secretariat for the smooth relocation of the Centre from New York to Kathmandu. I would like to take this opportunity to reiterate Nepal's commitment to make this Centre successful through the cooperation of all the countries concerned.

Over the years, peacekeeping has evolved as the soul of the United Nations. With this in mind, Nepal has been regularly sending its peacekeepers at the call of the United Nations since 1958. We are celebrating the 50th anniversary of Nepal's continuous participation in the UN peacekeeping operations; I take this opportunity to reiterate Nepal's commitment that we will continue to provide our troops for the cause of peace worldwide. Today, Nepal is the fifth largest contributor of troops and police personnel to UN's peacekeeping operations. We are glad that they have earned accolades for their professional competence and performance both at home and abroad. We consider this as our modest contribution to international peace and security.

Enjoyment of universal human rights is absolutely essential in creating the environment of peace, justice, democracy and development. As a democracy, Nepal is fully committed to protect and promote the human rights of its people under all circumstances with constitutional and legal guarantees and implementation of the international human rights instruments to which Nepal is a party. The government is committed to end the environment of impunity. The proposed Truth and Reconciliation Commission, which will seek to arrive at a necessary balance between peace and justice, so that there is justice, and that the centrality of the peace process is preserved. We will continue to strengthen the National Human Rights Commission so that it can take up its statutory responsibility for protection and promotion of human rights in the country even more effectively. It goes without saying that the environment for the protection and promotion of human rights in Nepal has significantly improved, especially after the signing of the comprehensive peace agreement in November 2006.

As a least developed country that entered the World Trade Organization not too long ago, Nepal is concerned at the lack of tangible progress in negotiations on the Doha Development Agenda. We think that the opportunities in world trade through multilateral trading framework of the WTO should not be delayed any further. The least developed countries deserve a duty free and quota free market access for all their tradable products from all the major countries with sincerity, together with more favorable rules of origin and the support for enhancing their supply side capacity. Only then the Doha Round would be a development round in the real sense of the word. Without meaningful integration of the LDCs into the global regime, I do not know how we can make the global trading regime sustainable, equitable and inclusive. Similarly, the least developed countries need more aid for trade and trade facilitation measures to enhance their trading capacity.

Today, the United Nations needs to reform and democratize itself to take on the numerous challenges in international peace and security effectively. And it should also reflect the current realities of the world. We should also give the necessary credibility, legitimacy, competence and effectiveness to the world body in solving the global problems. I take this opportunity to reiterate Nepal's solemn faith and commitment to the purposes and principles of the United Nations Charter. On behalf of the people and government of Nepal, I pledge to work with all of you to take on the global challenges through the United Nations in a spirit of goodwill, cooperation and mutual solidarity. It is with this belief that we have adopted them as one of the tenets of Nepal's foreign policy. Nepal is an example of how swords have been turned into the ploughshares. That is what the United Nations believes in. Therefore, as I address this gathering here, I have a special feeling about the whole objectives and ideals that the United Nations stand for and the co-relationship between those ideals and the political, economic and social transformation that we would like to achieve in our country. May we all succeed in attaining our common objectives through our collective and sincere efforts as the united and inseparable members of a single global family.

(*Source*: www.mofa.gov.np)

## Development in Nepal: Opportunities and Constraints[2]

September 25, 2008

*Nepal's Prime Minister, Pushpa Kamal Dahal, in a statement at the Round Table on Millennium Development Goals, UNGA, brought to focus the lack of development aid provided to Nepal. He noted that the development partners had provided only 0 .28 percent of their GNP as aid, as against the committed 0 .7 percent. He expressed concern over the agricultural subsidy policies of developed countries, which he stated was jeopardizing the agricultural sector of Nepal. Applauding the initiative of the Secretary General on the establishment of Task Force to address global food crises, he stressed the need for investment in the agricultural sector, which he considered essential, if Nepal had to achieve the targets set by Millennium Development Goals.*

In 2000, the world leaders adopted goals and targets, Millennium Development Goals (MDGs), as the collective commitment of the international community to take on poverty, hunger, diseases and many of the development challenges confronting the world.

Despite such solemn pledge, it is ironic that more than a billion people, the so-called "bottom billion", mostly in developing countries, are still

2. Statement by Pushpa Kamal Dahal 'Prachanda', Prime Minister of Nepal, at the UN General Assembly High-Level Event on the Millennium Development Goals Round Table: Poverty and Hunger, September 25, 2008.

trapped in conditions of grinding poverty with an income of less than a dollar a day. This is unbecoming of the contemporary human civilization, which has so much of affluence and prosperity at its disposal.

Let us acknowledge the stark reality, which has been pointed out by the UN Task Force in identifying the gaps in implementation of the goals. The developed partners have provided only 0.28% of their GNP as development aid up to this mid-point, as against the commitment to provide 0.7%. So far, only eight countries have met their commitment to make available 0.15% - 0.2% of the GNP to the least developed countries (LDCs). In fact, development aid has declined in actual terms. The Paris commitments for improving aid effectiveness remain largely unimplemented. The failure to conclude the "development round" of trade negotiations is disappointing. Preferential access to the products from least developed countries is eroding, despite the commitment in the WTO to allow access to 97% of their products. The pledged "aid for trade" initiative lacks operational clarity and very few countries have actually benefited from it. Most of the least developed countries are still outside the debt relief initiatives. Under such conditions, the target of reducing poverty and hunger and meeting other MDGs will be very difficult.

I agree with the Secretary General that the year 2008 should mark a turning point in progress towards the MDGs. I think this high-level event should be that turning point. I am confident that we can chart that course to achieving the MDGs in full, if we recommit ourselves to redirect our combined efforts and resources towards achieving them.

Nepal has a mixed result on the achievement of the MDGs. We are on track of achieving goals related to halving the poverty by 2015, achieving universal primary education, reducing under-five child mortality, and providing safe drinking water. Despite internal conflict, the percentage of people living in poverty has been reduced to 31%. Nepal has made significant progress in improving access to education and health services.

But we have numerous challenges to address. The biggest challenge is effectively addressing mortality among new borns and reducing hunger among the children under five. We have to address the problem of inequality and exclusion, which is denying the distribution of fruits of development to the people, who often live in the periphery of the state and the economy. The current government is therefore committed to put the people, who have been traditionally marginalized, at the centre of its development strategy and initiate collective interventions at various levels. As signatory to International health partnerships, we have prepared a national compact. With the support of the partners, we seek to intensify free health care and motivate health workforce to reach all including the marginalized groups.

We feel that MDGs on their own cannot be achieved by all and more specifically by the LDCs. We can meet them only with global political support, stronger partnerships and coordinated efforts of all. Our achievements, including in reducing poverty, are likely to be thwarted by the rising food and oil prices and threats of climate change. We need short term relief and long term measures to deal with them in a comprehensive manner.

We welcome the initiative of the Secretary General for establishing a Task Force under his leadership on the global food crisis. Similarly, we also welcome the recommendations of the World Food Summit held in Rome earlier this year. We hope some concrete action will be taken under these initiatives. Unless we invest systematically in the agriculture sector and develop it, the achievement of the MDGs will neither be possible nor sustainable.

It is alarming that the increasing use of bio-fuels has shifted the focus from crops for food to that for fuel and has triggered the rise in food prices. The artificial barriers such as agricultural subsidies are causing the food prices to be distorted globally. This must be corrected.

The commitment to "making poverty history" will sound empty without a genuine support and cooperation from the developed countries

We think the review conference on the Financing for Development to be held in Doha later this year should be utilized as an opportunity to recommit ourselves to the cause of attaining MDGs through stronger support from developed countries. Financing for development should not be an obstacle when there is so much political will around this Assembly.

The situation we are facing demands visionary and strategic choice to be made globally. It is about time that this Assembly rose up to its challenge and adopted that strategic choice. After all, investment in development in the poorer countries is an investment in the peace and stability of the world. Our choice should be guided by this imperative. I think it is yet another opportunity for this Assembly to stand up to the challenge of poverty and hunger.

On behalf of the people and the Government of Nepal, I would like to pledge to work together in a spirit of partnership. In the same vein, I would like to urge our development partners for enhanced level of targeted cooperation for sustained socioeconomic development, for the reduction of poverty and for addressing all development challenges. Working together, we can effectively deal with the current challenges. We have to employ all our collective energy to attain our collective objectives, as only a short time is available for us to meet the MDGs.

(*Source*: www.mofa.gov.np)

# PAKISTAN

# 17.

# BILATERAL RELATIONS WITH INDIA

## Pakistan on Mumbai Bomb Blasts-I[1]

28 November, 2008

> *Pakistan at the highest levels has strongly condemned the horrific terrorist attacks in Mumbai (26 November, 2008) and the President and the Prime Minister conveyed to the Indian leadership their sense of shock and deep sorrow on the loss of life. The Foreign Minister who is presently visiting India has also, in unequivocal terms, conveyed to the Indian leadership, the abhorrence and distress of the Government and people of Pakistan at these dastardly attacks.*

In separate telephone calls today to the Indian Prime Minister, the President and the Prime Minister reiterated Pakistan's strong condemnation and indignation on the terrorist attacks in Mumbai and expressed Pakistan's readiness to extend every assistance and cooperation that the Government of India may require in investigating these incidents. Director General (ISI) will visit India in this regard.

Earlier Pakistan had proposed closer intelligence cooperation and meetings between the intelligence chiefs of the two countries. Pakistan and India have established mechanisms of cooperation for combating terrorism. Joint anti-terrorism mechanism exists. At its meeting in New Delhi in October, it was decided to make it more effective. Anti-terrorism cooperation is also an item in the Composite Dialogue process. Both countries have also broad ranging cooperation on a range of issues relating to terrorism, crime and drug trafficking. The meeting of Interior/Home Secretaries of the two countries held in Islamabad on 25-26 November was productive. It was decided that severe action will be taken against any elements involved in terrorist attacks.

Pakistan, itself a victim of terrorism, has ongoing cooperation in combating terrorism with several countries of the world. Terrorism is a

1. Mumbai Tragedy, 28 November, 2008.

global problem and needs to be combated in all its forms and manifestations through serious, sustained and pragmatic steps.

Pakistan is prepared to deepen its engagement with India, including on combating terrorism. It is however, important to avoid blame game and knee jerk reactions. We are confident that the Government of India will respond positively to Pakistan's offer to cooperate in the investigation of the Mumbai attacks. It is in the interest of Pakistan and India to enhance multi-track cooperation in anti-terrorism.

(*Source*: http://www.mofa.gov.pk/Press_Releases/2008/Nov/PR_363_08.htm)

## Pakistan on Mumbai Bomb Blasts-II[2]

28 November, 2008

*Following are the condolence messages from the President and the Prime Minister of the Islamic Republic of Pakistan to the President and the Prime Minister of India on the terrorist attacks in Mumbai.*

**Quote**

Excellency,

On behalf of the people and Government of Pakistan and on my own behalf, I wish to express our deep shock and sorrow at last night's terrorist attacks in Mumbai.

The people of Pakistan join you in mourning the loss of so many precious lives. We offer our heartfelt sympathies and condolences to the family members of all those who have lost their lives or have been injured in these incidents.

Pakistan strongly condemns these acts of terrorism. Terrorism is a scourge of humanity, which needs to be rooted out.

Please accept, Excellency, the assurances of my highest consideration.

(Asif Ali Zardari)
President of Pakistan

Her Excellency,
Mrs. Pratibha Devisingh Patil,
President of the Republic of India,
**New Delhi.**

**Unquote**

**Message from the Prime Minister**

**Quote**

Excellency,

I am shocked to learn of the deadly terrorist attacks in Mumbai last night which have caused enormous loss of lives.

2. Condolence Messages on the Terrorist Attacks in Mumbai, 27 November 2008.

Please accept our deepest condolences on these dastardly attacks.

Such acts of violence and terrorism are totally unacceptable in any civilized society. The Government and people of Pakistan unequivocally and strongly condemn these heinous acts of terrorism.

Please accept, Excellency, the assurances of my highest consideration.

(Syed Yousuf Raza Gilani)
Prime Minister of Pakistan

H.E. Mr. Manmohan Singh,
Prime Minister of the Republic of India,
**New Delhi**

(*Source*: http://www.mofa.gov.pk/Press_Releases/2008/Nov/PR_363_08.htm)

## India and Pakistan: Spaces for Mutual Cooperation[3]

November 27, 2008

*In his address at the Centre for Research in Rural and Industrial Development (CRRID), Chandigarh, the Foreign Minister stated that Pakistan desires close, cooperative and friendly relations with India and pointed out that much as India has a stake in Pakistan's prosperity, Pakistan has a stake in India's progress and development. While stating that Pakistan and India were constructively engaged in a Composite Dialogue process both countries were also committed towards combating terrorism. He pointed out that low agricultural productivity and lack of adequate access to water; inadequate infrastructure, substandard public service delivery, and lack of direct access to market by farmers were the main challenges for Pakistan. He emphasized that Pakistan hoped to have peaceful and friendly relations with India.*

The importance of peace and cooperative development for the future of our region cannot be overstated.

Pakistan desires close, cooperative and friendly relations with India. We believe that a sustained engagement between Pakistan and India will not only help in promoting peace but also bring the fruits of bilateral cooperation and regional collaboration to the whole of South Asia.

Pakistan wishes the people of India peace and prosperity. Much as India has a stake in Pakistan's prosperity, Pakistan has a stake in India's progress and development. There is much that is common between our two peoples.

---

3. Statement by Mr Makhdoom Shah Mahmood Qureshi, the Foreign Minister of Pakistan at the Centre For Research in Rural and Industrial Development (CRRID) - Chandigarh, November 27, 2008.

These sentiments of goodwill have been conveyed to India at the highest level including during my interaction with His Excellency Pranab Mukherjee yesterday.

We welcome the statement made by Prime Minister Manmohan Singh in Srinagar last month (10 October) that India seeks "normalization of relations with Pakistan and a solution of all issues that cause estrangement, including Jammu and Kashmir, through dialogue and peaceful negotiations in an atmosphere free of violence". We reciprocate these sentiments.

I believe that peace does not accrue only through covenants and treaties; it must lie in our hearts and minds. I am reminded of a statement attributed to President Kennedy that "it is not enough to say we must not wage war; it is necessary to love peace and sacrifice for it".

Pakistan and India must transform the dynamics of our region from conflict and confrontation to engagement and cooperation for the larger good of our people.

I believe that the future we seek is the future we would get.

Achieving peace in our region in not only desirable it is also doable. We are fortunate that at this point in time political leadership in both countries, across the board, wants peaceful cooperative relationship between our two countries.

All political parties, the Parliament and the elected government in Pakistan sincerely desire improvement of relations with India. I have often said this, and it bears repetition, that we must avail of this propitious political consensus and transform this relationship into one of peace, harmony and broad-ranging cooperation.

A democratic Pakistan is the best insurance against conflict in our region and your best interlocutor for a meaningful dialogue. Shaheed Mohtarma Benazir Bhutto once said that "democracy needs support and the best support for democracy comes from other democracies. Democratic nations should come together in an association designed to help each other and promote what is a universal value – democracy".

In South Asia today, we have a shared responsibility to channel our energies towards the betterment of our people who constitute one fifth of this planet's population.

Importantly, Pakistan and India are constructively engaged in a Composite Dialogue process. Four rounds of the Dialogue have been held. As decided at the meeting of President Zardari with Prime Minister Manmohan Singh in New York last September, meetings under the fifth round of the Composite Dialogue would be completed in the near future.

Earlier, Prime Minister Gilani met the Indian Prime Minister in Colombo in August on the sidelines of the SAARC Summit. Similarly, the two Prime Ministers met in Beijing last month. Our National Security Advisors and Deputy Chairmen Planning Commission have also met. These high level interactions help to carry the relationship forward.

The opening of the cross LOC trade last month, visit to Srinagar by a delegation from the AJK Chamber of Commerce and increase in the frequency of the Srinagar-Muzaffarabad and Poonch-Rawalakot bus services from fortnightly to weekly basis are welcome developments.

The resolution of the issue of Jammu and Kashmir is important. The solution to the problem has to be found through the collective political will of the leaderships of Pakistan and India in accordance with the wishes of the people of Jammu and Kashmir.

India and Pakistan spend enormous amounts on maintaining their troops in Siachen. Both countries also feel that the resolution of the issue of Sir Creek is not difficult. I believe we need to move forward on these two resolvable issues.

We would also like to see forward movement on the issue of Chenab water flows. The Indus Waters Commissioners held a meeting in New Delhi last month. Now, the Indus Waters Commissioner is expected to visit Pakistan. We welcome the statements at the highest level in New Delhi that India would honor the Indus Waters Treaty in letter and spirit.

Like India, Pakistan is committed to combating terrorism. Both the countries are a victim of this malaise. We are happy to note the Pakistan-India Joint Anti Terrorism Mechanism meeting was held in New Delhi last month followed by the discussions in Islamabad during the meeting of the Interior Secretaries under the fifth round of the Composite Dialogue. These are important avenues to address our mutual concerns.

Pakistan-India economic cooperation has progressed at a satisfactory pace. Bilateral trade, which was around US$ 300 million in 2002, has crossed US$ 1.98 billion now. Informal trade is estimated to be even higher. Secretaries Commerce of the two countries will be meeting soon for talks on promoting economic cooperation under the Composite Dialogue process.

The idea of agricultural cooperation and rural development, in particular, is of considerable importance for countries in South Asia. In both, Pakistan and India, rapid population growth has been accompanied by a slow growth in agriculture productivity. This has resulted into socio-economic inequalities within the rural areas and between the rural and urban regions. This increasing level of inequality has serious implications for stability and development of our economies.

Key factors hindering growth in agriculture sector in both our countries are:

1. low agricultural productivity,
2. lack of adequate access to water,
3. inadequate infrastructure,
4. substandard public service delivery, and
5. lack of direct access to market by our farmers. In addition, the

environmental issues, including water scarcity, changing weather cycles, etc. have compounded the mounting challenges.

Food security has emerged as a major challenge to the governments, farmers, agri-scientists, economists, and consumers. This is happening at a time when the world is gripped with an ongoing global financial crisis. Millions of people are at the risk of falling below poverty line. Poverty, hunger, illiteracy, and disease accentuate this vicious cycle. These challenges have been researched and plausible solutions proffered. However, owing to the traditional mindset in our rural areas, it has been difficult to bring about a significant change at the required pace. The contemporary challenges, some of which I have outlined above, in particular climate change and food insecurity, require drastic re-orientation of our traditional agricultural patterns.

We need to think innovatively and work cooperatively. This can be done by the right mix of policy incentives supported by investments in agriculture. We should improve the asset position of the rural poor, make small-holder farming more productive, competitive and sustainable and invest in rural non-farm economy. According to the World Development Report 2008, the growth originating in agriculture is four times more effective in reducing poverty than the growth coming from non-agriculture sectors. And it is in this larger context of turning challenges into opportunities that I believe that we can learn from each other's experiences and good practices for our common good. A cooperative relationship between the farmers and agricultural related research institutes of the two countries in the fields of research, education, and agriculture extension can, for instance, be mutually beneficial.

I would like to invite CRRID and the Farmers Associates of Pakistan to work together to identify possible areas for economic and commercial cooperation between our two countries focusing on the field of agriculture. Besides sharing of information, knowledge and experiences, we could also explore the possibility of transfer of technology and capacity building through developing institutional linkages. We should also expeditiously consider visa liberalization for professionals. Our priority in Pakistan is to promote peace and security in the region and beyond. This priority stems from the conviction that a conflict-free and secure regional environment would contribute towards high and sustainable economic growth and development for our countries. We also need to work together to contribute towards economic integration at the regional level. Establishment of SAARC Food Bank and the recently held Meeting of SAARC Agricultural Ministers are welcome developments. Let me conclude by emphasizing that Pakistan wishes to have peaceful and friendly relations with India. We seek peaceful settlement of all outstanding issues and take our relationship to a new higher plane.

(*Source*: http://www.mofa.gov.pk/Press_Releases/2008/Nov/PR_360_08.htm)

## Joint Statement Issued at the End of the Home/Interior Secretary Level talks between India and Pakistan in Islamabad on 25-26 November 2008

November 26, 2008

*In a joint statement between India and Pakistan, both countries discussed the issues related to terrorism and drug trafficking and reviewed the implementation of decision. The countries condemned terrorism in all its forms and manifestations and affirmed their resolve to cooperate with each other to combat the menace of terrorism. The MoU on Drug Demand Reduction and Prevention of Illicit Trafficking in Narcotics Drugs/Psychotropic Substances and Precursor Chemicals and Related Matters, was initialed by the countries. The countries decided that Federal Investigation Agency of Pakistan and the Central Bureau of Investigation of India would work out ways of cooperation in addressing the issues of human trafficking, illegal immigration, and counterfeit currency, along with Red Corner Notices (RCN) subjects.*

1. The fifth round of Interior/Home Secretary Level Talks between Pakistan and India on Terrorism and Drugs Trafficking was held in Islamabad on 25th and 26th November 2008 as a part of the Composite Dialogue. The Pakistan delegation was led by Syed Kamal Shah, Secretary, Ministry of Interior, while the Indian delegation was headed by Mr. Madhukar Gupta, Home Secretary of India.

2. The meeting was held in a cordial and friendly atmosphere.

3. Both sides discussed the issues related to terrorism and drug trafficking and reviewed the implementation of decisions taken during the last round. Both sides noted with satisfaction the progress made and identified ways to further promote cooperation in a number of areas.

4. Both sides condemned terrorism in all its forms and manifestations and affirmed their resolve to cooperate with each other to combat the menace of terrorism. It was agreed that terrorism must be prevented and as directed by the leadership of the two countries at the meeting in New York on 24 September 2008, severe action be taken against any elements involved in terrorist acts.

5. Both sides welcomed the release of prisoners and fishermen by each other on the eve of these talks as a gesture of goodwill and on humane considerations. It was agreed to exchange by 31st December 2008, names of those civil prisoners, who have completed their sentence and whose national status has been confirmed, with a view to facilitating their release in January. It was further agreed that, henceforth, verification of nationality status would be completed within six weeks of provision of consular access.

It was also agreed to facilitate the expeditious release of fishermen and boats.

6. Both sides welcomed the signing of Agreement on Consular Access during the review of the Fourth Round of Pakistan-India Composite Dialogue, and affirmed full implementation of the Agreement.

7. Both sides commended the work done by the Judicial Committee on Prisoners for the release, repatriation and humane treatment of prisoners and agreed on the need for the continuation of the work of the Committee.

8. Both sides underscored the need for visa liberalization. In this context, useful discussions were held on draft Visa Agreement. The Indian side would propose a draft Visa Agreement within four weeks, based on parameters discussed.

9. Both sides agreed that the issue of inadvertent crossers be viewed from a humanitarian dimension and recommended early finalization of the draft agreement regarding inadvertent crossings by the expert group on Conventional CBMs which is due to meet soon.

10. Both sides noted that Protocol of 1974 on visits to religious shrines was due for revision along with lists of religious shrines in both countries. The subject will be discussed under the segment of Secretary Culture level talks on Promotion of Friendly Exchanges which is likely to take place soon. It was recommended that a revised Protocol and the list of shrines should be finalized as early as possible and the Pakistan side agreed to furnish its comments on the lists before the talks on Friendly Exchanges.

11. Both sides assessed as positive the existing cooperation and information sharing between the Anti Narcotics Force of Pakistan and the Narcotics Control Bureau of India and agreed that both Agencies would enhance mutual cooperation in terms of effective and sustained steps to control drugs trafficking.

12. The MoU on Drug Demand Reduction and Prevention of Illicit Trafficking in Narcotics Drugs/Psychotropic Substances and Precursor Chemicals and Related Matters, was initialed. Both sides welcomed this development and agreed that the MoU will further promote bilateral cooperation in this field. It was agreed that Director General ANF of Pakistan and Director General of NCB of India will meet as early as possible to discuss ways of furthering cooperation.

13. It was decided that the Federal Investigation Agency of Pakistan and the Central Bureau of Investigation of India will schedule a meeting at an early date to discuss ways of cooperation in addressing the issues of human trafficking, illegal immigration, and counterfeit currency, along with Red Corner Notices (RCN) subjects.

14. The Home Secretary of India also called on the Advisor to the Prime Minister on Interior/Minister and discussed issues of mutual interest.

15. It was agreed to continue the discussions within the framework of the Composite Dialogue.

(*Source*: http://meaindia.nic.in/)

## Joint Press Statement issued after the Special Meeting of the Joint Anti-Terrorism Mechanism

October 24, 2008

*A Special Meeting of the Joint Anti-Terrorism Mechanism, as directed by the Prime Minister of India and the President of Pakistan was held in New Delhi on 24th October 2008. Information on issues of mutual concern including the bombing of the Indian Embassy in Kabul was exchanged*

A Special Meeting of the Joint Anti-Terrorism Mechanism, as directed by the Prime Minister of India and the President of Pakistan in New York on 24th September 2008, was held in New Delhi on 24th October 2008. The Indian delegation was led by Shri Vivek Katju, Special Secretary, Ministry of External Affairs and the Pakistan delegation by Mr. Aizaz Ahmad Chaudhry, Additional Secretary, Ministry of Foreign Affairs.

Information on issues of mutual concern including the bombing of the Indian Embassy in Kabul was exchanged. The Meeting was held in a positive, constructive and forward looking atmosphere.

(*Source*: http://meaindia.nic.in/)

## India- Pakistan Joint Press Statement Issued after Meeting of the Prime Minister with the President of Pakistan in New York

September 24, 2008

*India and Pakistan in a joint statement, welcomed several positive outcomes of the four rounds of the Composite Dialogue, and stated that the dialogue has brought their people, businesses and institutions closer together. Both countries agreed to work for an early and full normalization of relations between India and Pakistan, on the basis of mutual respect, peaceful coexistence and non-interference.*

The President of Pakistan and the Prime Minister of India met during the 63rd UNGA session in New York.

Prime Minister Singh congratulated President Zardari on his election and the victory of democracy in Pakistan. He expressed the hope that this would pave the way for a profound transformation of the bilateral relationship, so that India and Pakistan could work together on their shared objectives of peace, prosperity and security.

Both leaders welcomed the several positive outcomes of the four rounds of the Composite Dialogue, which have brought their people, businesses and institutions closer, while permitting sustained efforts to be made to resolve all outstanding issues; these gains need to be consolidated. They agreed to work for an early and full normalization of relations between India and Pakistan, on the basis of mutual respect, peaceful coexistence and non-interference.

Both leaders acknowledged that the peace process has been under strain in recent months. They agreed that violence, hostility and terrorism have no place in the vision they share of the bilateral relationship, and must be visibly and verifiably prevented. Severe action would be taken against any elements directing or involved in terrorist acts. President Zardari reassured Prime Minister Singh that the Government of Pakistan stands by its commitments of January 6, 2004.

Both leaders agreed that the forces that have tried to derail the peace process must be defeated. This would allow the continuation and deepening of a constructive dialogue for the peaceful resolution and satisfactory settlement of all bilateral issues, including Jammu and Kashmir.

The two leaders agreed that:

The Foreign Secretaries of both countries will schedule meetings of the Fifth round of the Composite Dialogue in the next three months which will focus on deliverables and concrete achievements.

The ceasefire should be stabilized. To this end, the DGMOs and Sector Commanders will stay in regular contact.

A special meeting of the Joint Anti-Terror Mechanism will be held in October 2008 to address mutual concerns including the bombing of the Indian Embassy in Kabul.

The expansion of people to people contacts, trade, commerce and economic cooperation provides an effective platform to develop and strengthen bilateral relations. Towards this end it was decided to:

Open the Wagah-Attari road link to all permissible items of trade.

Open the Khokrapar-Munabao rail route to all permissible items of trade.

Continue interaction between the Planning Commissions of both countries to develop mutually beneficial cooperation including the energy sector.

Commence cross-LoC trade on the Srinagar-Muzaffarabad and Poonch-Rawalakot roads on October 21, 2008.

Modalities for the opening of the Skardu-Kargil route will be discussed soon.

(*Source*: http://meaindia.nic.in/)

## Joint Press Statement after the 3rd Meeting of Pakistan-India Judicial Committee on Prisoners

August 18-23 2008

*In the Joint Press Statement by Pakistan-India Judicial Committee, both the countries agreed to repatriate prisoners, whose travel documents were available. The Committee also decided to repatriate women and juvenile prisoners, on humanitarian grounds. Provision of legal aid was also made mandatory at all stages of the cases. The Committee also appreciated release of 131 Indian fishermen and 6 civil prisoners, (including 35 Juvenile fishermen) by Pakistani authorities, and 14 Pakistani fishermen and 3 civil prisoners by Indian authorities.*

1. Pakistan-India Judicial Committee on Prisoners visited jails in Amritsar, Delhi and Jaipur on 18-23 August 2008. The Members of the Committee are Justice (Retd) Mr. Abdul Qadeer Chaudhary, Justice (Retd) Mr. Fazal Karim, Justice (Retd) Mr. Nasir Aslam Zahid and Justice (Retd) Mr. Mian Muhammad Ajmal from the Pakistan side and Justice (Retd) Mr. Nagendra Rai, Justice (Retd) Mr. Amarjeet Choudhary, Justice (Retd) Mr. A.S. Gill and Justice (Retd) Mr. M.A. Khan from the Indian side.

2. As per the agreement on Consular Access, the lists of prisoners were exchanged in July 2008. According to Indian authorities, 378 Pakistani prisoners were in different jails throughout India. However, according to Pakistani authorities, there were 644 Pakistani prisoners in custody in India. According to Indian authorities, there were 687 Indian prisoners including 412 fishermen in various jails in Pakistan, as against which, Pakistani authorities confirmed that there were 470 Indian prisoners including 412 Indian fishermen. (Out of the 412 Indian fishermen, 35 juvenile Indian fishermen have since been released by Pakistan authorities).

3. The Committee reiterates its earlier recommendation that a consolidated list of prisoner with full particulars be reconciled and exchanged. This should be done expeditiously and in any case before the next meeting of the Committee.

4. During its current visit, 131 Pakistani prisoners were produced before the Committee who were confined in the three jails visited by the Committee in India

5. The Committee recommends the following:

- ll prisoners who have completed their sentences and whose travel documents are available should be repatriated to their respective countries immediately and in any case before 30 th September 2008.
- The Committee strongly reiterates its earlier recommendations that women and Juvenile prisoners, prisoners terminally ill or suffering from serious illness or physical disability, mentally disabled persons

and prisoners involved in minor offences like violation of Foreigners Act, border crossing, visa violation like overstaying or visiting places not covered by the visa deserve compassionate and humanitarian consideration. Its recommendation that such prisoners, whether under trial or convicts, be repatriated to the country of their origin at the earliest and, for that purpose, necessary action be taken for withdrawal of prosecution or for remission of the balance sentence as the case may require, be implemented by the Governments.

- Consular access should be provided immediately to all those prisoners who have not been given consular access, but not later than 30 th September 2008. The Committee also desires that both the countries should follow the commitments made in the Agreement on the Consular Access signed between them in May 2008.
- ll the prisoners shall be provided legal aid at all stages of their cases.
- The Committee reiterates its earlier recommendation for supply of copy of Post Mortem Report to the respective High Commission in the unfortunate event of the death of a prisoner in custody.
- During the next visit of the Judicial Committee to various jails, prisoners who are lodged in the different jails of the same Province/State should be brought to the jail to be visited by the Committee in that Province/State. Efforts should also be made to produce prisoners from other Provinces/States, for meeting the Committee.
- The respective courts be requested for expeditious trial of all the under-trial prisoners for early disposal of their cases.
- The Committee appreciates the release of 131 Indian fishermen and 6 civil prisoners, (including 35 Juvenile fishermen) by Pakistani authorities, and 14 Pakistani fishermen and 3 civil prisoners by Indian authorities on its recommendation and further expects that its earlier recommendations for the repatriation of remaining fishermen and other prisoners be implemented at the earliest.
- Both the Governments should facilitate the prisoners to correspond with their family members.
- The Committee strongly recommends that the Home/Interior Secretaries of the two countries should meet at the earliest for issuance of directions for implementation of recommendations of this Committee.
- The Committee suggests that their further visits to jails in both the countries be decided early through diplomatic means in consultation with the members of the Committee.

(*Source*: http://www.mofa.gov.pk/Press_Releases/2008/Aug/PR_256_08.html)

## Joint Statement issued after the meeting of India-Pakistan Working Group on Cross-LoC CBMs

July 18, 2008

*The meeting of India-Pakistan Working Group on Cross-LoC CBMs was held in Islamabad on 18 July 2008. The two sides discussed modalities for implementation of the decisions taken by the Ministerial meeting of 21 May 2008 on cross-LoC travel and trade. They also reviewed measures to ensure effective implementation of the existing cross-LoC measures.*

1. The meeting of India-Pakistan Working Group on cross-LoC CBMs was held in Islamabad on 18 July 2008. Indian delegation was led by Mr. T.C.A Raghvan, Joint Secretary (PAI), Ministry of External Affairs while the Pakistan side was headed by Mr. Aizaz Ahmed Chaudhry, Director General (South Asia & SAARC).

2. The meeting was held in a cordial and constructive atmosphere.

3. The two sides discussed modalities for implementation of the decisions taken by the Ministerial meeting of 21 May 2008 on cross-LoC travel and trade. They also reviewed measures to ensure effective implementation of the existing cross-LoC measures.

4. Joint Secretary (PAI) also called on the Foreign Secretary of Pakistan.

(*Source*: http://meaindia.nic.in/)

## Joint Press Conference of External Affairs Minister of India Shri Pranab Mukherjee and Foreign Minister of Pakistan Mr. Makhdoom Shah Mehmood Qureshi, New Delhi

June 27, 2008

*The Indian Foreign Minister, Pranab Mukherjee, pointed out that issues of energy security, food security, poverty alleviation were the main challenges confronting both countries. He also highlighted prospects for cooperation in areas of wind and thermal energy. He pointed out that the meeting on Joint Anti–Terror Mechanism had been constructive and issues related to the same would be held at level of Home Secretaries. Foreign Minister of Pakistan, Mr. Makhdoom Shah Mehmood Qureshi, stated that Jammu and Kashmir and importance of ceasefire on the Line of Control and the International Border were topics of discussion. He stated that both the countries could reach a conclusion on the resolution of Sir Creek and on Siachen . Trade, energy and SAARC were some other issues highlighted by the Minister.*

**External Affairs Minister of India (Shri Pranab Mukherjee):**

I am glad to welcome Foreign Minister Qureshi on his first visit as Foreign Minister of Pakistan to India. Although this is his first visit as Foreign Minister, he is no stranger to India and has visited us many times in the past. I am glad that, during this visit, he will also be able to take the time to visit Jaipur, Ajmer and Chandigarh.

As you are aware, I visited Pakistan last month for meetings with the leadership of Pakistan and for consultations with my colleague, Foreign Minister Qureshi, on the Composite Dialogue. We had noted then that the Composite Dialogue process has substantial achievements to its credit. This process has proved to be a useful instrument for developing and enhancing our bilateral relations. It is our expectation that the 5th Round of this process, to be launched in July, will be even more fruitful than the earlier rounds.

Since my visit to Pakistan, we have had a visit by the Deputy Chairperson of the Pakistan Planning Commission to India for discussions with our Planning Commission. There was a very useful exchange of views and the realization that both countries can benefit from each other's experience substantially. Issues of energy security, food security, poverty alleviation, amongst others, are challenges which confront both our countries. Our cooperation in these areas fruitfully contributes to the ongoing process within SAARC. I am happy to note that certain ideas for cooperation are emerging in the areas of wind and thermal energy.

The Joint Anti–Terror Mechanism also met in Islamabad recently and the discussions in that meeting were constructive. Terrorism is a threat to the stability of our respective democratic frameworks. Whatever may be our political differences, we have to be unambiguous in addressing the terrorist threat. We hope that in its future meetings, as well as through the Home Secretary level dialogue on terrorism, concrete results, including exchange of information on terrorists and terrorist incidents, will emerge. On our part, we are committed to peace, friendship and good neighbourly relations with Pakistan and to develop these relations in an atmosphere free of violence or the threat to use violence. Such an atmosphere has to be positively promoted.

We have had a useful exchange of views today, both as a follow up to our meeting in Islamabad in May and also to build on developments since then. Our discussions covered different aspects of our relationship, including economic and commercial cooperation, political issues, promoting people-to-people contact as also a very useful exchange of views on the regional situation. I believe we both have certain ideas on the table for detailed technical follow up in the Composite Dialogue once the Fifth Round begins at the Secretaries' level.

The resurgence of democracy and popular participation in Pakistan is a positive factor for our bilateral relationship and indeed for our whole region. The scope for cooperation is immense and covers all fields. We need to deepen the levels of our cooperation in the economic and commercial fields. What has been achieved is significant, but represents no more than a small fraction of our potential. We hope that in the Fifth Round of the Composite Dialogue, concrete achievements will continue and pave the way for a qualitative transformation of our bilateral relations.

I will now read the agreed outcomes of our meeting after which, I will invite the Foreign Minister of Pakistan to make his remarks:

**Agreed Outcomes**

1. The Vth Round of the Composite Dialogue would be launched on 21-22 July 2008 with discussions on:

(*i*) Peace and security including CBMs.

(*ii*) Jammu and Kashmir

The Foreign Secretary of Pakistan will visit New Delhi for this meeting.

2. The Technical Working Group on cross LoC Confidence Building Measures will meet in Islamabad on 10 July, 2008 to concretize decisions regarding bus services, trade and truck services across the LoC announced in May, 2008.

3.The Technical Working Groups of the India Pakistan Joint Economic Commission complete their meetings such that the Joint Commission could meet by the end of the year.

4.The respective Deputy Chairs of the Indian and Pakistan Planning Commission had felt that an institutional mechanism for regular dialogue and exchange of views between them would be useful. The modalities and framework can be evolved through mutual consultations.

5. We also noted the detailed discussions which took place on issues such as wind and thermal power and power supply arrangements and issues. The mutually beneficial cooperation in Rapid Mass Transport Systems – in particular the Metro – was also noted. We hope that these discussions will be followed up by concrete proposals for bilateral cooperation.

6. After completing their visit to jails in Pakistan, the India Pakistan Judicial Committee on Prisoners will now visit jails in India in the month of July to make further recommendations with regard to issues concerning prisoners and fishermen in custody. We agreed that the work of the Judicial Committee has proved to be an effective way to proceed with the issues arising from prisoners and fishermen in custody and hope that the implementation of the recommendations of the Committee would speedily address the humanitarian aspects of this issue.

7. We noted that the Railway authorities had agreed to increase interchange of rakes to five daily from current levels of two daily. The proposal of opening the Kokhraphar – Munabao route in freight was also discussed and will be examined.

8. We noted that the third meeting of the Anti-Terrorism Mechanism was held in Islamabad on 24th June. We decided that the meetings would henceforth be held regularly.

I am very glad once again to welcome the Foreign Minister of Pakistan and his distinguished delegation to India. I look forward to our continued engagement and interaction.

**Foreign Minister of Pakistan (Mr. Makhdoom Shah Mehmood Qureshi):**

I want to emphasize that the talks that took place between us were cordial and friendly and they were in continuation of the talks that we held in Islamabad. I am of the view that such interaction at this level will advance our relationship and will promote shared interest between the two countries.

We discussed a host of issues – bilateral issues. Obviously, as the Minister for External Affairs has said, the Foreign Secretaries will be meeting on the 21st and 22nd of July, that is very very soon. They will be discussing a number of issues. In Jammu and Kashmir, peace and security are issues that will be focused on in those talks. But we also, in our talks, exchanged the significance and importance of ceasefire on the Line of Control and the International Border. And we are both of the view that that has by and large been upheld by both sides, respected by both sides; and it is in our mutual interest to maintain that.

While acknowledging the progress that we have made in the four rounds of talks, I urged the Minister for External Affairs to give serious thought to outstanding disputes that need our consideration. I have come to India with a very positive agenda, with a very positive frame of mind; and I have come representing a democratically elected government; I have come representing a coalition of political parties that feels that a positive movement towards peace and stability and normalization is in our mutual interest. We both stand to gain if our bilateral relations improve on the political as well as the economic front.

As Foreign Minister has said, for the Fifth Round the dates have been announced. And I also want to share with you that the commitments made by the Government of Pakistan on the 21st of May in Islamabad have been honoured. We had said that the Joint Anti-Terrorism Mechanism Committee meeting will take place and it did take place on the 24th of June. And in our discussions we have concluded that a regular exchange will be mutually beneficial. We had agreed upon that the meeting of the

Working Groups on Cross LoC CBMs is to take place and it will take place. Pakistan will host this on the 8th of July.

As I said earlier on, I have come with a very realistic agenda. I personally feel that people on both sides want movement. They want progress; they want peace; they want stability; because they realize that South Asia is lagging behind. South Asia is lagging behind because both of us have not been able to fully concentrate on our social sectors, on developing our infrastructures to the extent that we could have. This region has a huge potential and we should optimally utilize that potential. And we can only do so if there is stability and there is peace.

I am of the view that the areas that we can very quickly move on, which will have a very positive impact on South Asia and the whole environment, are four in nature, and I discussed them in my talks with the Minister for External Affairs. I personally feel resolution of Sir Creek is doable. I am of the view that Siachen issue can be resolved. I am of the view that liberalization of visas is to our mutual advantage and will promote people-to-people contact. And the experience that we have had in people-to-people contact is that people when they visited each other have come back with fond memories and have developed friendships, and want to come back again and want to go back to each other's countries. The fourth area I think is economic cooperation and trade. We have recognized the fact that there has been movement, there has been considerable progress, but we are nowhere near the vast potential that exists between the two countries.

We also discussed how to revitalize SAARC as a forum for regional cooperation and mutual benefit, and I have suggested that in the Summit that will take place in Colombo we will put forth certain ideas on a number of focused areas.

I also urged and laid emphasis on a decision, for a quick decision on the IPI gas pipeline which I feel is to our mutual benefit. Both sides stand to gain and this pipeline can be a pipeline of peace and a new bond.

On the issue of prisoners, I did bring to the notice of the Minister for External Affairs certain mishandling and unfortunately the coverage that was reported in the press. It is a humanitarian issue. We have agreed to a mechanism and the recommendations of the Judicial Committee on Prisoners and the Consular Access Agreement that we have signed in Islamabad should be followed in letter and spirit.

In conclusion, what I want to say is that the political environment to make the peace process result-oriented is right on both sides. And as I said earlier on, I am of the view that the people on both sides are ahead of the Governments. The Governments have to show the political will and they have to give leadership to this process which is to our mutual advantage.

I feel this is a unique opportunity because all the major political players, whether on this side of the border or that side of the border, are supportive of this movement. Whether it is the Congress-led coalition in Delhi or it is the PPP-led coalition in Pakistan, major players whether it is the BJP, the Opposition here, or major opposition parties in Pakistan, there is a virtual consensus on movement and normalization. We must cease this opportunity, we have the right environment. And we must not miss this opportunity. It will be a great loss, if we fail and miss this opportunity.

I think a positive movement will give confidence and revitalize the faith of the people in the process. We are political parties; we are political leaders; and we have to carry our people along. And I think the people will support this positive movement.

I once again expressed our very keen desire that Prime Minister Manmohan Singh visits Pakistan. His visit is long overdue. We are looking forward to his visit to Islamabad. And we feel that that visit could be positive and add a new chapter in our relations.

Question (Mr. Khalid Ahmed, Express TV, Pakistan): My question is addressed to Mr. Mukherjee.

What is the future of the IPI gas pipeline? Will India be committed to this project?

External Affairs Minister of India: We have discussed Iran-Pakistan-India gas pipeline during my visit and during this visit. We are hopeful that it would be possible to resolve this issue both on technical, commercial and all other aspects so that it contributes substantially to resolve the problem arising out of the high energy prices all over the world and also to resolve to some extent the energy crisis which many countries including ours are facing.

Foreign Minister of Pakistan: May I add to that? I am of the view, and I discussed it with the Minister for External Affairs, that the energy prices have gone berserk and both countries are suffering on account of that. You know, the subsidies both countries are providing on petroleum products are immense and really are contributing to our fiscal problems. This is a project that can help us mitigate our problems vis-à-vis energy shortages. Pakistan's requirements are growing at seven per cent per annum and so are India's. Indian economy is growing at a rapid pace. We need energy and this is a project which is a doable project. It so happens that I am holding the portfolio of Petroleum and Natural Resources as well, and later in the day I will be meeting the Minister for Petroleum Mr. Murli Deora and I will discuss in detail this project. Pakistan is keen to move ahead and I would want to seek his input whether India is ready to fully engage with us or would they like to spend some more time thinking about it.

Question (Mr. Srinjoy Choudhuri, Times TV, India): Question for the Foreign Minister of Pakistan. Sir, you have spoken about the abolition of the death penalty. Where does that leave Sarabjit Singh? Is the Government of Pakistan actively considering commuting the sentence?

And question for External Affairs Minister. Sir, the Government of India has spoken about being determined to go to Vienna and signing the Safeguards Agreement. Can you give us a timeline? Also, is the Government talking with the Samajwadi Party?

Foreign Minister of Pakistan: My answer is a very brief one. Yes, Sarabjit Singh's case is under consideration.

External Affairs Minister of India: You are aware that we are currently engaged in resolving these issues and I do hope through the discussions of all the parties concerned it will be possible to arrive at an acceptable solution. Of course, I am aware about the constraints of time. But at the same time we shall have to keep in view the concerns expressed from different sections are to be addressed adequately.

Question (Geo TV, Pakistan): My question is addressed to Pranab Mukherjee. Prime Minister of India Manmohan Singh is visiting Pakistan, as we understand from media and Minister Qureshi already talked about the visit, do you think that the resolution of such kind of less complicated issues like Siachen and Sir Creek will be possible before his visit and during his visit to Pakistan? Is there any possibility?

External Affairs Minister of India: Prime Minister has accepted the invitation from Pakistan and he has agreed to visit Pakistan. We are working out on the date of his visit as per mutual convenience. I do hope shortly we will be able to finalize the date.

Question (Ranjit Kumar, Navbharat Times, India): My question is addressed to the Foreign Minister of Pakistan. It is related to the Siachen issue which has just been asked. You said that the Siachen issue can be resolved. I want to know as to why it has still not been possible to resolve. What are the areas of difference between the two countries?

Foreign Minister of Pakistan: Well, it is certainly not going to be resolved in front of the press in Delhi right now. But I think, as I said earlier on, we were close to a resolution. I think it is a resolvable issue. It is a doable question. I think both sides stand to gain if this issue is resolved. There is a huge financial and human loss being incurred on both sides. There are environmental issues that need to be considered. But there is a forum to discuss that and this is not the forum.

Question (Pak Media): My question is about the CBMs across the LoC. Do you think that during your discussion today, both in the delegation-level talks and your one-to-one meeting, some new initiatives were discussed? What about the implementation of those which have been pending for two-three years?

External Affairs Minister of India: Yes, confidence-building measures on the cross-LoC issues are being considered and we have taken certain steps. As you are fully aware, certain positive and concrete steps have been taken to ease the problem, particularly to facilitate the people-to-people contacts across the LoC. We have peace and tranquility on the border all along the LoC since November, 2003. Of course, in the recent weeks there have been some aberrations. But we do hope it would be possible for us as both countries are trying to restore the normalcy and to maintain peace and tranquility on the border, and to address these issues at the expert level; and thereafter of course the final solution will be taken at the political level.

Foreign Minister of Pakistan: May I just add to what the External Minister has said on the cross LoC CBMs?

We are of the view, Pakistan is of the view, that they have been useful, and they have been beneficial, and there is need for more such CBMs; and we will look into other CBMs that will promote this kind of environment. We also need to examine the status of implementation of the CBMs that are already in place and I am sure the Working Group constituted for this purpose will certainly look into this.

Question (D'Souza, Headlines Today, India): My question is to Pakistan Foreign Minister. Sir, you speak of speeding up decision on the gas pipeline. But as far as India is concerned there have been two areas of concern that of the short supply and security. Could you tell me what assurances have you given the Indian Government on these two fronts? My second question is, can you give us some clarity on the situation in Peshawar? What is the security situation as of today?

Foreign Minister of Pakistan: Let me address the pipeline first. You see, we are not trying to reinvent the wheel here. There are many such international experiences in front of us, and international securities can be built into. The will is there, the desire should be there, and the need is there. Given that, I think we can do it. There are mechanisms in the past that have worked well. They have worked well under testing conditions. And let me add, the mechanism of resolution of the water dispute that we have had, the Indus Waters Treaty, has withstood the test of time. If we can work out issues as complicated as water, then the gas pipeline is chicken feed according to that.

Responding to the second part of the question, yes, Pakistan is dealing with this menace of terrorism and we are dealing with it in a very effective manner. We have evolved a new strategy, a three-pronged strategy. And that is: we will engage politically with the positive element that does not believe in violence that does not believe in taking up arms, we would concentrate on socioeconomic development of that area, tribal belt and the border area; and if required, we will use force when required. As far as Peshawar is concerned, Peshawar is secure and we will defend our integrity and our borders; and we know how to do that.

(*Source*: http://meaindia.nic.in/secframe.php?sec=ta)

## Joint Statement issued after Foreign Minister Level Review of the Fourth Round of Composite Dialogue, Islamabad

May 21, 2008

*The Foreign Minister of Pakistan, Makhdoom Shah Mahmood Qureshi, and External Affairs Minister of India, Mr. Pranab Mukherjee, met in Islamabad to review the progress made in the Fourth Round of Pakistan-India Composite Dialogue. The two sides signed the Agreement on Consular Access, which was finalised during the fourth round of Composite Dialogue. Both sides exchanged views on Siachen and reiterated their commitment towards seeking an early amicable solution. Both sides emphasized the need for further strengthening cooperation to eliminate drug trafficking and welcomed the finalization of an MOU on Cooperation between Pakistan's Anti-Narcotics Force and Narcotics Control Board of India. The two Foreign Ministers also exchanged views on promoting the Pakistan-India peace process, reinvigoration of SAARC and agreed to work towards promoting regional cooperation for enabling South Asia to realize its full development potential.*

1. The Foreign Minister of Pakistan, Makhdoom Shah Mahmood Qureshi, and External Affairs Minister of India, Mr. Pranab Mukherjee, met in Islamabad on 21 May 2008 to review the progress made in the Fourth Round of Pakistan-India Composite Dialogue. This was preceded by a meeting between the Foreign Secretary of Pakistan, Mr. Salman Bashir and Foreign Secretary of India, Mr. Shivshankar Menon, on 20 May 2008.

2. The talks were held in a friendly and constructive atmosphere.

3. They reviewed the progress made in the Fourth Round of the Composite Dialogue encompassing (i) Peace and Security, including CBMs; (ii) Jammu and Kashmir; (iii) Siachen; (iv) Sir Creek; (v) Wullar Barrage/Tulbul Navigation Project; (vi) Terrorism and Drug Trafficking; (vii) Economic and Commercial Cooperation; and (viii) Promotion of Friendly Exchanges in Various Fields.

4 They noted the positive contribution to improvement of relations by the Composite Dialogue process since its resumption after the joint statement of 6 January 2004 and the subsequent Summit Statements of 25

September 2004, 18 April 2005, 14 September 2005 and 16 September 2006. The Ministers reaffirmed their determination not to let terrorism impede the peace process and take all necessary steps to eliminate this scourge against humanity. They further resolved to carry forward the peace process and to maintain its momentum.

5. The Ministers noted that in 2007 and over the course of the Fourth Round of Composite Dialogue there had been a number of important bilateral achievements, including:

- MoU to increase the frequencies, designated airlines and points of call in either country.
- Agreement for the trucks from one side to cross the border up to designated points on the other side at the Wagah-Attari border.
- Increase in frequency of Delhi- Lahore bus service from two to three trips per week.
- Signing of Agreement on 'Reducing the Risk from Accidents relating to Nuclear Weapons'.
- MoU between the Securities and Exchange Board of India (SEBI) and Securities and Exchange Commission of Pakistan (SECP) to facilitate the sharing of information between two agencies.
- Completion of the Joint Survey of Sir Creek and adjoining areas.
- Two meetings of the Joint Anti-Terrorism Mechanism.

6. The two sides signed the Agreement on Consular Access, which was finalised during the Fourth round of Composite Dialogue.

7. They exchanged views on the issue of Jammu and Kashmir and agreed to continue discussions to build on convergences and narrow down divergences. They also agreed to continue with the implementation of Cross-LoC CBMs with a view to enhancing interaction and cooperation across the LoC. In this regard, they decided:

a) To increase the frequency of Muzaffarabad -Srinagar and Rawalkot-Poonch Bus service from a fortnightly to a weekly basis.
b) To finalize modalities for intra-Kashmir trade and truck service as early as possible.
c) To implement other measures to expand and facilitate travel a meeting of Working Group on Cross-LoC CBMs would be convened within two months.

8. They reaffirmed the importance of ceasefire in place since November 2003 and the commitment of both sides to cooperate to safeguard it.

9. They agreed that progress has been made under the Composite Dialogue process on promoting a stable environment of Peace and Security including CBMs. The Expert Groups on Nuclear and Conventional CBMs

should consider existing and additional proposals by both sides with a view to developing further confidence building measures in the nuclear and conventional fields.

10. Both sides exchanged views on Siachen and reiterated their commitment to seeking an early amicable solution.

11. Both sides expressed satisfaction on the progress made on Sir Creek, with the completion of the joint survey, the exchange of maps, and the discussions thereafter. They agreed to further facilitate the process for an early resolution of this issue.

12. Both sides reiterated their commitment to fight terrorism in all its forms and manifestations, and re-emphasized the need for effective steps for the complete elimination of this menace. In this context, it was agreed to continue cooperation in the Joint Anti-Terrorism Mechanism whose next meeting would be held within two months. Both sides agreed to refrain from hostile propaganda.

13. Both sides emphasized the need for further strengthening cooperation to eliminate drug trafficking and welcomed the finalization of an MOU on Cooperation between Pakistan's Anti-Narcotics Force and Narcotics Control Board of India.

14. Both sides reiterated the importance of enhancing mutually beneficial economic and commercial cooperation and agreed to discuss further steps for facilitating trade and redressing the trade imbalance. In this regard, Indian and Pakistan Railway officials would meet in June for resolving all technical issues to enable increase in to and fro freight movement. They also agreed to facilitate the process of early opening of bank branches in the two countries.

15. Both sides appreciated the work being done by the Judicial Committee on Prisoners, which will meet in Pakistan shortly; welcomed the finalization of the Consular Access Agreement that will help addressing humanitarian aspects relating to persons under detention in each other's country and; agreed to provide on a regular basis updated and comprehensive list of prisoners in each other jails.

16. Both sides agreed to the need for promoting friendly exchanges between the two countries.

17. Both sides agreed to the early finalization of the Visa Agreement which will help liberalize the visa regime and facilitate people-to-people contacts.

18. The two Ministers reiterated their commitment to the Iran-Pakistan-India gas pipeline project and had a useful exchange of views in this regard.

19. The two Foreign Ministers also exchanged views on promoting the Pakistan-India peace process, reinvigoration of SAARC and agreed to work towards promoting regional cooperation for enabling South Asia to

realize its full development potential. It was agreed to work for promoting sustainable development and food and energy security.

20. It was decided that the two Foreign Secretaries will launch the Fifth Round of the Composite Dialogue in New Delhi in July 2008.

21. The External Affairs Minister of India, Mr. Pranab Mukherjee, called on the President and the Prime Minister of Pakistan.

(*Source*: http://meaindia.nic.in/)

## Joint Press Statement after the first meeting of the India-Pakistan Joint Judicial Committee on Prisoners

February 27, 2008

*The first meeting of the India-Pakistan Joint Judicial Committee on Prisoners was held in New Delhi on 26th February 2008. It agreed to visit jails in Pakistan in April 2008 through diplomatic channels.*

The first meeting of the India-Pakistan Joint Judicial Committee on Prisoners was held in New Delhi on 26th February 2008. The Committee was formed in January 2007 by the External Affairs Minister of India and the Foreign Minister of Pakistan to recommend steps for humane treatment and expeditious release of prisoners of the respective countries in each other's jails.

The members of the Committee are Justice (Retd) Mr. Nagendra Rai, Justice (Retd) Mr. Amarjeet Choudhary, Justice (Retd) Mr. A.S. Gill and Justice (Retd) Mr. M.A. Khan from the Indian side and Justice (Retd) Mr. Abdul Qadeer Chaudhary, Justice (Retd) Mr. Fazal Karim, Justice (Retd) Mr. Nasir Aslam Zahid, and Justice (Retd) Mr. Mian Muhammad Ajmal from the Pakistan side.

The Committee recommended to the two Governments that:

a) A consolidated list with full particulars and their present status of nationals in each others' jails be exchanged on 31st March 2008;
b) Prisoners who have completed their sentences and whose national status has been verified be released forthwith;
c) Special consideration, on compassionate and humanitarian basis, be accorded to women, juvenile and disabled prisoners for their repatriation;
d) As agreed between the two Governments, those fishermen in custody whose nationality status is confirmed be released forthwith and in remaining cases, Consular Access be provided by 31st March 2008;
e) All efforts be made to arrange early release of all those prisoners, accused or convicted of minor offences, once their nationality status is confirmed; and

f) Each country may immediately notify the other of the arrest of its nationals and provide Consular Access expeditiously.

The Committee also agreed to visit jails in Pakistan in April 2008 on dates agreed through diplomatic channels. This would be followed by a return visit to Indian jails.

(*Source*: http://meaindia.nic.in/)

## Joint Statement after the first meeting of the India-Pakistan Standing Committee on Bus Services

February 21, 2008

*The first meeting of the India-Pakistan Standing Committee on Delhi–Lahore, Amritsar-Lahore and Amritsar-Nankana Sahib Bus Services was held in New Delhi on February 21, 2008. It has been decided to increase the frequency of Delhi – Lahore bus service from two trips per week to three trips per week from each side.*

1. The first meeting of the India-Pakistan Standing Committee on Delhi–Lahore, Amritsar-Lahore and Amritsar-Nankana Sahib Bus Services was held in New Delhi on February 21, 2008. The Indian delegation was led by Mr. Saroj Kumar Dash, Joint Secretary (Transport), Ministry of Shipping, Road Transport and Highways and the Pakistan delegation was led by Mr. Mohammad Abbas, Additional Secretary, Ministry of Communications.

2. Both sides noted with satisfaction the continuing operations of the bus services and discussed further measures for its improvement. It has been decided to increase the frequency of Delhi – Lahore bus service from two trips per week to three trips per week from each side. It was also decided to rationalise the bus fare. In addition, the quota for the return tickets would be increased from the existing 6 (six) seats to 10 (ten) seats.

3. The two sides agreed that enroute, the Amritsar – Nankana Sahib bus service would make a halt at Lahore to enable the passengers to disembark/embark whereas, Lahore- Amritsar bus service would continue to operate as per existing arrangement.

4. It was decided that the concerned financial officials of the two sides would meet every year, alternately in Delhi and Lahore, in July for reconciliation of accounts.

5. The new arrangements will come into effect from March 17, 2008.

6. The meeting was held in a friendly and cordial atmosphere.

(*Source*: http://meaindia.nic.in/secframe.php?sec=js)

## MOU on Air Service Agreement between Pakistan and India

February 15, 2008

*The MoU on Air Service Agreement between Pakistan and India took review of the aviation industry, emphasizing the connectivity between two countries. Against the two destinations presently available to the designated airlines in each other's territory, Chennai was added for the designated airlines of Pakistan and Islamabad was added for the designated airlines of India.*

1. The delegations representing the Government of the Islamic Republic of Pakistan and the Government of the Republic of India met in Rawalpindi on 14-15 February, 2008 for consultations on air services matters. The Pakistan delegation was headed by Major General Mir Haider Ali Khan, Additional Secretary, Ministry of Defence, whereas the Indian side was led by Mr. Kanu Gohain, Director General Civil Aviation. The consultations were held in a friendly and cordial atmosphere.

2. Both delegations recognized that in the wake of developments which have taken place in the aviation industry during the past few years, the existing Air Services Agreement needs to be reviewed and updated.

3. It was agreed that each country shall henceforth be entitled to designate three airlines each to operate the agreed services on the specified routes. Presently only one airline each operates between India and Pakistan.

4. It was also agreed to increase the frequency of flights per week from 12 to 28 for each side.

5. Against the two destinations presently available to the designated airlines in each other's territory, it was agreed to add Chennai for the designated airlines of Pakistan and Islamabad for the designated airlines of India, as third destination. This also enables direct air connectivity between the capitals of the two countries.

6. Both delegations also agreed to meet again at a mutually convenient date within one year to review the capacity / frequency framework and additional destinations in each others territory, keeping in view the market demand.

7. A Memorandum of Understanding (MoU) was signed by the leaders of the two delegations today containing the above agreed elements.

8. Both sides expressed satisfaction that the new arrangement would further the objective of facilitating people to people contact, business and trade activities between the two countries.

(*Source*: http://www.mofa.gov.pk/Press_Releases/2008/Feb/PR_030_08.htm)

# 18.

# BILATERAL RELATIONS WITH AFGHANISTAN

## Afghanistan-Pakistan: Shared Security and Development Concerns[1]

October 27, 2008

*The Foreign Minister of Pakistan, Mr Shah Mehmood Qureshi pointed out that no two countries are as closely linked as Pakistan and Afghanistan and emphasized that the new democratic government of Pakistan would be deeply committed to the cause of peace, stability and prosperity not only in Pakistan, but in the whole region. Highlighting the common challenges faced by both the countries, the Minister stated that Afghanistan and Pakistan had both suffered immensely and continue to suffer at the hands of extremism, militancy and terrorism. The Minister stated that Pakistan fully subscribed to the Jirga process and the decisions of the 'Kabul Peace Jirga' and pointed out that both Afghanistan and Pakistan needed peace.*

No two countries are as closely linked as Pakistan and Afghanistan. Our ties are abiding and deep. Our cultures and customs, folklore, languages and literature, our heroes and histories are all common. Above all we share our glorious and eternal faith – Islam. Our concerns and aspirations are common.

When calamity afflicts one country, the other cries in pain. Our destinies are interlinked. Therefore, be it the Soviet occupation of Afghanistan, or the tragic earthquake of October 2005, throughout history, our two peoples have stood resolutely by each other.

As you all are aware, since the holding of the Joint Peace Jirga last year in Kabul, Pakistan has undergone a major transition to full democracy. The new democratic government of Pakistan is deeply committed to the

1. Statement by the Foreign Minister of Pakistan at the Inaugural Session of the Pak-Afghan Jirgagai, October 27, 2008.

cause of peace, stability and prosperity not only in Pakistan, but in the whole region.

Our government has already made a new beginning in the Pak-Afghan relations, restoring a climate of trust and confidence. Today, both countries are constructively engaged with each other in all spheres. Together we are developing a forward-looking vision of peace, prosperity and development for our peoples and the region.

Afghanistan and Pakistan have both suffered immensely and continue to suffer at the hands of extremism, militancy and terrorism. This is the gravest threat to both countries. Pakistan and Afghanistan, therefore, need to cooperate closely to effectively counter and completely eliminate this curse.

Thirty years ago, when a superpower marched into Afghanistan, the landscape of our region changed tragically and irrevocably. Afghanistan got mired in a prolonged conflict as the last theater of the cold war. Millions of innocent Afghans lost their lives. Millions others were displaced from their homes and forced to seek refuge outside their homeland. It was a humanitarian catastrophe of unprecedented scale. With open hearts and open arms, Pakistanis welcomed their Afghan brethren, and did everything within their means to mitigate their suffering. Your pain was our pain; your anguish was our anguish.

The Afghan jihad altered the course of history. The cold war came to an end and the Soviet Union unraveled. Yet as the world enjoyed the dividends of peace, the valiant Afghan sacrifices went unacknowledged and uncelebrated. Afghanistan, and with it Pakistan, suffered at the hands of international neglect. Our societies suffered deeply as a result of free flow of weapons, drugs and the insidious spread of extremist ideologies. This in turn led to the spread of militancy and terrorism.

Pervasive poverty, widespread illiteracy and lack of employment opportunities provided fertile ground for the rapid growth of extremism and terrorism.

Afghanistan, which was the main theater of jihad against the Soviet Union, in the eighties converted into a stage of intense infighting following the Soviet withdrawal. The political vacuum thus created, led to the Talibanization of Afghanistan.

The Taliban in Afghanistan were subsequently hijacked by Al-Qaeda converting Afghanistan into a breeding ground of extremism and terrorism. All these developments not only devastated Afghanistan but also had serious negative implications on Pakistan. Afghanistan and Pakistan have suffered together and together they need to reverse the tragic legacy of the past three decades.

The Joint Peace Jirga held in Kabul, in August, last year was a historic first people-to-people contact. It was a bold initiative to address the challenges of insecurity, militancy, terrorism and to redress a wide range of socio-economic and developmental issues concerning both countries.

The Peace Jirga Declaration, concluded on the basis of time-tested tribal traditions, customs and Revaj, reflected an overwhelming consensus among our two peoples for partnership and peace, stability and progress in the region.

It recognized terrorism as an anti-humanity phenomenon and against the spirit and essence of our eternal faith – Islam. It further recognized terrorism and extremism as a common threat to both countries. It called for a concerted campaign against terrorism. It also took note of the nexus between terrorism and narcotics.

The Peace Jirga emphasized the importance of brotherly relations in pursuance of policies of mutual respect, non-interference and peaceful coexistence.

In short, it laid a broad framework for the two countries to move forward, in a constructive, cooperative and meaningful manner.

Pakistan fully subscribes to the Jirga process and the decisions of the 'Kabul Peace Jirga'. The democratic government in Pakistan accords top priority to effectively deal with the menace of terrorism and enjoys broad-based support in this regard. It is also the resolve of the Government of Pakistan to cooperate closely with the brotherly people and the Government of Afghanistan in overcoming their difficulties emanating from terrorism.

Our government has always stood up to its responsibility of resolutely tackling extremism and terrorism. Thousands of innocent civilians have fallen victim to terrorism in Pakistan. The tragic loss of our great leader Mohtarma Benazir Bhutto Shaheed has strengthened our determination to close our ranks against this lethal threat. Our armed forces and people have joined hands and are fully mobilized against it. A democratic polity draws its strength from the mandate of the people. It has a much greater chance of success than a dictatorship. Today, Pakistan is more committed than ever not to allow anyone to use its soil for nefarious activities against its own or Afghanistan's interest.

A few days ago, the Parliament of Pakistan spoke decisively on the issue of terrorism. Representatives of the people of Pakistan unanimously declared the nation's firm resolve to stand united against this growing menace, and to address its root causes. Pakistan's territory shall not be used for any kind of attacks on other countries, and foreign fighters, if found, will be expelled from our soil. At the same time, Pakistan's sovereignty and territorial integrity shall be safeguarded at all costs. Dialogue will be given high priority with all those willing to abide by the Constitution of Pakistan and rule of law and development of the affected areas will be expedited.

The charter given to this Government by the Parliament will henceforth guide our actions and policies. We shall not deviate from this course.

The Jirgagai is being held in pursuance of the decisions of the Peace Jirga. Its mandate is clear. You have been tasked to expedite the on-going process of dialogue for peace and reconciliation with the opposition, to monitor and oversee implementation of the decisions of the Joint Peace Jirga and plan and facilitate the convening of the next Grand Peace Jirga. The mandate of Jirgagai is short in words but vast in scope.

There is an increasing realization that the use of force alone cannot yield the desired results. For lasting success, negotiations and reconciliation must be an essential part of the process. The wrongs and neglect of the past must be corrected. Political, economic and social reforms must proceed hand in hand. We must not shut doors of negotiations to those sons of the soil willing to forsake the path of violence. With a patient ear, we must listen to them, and let them be heard.

I have full faith in your sagacity and wisdom as revered leaders. You represent a wide spectrum of political, regional and ethnic mix in both countries. The distinguished Jirgagai members imbibe the true spirit of tribal traditions and wisdom in peacefully resolving complex issues. We have full trust in your collective wisdom and your ability to navigate your way to success.

Both Afghanistan and Pakistan need peace. Both need a healing touch. We owe it to posterity to work towards it. Peace will lead to prosperity. In my mind, a day will come InshaAllah, in the not too distant a future, when Pakistan and Afghanistan will serve as an integrated gateway for the region and beyond.

When gas pipelines and transit corridors will traverse our territories. When the peoples of the two countries will enjoy the fruits of peace and prosperity, and when narcotics and terrorism will be but a distant memory.

The future I foresee is well within our reach. The Jirga process holds the promise of morphing this vision into reality. I wish you great success.

(*Source*: http://www.mofa.gov.pk/Press_Releases/2008/Oct/PR_328_08.htm)

## Transcript of Foreign Minister Makhdoom Shah Mahmood Qureshi's Statement at the Joint Press Statement with Afghan Foreign Minister Dr. Rangin Dadfar Spanta

June 6, 2008

*The Foreign Minister of Pakistan pointed out that he along with Dr. Rangin Dadfar Spanta, the Afghan Foreign Minister had decided to reinvigorate ties between the two countries with the aim of nurturing mutual trust and understanding. He emphasized as militancy and extremism were a common threat to both the countries, the progress on the Joint Peace Jirga process would be an ongoing effort undertaken with the aim of confidence building between the two countries. He added that the prospects of Afghanistan being the land bridge for Asia should be explored.*

It is a matter of profound pleasure for me to visit Afghanistan on the invitation of my friend and colleague, Foreign Minister Dr. Rangin Dadfar Spanta. This is my maiden visit to Kabul, and among the first few I have undertaken after taking over as Foreign Minister of Pakistan. I am most impressed by the traditional warmth and hospitality that has been extended to my delegation. For this, may I express my gratitude.

Besides having discussions with the Foreign Minister, I will have the privilege of calling on President Karzai, and benefiting from his wise counsel.

I have come here to underscore the immense importance the new leadership of Pakistan attaches to relations with Afghanistan. In April earlier this year, Dr. Spanta and I had decided to reinvigorate our two countries' age-old ties, and pursue mutually beneficial cooperation with a renewed sense of vigour, and in a spirit of complete mutual trust and understanding.

This morning, I am happy to report that we have taken forward this process. Our consultations have covered the entire gamut of bilateral relations, as well as a range of issues of mutual concern, and regional significance.

Militancy and extremism pose a grave challenge to the security of both our countries. Dr. Spanta and I have agreed on the need for broad based and coordinated efforts to curb this twin menace. To this end, we have reviewed progress on the Joint Peace Jirga Process. This will not be allowed to lose momentum. Pakistan will shortly host the next meeting of the mini Jirga in Islamabad .

Pakistan and Afghanistan are facing the common challenge of terrorism and extremism. In Pakistan's view peace is indivisible. I have explained that the recent peace deals in the Tribal Areas were not made with the militants but with the tribal elders, and are aimed at weaning the hard core militants away from those willing to negotiate. While pursuing the political tract, Pakistan has not forgone the military option, nor have we been negligent of our obligation towards peace and stability in Afghanistan. We have not, and will not negotiate with those who are unwilling to forsake the path of violence and destruction. In tackling terrorism in our region, we do not make any distinction between the interests of Pakistan and those of Afghanistan. Pakistan also supports Afghan government's efforts for national reconciliation.

We have also availed this opportunity to discuss the agenda of the forthcoming Paris Conference, where I will be leading the Pakistan delegation. At the Conference, Pakistan will join Afghanistan in calling for international assistance to be channeled through the Afghan Government, in accordance with its wishes and the needs of its people. Pakistan and Afghanistan will speak with one voice in the Paris Conference.

Pakistan will be hosting later this year, the Third Regional Economic Cooperation Conference on Afghanistan (RECCA). Besides discussing other aspects, the Conference will highlight the prospects Afghanistan holds as Asia's land bridge.

The meetings I have had earlier today are part of a series of consultations which I hope, we will hold regularly with Afghan side. I look forward to working in partnership with my distinguished colleague to explore new horizons for mutually beneficial cooperation. It will be our endeavour to expand our multifaceted ties, even further, to the benefit and advantage of our two peoples.

(*Source*: http://www.mofa.gov.pk/Press_Releases/2008/June/PR_156_08.htm)

# 19.

# BILATERAL RELATIONS WITH CHINA

## Joint Statement between the Islamic Republic of Pakistan and the People's Republic of China

April 15, 2008

*Some of the important issues discussed between China and Pakistan included enhancing cooperative ties in economy, trade, science & technology, culture, and people to people relations. While China expressed its full support to Pakistan to promote its socio-economic development through projects under the Pakistan-China Joint Five Year Economic and Trade Cooperation Plan, Pakistan reiterated its full support for the One China Policy as well as its condemnation and rejection of the three evil forces i.e. secessionism, separatism and terrorism. Some of the MoUs signed between the two countries relate to issues of water, science and technology, culture and communication, amongst many others.*

President Pervez Musharraf visited China on 10-15 April 2008 on the invitation of President Hu Jinta. He was accompanied by Begum Sehba Musharraf.

During the State visit, President of Pakistan held officials talks with President Hu Jintao in Sanya; met Chairman NPC Standing Committee Mr. Wu Bangguo, Premier Wen Jiabao, and Chairman CPPCC Mr. Jia Qinglin in Beijing as well as the leadership of the Xinjiang Uygur Autonomous Region in Urumqi.

In their warm and friendly discussions, the leaders of Pakistan and China underscored the importance of the special relations that so happily exist between the two countries as well as their determination to take Pakistan-China friendship and strategic partnership to new heights.

Both sides expressed complete satisfaction on the development of comprehensive cooperation in all fields and agreed to further enhance their cooperative ties in economy, trade, science & technology, culture, and people to people relations.

China expressed its full support to the efforts of the Government of Pakistan to promote socio-economic development and in this regard expressed its readiness to assist Pakistan for the development of the energy, expressed its readiness to assist Pakistan for the development of the energy, mineral and mining sectors; enhance financial and banking sector cooperation; and extend support for "projects" under the Pakistan-China Joint Five year economic and Trade Cooperation Plan. Both sides agreed to work together to achieve the trade target of $ 15 billion as early as possible.

Both sides also agreed to optimally utilize the bilateral FTA. It was agreed that FTA on Trade in Services will be completed as early as possible.

Both sides agreed to enhance coordination and cooperation between relevant departments and agencies so as to facilitate overland trade between Pakistan and China .

Both sides also agreed to take steps for upgrading transportation and communication networks overland with a view to enhancing connectivity between the bordering regions for mutual benefit. Both sides also agreed to cooperate closely in the fields of water management, environmental protection and bio-diversity.

Both sides agreed to further strengthen defence cooperation and enhance collaboration between their respective defence industries.

China expressed its full support for Pakistan's efforts to preserve its sovereignty, independence, territorial integrity and expressed appreciation for Pakistan's important role in promoting peace, stability and security and its contribution to counter terrorism.

Pakistan reiterated its full support for the One China Policy and the return of Taiwan to motherland as well as its condemnation and rejection of the three evil forces i.e. secessionism, separatism and terrorism.

Both sides exchanged views on regional and global issues and reached common understanding. They agreed to work together closely in global and regional forums to promote the cause of peace and development.

Pakistan warmly congratulated the Chinese leaders and people on their great national accomplishments and expressed joy at the celebrations of the three decades of the policy of economic reforms and opening up.

Pakistan also expressed its appreciation for the excellent arrangements made by the Government and people of China for the holding of the Beijing Olympics and expressed its fullest cooperation and support to the Chinese Government.

President Hu Jintao accepted with pleasure the invitation extended by the President of Pakistan to visit Pakistan at his convenience.

Following Agreements/MOUs were signed during the visit:

- Memorandum of Understanding between the Ministry of Water and Power of the Islamic Republic of Pakistan and the Ministry of Water Resources of the People's Republic of China.
- Memorandum of Understanding on Cooperation in Engineering and Technological Sciences between the Ministry of Science and

Technology of Islamic republic of Pakistan and the Chinese Academy of Engineering of the People's Republic of China.

- Agreement on Sports Cooperation between the Ministry of Sports of the Islamic Republic of Pakistan and the General Administration of Sport of the People's Republic of China.
- Memorandum of Understanding on Cooperation between the Ministry of Finance of the Islamic Republic of Pakistan and Ministry of Finance of the People's Republic of China.
- Memorandum of Understanding for Cooperation on Architectural Design, Research and Constructions between Capital Development Authority (CDA), Islamabad, Pakistan and The Consortium of China Architecture Design & Research Group and Institute of Architecture Design and Research, Chinese Academy of Sciences.
- Memorandum of Understanding for Cooperation in the field of exchange of news between Pakistan Television Corporation and China Central Television Network of the People's Republic of China.
- Memorandum of Understanding for the establishment of Pakistan Culture and communication centre at Tsinghua University .
- Memorandum of Understanding on Economic and Trade Cooperation between the Ministry of Commerce of the Islamic Republic of Pakistan and Foreign Trade and Economic Cooperation Bureau of Xinjiang Uygur Autonomous Region, People's Republic of China.
- Memorandum of Understanding between Board of Investment of the Islamic Republic of Pakistan and China Council for International Investment Promotion on Cooperation in Investment.
- Memorandum of Understanding on establishing relations of Friendship and Good Neighbourly Cooperation between the North West Frontier Province (NWFP) of Islamic Republic of Pakistan and Xinjiang Uygur Autonomous Region.

(*Source*: http://www.mofa.gov.pk/Press_Releases/2008/April/PR_090_08.htm)

# 20.

# BILATERAL RELATIONS WITH UNITED KINGDOM

## Peace & Prosperity in South Asia-Pakistan's Perspective[1]

July 24, 2008

*The Foreign Minister of Pakistan touching upon his country's relations with U.K. noted that U.K. is Pakistan's largest trading partner within the European Union. Food and Energy Security were two themes he extensively focused on. He emphasized that Pakistan is seeking international gas-pipeline option, with which it aims to position itself as an energy hub for South Asia and possibly China through the port of Gwadar. The Minister reiterated his commitment to fight terrorism, and stated that regionally, Pakistan is faced with challenges on two fronts, with Afghanistan on one end and the unresolved Kashmir dispute on the other. He emphasized that resolution of these issues is an imperative for peace and economic prosperity of the region and its people. The Minister also pointed out that Pakistan's nuclear capability must be viewed in the context of India's pursuit of the nuclear option and the overall security concerns.*

I am happy to note that my presence today at this august gathering coincides with the 50th anniversary of the International Institute of Strategic Studies. I may also add that we are pleased to be a dialogue partner of the IISS. The IISS entered into this partnership with our Ministry of Foreign Affairs last year and we already have had our first round of discussions. We are keen to closely cooperate with the IISS and to benefit from its expertise and analysis.

Today I have the pleasure to share my thoughts with you on "Imperatives for Peace & Prosperity in South Asia" from our perspective. I will be glad to answer all your questions at the end. But first a few words on our excellent and long standing relations with the United Kingdom .

Our friendly relations are rooted in a long historical association, which predates our independence. We share many parallels in institutions–

1. Foreign Minister's Address at IISS, London, July 24, 2008.

political, administrative, military and in the education field. These provide a sound basis for mutual understanding and cooperation. Nurturing relations with the UK is a corner stone of our foreign policy. Pakistan views the UK as a key industrialized country with sound opportunities for trade and investment, an important member of the G-8 and the EU, and a comrade in the Commonwealth. The UK is Pakistan's largest trading partner within the EU and the second largest foreign investor. Last but not the least, the presence of around one million Pakistanis in Britain gives added strength to the traditional relationship.

Since 9/11 new chapters have been added to Pakistan-UK relations. These new dimensions include our strategic partnership in the fight against terrorism and extremism and the common endeavour to bring peace and stability to Afghanistan. Our relationship is characterized by numerous exchanges at the political level. New and revived institutional forums for interaction include annual summits, annual bilateral consultations between the Foreign Ministries, Pakistan-UK Defence Cooperation Forum, Joint Judicial Cooperation Working Group, Pakistan-Britain Trade and Investment Forum and Working Group on Counter Terrorism Cooperation. All these forums have held meetings regularly. It is worth mentioning that the UK was the first European country to establish high level contacts with the new democratic government in Pakistan. Several Ministerial level visits have since taken place. I came to the UK in the same spirit of friendship and camaraderie.

Reverting to our topic of discussion today, let me mention that the South Asian region has a concentration of about 1.5 billion people with its woes that are deep-rooted and a cause for human sufferings for decades. Mired in poverty and backwardness, its people have suffered for long and have paid in terms of economic deprivation, adversely affecting the very social fabric of South Asian societies.

I need not elaborate before this gathering of scholars and intellectuals, how poverty and societal fragmentation impact upon t he overall security situation in the region.

The issues and challenges, which are as much of concern to us as they are to you and the world community, are poverty, food and energy security, rampant inflation, rise in oil prices, environmental degradation, illiteracy, unemployment, terrorism and extremism, regional rivalries and conflicts and nuclear non-proliferation.

The new democratic government which took office in Pakistan only a few months back is faced with daunting challenges that it inherited from the previous government. The tragic assassination of our leader Mohtarma Benazir Bhutto Shaheed underscored the serious situation facing the country in terms of extremism and terrorism.

The country is now passing through a transition phase with the government laying the foundation of a long term strategy to address the complexities and challenges that I just mentioned. The government is working out short, medium and long term strategies to grapple with these issues. We are confident that we will overcome these problems with the support and resolve of the people as well as our allies and partners.

**Food & Oil Crises**

For the first time since 1973, the world has been hit by a combination of record high oil prices and food shortages. This has had a destabilizing effect on the global economy which was already facing a slow-down. Food shortages have a severe impact on income distribution, inflation and the incidence of poverty. The challenge to craft appropriate policy responses to the food crisis is made even more difficult by the grave nature of the crisis we face today.

According to FAO statistics, 527 million people are suffering from chronic hunger in South and East Asia. 60% of the world's undernourished population lives in this region. The issue is exacerbated in South Asia where Afghanistan has already appealed for foreign help to combat a wheat shortage while Bangladesh recently warned that it faced a crisis over rice supplies. The United Nations reported in June that Nepal, which imports much of its rice, has 2.5 million people in immediate need of assistance and 3.9 million more whose welfare may be compromised by rising prices.

The paradox is that most of the economies of South Asia are agro-based economies, which have been suffering because of a shift away from agriculture.

Wheat is Pakistanis' staple food. Until the 1980s we were a wheat exporting country. Now, we have to import wheat for domestic consumption. Rising food prices and low purchasing power are leading to increased food insecurity in our country. The situation had been aggravating due to poor government policies in the past, incoherent market prices and exploitation by the traders. The situation in other South Asian countries is no better.

To address this issue the government has announced effective measures such as maintaining price uniformity, checking smuggling and hoarding, providing agricultural incentives, crop insurance and wheat monitoring. Wheat demand from the disadvantaged provinces of NWFP and Balochistan have been given priority.

South Asia is also gravely affected by the energy crisis. The world wide quest for accelerated growth in industry, services and agriculture gives rise to increase in demand for energy.

In this context Pakistan is seeking to pursue international gas-pipeline options, with which we hope we will position ourselves as an energy hub for South Asia and possibly China through the port of Gwadar.

We have a planned gas pipeline from Iran, crossing Pakistan and heading on to India. This project offers not just energy to both nations but could also serve as an incentive for stability in the region. Another pipeline project is from Turkmenistan through Afghanistan into Pakistan and, possibly, onward to India .

We are also making a major endeavour to exploit our substantial coal and hydel resources to meet our energy needs. This is being done both through indigenous and foreign sources. In addition, we are also exploiting, as outlined in our Medium Term Development Framework, wind and solar energy.

**Extremism & Terrorism**

We are playing an active role in the international campaign against terrorism as a frontline State. Pakistan has been a victim of terrorism for decades. Our counter terrorism efforts predate the events of 9/11.

Our commitment to fight terrorism has been unswerving notwithstanding the threats terrorism poses today and the terrorist attacks Pakistan has had to face due to its principled position.

Since last year we have suffered thousands of casualties in various terrorist incidents across Pakistan. In the armed confrontation with the militants more than a thousand of our soldiers have sacrificed their lives.

Our message to terrorists is clear and unequivocal. We will not allow our territory to be used by terrorists and we will not be daunted by the threats of terrorism. At the same time, let me also make clear that Pakistan will not allow foreign troops to operate inside its territory. Military action within our territory is the sole prerogative of the Pakistani armed forces.

We have subscribed to a comprehensive strategy to counter terrorism that includes political, economic and military measures to find immediate and long term solutions to the problem. We wish to address the root causes of terrorism and to suppress it for the long term.

The threat of terrorism transcends national borders. It requires a coordinated and cooperative approach from all States. A long-term strategy needs to be evolved to address the factors which contribute to the growth of terrorism. In my view, primary among these factors are poverty, economic depravation and denial of rights, which fuel extremist tendencies.

The international community will have to ensure that the right of peoples to self-determination is not de-legitimized by associating it with terrorism. The two are clearly distinct and this distinction needs to be maintained through an agreed legal definition of terrorism.

**Afghanistan**

Regionally, Pakistan is faced with challenges mainly on two counts; the conflict in Afghanistan and the unresolved Kashmir dispute. Resolution of these issues is an imperative for peace and economic prosperity of the region and its people.

Afghanistan is a country with which we share ties of religion, history, culture and language. Peace and stability in Afghanistan is of vital interest to Pakistan as it impinges on our own well being and development.

Afghanistan came to centre stage following the Soviet military intervention in 1979. With the exit of the Soviets in 1990, the world attention shifted to Eastern Europe and the disintegration of the Soviet Union. Afghanistan suffered international neglect. Internecine conflict led the country into chaos. As a consequence of thirty years of war a whole generation of Afghans has missed out on education. Pakistan also suffered the consequences of the Afghan war. Firstly, we were burdened with 4 million Afghan refugees. Secondly, Afghanistan became a base for extremist forces, comprising mostly of foreign elements who had come to oust the Soviet Union.

In the transformed post - 9/11 circumstances, the international community has recommitted itself to assist Afghanistan. We have all along supported the Bonn Process and the government of President Karzai and his efforts to help restore normalcy and stability in Afghanistan. An Afghanistan at peace with itself is important for Pakistan and vital for the stability and economic progress of the entire region. We therefore call upon the international community to help restore Afghanistan's past glory and to help in its reconstruction and rehabilitation.

Despite our limited resources, we are contributing to this process and have accorded unrestricted transit access to land-locked Afghanistan, invested heavily in the Afghan economy and are helping to re-build its infrastructure. We recently responded to their call to meet their wheat requirements despite shortage in our own country.

Pakistan is fully aware of the threat to Afghanistan's sovereignty and territorial integrity. We are doing all we can to ensure that our territory is not used as a staging ground for attacks into Afghanistan. We have deployed more than 100,000 troops on our common border for this purpose. We have good intelligence sharing cooperation with Afghanistan in order to apprehend terrorists on both sides of the border.

However, it deeply hurts us when there are accusatory statements from Afghanistan that we are endangering their peace and sovereignty. Nothing can be far from the truth. We want a stable and viable Afghanistan to play its due role in the betterment and development of the region.

**India**

Our quest for enhancing peace and security in South Asia remains unflinching, sincere and steadfast. In the interest of peace and progress in South Asia there has to be a normalization of relations between Pakistan and India. We are working with India through a composite dialogue process to resolve all issues including Kashmir to ensure durable peace in the region. We have demonstrated an unwavering commitment to the dialogue process with India. It was due to our sustained efforts that this process was resumed in January 2004 and has contributed towards an appreciable improvement in the atmospherics between the two countries.

The improved state of relations between Pakistan and India provide a precious opportunity for our two countries to work for resolution of the difficult issues between us, in particular the unresolved Kashmir dispute. This outstanding issue must be resolved keeping in view the aspirations of the Kashmiri people.

We have demonstrated sufficient resolve and flexibility in order to seek a peaceful solution of this problem. It is upto India to do same so that the people of South Asia can have the opportunity to live in an atmosphere of peace, stability and prosperity.

The international community can help the process by encouraging all parties to stay the course and to demonstrate courage, determination and sincerity.

It would not be out of context to mention that Pakistan-India relations have in the past been a major impediment in the progress and prosperity of the South Asian region.

Asia is the emerging engine of growth for the global economy, with China in the lead. We favour economic integration of the various sub-regions of Asia for shared prosperity for all regions and all societies. It is our effort to link up with the important processes of regional cooperation in the Asia-Pacific region.

We would like to see regional groupings such as the South Asian Association for Regional Cooperation (SAARC) and the Economic Cooperation Organization (ECO), to which we belong, become effective. We have offered an energy corridor to India. We are developing roads and infrastructure linkages to provide Central Asia the shortest access to the sea. The construction of Gwadar Port is an important landmark in that direction. In short we are working on a multi-pronged approach to inspire regional progress and development.

Pakistan's capacity to play an effective role in promoting regional peace and security has been enhanced by our close relations with the countries of the region.

## Nuclear Non-Proliferation

Pakistan's nuclear capability must be viewed in the context of India's pursuit of the nuclear option and our overall security concerns. Pakistan does not seek regional domination or great power status. We do not threaten any country and wish to live in peace. Our strategic capabilities have been developed in self-defense following the Indian nuclear test of 1974 that disrupted the security balance in South Asia and provided a nuclear edge to India .

The establishment of deterrence was important. Pakistan's atomic tests made South Asia more secure and helped prod India and Pakistan to better relations and to commence talks on Kashmir.

As a nuclear weapon state, we adhere to a doctrine of minimum credible deterrence and are opposed to any nuclear proliferation as well as arms race in the region. Accordingly, we have proposed a Strategic Restraint Regime to India. We also believe that induction of antiballistic missiles would have a destabilizing impact on the entire region.

Pakistan is committed to the prevention of nuclear proliferation and has developed a fool proof command and control structure to protect our strategic assets. Furthermore effective export controls are in place. At the same time, we believe that no restrictions should be imposed on civilian nuclear cooperation under appropriate safeguards. As a fossil fuel deficit country, we need nuclear power generation to meet the growing needs of energy for our growing economy. We are prepared to accept all safeguards on our civilian nuclear power sector.

Allow me to conclude by emphasizing that South Asia is not a unique region. The imperatives for peace and prosperity in South Asia are not different from other regions across the world.

The first step is to acknowledge the root causes of conflicts. Then, we must have the will to address them peacefully. Difficult decisions cannot be put on hold forever. Unless there is tangible progress towards settling core issues, confidence building measures are bound to collapse under their own weight.

Big or small, rich or poor, states are sensitive to their sovereignty and expect to be treated with respect. It is only through mutual respect that inter-state relations can be built and nourished.

South Asia faces many serious challenges of all kinds, which individual countries cannot address on their own. Even the level of current economic growths will be difficult to sustain unless the countries of the region are at peace. This dilemma is real and cannot be wished away.

Let me say that it is time for action. Pakistan is ready to play its part seriously and sincerely in building a peaceful and prosperous South Asia. We have lost many years in mutual acrimony and contention, squandering our energies and resources.

The people of South Asia deserve a far better future. To this end, you will find the democratic government in Pakistan fully committed and dedicated.

(*Source*: http://www.mofa.gov.pk/Press_Releases/2008/July/PR_221_08.htm)

# 21.

## BILATERAL RELATIONS WITH UNITED STATES OF AMERICA

### Joint Statement on Pakistan - United States Strategic Dialogue

September 30, 2008

*In a joint statement, the United States of America and Pakistan, reaffirmed their commitments to a wide-ranging, substantive and long-term strategic partnership between them. While the United States committed itself towards providing Pakistan with training and equipment to fight terrorism, including support to enhance Pakistan's counterinsurgency and counterterrorism capabilities; Pakistan on the other hand expressed its appreciation for the $4 million the U.S. has committed for flood relief and for humanitarian assistance to those displaced by fighting in Bajaur. It also appreciated the new Friends of Pakistan initiative. The two sides also emphasized the need for improved regional cooperation and integration in the energy sector and science and technology.*

The Governments of Pakistan and the United States held the third round of the Pakistan-U.S. Strategic Dialogue on September 29 at the Department of State in Washington, D.C.

Foreign Minister Makhdoom Shah Mahmood Qureshi led the Pakistani delegation. Deputy Secretary of State John Negroponte led the U.S. delegation. The Pakistan-U.S. Strategic Dialogue was last held in Islamabad in September 2007.

Foreign Minister Qureshi and Deputy Secretary Negroponte reaffirmed their commitments to a wide-ranging, substantive, and long-term strategic partnership between Pakistan and the United States, which is based on shared values and a common effort to promote enduring peace, security, stability, freedom, and prosperity of Pakistan and of the region. Both sides exchanged views on ways to deepen their bilateral cooperation and to make the Strategic Dialogue more effective and productive.

Pakistan and the United States both strongly condemned the terrorist attack at the Marriott Hotel in Islamabad, on 20 September. Both Foreign

Minister Qureshi and Deputy Secretary Negroponte offered their condolences to the families of all of those who lost their lives in the vicious attack. They acknowledged that terrorism and violent extremism pose a common threat to Pakistan, the United States, and the international community.

The United States affirmed its support for Pakistan's sovereignty, independence, unity, and territorial integrity. The United States is dedicated to providing Pakistan with the training and equipment it needs to fight terrorism, including support to enhance Pakistan's counterinsurgency and counterterrorism capabilities and increased cooperation with Pakistani security forces. Both sides renewed their intention to work together to combat the threat of terrorism and violent extremism by expanding security cooperation, and to work together to develop and modernize the Federally Administered Tribal Areas. Pakistan expressed its appreciation for the $4 million the U.S. has committed for flood relief and for humanitarian assistance to those displaced by fighting in Bajaur.

During the Strategic Dialogue, the two sides discussed regional and international issues of common interest. The U.S. expressed support for continued dialogue and improved relations between Pakistan and its neighbors. The U.S. expressed support for the resumption of the Jirga process with Afghanistan and for Pakistan's commitment to hold the next Regional Economic Cooperation Conference meeting in Islamabad later this year.

The Pakistani Government expressed its appreciation for the new Friends of Pakistan initiative, which will help Pakistan face its challenges in the years ahead.

Building on the August 2008 bilateral Economic Dialogue, both sides reaffirmed their commitment to increased bilateral economic cooperation. Pakistan outlined its economic stabilization measures and reforms to foster economic growth and opportunity. The U.S. expressed support for Pakistan's plan to stabilize its economy and welcomed Pakistan's commitment to implement comprehensive reform measures.

The U.S. expressed its determination to continue efforts to promote Reconstruction Opportunity Zones legislation, currently pending in Congress. The establishment of such zones would improve stability and security by stimulating jobs, infrastructure and legitimate economic alternatives in underdeveloped areas.

The two sides emphasized the need for improved regional cooperation and integration in the energy sector. They reaffirmed their commitment to address Pakistan's growing energy needs by expanding technical assistance and promoting investment in Pakistan's energy sector.

Cooperation in education and science and technology were reviewed, and both resolved to make best efforts to hold Energy and Education Dialogues by the end of the year.

In keeping with the commitment made by Prime Minister Gillani and President Bush during their July meeting in Washington, the delegations began discussions focused on agricultural cooperation that would help Pakistan strengthen its agricultural sector and enhance its food security. The two sides committed to work together to realize their long-term vision of the Pakistan - U.S. Strategic Partnership.

*Source*: http://www.mofa.gov.pk/Press_Releases/2008/Sep/PR_304_08.htm

## Joint Statement on Pakistan-United States Strategic Partnership

July 28, 2008

*The joint statement issued during the visit of Pakistan's Prime Minister to the United States reaffirmed the strategic partnership between both the countries, and decided on the comprehensive strategy in fighting terror, while acknowledging the denial of any space to militants or terrorists through increased cooperation. The United States proposed to provide $115.5 million in food security assistance to Pakistan, including $42.5 million for the consecutive nine months. The joint statement also mentions the establishment of Reconstruction Opportunity Zones which would help expanding trade opportunities in parts of Pakistan and Afghanistan*

President George W. Bush welcomed Prime Minister Syed Yousaf Raza Gillani to Washington today for his first visit to the United States as the leader of Pakistan's democratically-elected civilian government. The President and Prime Minister reaffirmed their commitment to the long-term Strategic Partnership between the United States and Pakistan, which is based on shared values and holds immense potential for the enduring peace, security, stability, freedom, and prosperity of Pakistan and of the region. The President affirmed his support for Pakistan's sovereignty, independence, unity, and territorial integrity. The two leaders agreed that the focus of the broad-based Pakistan-U.S. relationship should remain on ensuring the well being of the people by assisting Pakistan to implement its national development agenda in a comprehensive manner. Pakistan and the United States will work together to eliminate the threat of extremism, build strong democratic institutions, modernize education, and increase economic growth and opportunity.

President Bush and Prime Minister Gillani reaffirmed their condemnation of terrorism in all its forms and manifestations. They acknowledged that terrorism and violent extremism pose a common threat to Pakistan, the United States, and the international community. The two leaders pledged to work together to address this threat and to deny any space to militants or terrorists through increased cooperation. The President recognized the sacrifices the people of Pakistan and the Pakistani security forces have made in the ongoing fight. The President and Prime Minister reiterated that success in countering terrorism will require a comprehensive strategy, including increased security, improved governance, and opportunity for socio-economic development for the people especially in the less-developed regions of Pakistan. The President and the Prime Minister expressed deep sympathy for the families of those who have fallen victim to suicide and other terrorist attacks in Pakistan. The Prime Minister expressed appreciation for U.S. efforts to promote peace and stability in the region. The United States is dedicated to providing Pakistan with the support and tools it needs to lead the fight against terrorism.

The two leaders also committed to increased bilateral economic cooperation to include expanded trade, an improved investment climate, promoting cooperation in the public and private sectors, and agreed to work together to ensure food and energy security as well as facilitate investment in infrastructure and social sectors in Pakistan.

In reaffirming the Strategic Partnership, President Bush and Prime Minister Gillani attached importance to the next round of the Strategic Dialogue, which will be co-chaired by the U.S. Deputy Secretary of State and Pakistan's Foreign Minister, in September 2008 and regularly thereafter to review issues of mutual interest. In addition, the two leaders committed both countries to undertake the following steps in development, counterterrorism, economic, and regional cooperation:

Focus on the needs of the Pakistani people: Food, Health, Education, Energy, and Democratic Governance

* The two leaders welcomed recent efforts in the U.S. Congress to extend the United States' assistance commitment to Pakistan to help address Pakistan's most urgent needs, including education, agriculture, and energy. The President will continue to work with Congress to ensure the continued support of the United States to Pakistan over the long term.
* The two leaders agreed to institute a separate track for agricultural cooperation under the Strategic Dialogue.
* The United States will provide $ 115.5 million in food security assistance to Pakistan, including $ 42.5 million over the next nine months.
* The United States will assist with disease control activities in Pakistan to augment the Prime Minister's initiative to combat the spread of hepatitis and other infectious diseases.
* The United States highlighted its $30 million Pakistan Energy Development program focused on improving power availability, affordability, and efficiency.

* The United States and Pakistan will hold the next round of the U.S.-Pakistan Energy Dialogue this fall to help Pakistan meet its vast and growing energy needs.
* The two leaders agreed to hold the next round of the U.S.-Pakistan Education Dialogue later this year.
* The two leaders agreed to continue and enhance robust collaboration in science and technology under the successful bilateral Science and Technology Framework Agreement.
* The United States highlighted its support for democracy-building and improved governance through project funding.

**Expand Bilateral Trade and Improve the Business Climate**

* The two leaders renewed a joint commitment to pursue steps to establish Reconstruction Opportunity Zones that will expand trade opportunities in parts of Pakistan and Afghanistan.
* The United States and Pakistan will work together toward a goal of establishing direct non-stop flights between the two countries before the end of 2008, expanding people-to-people ties and improving the investment climate to the benefit of the people of both countries.
* The United States and Pakistan agree to convene officials promptly to review the status of bilateral investment treaty negotiations.
* The two countries will reconvene the Joint Council under the Trade and Investment Framework Agreement in September 2008.
* The U.S.-Pakistan Economic Dialogue will be held on August 11 in Islamabad.

**Expand Security and Counterterrorism Cooperation**

* The two leaders agreed to strengthen the long-term security relationship with a view to enhancing Pakistan's defense capabilities, especially in the field of counterterrorism, through training and equipment.
* Reconvene the bilateral Defense Consultative Group this fall with a renewed focus on counterinsurgency and counterterrorism.
* Renew cooperative efforts to root out extremism along the Pakistan-Afghanistan border, including the Northwest Frontier Province, the Federally Administered Tribal Areas, and Balochistan.
* Expand cooperation between the United States and the Pakistani Frontier Corps and other Pakistani security forces on the front lines in the fight against violent extremism.
* Focus U.S. security assistance on efforts to enhance the counterterrorism capability of Pakistan's military forces.

**Work Together to Enhance Regional Peace, Security, and Stability**

* Strengthen the Tripartite Commission between the International Security Assistance Force, Pakistan, and Afghanistan.

* Support the efforts of Pakistan and Afghanistan to hold the next joint jirga this fall.
* Hold the next Regional Economic Cooperation Conference in Islamabad this fall.
* Encourage the Pakistan-India Composite Dialogue process to reduce tensions, build trust, and resolve all outstanding issues.

Prime Minister Gillani thanked President Bush and the people of the United States for the hospitality accorded to him, Mrs. Gillani, and the members of the Prime Ministerial delegation during their stay in the United States.

(*Source*: http://www.mofa.gov.pk/Press_Releases/2008/July/Joint_Statement.htm)

## Pakistan-United Sates of America: Challenges Ahead[1]

July 11, 2008

*In his address at the Brookings Institution, Foreign Minister, Makhdoom Shah Mahmood Qureshi raised some key points regarding developments in Pakistan. While pointing that Pakistan was looking forward to United States for combating challenges like terrorism, extremism, poverty, hunger, illiteracy and disease; the Minister emphasized that in the long-term, socio-economic development would be the key for winning the hearts and minds of the people. He also spoke about U.S. contribution of about US $2 billion which he said was focused towards the development of the FATA region. He stated that such efforts would relieve the tribal people from the clutches of poverty, illiteracy and underdevelopment. He also proposed the signing of a Bilateral Investment Treaty, with the United States, which he emphasized, would be beneficial for the country.*

I express my deep appreciation to Mr. Strobe Talbot, President of the Brookings Institution, Steve Cohen, and Bruce Riedel, for a warm welcome extended to me in this prestigious institution. I take this opportunity to share my thoughts on "Opportunities and Challenges of Pakistan's Foreign Policy."

We have recently seen a difficult period in our history, and we continue to mourn the death of our icon of democracy Shaheed Benazir Bhutto. But from challenge has come the strength. We are more determined than ever in our history to promote the ideals of peace, security, development and reconciliation between cultures, values and societies.

In the past, the United States and Pakistan have stood side by side through perilous times. We look forward to continue to work with you and

1. Address by Makhdoom Shah Mahmood Qureshi, Foreign Minister of Pakistan, at the Brookings Institution, Washington, DC, July 11, 2008.

your great country in confronting the problems that nations face in this millennium – terrorism, extremism, poverty, hunger, illiteracy and disease.

The United States and Pakistan have also been longstanding allies. Pakistan's founder Quaid-i-Azam Muhammad Ali Jinnah laid the foundation of this relationship immediately after our nation's independence in 1947. Together, we now look forward to building a new, more mature, long-term partnership based on common values and common goals.

During the visit of President Bush to Islamabad in March 2006, our two countries affirmed a "Strategic Partnership" focused on strengthening the foundation for a strong and enduring relationship, and promoting multifaceted cooperation. We are cooperating in various fields including trade and economy; defence and security; health and education; science and technology; and counter-terrorism and non-proliferation.

We believe that a deeper and sustained economic partnership between our two countries would contribute to combating extremism — by strengthening our economic growth trajectory, by fulfilling the social and economic needs of our people, and by consolidating democratic governance in Pakistan.

Pakistan believes that there is an intrinsic link between peace and development. Peace on our borders can strengthen stability and bring economic development as well as the much needed improvement in the quality of life of our people.

Pakistan has suffered twice for Afghanistan – first, when we supported the world's efforts to drive out the Soviets which made a vital contribution to the success of freedom movements in Eastern Europe and elsewhere, and then more recently, after 9/11. Pakistan can realize its dream of becoming a regional trading and energy hub only if Afghanistan is politically and economically stable. We wish Afghanistan peace and stability for their sake and for our own sake.

The fight against terrorism is not America's fight alone. We, in Pakistan, have been the victims of terrorism and extremism, and we have paid a heavy price, and more than 1,000 of our brave soldiers have made the ultimate sacrifice while confronting this menace. But the fight against terrorism is a multifaceted fight, not just a military one. Our comprehensive strategy seeks to isolate and marginalize the extremists and combines political engagement, economic development and social reforms.

In the long-term, socio-economic development is the key to winning the hearts and minds of the people. And because of the democratic elections that took place in Pakistan this year, our government now has a legitimate mandate from the people to confront the forc es of terrorism wherever they rear their ugly heads, and to build a just and equitable society where parents have faith that their children's lives will be better than their own.

Our effort is to mobilize our people behind the policies of the government as we move forward with a political dialogue to complement our military strategy, aimed at achieving peace agreement with those who desire peace and are willing to lay down their arms. Pakistan will not negotiate with terrorists. And Pakistan will not permit its territory to be used by anyone against any country.

While we prefer dialogue over use of force, for obvious reasons, we are not shy to employ force where it is required, as is evident from the recent operations in Khyber Agency.

The challenge of terrorism is such that no single country, howsoever strong, can deal with it alone. This is a global challenge that requires a global response and global strategy. As allies, Pakistan and the U.S. need to coordinate closely and cooperate closely. This is essential in order to be able to deal with challenge in the short-term perspective as well as the long-term perspective.

The ROZs legislation that was recently introduced in the US Congress is an example of how we can help each other. I am confident that an effective ROZs plan would surely go a long way in helping us expand economic opportunities and wean the innocent people away from the appeal of extremism and terrorism. Similarly, the $2 billion FATA Development Plan, to which the U.S. is contributing $750 million over a five-year period, would help accelerate economic growth and social sector development in the Tribal Areas, thus contributing to the efforts to deliver the tribal people from the clutches of poverty, illiteracy and under-development.

For too long, our bilateral relationship has hinged heavily on cooperation in security areas. But luckily, a clear realization from both sides in the post 9/11 phase is of the need to broaden and deepen the relationship, through expanding cooperation across a broad spectrum — from agriculture to trade to energy to education to science & technology. We already have institutional mechanisms for promoting cooperation in these areas. The results achieved so far are below potential. The new government of Pakistan is determined to realize that potential.

Nothing can be more effective in truly broadening the base of our relationship than an expansion in bilateral trade. And nothing can be more helpful in enabling Pakistan achieve its goals of lifting millions out of poverty and keeping the economy on a sustainable trajectory of stability and growth than market access. For these reasons, there is no alternative to the two countries signing an Free Trade Agreement (FTA) of which a Bilateral Investment Treaty (BIT) can be a part, as the U.S. has done with several countries.

And, while all key areas are of utmost importance, Pakistan-U.S. collaboration to meet our energy shortages and to strengthen our energy security could hardly be overemphasized.

In Afghanistan, Pakistan has a vital stake in peace and stability. We cannot think of a scenario where Pakistan can benefit from the continuing turmoil in Afghanistan. For that reason, it is baffling when we come across the insinuations that Pakistan was in any way responsible for the present or past crises in Afghanistan. We will, nevertheless, continue our support for Afghanistan's political stability, economic development, and social progress — for reasons of our own vested interest.

We are also committed to continuing the process of composite dialogue with our eastern neighbor, India. The time is now for taking bold steps to take the two countries out of the cycle of hostility, acrimony, and mutual suspicion.

It is our hope that the leadership of the two countries would not shy away from taking such steps and move beyond the CBMs to engaging in a serious dialogue to address the real issues, notably the core issue of Jammu and Kashmir.

Pakistan, as you know has shown flexibility and emphasized the need for out-of-box thinking. There is a general feeling and public perception in Pakistan that a matching response should come from India. The India-Pakistan dialogue should now move for resolving the conflicts rather than lingering on with them.

And the two countries, despite their best efforts, would not succeed in achieving any real breakthrough, without the support and encouragement of their friends.

We appreciate the constructive role that the United States has played in encouraging the peace process in South Asia. But its role should not remain confined to conflict management and should also extend to facilitating conflict resolution.

We have seen in the past that democracy in Pakistan has invariably led to a better relationship between the two countries. Both Pakistan and India have posted the highest rates of growth in the region in the past several years and their economic performance has been startling. Better diplomatic, cultural and trade relations will only help boost their progress.

However, given the past history of distrust, dramatic changes cannot be expected very quickly. But the trend is certainly positive and is likely to continue under the new government. My recent visit to New Delhi was a step forward in this direction.

China would continue to figure prominently in Pakistan's foreign policy. Our time-tested relationship with China continues to expand in all fields including trade, investments, economic cooperation, security, energy and telecommunications. China has also been a key partner in developing the Gwadar port in the southwest of Pakistan which has already become operational.

Some speculative theories notwithstanding, Gwadar is an economic project designed to help speed the process of economic development through tapping the opportunities of regional cooperation in transit and trade.

Pakistan's relations with the Middle Eastern countries are deeply rooted in the religious and cultural affinities, geographical proximity and shared historical experiences. These brotherly relations are marked by identity of views and a commitment of mutual sup port on vital issues.

We firmly believe that a just and peaceful resolution of the Palestine issue is important for durable peace and stability in the Middle East. Pakistan has consistently extended support to the two-state solution whereby both Palestine and Israel can live side by side.

This will require withdrawal of Israel from occupied Arab territories including Jerusalem and the establishment of an independent Palestinian state in accordance with the relevant UN resolutions. Pakistan supports the Quartet's Roadmap and the Arab Peace Plan based on a two-state solution. We also support the understanding reached at Annapolis for the establishment of an independent Palestinian State, addressing all core issues, with a timeline of end-2008 and for following the Syrian and Lebanese tracks. Urgent efforts are also needed to address the Gaza situation and mitigating the enormous sufferings of the Palestinian people there. The international community, particularly the United States, must help to ensure a just and equitable solution of the long festering Palestinian dispute.

The situation in Iraq remains a matter of concern to the Muslim world. Pakistan attaches great importance to Iraq's sovereignty and territorial integrity, and wishes to see an early end to the violence and return of stability and normalcy to Iraq .

Pakistan also attaches great significance to the Organization of the Islamic Conference (OIC) as a representative organization of 57 Muslim states and the millions of Muslims living as minorities around the world. Pakistan has a central and leadership role within the Organization of the Islamic Conference (OIC). Last year, Pakistan chaired the Islamic Conference of Foreign Ministers.

Our focus has been to make the Organization more effective and dynamic in order to represent and advance the interests of the Muslim world at the global level and that it should also be a vehicle of greater economic integration in the Muslim world.

The newly elected government of Pakistan faces a host of daunting challenges, both political and economic. But there are exciting opportunities as well. We are confident that we will succeed in meeting these challenges head on and in realizing our full potential with the support of the people of Pakistan. The support and cooperation of our friends and allies, notably the United States, would be important.

(*Source*: http://www.mofa.gov.pk/Press_Releases/2008/July/PR_211_08.htm)

# 22.

## INTERNATIONAL DOCUMENTS

### UNHCR repatriates 2,50,000 Afghans[1]

October 7, 2008

*The UNHCR press release noted that over 2,50,000 Afghan refugees have returned home from Pakistan and Iran. The release states that around 30,000 Afghan refugees been living in five makeshift settlements in Nangarhar and Laghman provinces, since their repatriation. On its part UNHCR provides a cash grant of US$100 per person also offering shelter assistance to the most vulnerable returnees, while also coordinating efforts to establish water and sanitation facilities and other basic infrastructure.*

KABUL, Afghanistan, October 7 (UNHCR) – More than 250,000 Afghans have returned home with UNHCR help so far this year from Pakistan and Iran, many of them reportedly due to economic and security uncertainties faced in exile.

Since January, the UN refugee agency has assisted a total of 251,880 registered Afghans to repatriate from neighbouring Pakistan (248,951) and Iran (2,929). Many said they returned to Afghanistan because they could not afford the high cost of living in exile amid the current food and fuel crisis. Others cited security uncertainties as a reason for leaving Pakistan's North West Frontier Province.

The majority of this year's returnees (63 percent) have gone to eastern Afghanistan, while 13 percent have returned to the capital, Kabul. Another 6 percent have returned to the central region, 13 percent to the north and 6 percent to the south and south-east.

Many of them have returned to their places of origin, but some are unable to go back to their villages as they have no land, shelter, job opportunities or security there. These include more than 30,000 Afghans who have been living in five makeshift settlements in Nangarhar and

1. UNHCR helps more than 250,000 Afghans return home since January, October 7, 2008.

Laghman provinces since they repatriated this summer with the closure of Jalozai refugee village in Pakistan's north-west.

The UNHCR-assisted voluntary repatriation operation from Pakistan to Afghanistan will be temporarily suspended at the end of October for the annual winter break. Assisted returns will resume in March 2009.

Ewen Macleod, UNHCR acting representative in Afghanistan, stressed the voluntary nature of UNHCR's repatriation programme.

"Afghanistan's capacity to absorb additional returns sustainably has limitations. There are substantial migration flows out of Afghanistan. This is one of the key factors behind UNHCR's position that repatriation must remain voluntary and gradual in order to ensure that it is a durable solution," he said.

More than 5 million Afghans have returned home since the fall of the Taliban regime in late 2001. Some 4.3 million of them went back with UNHCR assistance, mostly from Pakistan and Iran. Afghanistan has been struggling to absorb these massive returns.

Many returnees are facing reintegration difficulties, including lack of land, shelter, water and basic services such as health care and education. Job opportunities are also scarce.

UNHCR provides a cash grant averaging US$100 per person upon their return to Afghanistan. The agency also offers shelter assistance to the most vulnerable returnees, and coordinates efforts to establish water and sanitation facilities and other basic infrastructure in areas of high return.

But these are just short-term measures to help returnees reintegrate. The medium-term solution is to incorporate their needs into the Afghanistan National Development Strategy, particularly national programmes in key sectors like health, education, water and sanitation and employment.

To address these issues, Afghanistan's Ministry of Foreign Affairs and UNHCR will co-host an international conference in Kabul on return and reintegration on November19 in Kabul.

The conference seeks to reconcile the repatriation targets and time lines proposed by the neighbouring countries with the increasingly challenging operational environment in Afghanistan. It will also be a forum to mobilize additional resources for a comprehensive, integrated approach and multi-year funding delivered through the framework of the National Development Strategy.

(*Source*: http://www.unhcr.org/news/NEWS/48eb80d02.html)

## SAARC-Regional Space for Cooperation: Perspectives from Pakistan[2]

July 31, 2008

*Makhdoom Shah Mahmood Qureshi, Foreign Minister of Pakistan, in his statement at the 30th Meeting of the SAARC Council of Ministers, stated that socio-economic development was intricately linked towards the establishment of peace and stability. Food security, SAARC Development Fund were identified by the Minister as important areas for cooperation. The Foreign Minister also spoke of granting an observer status to Myanmar, E.U and Australia.*

We welcome the theme of the Summit chosen by Sri Lanka: "Partnership for growth for our people". We share the conviction that people should be at the heart of all SAARC processes. Socio-economic development is linked, in large measure, to the creation of peace and stability. We are confident that the Colombo Summit would contribute to building trust and according a pragmatic impetus to regional cooperation in South Asia.

Since its establishment in 1985, SAARC has come a long way. From the initial tentative steps limited to technical cooperation, SAARC now has grown into a vibrant organization tackling the challenging subjects of social uplift, regional connectivity, food security, energy cooperation, and human resource development. It must continue to surge ahead and become an effective vehicle for regional cooperation. The coming years would surely test our collective resolve as we embark on addressing the difficult but vital questions related to inter-dependence and integration.

Pakistan is committed to the SAARC objectives. We have made substantial contribution towards various SAARC processes and taken a number of initiatives in furthering the goals of close regional cooperation.

Pakistan believes that SAARC can enhance its relevance to the peoples of our region by pursuing people-centered and result oriented approach. In this regard, we find merit in many of the recommendations given by the Secretary General in his detailed analysis report.

We agree with the Secretary General that poverty alleviation and achievement of SAARC Development Goals (SDGs) should be a priority for SAARC. Pakistan has taken a number of steps for the attainment of this objective. We have also aligned our national goals to SDGs.

The rising food prices have placed an added stress on our efforts to achieve SDGs, in particular poverty alleviation. Achieving food security in our region should be a matter of high priority for us.

---

2. Statement by Makhdoom Shah Mahmood Qureshi, Foreign Minister of Pakistan, at the 30th Meeting of the SAARC Council of Ministers, Colombo, July 31, 2008.

Pakistan, therefore, strongly supports early operationalization of SAARC Food Bank. Besides, SAARC needs to develop a comprehensive and holistic regional strategy on food security, which should include sharing of best practices in agricultural sector, technology transfer and efficient irrigation system.

In this regard, I had shared my ideas with you. I am pleased to learn that our Foreign Secretaries have finalized the text of a separate Declaration: "Colombo Statement on Food Security", which expresses our resolve to take urgent actions to ensure food security in our region. We should commend this Declaration to our Leaders for approval.

Likewise, the rising prices of fossil fuel in international market warrant SAARC to step up its efforts for regional energy security through sharing of indigenous sources of energy, i.e. solar, wind, bio, and hydro.

We hope that the ADB study on options/benefits and constraints of intra-SAARC energy trade will contribute to our endeavours in this field.

I had proposed to all colleagues in the Council of Ministers that SAARC may consider concluding a regional inter-governmental framework agreement to provide an enabling environment for such cooperation. I am pleased to note that the draft SAARC Declaration prepared by the Foreign Secretaries adequately addresses this important subject.

The fourteenth SAARC Summit had directed SAARC to move from declaratory to implementation phase. SAARC should, therefore, focus on project-based cooperation.

SAARC mechanisms should identify regional and sub-regional projects in priority areas. Each Member States should adopt at least one project as the lead country.

We should also involve SAARC Observers and other relevant international organizations in the implementation of projects. I believe these ideas have been duly reflected in the draft Declaration prepared for adoption by our Leaders.

Fourteenth SAARC Summit had stressed the need for regional connectivity. It is important to take early action on development of transport and communication infrastructure to link SAARC countries with each other as well as with other regions. These are essential pre-requisites for regional trade and economic cooperation.

SAFTA is progressing well. We can strengthen the efficacy of SAFTA by complementing it with other trade facilitation measures including elimination of all non-tariff and para-tariff barriers.

We are happy to note that the SAARC Ministerial meeting on climate change held in Dhaka earlier this month has evolved a comprehensive plan of action on climate change. Our efforts to protect the environment and climate change should include measures to protect melting of the glaciers of the Himalayas and the Karakoram, which are the major source of fresh water in the region.

We note the progress made with regard to SAARC Regional Multi-model Transport Study (SRMTC). We support the development of pilot projects through consultations.

Pakistan supports early operationalization of SAARC Development Fund (SDF). Pakistan has offered to host the Secretariat of the SDF. The Secretariat of its predecessor organization, South Asia Development Fund (SADF), was also based in Pakistan.

As a front-line state in the global fight against terrorism, Pakistan attaches great importance to regional cooperation to combat terrorism, drugs and human trafficking. Pakistan has taken a number of measures, backed by appropriate legislation, to counter the menaces of drugs and human trafficking and terrorism. We have formal mechanisms with 39 countries on issues relating to terrorism.

We welcome the finalization of the SAARC Convention on Mutual Assistance in Criminal Matters.

Pakistan advocates the need for SAARC to open up to the world and enter into collaborative arrangements with international and regional organizations. In this spirit, we had supported granting observer status to important countries and EU. We also welcome the interest shown by Australia and Myanmar for obtaining observer status with SAARC. We believe we should now think of going beyond observer status and think of dialogue partnerships with those Observers who wish to actively associate with SAARC programmes, activities, and projects. In this regard, we commend the Standing Committee for preparing the requisite Guidelines for cooperation with Observers and Inter-Governmental Organizations. This would indeed enrich the work of our Organizations.

In conclusion, let me state that in its third decade SAARC must mould itself into an effective regional organization that is responsive to the aspirations of its peoples. We must introspect, constantly evaluate what we have achieved so far, and clearly identify our priority areas for further action. We have tremendous potential. We can leverage it to avail of the opportunities available and overcome our challenges.

I hope that our deliberations in this session would give a new push to the multifaceted regional cooperation. Pakistan would always be ready to provide its full support to this shared objective.

I have touched upon all important issues on our agenda today. We can discuss these issues further as we take up these items as per the agenda of the meeting.

(*Source*: http://www.mofa.gov.pk/Press_Releases/2008/July/PR_236_08.htm)

## Pakistan-Afghanistan Cooperation Framework[3]

June 12, 2008

*The Foreign Minister of Pakistan, urged the internal community to provide full support to Afghanistan especially in areas related to polity, governance, security and reconstruction and drug control. He said that Pakistan with security cooperation with Afghanistan under the "Tripartite Military Commission" should take all measures to stabilize the situation on border with Pakistan.*

First of all I would like to thank the hosts and organizers for the excellent arrangements that they have made for holding this conference.

I would also like to take this opportunity to place on record, Pakistan's deep appreciation for the leaderships of France, Afghanistan and the United Nations for convening this conference.

It has provided a timely opportunity to the international community, for taking stock of the situation, reaffirming its commitment, and accelerating its efforts, for building stability, peace and progress in Afghanistan.

Towards that end, we have to assess how far the goalposts laid down by 'London Compact' have been achieved. And how much remains to be achieved.

In Pakistan's view, London Compact's principal achievement has been the assistance to Afghanistan, for putting in place its physical, institutional and political infrastructure and enhancing, and preventing the Bonn Process from getting derailed.

Having said that, we need to revisit the strategy and corresponding means, worked out by the London Compact, and see where these need improvement and reinvigoration.

In doing so, first and foremost, we have to be guided by the view of the Afghan government. On this score, we have greatly benefited from the analysis and prognosis given by our Afghan friends today.

Now we have to see where and how much we could be of further assistance to them. This brings us to the question of greater international assistance to Afghanistan .

In the areas related to capacity building of the Afghan polity, governance, security and reconstruction and drug control.Pakistan hopes the international community would not be found wanting in responding to Afghanistan's requirements.

The complex problems in Afghanistan are not going to lend themselves to quick and neat solutions. However, greater economic assistance can help in ensuring that Afghanistan, stays the course.

3. Statement for the Foreign Minister, Makhdoom Shah Mahmood Qureshi at the Paris Conference on Afghanistan, June 12, 2008.

Moreover, it would also send the signal that the people of Afghanistan are not alone. The international community is with them.

The international community can not be deterred by extremists and terrorists from coming to the help of Afghanistan .

And that the international community was determined to break the vicious circle of "less security - less development", and make sustainable development — "the overwhelming dynamic" in Afghanistan.

In this context, Pakistan is also of the view, that the international assistance to Afghanistan needs to be channeled more through its government.

We need to appreciate that in a situation like Afghanistan, the leading role by the government in reconstruction and economic development, is also essential for strengthening and enlarging the writ of the State.

It also needs to be sufficiently understood that the challenges of reconstruction, reconciliation and governance in Afghanistan, are interlinked and the strategy to overcome these challenges needs to be based on the capacity of the State.

Without Afghan ownership, it is doubtful that significant success can be achieved in any of these areas.

Pakistan on its part, will continue to have security cooperation with Afghanistan, under the mechanism of the "Tripartite Military Commission".

Pakistan will take all feasible measures to stabilize borders with Afghanistan. But matching measures are needed by both sides. Pakistan's commitment in war against terror is unwavering. It should not be doubted. More then one thousand Pakistani soldiers have laid down their lives in war against terror. If adding of one battalion soldiers in the fight against terror is a reason for pride, then Pakistan has more reason to be proud of in the struggle against terror.

Pakistan will also extend assistance in the construction work in Afghanistan. Moreover, it will not only revive but reinvigorate the process of 'Joint Peace Jirga" that is a traditional mechanism for reconciliation through dialogue.

We believe, that in the given situation, for building peace and stability, dialogue should have the primacy.

It is only when dialogue fails or starts giving diminishing returns, that other options could be revisited.

For these reasons, Pakistan hopes that avenues of dialogue, with those who are amenable to it, may be fully explored.

In the field of governance, Pakistan would like Afghanistan to avail the training programmes in the disciplines of judiciary and police, that are on offer to it for sometime.

Pakistan has been host to millions of Afghan refugees for the last three decades. Currently there are around 2.2 million of them in Pakistan.

To facilitate their repatriation, maintain their honour and security and help in their resettlement in Afghanistan, it gives me great pleasure to pledge US$ 20 millions to Afghanistan .

Pakistan would also appeal to the international community to enhance assistance for their early and safe repatriation and sustainable settlement inside Afghanistan .

Pakistan is sanguine that on their return, these proud Afghans will singularly contribute to the reconstruction and development of their homeland.

The Afghan Presidential elections scheduled in 2009 and Parliamentary elections in 2010, hold great promise for further strengthening of the democratic dispensation over there.

Afghans deserve financial and technical assistance of the international community, for holding these elections smoothly and successfully.

Recently, Pakistan also held elections in the face of serious security challenges in some of its areas.

For this reason, we feel confident in offering our experience and expertise to Afghanistan, in holding of its elections.

To conclude, I would like to emphasize that as a close neighbour of Afghanistan, having bonds of shared faith, history, heritage and indeed of common geography – the security, progress and prosperity of Afghanistan, is of vital and abiding interest to Pakistan.

And with the new and democratic government in place in Pakistan, we would like to build further on our existing brotherly ties with Afghanistan .

We believe that close and cooperative relations between Pakistan and Afghanistan are not only in the mutual interest of the two countries and its peoples, but could also become a powerful dynamic of regional cooperation.

(*Source*: http://www.mofa.gov.pk/FM_Speeches_Briefings/FM_Statement_Paris.htm)

## Pakistan: Views on the Islamic World[4]

July 10, 2008

*The Foreign Minister of Pakistan, Makhdoom Shah Mahmood Qureshi, in his statement at the OIC Ambassadorial meeting, focused on the changing perceptions towards the Muslim community. Stating that Pakistan would continue its efforts to transform the OIC into a more coherent and strong organization the minister*

4. Statement by Mr. Makhdoom Shah Mahmood Qureshi, Foreign Minister of Pakistan to the OIC Ambassadorial Meeting, July 10, 2008.

> *flagged some key focal points to be addressed. Some of these were human rights, islamophobia, terrorism, disarmament, development and UN reform. Stating that Pakistan had been one of the principal victims of terrorism and violent extremism, the minister asserted that any act of terrorism or cross-border attack in Afghanistan from Pakistani soil would not be tolerated*

Your presence here at short notice is a testimony of your affection for and solidarity with Pakistan. This is my first visit to New York after assuming responsibilities as the Foreign Minister of Pakistan.

Just a few weeks ago, I had the honour to attend the 35th Islamic Conference in Kampala, Uganda. I wish to congratulate Uganda on the success of this Conference and on assuming the OIC Chairmanship.

I wish to take this opportunity to share with you my thoughts on some of the vital issues that confront the Islamic Ummah.

The Islamic world, unfortunately, is in the vortex of several volatile political and economic transitions. Muslim lands remain under occupation. Our noble faith is repeatedly attacked and insulted in a systematic campaign of Islamophobia. Our youth are being misguided to a path of extremism and violence. Our societies are battling against internal and external threats. Many of our countries remain underdeveloped, economically, socially and technologically. The new onslaughts of food crisis and high energy prices are aggravating the multiple challenges facing our countries.

Most of these threats affect us collectively and threaten the peaceful existence of our countries. It is necessary to respond to them collectively and wisely. We should endeavour jointly to address the underlying political and security challenges facing the Islamic countries. We should try to play a more active role at the United Nations and other organizations to resolve the issues of Palestine, Islamophobia, international terrorism, and development.

Pakistan has always been at the forefront in advancing the causes of the OIC, particularly the legitimate cause of Palestine. We desire a just and comprehensive peace in the Middle East and an end to the occupation of all Arab territories.

I wish to also thank the members of the OIC for their continued support to the just cause of the people of Jammu and Kashmir and for their internationally recognized right to self-determination. Tangible progress on this issue will contribute to Pakistan's endeavour to build cooperative relations with India and to enable South Asia to emerge as a zone of prosperity and peace.

It is a matter of pride for us that during the tenure of Pakistan's chairmanship of the Islamic Conference of Foreign Ministers, our Organization was able to secure the adoption of the new OIC Charter. We hope that the ratification of the new Charter by all member States will help to transform our Organization into a more relevant and vibrant entity that can help the Islamic countries to respond the challenges of the 21 st century.

Pakistan has and will continue its efforts to transform the OIC into a more coherent and strong Organization, able to advance the objectives of the Islamic world. During the last year, the OIC Group in New York has set up informal working groups which have helped to consolidate the OIC positions on important issues, such as human rights, Islamophobia, Terrorism, Disarmament, Development and UN Reform. The OIC Group in New York has also adopted a number of statements on the core problem of Palestine and other Arab occupied lands as well as on instances of Islamophobia.

We have every confidence that during the Chairmanship of Uganda, the solidarity and cooperation of the Islamic countries in all relevant UN bodies will be intensified and enlarged in accordance with the decisions of our leaders.

The active and constructive role of OIC members at the United Nations is vital to safeguard and promote our national and collective interests. Many members of our Organization are playing prominent roles in new UN entities, such as the Peace Building Commission and the Human Rights Council.

Our countries should also play a significant role in the Security Council and in its reform and expansion. The OIC constitutes more than one-fourth of the UN membership; it should have proportional representation on an expanded Security Council, especially since the Council's agenda contains many items of direct concern to the Islamic countries. In our joint statements, the Islamic Foreign Ministers have categorically stressed that any reform of the Security Council in any category of membership must ensure adequate representation of the OIC member States. This should remain the minimum goal for our Group in the future discussions of this issue at the United Nations.

The continued misrepresentation of Islam and repeated insults to our Faith is another significant challenge we face today. We cannot accept malicious attempts to defame our religion under the cover of the freedom of speech. In this context, I would like to recall the historic decision of the last Annual Coordination Meeting of the OIC Ministers in New York to combat Islamophobia in a comprehensive manner. It called for the finalization of a legally binding instrument on discrimination and instigation of hatred against any religion. This decision was emphatically endorsed by the 11 th Islamic Summit in Dakar. The OIC should vigorously engage the Western and other countries to promote this objective.

Another major challenge faced by the Ummah today is terrorism and violent extremism. Both pose a serious threat to our societies and countries and to our regions and the world. Pakistan has been one of the principal victims of terrorism and violent extremism. Just the day before I left for

New York, we faced a new spate of bombings in Islamabad and Karachi.

Terrorism can never be justified and must be condemned in all its forms and manifestations. In our collective efforts to eliminate this menace, however, we need to address some deeper questions including the root causes of terrorism. We must evolve a holistic and multi-dimensional strategy to tackle the challenge of terrorism and extremism.

Pakistan's contribution to the fight against Al-Qaeda and Taliban terrorism and extremism is well known. We are pursuing such a comprehensive strategy in our frontier regions. Our priority is to promote political reconciliation and economic reconstruction and development in Pakistan's tribal areas to win over the people, the tribes and the moderate forces and to isolate and eventually eliminate the terrorists and violent extremists. However, I would like to stress and clarify that our pacification moves and negotiations are only with tribal elders and other influentials in the region and not with terrorists nor those who do not eschew violence.

In our efforts to restore peace through dialogue and development, any act of terrorism or cross-border attack in Afghanistan from Pakistani soil will not be tolerated. If any such violation occurs, our government will take forceful action to eliminate that. On the other hand, Pakistan will not allow any foreign troops on its territory.

We believe that peace and stability between Pakistan and Afghanistan are indivisible. It is in the vital interest of our two countries which are bound by geography, history, faith and culture, to cooperate closely to defeat the menace of terrorism. Peace in our countries will enable Pakistan and Afghanistan to serve as the hub for trade and economic cooperation in the regions of South Asia and Central Asia, China and the Gulf. We can succeed in realizing these objectives only with the good wishes and support of the Islamic countries and the unconditional cooperation of the international community.

(*Source*: *http://www.*mofa.*gov.pk/Press_Releases/2008/July/PR_209_08.htm*)

## Conflict in Afghanistan: Perspective from Pakistan[5]

July 9, 2008

*The Foreign Minister, Makhdoom Shah Mahmood Qureshi, in his statement at the Security Council stated that political changes in Pakistan, equip the country to deal with the challenges posed by the conflict in Afghanistan. Condemning the attacks on the Indian embassy, he stated that Pakistan would give full support to*

---

5. Statement by Mr. Makhdoom Shah Mahmood Qureshi, Foreign Minister of Pakistan, in the Meeting of the Security Council on the situation in Afghanistan, July 9, 2008.

> *UNAMA. The Minister pointed out that though considerable progress had been made in Afghanistan since the Bonn Agreement, Pakistan had been directly facing the spillover effect of hosting over 3 million refugees. The Foreign Minister also spoke in length about the political relations and underscored the economic relations with Afghanistan which amounted to around one billion. Stating that Pakistan had committed around $ 300 million for Afghanistan's reconstruction, it had also authorized the export of 50,000 tons of wheat to Afghanistan at subsidized rates. He pointed that Pakistan would host the next meeting of the Afghan Regional Economic Cooperation forum in Islamabad from 28-30 August, 2008.*

The new democratic government of Pakistan has inherited imposing political, economic and security challenges. We are addressing these challenges democratically and effectively. None among these challenges is as critical as the threat posed by terrorism and extremist violence – a threat we face in common with our neighbour, Afghanistan

I have condemned the terrorist attack against the Indian embassy in Kabul. We deeply regret the loss of life and damage caused by this unacceptable suicide bombing. Any attack on civilians or diplomatic missions is highly reprehensible. As you know, a day earlier, a suicide bomber in Islamabad, killed twelve policemen and civilians and wounded scores of people. Again, a day later, there was a series of terrorist bombings in Karachi. We welcome the condemnation of these terrorist attacks by the Security Council.

I am, therefore, grateful for this opportunity to address the Security Council on the situation in Afghanistan. I would like to thank the Special Representative of the Secretary-General, Mr.Kai Eide, for his briefing this morning and to assure him of our cooperation. Pakistan supports the central coordinating role of the United Nations Mission in Afghanistan in accordance with its mandate, which is specific and limited to Afghanistan. Bilateral relations between Pakistan and Afghanistan will continue to be conducted between the democratically elected governments of the two countries.

Since the Bonn Agreement, considerable progress has been made in Afghanistan. We need to consolidate these gains and effectively address the outstanding challenges, in particular the intensifying threat posed by terrorist violence and militant insurgency. The continuing insecurity and violence in several parts of Afghanistan can be attributed to a complex interplay of several factors – Taliban, Al-Qaeda, lingering warlordism, factional rivalries and criminal activity including, but not limited to, the drug trade.

Peace and Stability in Afghanistan are in Pakistan's vital interest. The bonds of geography, history, faith and culture inextricably link the destinies of our two nations. We face a common threat of extremism and terrorism. Peace and stability are essential to enable Pakistan and Afghanistan to serve as the hub and corridor for trade and economic cooperation between the dynamic regions of South Asia, Central Asia, China and the Gulf.

Apart from the Afghan people, the people of Pakistan have suffered the most from the decades of conflict in Afghanistan. We have hosted over 3 million refugees. We have been afflicted with drugs and arms. And our frontier regions, which were previously peaceful, have been inflamed by the three decades of war and instability in Afghanistan specially after 2001, when many Al-Qaeda and Taliban elements crossed the border into Pakistan .

Pakistan's contribution to the fight against terrorism and extremism is well known. Much of the success against Al-Qaeda and Taliban has been achieved with our support and cooperation. We have lost more soldiers than any other country in the effort. Yet, we remain determined to defeat and eliminate terrorism and its root causes. An end to conflict in Afghanistan will help to restore normalcy on our side of the border and conversely, we recognize, that our efforts to stabilize, pacify and promote development in our frontier region will also have a positive impact on the situation across the border.

Pakistan has taken several measures to prevent cross-border infiltration by terrorists and insurgents. These measures have curbed such cross-border movement. But, the security environment on our side deteriorated sharply as a result of our role in the counter-terrorist campaign. In 2007, Al-Qaeda and some Taliban-linked groups turned on Pakistan and its security forces. Last year, there were a larger number of suicide bombings in Pakistan than Afghanistan, resulting in 2000 civilian casualties. Pakistan lost Mohtarma Benazir Bhutto – a leader of great stature and vision – to terrorist attack. This terrorist onslaught continues. The recent suicidal attack in Islamabad suggests that terrorist's threat to Pakistan is far from over. Naturally, this has led to growing popular concern and questioning by some of the excessive reliance on the military option. However, there is also popular disenchantment in Pakistan, including in our frontier region, with the terrorists and extremists, as evident from the success of mainstream political parties, in the region in our February 18 elections.

The new democratic government in Pakistan cannot but be sensitive to the sentiments of our people. The new holistic strategy we have evolved seeks to restore peace in our frontier regions, halt and reverse extremism, and eliminate terrorism and violence through political dialogue and socio-economic measures but retaining the option to use force, whenever required. We remain committed to cooperation with Afghanistan and the Coalition forces to stabilize Afghanistan. Political reconciliation and economic reconstruction and development are our priority options to win over the people, the tribes and the moderates, and to isolate the terrorists and violent extremists. In the context of these pacification efforts, it is important to note that the problems and threats in each area and region of our frontier – as across the border – differ from region to region. Pacification will, therefore, require painstaking efforts, region by region, to win the trust and support of local people and their leaders. We are negotiating with tribal leaders and other influentials in these regions; not with the terrorists, nor with those who do not eschew violence.

Reconciliation and reconstruction are the only sustainable solution to insurgent violence and instability. We plan massive investment for the reconstruction of the area and its incorporation into the domestic political mainstream of the country. We welcome the commitment by the U.S. to the creation of Reconstruction and Opportunity Zones in the region and its pledge to provide $ 750 million over 3 years to support these Zones.

While we seek peace through dialogue and development, challenges to the authority of the government, acts of terrorism, or cross-border attacks in Afghanistan, will not be tolerated. Where such challenges and violations occur, the government will take forceful action to eliminate them. We are currently doing so in the Khyber Agency against certain violent and criminal extremist militias. The Chief of Army Staff has been given the authority to decide on the application of such military action when required. Pakistan will not allow its territory to be used against other countries. However, no foreign troops will be allowed to operate inside Pakistan .

We can assure greater success in containing, terrorism and insurgency on both sides of the border through more effective cooperation and matching military measures. This is a joint responsibility. Pakistan will continue active cooperation within the Tripartite Commission. We are prepared to consider suggestions to enhance the effectiveness of such cooperation. At the same time, we feel that our partners too could contribute to enhancing operational cooperation by undertaking the following measures:

- expansion military deployments and check posts on the Afghan side of the border to match Pakistan's 100,000 military personnel and 1200 check-posts:
- real time intelligence sharing;
- caution in the use of artillery and aerial attacks, to avoid accidents or territorial violations;
- supply of counter-insurgency equipment requested by Pakistan;
- more effective check of the 40,000 daily legal crossings, including through use of biometric I.D. cards;
- relocation of Afghan refugee camps close to the border from Pakistan to controlled sites in Afghanistan.

The bonds that bind the peoples of Pakistan and Afghanistan, the mutuality of our strategic interests, the democratic mandates of our governments dictate that political relations between our countries should be much better than have been in recent months. Foreign Minister Spanta and I have made a beginning, by exchanging visits during the last two months. President Karzai, who I had the honour to meet in Kabul, was one of the last people to see our martyred leader, Benazir Bhutto, hours before her tragic assassination.

Yet, clearly, we need to do more to overcome suspicion and distrust. We will do our best to reassure our Afghan brothers and sisters that our government is inspired by nothing but goodwill towards them. They too should make every effort to address our concerns.

I would suggest that we take some initial steps such as:

- declaring mutual respect for each other's sovereignty and territorial integrity, in accordance with the Kabul Declaration;
- not allow our respective territories to be used against each other;
- avoid provocative statements;
- intensify the frequency of mutual visits at all levels;
- revive and reinvigorate the Jirga process. Pakistan will soon convene the smaller Jirga meeting we have agreed on;
- support the Ankara Process as well as the Afghanistan – Iran – Pakistan Tripartite cooperation;

The economic relationship and cooperation between Pakistan and Afghanistan is already intimate and intense. Our trade amounts to around one billion. Its potential is far more. We want to realize its full potential. Most of Afghanistan's trade transits through Pakistan. Pakistan has committed $ 300 million for Afghanistan's reconstruction. We have pledged additional $ 20 million for the resettlement of Afghan refugees. Responding to the food crisis, and despite shortage in Pakistan, we have authorized the export of 50,000 tons of wheat to Afghanistan at subsidized rates. Pakistan supports the Afghan National Development Strategy, endorsed in Paris, as the engine for economic growth and equitable development. We will host the next meeting of the Afghan Regional Economic Cooperation forum in Islamabad from 28-30 August, this year.

Pakistan and Afghanistan must press forward on all possible avenues to exploit the significant potential for mutual economic cooperation, for example by:

- jointly establishing Reconstruction Opportunity Zones along the border, in which Pakistan entrepreneurs would be prepared to invest;
- implementing Pakistan's plans to import electricity from Central Asia ;

- implementing the Turkmenistan-Afghanistan-Pakistan-India gas pipeline project.

Afghanistan and Pakistan can succeed in achieving their objective of peace, stability and prosperity through mutual cooperation. They can succeed only if they enjoy the unconditional support of the international community.

This debate is a good opportunity to commence an honest and objective evaluation of the challenges we face in Afghanistan and to devise a cooperative strategy for success. This strategy must combine military containment with political reconciliation, administrative control and rapid socio-economic development. The military option should be used but as a last, and not the first, resort. Military tactics should not create more alienation, more opposition and more enemies. We are convinced that dialogue and reconciliation together with calibrated use of force, are the best means to promote peace. To win this war, it is vital to win the hearts and minds of the people. We must build peace in Afghanistan in a bottom-up approach – village by village, district by district – offering incentives and disincentives to win the cooperation and support of the local population. Most importantly, our strategy for success must accelerate reconstruction and development. It must offer hope to the people – hope for peace, for jobs, for better lives, for themselves and their children.

(*Source*: http://www.mofa.gov.pk/Press_Releases/2008/July/PR_208_08.htm)

## Pakistan on Developing-8

July 8, 2008

*In his statement at the sixth D-8 Summit, Kuala Lumpur, Prime Minister Syed Yousuf Raza Gilani, expressed satisfaction over the progress made by Developing-8 countries. He lauded the signing of the of agreements on Preferential Trade Agreement, mutual assistance in Customs matters, and simplification of visa procedures for businessmen of member states, stating that intra D-8 trade, amounted to US$ 60.5 billion. Knowledge-based societies, promoting human resource development, skill development, education and research, and learning from each other's experiences and good practices were some areas he identified for further cooperation. Highlighting Pakistan's strategic location at the confluence of South Asia, Central Asia and South-West Asia, the prime minister pointed out that Pakistan could become a potential energy, trade and communication corridor for the entire region.*

It is an honour for me to address this eminent and distinguished gathering. I wish to congratulate you, Mr. Prime Minister, on assuming the

Chairmanship of the Developing-8. We are confident that under your able and dynamic leadership, this organization will make further progress in achieving our common objective of development cooperation.

We are thankful to the people and the Government of Malaysia for the warm welcome and gracious hospitality extended to us since our arrival in this beautiful city.

I avail myself of this opportunity to express my deep appreciation to Indonesia for providing excellent leadership to this organization over the last two years.

Our Secretary General H. E. Dr. Dipo Alam deserves our commendation for his strenuous efforts in promoting the objectives of the organization.

The sapling of the D-8 planted eleven years ago in Ankara, is growing steadily. Our vision in 1997, under the leadership of Turkey, was to make collective efforts for development cooperation among us. Though we are spread over in three continents, we have the bonds of affinity through close friendship.

Today, as we gather in this beautiful city of Kuala Lumpur, we renew our collective pledge and determination to build a better, peaceful and prosperous future for our people. Ours is an organization with a global reach, with abundant natural resources, and youthful population.

We are happy to see progress in promoting economic cooperation by promoting trade among D-8 countries. The signing of Agreements on Preferential Trade Agreement, Mutual Assistance in Customs Matters, and Simplification of Visa Procedures for Businessmen of Member States, are commendable steps in the right direction. Early implementation of these agreements will give impetus to promotion of intra D-8 trade, which is at present only US$ 60.5 billion.

Today, as we enter into the second decade of D-8, it is important to review our achievements and lay down a clear roadmap for adding value to our endeavours. Let me share my views in this regard.

In the last 11 years, the D-8 has made steady progress. However, the progress achieved so far does not reflect the true potential of D-8 countries. We need to look into the challenges before us, analyze them and convert them into opportunities to the advantage and betterment of our people.

Pakistan is committed to the success of D-8. Pakistan's trade with D-8 countries accounts for 8.14 percent of its overall trade, which is the highest as compared to the trade of other D-8 States with members of the organization. We need to do more to enhance economic opportunities that exist amongst us.

The D-8 can become a model of progress, development, cooperation and partnership. This organization has a great promise with more than 930 million people and vast natural resources. We need to build knowledge-based societies, promoting human resource development, skill development, education and research, and learning from each other's experiences and good practices. We need to promote greater connectivity, people-to-people contacts, networking and linkages exploiting the opportunities rendered by the Information Age.

We have the D-8 Roadmap for Economic Cooperation in the Second Decade of Cooperation among Member States. This is a useful document containing a blue print of D-8 cooperation in diverse fields. I would like to suggest that we should prioritize areas of cooperation and focus on some selected projects with timelines and verifiable indicators for effective monitoring and evaluation. Our first and foremost priority should be the promotion of intra D-8 trade. We hope all of us will soon implement the three agreements that we have signed for facilitation of trade promotion.

Pakistan would like the D-8 to rapidly grow and become a vibrant and effective organization. In order to achieve success and move forward, we need to provide the requisite human and financial resources to the D-8 Secretariat. We support the endeavours of the Secretary General in strengthening of the Secretariat that is commensurate with its mandate.

We welcome the association of private sector with the D-8, which will enrich our cooperation in various fields. The holding of Business Forum on the sidelines of this Summit to deliberate on issues like biotechnology, halal industry, and renewable energy, is commendable. This offers an occasion for the private sector and businessmen from D-8 countries to interact with each other and explore ways and means to further enhance intra D-8 trade.

The top most priority of my Government, which is democratically elected and enjoys overwhelming mandate of the people, is economic development for poverty alleviation in Pakistan. This overarching objective determines our economic reform process. Today we have a liberalized market oriented economy with abundant opportunities for businessmen and investors. We have established special economic zones with special incentives for foreign companies to invest in Pakistan .

Pakistan is strategically located at the confluence of South Asia, Central Asia and South-West Asia, with immense human and natural capital. It can serve as an energy, trade and communication corridor for the entire region. The wealth of our human and material resources is available to our brothers in the D-8 for enhancing mutually beneficial cooperation and integration of our fast growing economies.

The world is facing today the menace of extremism and terrorism, which has affected our socio-economic development. Pakistan has suffered the most due to this scourge. Our great leader former Prime Minister Shaheed Mohtarma Benazir Bhutto was martyred by terrorists. However, such cowardly acts will never dampen our firm resolve to fight terrorism and extremism with iron fist. We are following a multi-pronged approach in dealing with extremism that combines use of political, economic, administrative, and military measures.

Peace and stability are indispensable for socio-economic progress. We have made positive progress in recent years in our dialogue with India. We are seeking peaceful resolution of all our outstanding issues, including the core issue of Jammu and Kashmir in accordance with the aspirations of the Kashmiri people. Pakistan is committed to peace and stability in our region. However, we are of the view that there is a need to move from conflict management to conflict resolution to achieve durable peace and security in South As

On behalf of the Government and the people of Pakistan, I avail myself of this opportunity to assure your government and the people of Malaysia of our full cooperation in our collective efforts within D-8 to achieve tangible results in socio-economic development of our people.

(*Source*: http://www.mofa.gov.pk/Press_Releases/2008/July/PR_206_08.htm)

# 23.

## MISCELLANEOUS

### Building Political and Economic Linkages between South Asia and Central Asia[1]

October 2, 2008

*Foreign Minister Makhdoom Shah Mahmood Qureshi spoke on Building Political and Economic Linkages between South Asia and Central Asia and touched upon opportunities for regional cooperation within the South Asian region and drew attention towards the scope and potential offered by Central Asian Republics. Underlining the vast potential, Pakistan offered as the hub for inter-regional economic and political activity, he stated that the need for cooperation between South Asia and Central Asia was also reinforced by the common challenges faced by the two regions. Talking of inter-regional initiatives, he drew attention towards the Central Asia–South Asia Regional Market (CASAREM), which he said would improve the energy security situation of Pakistan and possibly some other energy deficient countries of South Asia. He pointed out that the initiative would also integrate the economies of South Asia and Central Asia. The Minister pointed out that Pakistan was also a party to ECO's Transit Transport Framework Agreement and was pursuing import of hydroelectricity and natural gas from Central Asia to South Asia. He stated that Pakistan's leading role both in SAARC and ECO and Observer status in the Shanghai Cooperation Organization (SCO) offered important platforms to Pakistan for promoting ties between Central Asia and South Asia.*

South and Central Asia have interacted over centuries through the fabled Silk Route. The route facilitated not just traders and invaders but also

---

1. Address by Foreign Minister Makhdoom Shah Mahmood Qureshi "Building Political and Economic Linkages between South Asia and Central Asia" at Institute of Regional Studies, Islamabad, October 2, 2008.

philosophers, saints, thinkers and artisans. This interaction was intense and spread over millennia. As a result, today, no two regions and their people have so much cultural, linguistic, ethnic and spiritual commonalities as South Asia and Central Asia .

These commonalities are even more pronounced in case of Pakistan. Our cultural traditions, language, cuisine, and even religious undercurrents have predominantly Central Asian roots.

The historic cross currents of ideas, civilization and culture between the two regions had been innately strong. Therefore, despite deliberate policies to isolate the two regions under over a century of British rule in South Asia and some seventy years of Soviet control of Central Asia, the similarities between the two regions remained. Under these colonial rules the historic and natural interaction between the two regions that was symbolised by travel, trade, migration and even conquest was assiduously curtailed. The Silk Route, both physically and in terms of ideas, lay idle. But this still failed to eliminate the inherent regional similarities. The effects of shared millennia of history could not be reversed by the antics of the Great Game.

Today, we are here to take stock of our common history. We need to build upon it. We need to deliberate upon the revival of the Silk Route. And we do all this not for the sake of history but for the sake of our people, for the prosperity and progress of our coming generations. The fabled Silk Route helped in sharing prosperity and cultural richness between South Asia and Central Asia in the past. Its revival - in its 21 st century reincarnation - should bring economic prosperity and provide opportunities to exchange ideas for the benefit of people of the two regions.

In my discourse today, I will briefly discuss regional cooperation within the South Asian region; will talk about the scope and potential offered by Central Asian Republics (CARs) in this regard, and underline the vast potential Pakistan offers as the hub for inter-regional economic and political activity. We are located at the cross-roads of the two regions and have much to offer to both.

The South Asian regional grouping SAARC was established in 1985. From its initial tentative steps limited to technical cooperation, SAARC now has grown into a vibrant organization addressing the challenging subjects of social uplift, regional connectivity, food security, energy cooperation, and human resource development.

SAARC has come a long way since its inception. It has gained considerable credibility at international level. Its global profile has been enhanced by the decision to grant observer status to USA, China, Japan, South Korea, Australia, European Union and Iran.

In recent years SAARC has also witnessed an increased collaboration with Association of South East Asian Nations (ASEAN), Asian Development Bank (ADB) and World Bank. Pakistan-India peace process has been a particularly useful development that has facilitated the growth of regional cooperation in South Asia .

An important milestone achieved by the South Asian countries is the operationalization of South Asian Free Trade Agreement (SAFTA).

We believe that three factors will by and large determine the full utilization of South Asia's potential in its external relations. Firstly, economic under-development, which leads to wide spread poverty, gross illiteracy and disease, is the greatest challenge faced by South Asia and needs to be addressed.

Second, South Asia's major strength lies in its demographics. The vast opportunities of globalization can bring benefit if our human resource is properly utilized. The quality of our population will determine our strength. Mere numbers will not account for much.

Third, it is important to develop transport and communication infrastructure to link SAARC countries with each other as well as with Central Asia. This, in fact, is an essential pre-requisite for inter-regional trade and economic cooperation.

The collapse of Soviet Union and emergence of independent republics of Kazakhstan, Kyrgyzstan, Uzbekistan, Turkmenistan, and Tajikistan have dramatically changed the political, economic and strategic landscape of Central Asian region.

The population of CARs is only about 65 million but they are extremely rich in energy resources and other raw materials, such as gold, uranium, iron and non-ferrous metals.

Central Asia has 150 billion barrels of crude oil and 1234 trillion cubic feet of natural gas reserves. South Asia affords a ready market for these resources.

Central Asia is land-locked. Its existing links to the sea are circuitous and time-consuming. South Asia potentially provides it an ideal route to the sea.

The Central Asian states have restructured their economies, improved their internal security and have emerged as stable political and geographic entities.

Central Asian states are members of the Economic Cooperation Organization (ECO) and Shanghai Cooperation Organization (SCO). With these organizations getting significance at world stage, CARs have also gained considerable weight in the international system.

The need for cooperation between South Asia and Central Asia is also reinforced by the common challenges faced by the two regions. These challenges are poverty, degradation of environment, food scarcity, threat of terrorism and extremism, narco trade, threat of epidemic diseases and the impact of global financial crisis. Working together, the two regions stand a better chance to meet these challenges.

Talking of inter-regional initiatives, I must point out that some inter-linkages between South Asia and Central Asia already exist. The Central Asia–South Asia Regional Market (CASAREM) is one such initiative. CASAREM is being developed in collaboration with the Asian Development Bank (ADB) and World Bank. Under this initiative, in the first instance, transmission lines will be laid from Tajikistan to Afghanistan and onward to Pakistan to transmit 1000–1200 MW of electricity. The project will improve the energy security situation of Pakistan and possibly other energy deficient countries of South Asia. Pakistan hosted an Inter-Governmental Ministerial Conference on the project in August 2008 in Islamabad. An Inter-Governmental Agreement was signed during the conference. CASAREM is to set up a permanent secretariat in Kabul .

TAPI (Turkmenistan-Afghanistan-Pakistan-India Gas Pipeline) project is another major initiative. The Steering Committee Meeting of TAPI had formally inducted India into the project in April 2008. This highly feasible project has tremendous potential and promise. Both regions will benefit economically. It will also integrate the economies of South Asia and Central Asia .

ECO's Transit Transport Framework Agreement (TTFA) has already entered into force. It lays down a comprehensive roadmap for establishing functional transit links across the region. Being a member of both SAARC and ECO, Pakistan could facilitate the extension of this initiative to South Asia .

An important field of mutual collaboration can be to synergize efforts being undertaken in the context of SAARC Regional Multi-model Transport Study (SRMTC) with those in progress within the framework of ECO's Transit Transport Framework Agreement (TTFA).

The two regions can jointly address the trans-border issues of environment and climate change. Melting glaciers of the Himalayas and Karakoram will change the climate and environment in both regions. We need to work together to avert this impending environmental degradation challenge. Likewise, Central Asian Republics can share their experiences in Aral Sea related environmental degradation with South Asia .

Like SAFTA in the context of South Asian countries, ECO countries have also concluded an ECO Trade Agreement (ECOTA). ECOTA has entered into force this year. With the finalization of lists, this important regional agreement is expected to be operational by January 2009. There is a need to strengthen the efficacy of these regional preferential trade arrangements by extending their territorial scope and by complementing these with other trade facilitation measures including elimination of all non-tariff barriers.

Pakistan follows the policy of supporting regional mechanisms that facilitate confidence building measures, preventive diplomacy, conflict resolution and peaceful settlement of all outstanding issues. This complements our vision to develop Pakistan as a hub of inter-regional economic activity .

Being founding member of SAARC and ECO, Pakistan is uniquely positioned to facilitate closer linkages between South Asia and Central Asia. Pakistan's geographic location provides a natural physical link between the two regions. *Pakistan is the bridge.*

Also, in geo-political, geo-strategic, and geo-economic terms, Pakistan is suitably positioned to play a key role in bringing the two regions closer. We will happily engage all the stake-holders to promote peace, stability, political harmony and economic development.

Over the years Pakistan has made steady progress towards improving potential trade and transit links through up-gradation of national transport infrastructure and establishment of functional region-wide transit corridors. This up-gradation has provided a viable option to the Central Asian Republics for transit links.

Gawadar seaport is a significant project in this regard. Future trade patterns envision substantial cargo from CARs and Afghanistan. Gawadar has opened new opportunities for CARs. Gawadar's role in oil transportation across the regions is also envisaged.

Karakoram Highway, built with the assistance of our great friend China, affords access to Central Asia through China. A Quadrilateral Agreement for Traffic in Transit brings together Pakistan, China, Kyrgyz Republic and Kazakhstan through KKH.

Pakistan is also a party to ECO's Transit Transport Framework Agreement. Unimpeded implementation of this and the Quadrilateral Agreement for Traffic in Transit will greatly boost regional commerce.

As I said earlier, Pakistan is also pursuing import of hydroelectricity and natural gas from Central Asia to South Asia. We have credible international backing for the two projects. World Bank and ADBP are the lead institutional support for import of energy from Central Asia .

Pakistan's leading role both in SAARC and ECO and Observer status in the Shanghai Cooperation Organization (SCO) proffer important platforms to Pakistan for promoting ties between Central Asia and South Asia.

We believe that convergence of economic and strategic interests will consume any real or perceived intra and inter regional differences. We should therefore aim for a free trade zone, and later even an economic community, for the countries of the two regions. Our focus should be close economic cooperation and integration, as in the Europe Union, or nearer home - ASEAN.

It is our firm belief that increased economic, political and human interaction will further the geo-economic potential of South Asia and Central Asia. Challenges are enormous but so are the opportunities. Let us focus on the latter.

(*Source*: http://www.mofa.gov.pk/Press_Releases/2008/Oct/PR_318_08.htm)

## The Transition in Pakistan and its impact on the War against Terrorism[2]

October 2, 2008

*Speaking on the political transition in Pakistan Mr Makhdoom Shah Mahmood Qureshi, Foreign Minister of Pakistan stated that elections were just the first step in an extensive and arduous process of rebuilding democracy and democratic-institutions in Pakistan. Talking on the refugee crises he pointed out that more than three million Afghanistan refugees poured into Pakistan and the present refugee population in Pakistan stands at nearly three million. He brought to attention the spillover effects of the U.S attack on the Taliban, which he said could be witnessed in the FATA region. On the issue of terrorist safe havens in border areas between Afghanistan and Pakistan, the Minister pointed out that Taliban and al-Qaeda elements in FATA constitutes a toxic brew of many elements - Taliban and Al Qaeda presence, ideology, ignorance, lack of economic, social and political opportunities, governmental neglect, marginalization and an insular way of life. He emphasized that force must be complemented by political, economic and social engagement. He stated that while democracy is inherently suited to deal with the complex challenges that confront nations, a strong economy is the key to winning the war against terrorism the long term.*

Pakistan has under gone a transition from an authoritarian government to a democratic dispensation since the general elections of February 2008. You are aware of the series of debacles that hit Pakistan in the run-up to the elections. President Musharraf about whose legitimacy the public had serious questions, declared emergency on 3 November 2007 to worldwide condemnation. Half of the judiciary was sacked. In December 2007 prior

2. Talk by Mr Makhdoom Shah Mahmood Qureshi, Foreign Minister of Pakistan at Princeton University, "The Transition in Pakistan and its impact on the War against Terrorism, October 2, 2008.

to vacating the office of the Army Chief he enacted a series of debilitating amendments to the Constitution granting himself immunity from his own unconstitutional measures.

These were calamities indeed for a country reeling under eight years of mismanagement and one man rule. However we could never have imagined the catastrophe that befell us on 27 December 2007 when Mohtarma Benazir Bhutto was assassinated in broad daylight. She was the icon of Pakistan's quest for democracy and rule of law. Her martyrdom was a rude shock to entire country. We have still not recovered from it.

The February elections were held under electoral machinery whose impartiality was open to question. However so great was the desire of the people of Pakistan for democracy that despite these handicaps their overwhelming verdict against the old order could not be masked by manipulation.

Two things were immediately clear. First, the people rejected the party President Musharraf had created to help him remain in power. Second, they unequivocally rejected the religious parties.

We are at present engaged in undoing the damage done to our society and polity in the nine years of dictatorship.

President Musharraf's government prided itself for its management. However in the year leading to the elections it was so obsessed with thwarting will of the people that it went into management hibernation. The international economic climate was steadily deteriorating all this time. There was a worldwide surge in food prices particularly of staples like wheat.

The price of oil began a steady and certain climb upwards. Nothing was done to deal with these serious challenges. The government did not anticipate the severest energy shortage in Pakistan's history. It failed to make the connection that economic growth needed a commensurate investment in energy. It also did nothing to correct a severely skewed macro-economic picture.

The elections were just the first step in an extensive and arduous process of rebuilding democracy and democratic institutions in Pakistan. The military regime had mutilated almost every institution of the State. The Constitution had suffered more than sixty amendments. There was the issue of the judges. Most of the leadership had been either in exile or in prison.

For instance President Zardari was in prison for a decade before being sent into exile. The present Prime Minister was in prison for six years. The leader of the other main political party the Muslim League was initially in prison and then sent into exile.

We have therefore had to relearn lost lessons. The institutions of the State have also had to relearn their functions and to work within established parameters. The primacy of the political leadership in setting national priorities has to be reestablished. The notions of personal and institutional accountability have to be reintroduced. These are not easy tasks.

However such is the enormity and number of challenges Pakistan faces that these are among our easier tasks. We have to undo the damage done to the Constitution.

There is friction among our federating units. Some feel neglected. Political frustrations have prompted resort to violence as in Balochistan. Then there are the real bread and butter issues. Inflation is galloping ahead at 24%, the highest that Pakistan has experienced in decades. The purchasing power of the average Pakistani has suffered a calamitous curtailment. The rupee has shed a quarter of its value over three months. There is a gap of 4500 megawatts between the peak supply and demand of electricity. It is no figure of speech when I say that the country has come to a stand still.

These are immediate challenges that we must overcome within the space of months or at the most a year or so. Only then can we afford to take a look at various developmental issues we face – provision of meaningful contemporarily relevant education, provision of healthcare, dealing with the dilapidated infrastructure and bringing Pakistan into the international economic mainstream.

So far I have not touched upon the single biggest challenge we face as a nation. I am of course referring to terrorism. The struggle against terrorism is the defining struggle of our times. When terrorists hit the twin towers in New York seven years ago it was not an attack on the US alone. It was an attack against all civilized societies. Terrorism poses a threat to all of us. It demands a response from all of us.

Unfortunately through a confluence of historical and geographical factors Pakistan finds itself the frontline state in the war against terrorism. It would be helpful if we can understand the genesis of the genie we are grappling with. We inherited the terrorism issue in the wake of the war against the Soviet invasion of Afghanistan. Pakistan and the US were partners in the endeavour that sowed the seeds of the eventual unraveling of the Soviet Union. Unfortunately while we won the war, we lost the peace. The spectacle of the Berlin Wall being breached and Soviet satellites gaining freedom in Europe claimed US attention and just when Afghanistan and Pakistan needed US and international support the most, it found itself abandoned.

The coming and rise of the Taliban was a natural corollary to developments in Afghanistan following the Soviet withdrawal and the US turning away. The Taliban's medievalism further alienated the international community. The isolated regime became a haven for the world's indigent terrorists and former jihadi warriors. Osama bin Laden, forced out of Sudan found welcome there. And it was from there that the 9/11 attacks were mounted.

As the immediate next door neighbour Pakistan was not totally insulated from what was going on in Afghanistan. Other than Afghanistan itself, no country has paid a higher price for the Soviet invasion and the war against that invasion than Pakistan.

The proliferation of weapons and drugs such as heroin in the Pakistani society is a direct consequence of that war. More than 3 million Afghanistan refugees poured into Pakistan. Rather than confining them in camps we allowed them to work. A whole generation of Afghans was born and reached adulthood in Pakistan without setting foot in their own country. The burden they imposed on our economy and society is incalculable. Even now there are nearly three million afghan refugees in Pakistan. Almost all Afghan leaders, including President Karzai, have at one time or another availed Pakistan's refuge and hospitality during the Soviet occupation of their country.

It did not help that the Pakistan Afghan border is one of the most difficult terrains to police. There is a historic free movement of people across this border as the people on both sides of it are ethnically the same. Following the US attack on the Taliban regime the defeated remnants of the Taliban and Al Qaeda crossed the porous Pak- Afghan border and entered our tribal areas – what the world now knows as FATA. There was no terrorist activity in those areas prior to October 2001.

The FATA had enjoyed autonomy in running their affairs since British times. They had their own laws and customs and the central government in Islamabad dealt with them through a Political Agent. The system had worked relatively well until the shock of the 9/11. Nevertheless in the immediate aftermath of the US attack on the Taliban we were able to apprehend or kill hundreds of Al Qaeda and Taliban cadres. Some of the most prominent terrorists in US custody including Khalid Sheikh Mohammad, the mastermind of the 9/11 attacks, was arrested by Pakistani authorities.

The government of Pakistan believing that the Taliban and Al Qaeda elements continued to remain in the FATA launched a full scale army operation in those areas in 2004. This was the first time in nearly a century that regular troops had entered those areas. While the operation was a success on many counts, it alienated the traditionally independent minded tribal population. The Taliban and the Al Qaeda fanned this alienation while coercing the more peaceable elements in the tribal society. When their situation grew desperate they resorted to indiscriminate killing of Pakistani civilians and armed personnel in the rest of Pakistan.

This is where we stand today. We are at war in FATA against the extremists. We have lost more than 1200 soldiers in this war. This includes one three star, one two star and a number of one star generals. Other than US casualties in Iraq this is the largest number of casualties sustained by any country fighting terrorism. Additionally thousands of civilians have been killed in suicide bombings and targeted killings. Pakistan is a victim of terrorism.

I must therefore confess to a degree of bewilderment when Pakistan is seen more as a problem in some US circles than as a partner in this defining struggle of our times. There is talk of terrorist safe havens in border areas between Afghanistan and Pakistan. I agree there are Taliban and Al Qaeda elements in those areas. The rising death toll bears the clearest testimony to their presence. However they are there despite our best efforts to dislodge them.

What more can I say to underline our commitment to reclaim our land and our way of life from the terrorists that we have not even hesitated from using airpower against them. However in FATA we are not only fighting the terrorists. We are fighting the terrain as well.

Force is certainly the most important ingredient in fighting any insurgency in the short term. However force alone will never be sufficient. The terrorism we see in FATA is a toxic brew of many elements - Taliban and Al Qaeda presence, ideology, ignorance, lack of economic, social and political opportunities, governmental neglect, marginalization and an insular way of life. The strategy to combat it must be equally comprehensive. The objective is to win the hearts and minds of the populace so that the Taliban and Al Qaeda find it difficult to hide in the population.

Single minded reliance on force will however result in further alienation of the populace. Admiral Mullen, US Joint Chiefs of Staff told Congress a few weeks back "It is my professional opinion that no amount of troops in no amount of time can ever achieve all the objectives we seek in Afghanistan. And frankly, we're running out of time."

Force must be complemented by political, economic and social engagement. We must not undertake any action that hardens the resolve of those already committed to violence or to sway the hostile neutrals to join them. I am afraid that a relatively recent element in this already difficult war threatens to undo what we have already achieved. I am referring to US attacks in Pakistani territory.

I have read a US legislator's comments as to why Pakistan opposes US incursions when in reality US troops are going into Pakistan in hot pursuit to fight the elements that threaten Pakistan. This is certainly one way of looking at this matter. However the Pakistani public rightly sees such attacks as a violation of Pakistan's sovereignty. It hurts us even more when the transgressor is our friend and ally, the US.. If there are actions to be taken those actions will be taken by Pakistan.

I can understand the US frustration. Things are going badly in Afghanistan. Ambassador Richard Holbrooke in an article published in the recent Foreign Affairs magazine sums up the difficulties confronting the US in Afghanistan in these words "Success will require new policies with regard to four major problem areas: the tribal areas in Pakistan, the drug lords who dominate the Afghan system, the national police, and the incompetence and corruption of the Afghan government". Admittedly the tribal areas are a factor in the difficult situation in Afghanistan. However we need to also devote the same kind of attention to intra-Afghanistan factors.

A large segment of the Pakistani public therefore believes Pakistan is being made the scapegoat for ISAF and Afghanistan government's failings. We are doing our share in stabilizing the situation in Afghanistan. Our brigade level operations in Bajaur attest to our commitment. However we must be honest to ourselves that the majority of Afghanistan's problems originate in and must be treated in Afghanistan.

The solution lies in closer coordination among the three principal parties – the US, Pakistan and Afghanistan. Each partner must also shed preconceived ideas and notions about the others' actions and motivations. The approach should be to address the problems rather than scoring media points. The capacity of both Pakistani and Afghanistan forces to fight the insurgents must be augmented. On the Pakistani side I can say that while we are quite effective during the day, we lose the initiative at night on account of limited night fighting capability. We need the means to gather real time intelligence and to mount a real time precision response in which there is minimal collateral damage. The US can help us in this area.

There should be a matching response on the Afghanistan side to the border control measures we have instituted. We have some 1100 posts along the border. There are about a hundred or so on the Afghanistan side. These posts and measures should act as a double net. Those that manage to evade one should be ensnared in the other.

We must also understand that progress against terrorism will be incremental. It is easy to lose patience in such a conflict. Disagreements can erupt between allies. However we must not forget that Pakistan and the United States are a team in this war. Neither can win this war easily without the other.

How is a democratic Pakistan better than an autocratic one in the fight against terrorism? I know there is no such thing as a panacea. However I believe that democracy is the closest thing to a panacea mankind has invented or discovered. There are few people more qualified to make this statement than us Pakistanis. In the course of sixty years of our existence as an independent nation we have suffered three major interruptions of the democratic process. The total time spent under authoritarian rule is more than our existence as a democracy. Each turn of the screw towards authoritarianism has left us institutionally weaker and our polity more brittle. The last nine years under General Musharraf were no different.

Authoritarianism is an attractive short cut. Democracy is the actual road where you have to make room for others and obey all signals. Yet in the final analysis it is the seemingly chaotic road of democracy that takes you to your destination.

A democratic system has a natural pressure release valve. All issues are hammered out in the Parliament. Opinions are expressed, consensus evolved and where consensus proves elusive compromises made. This process automatically takes the edge off the most extreme positions. There is an open airing of views, complaints and grievances. The remedies to these are also openly discussed. The government's priorities are set by the representatives of the people.

The representatives are answerable to their constituents. However interaction with the constituents is a two way street. The representatives can also educate their constituents about what is possible and what is not and why this is so. A democratic system is structurally more responsive to the real needs of the people. And neglect of the real needs of the people is what is behind the difficulties we face in FATA.

A democracy is inherently better suited to deal with the complex challenges that confront nations. Democracies are better at retaining and discharging their people's trust. If this were not the case then the world would be full of autocracies instead of democracies. In the final analysis it is only a democratic dispensation which can evolve the kind of national consensus needed to deal with a threat as existential as terrorism.

Democracy is the only cure of the difficulties Pakistan faces. Our first effort is to ensure the primacy of the Parliament. All policies and decisions must flow from the peoples' representatives. We have made headway here. We forced the resignation of President Musharraf through parliamentary means. There are now smoothly running democratic governments at the center and in the four provinces. There is a new found cordiality in relations between the treasury and the opposition benches. The institutions of the state are becoming used to the civilian leadership setting the nation's priorities.

In parallel to fighting the terrorists we must turn the flagging economy round. A strong economy is the key to winning the war against terrorism the long term. FATA is an area of special focus. We must generate employment there to give the youth of the area an alternative to Al Qaeda pay book. The ignorance that breeds extremism must be combated through schools imparting modern education. The people of FATA must have a stake in Pakistan's stability and prosperity. A person with steady employment and prospects of a better future for himself and his children is less likely to turn to violence and terrorism. The basic premise is that Al Qaeda and Taliban must not be able to find more recruits.

It is a long road. The journey is arduous. However it is a journey we must undertake if we are to become the country our founding father Quaid-e-Azam Mohammad Ali Jinnah wanted us to become – a modern Muslim nation at peace within and at peace without.

(*Source*: http://www.mofa.gov.pk/Press_Releases/2008/Oct/PR_307_08.htm)

# SRI LANKA

# 24.

## INTERNAL DEVELOPMENTS

### Official Statement in response to a Question on the Recommendations of the All Party Representatives Conference in Sri Lanka

January 24, 2008

*In response to a question on the recommendations of the All Party Representatives Conference in Sri Lanka, the official statement highlighted that the people of Sri Lanka would be solely responsible for the decisions and any solution regarding the devolution of powers would be under the framework of a united Sri Lanka.*

In response to a question on the recommendations of the All Party Representatives Conference in Sri Lanka, the Official Spokesperson said:

"The Government of Sri Lanka has been good enough to share with us the interim steps recommended by the All Party Representatives Conference in Sri Lanka for implementation of devolution provisions and official language provisions of the Sri Lankan Constitution. It has consistently been our view that a settlement of the issues in Sri Lanka is to be done by the Sri Lankan people themselves in a manner acceptable to all communities within the framework of a united Sri Lanka. The Government of India will continue to work with Sri Lanka and its people to bring about such a settlement of the issues in Sri Lanka. To the extent that the APRC proposals contribute to such a settlement, they are a welcome first step."

(*Source*: http://meaindia.nic.in/pressbriefing/2008/01/24pb01.htm)

### Official Response to Questions about Sri Lankan Government's Abrogation of Ceasefire Agreement of 2002, Official Spokesperson

January 4, 2008

*In response to questions about Sri Lankan Government's abrogation of Ceasefire Agreement of 2002, the Indian government while expressing concern over the human rights situation emphasized the importance of a settlement within the framework of "United Sri Lanka".*

For India, any step that leads to a reduction in levels of violence and human suffering in Sri Lanka is welcome. Unfortunately, what we have seen recently has been an increase in violence, tension and conflict in Sri Lanka. At the same time, we are acutely conscious that what is required in Sri Lanka is a settlement of political, constitutional and other issues within the framework of united Sri Lanka with which all communities in Sri Lanka are comfortable. It is only through such a settlement that a lasting peace can return to that troubled country. We strongly believe that there is no military solution to the issue.

(*Source*: http://meaindia.nic.in/pressbriefing/2008/01/04pb01.htm)

## Seventeenth Amendment

October 3, 2001

SEVENTEENTH AMENDMENT TO THE CONSTITUTION OF THE DEMOCRATIC SOCIALIST REPUBLIC OF SRI LANKA

[Certified on 3rd October, 2001]
L. D. - O. 47/2001.

AN ACT TO AMEND THE CONSTITUTION OF THE DEMOCRATIC SOCIALIST REPUBLIC OF SRI LANKA

BE it enacted by the Parliament of the Democratic Socialist Republic of Sri Lanka as follows:

**Short title**

1. This Act may be cited as the Seventeenth Amendment to the Constitution.

Insertion of Chapter VIIA in the Constitution of the Democratic Socialist Republic of Sri Lanka.

2. The Constitution of the Democratic Socialist Republic of Sri Lanka (hereinafter referred to as the "Constitution") is hereby amended by the insertion immediately after Article 41 of the Constitution of the following new Chapter, which shall have effect as Chapter VIIA of the Constitution:

**CHAPTER VIIA**
**THE CONSTITUTIONAL COUNCIL**

**Constitution of the Constitutional Council**

**41A.** (1) There shall be a Constitutional Council (in this Chapter referred to as the Council) which shall consist of the following members:

(a) the Prime Minister;

(b) the Speaker ;
(c) the Leader of the Opposition in Parliament ;
(d) one person appointed by the President ;
(e) five persons appointed by the President, on the nomination of both the Prime Minister, the Leader of the Opposition;
(f) one person nominated upon agreement by the majority of the Members of Parliament belonging to political parties or independent groups other than the respective political parties or independent groups to which the Prime Minister and the Leader of the Opposition belongs and appointed by the President.

(2) The Speaker shall be the Chairman of the Council.

(3) In nominating the five persons referred to in subparagraph (e) of paragraph (1) of this Article, the Prime Minister and the Leader of the Opposition shall consult the leaders of the political parties and independent groups represented in Parliament. Three of such persons shall, in consultation with the Members of Parliament who belong to the respective minority communities, be nominated to represent minority interests.

(4) The persons to be appointed or nominated as the case may be, under sub-paragraphs (d), (e) and (f) of paragraph (1) of this Article, shall be persons of eminence and integrity who have distinguished themselves in public life and who are not members of any political party.

(5) The President shall upon receipt of a written communication of the nominations under sub-paragraph (e) or sub-paragraph (f) of paragraph (1) of this Article, forthwith, make the respective appointments.

(6) (a) On the dissolution of Parliament, notwithstanding the provisions of paragraph (2) of Article 64 of the Constitution, the Speaker shall continue to hold office as a member of the Council, until a Member of Parliament is elected to be the Speaker under paragraph (1) of the aforesaid Article ;

(b) Notwithstanding the dissolution of Parliament, the Leader of the Opposition shall continue to hold office as a member of the Council, until such time after a General Election following such dissolution, a Member of Parliament is recognised as the Leader of the Opposition in Parliament.

(7) Every member of the Council appointed under sub-paragraph (e) and sub-paragraph (f) of paragraph (1) of this Article, shall hold office for a period of three years from the date of appointment as such member, unless he earlier resigns his office by writing addressed to the President, or is removed from office by the President on both the Prime Minister and the Leader of the Opposition forming an opinion that such member is physically or mentally incapacitated and is unable to function further in office, or is convicted by a court of law for any offence involving moral turpitude or if a resolution for the imposition of civic disability upon him has been passed in terms of Article 81 of the Constitution or is deemed to have vacated his office under paragraph (7) of Article 41E.

(8) In the event of there being a vacancy among the members appointed under sub-paragraph (e) or sub-paragraph (f) of paragraph (1) of this Article, the President shall, within two weeks of the occurrence of such vacancy and having regard to the provisions of the aforementioned sub-paragraphs, appoint another person to succeed such member. Any person so appointed, shall hold office during the unexpired part of the period of office of the member whom he succeeds.

(9) The member, appointed under sub-paragraph (d) of paragraph (1) of this Article shall, unless earlier removed from office by the President, hold office for a period of three years.

(10) A Member appointed under sub-paragraph (e) or sub-paragraph (f) of paragraph (1) of this Article, shall not be eligible for re-appointment under those sub-paragraphs.

(11) The appointments made by the President under sub-paragraph (d), sub-paragraph (e) and sub-paragraph (f) of paragraph (1) of this Article shall be communicated to the Speaker.

**Council to recommend appointments**

**41B.** (1) No person shall be appointed by the President as the Chairman or a member of any of the Commissions specified in the Schedule to this Article, except on a recommendation of the Council.

(2) The provisions of paragraph (1) of this Article shall apply in respect of any person appointed to act as the Chairman or a member of any such Commission.

(3) It shall be the duty of the Council to recommend to the President persons for appointment as Chairmen or members of the Commissions specified in the Schedule to this Article, whenever the, occasion for such appointment arises, and such recommendations shall reflect the different ethnic groups.

(4) No person appointed under paragraph (1) of this Article or a person appointed to act as the Chairman or a member of any such Commission shall be removed except as provided for in the Constitution or in any law, and where no such provision is made, such person shall be removed by the President only with the prior approval of the Council.

**SCHEDULE**

(a) The Election Commission.
(b) The Public Service Commission.
(c) The National Police Commission.
(d) The Human Rights Commission of Sri Lanka.
(e) The Permanent Commission to Investigate Allegations of Bribery or Corruption.
(f) The Finance Commission.
(g) The Delimitation Commission.

Council to approve appointments.

**41C.** (1) No person shall be appointed by the President to any of the Offices specified in the Schedule to this Article, unless such appointment has been approved by the Council upon a recommendation made to the Council by the President.

(2) The provisions of paragraph (1) of this Article shall apply in respect of any person appointed to act for a period exceeding fourteen days in any office specified in the Schedule to this Article.

(3) No person appointed to any Office specified in the Schedule to this Article or to act in any such Office, shall be removed from such Office except as provided for in the Constitution or in any law.

(4) In the discharge of its functions relating to the appointment of Judges of the Supreme Court and the President and Judges of the Court of Appeal, the Council may obtain the views of the Chief Justice and the Attorney-General.

**SCHEDULE**

**PART I**

(a) The Chief Justice and the Judges of the Supreme Court.
(b) The President and the Judges of the Court of Appeal.
(c) The Members of the Judicial Service Commission other than the Chairman.

**PART II**

(a) The Attorney-General.
(b) The Auditor-General.
(c) The Inspector-General of Police.
(d) The Parliamentary Commissioner for Administration (Ombudsman).
(e) The Secretary-General of Parliament.

**Secretary and other officers of the Council.**

**41D.** (1) There shall be a Secretary to the Council who shall be appointed by the Council.

(2) The Council may appoint such officers as it considers necessary for the discharge of its functions, on such terms and conditions as shall be determined by the Council.

**Meetings of the Council**

**41E.** (1) The Council shall meet as often as may be necessary to discharge the functions assigned to the Council by the provisions of this Chapter or by any other law, and such meetings shall be summoned by the Secretary to the Council in the direction of the Chairman of the Council.

(2) The Chairman shall preside at all meetings of the Council, and in the absence of the Chairman, the Prime Minister, and in the absence of the Prime Minister, the Leader of the Opposition shall preside at the meetings of the Council. Where the Chairman, the Prime Minister and the Leader of the Opposition are all absent from any such meeting, the members present shall elect a member from among themselves to preside at such meeting.

(3) The quorum for any meeting of the Council shall be six members.

(4) The Council shall endeavour to make every recommendation, approval or decision it is required to make by unanimous decision, and in the absence of an unanimous decision, no recommendation, approval or decision made shall be valid, unless supported by not less than five members of the Council present at such meeting.

(5) The Chairman shall not have an original vote, but in the event of an equality of votes on any question for decision at any meeting of the Council, the Chairman or other member presiding at such meeting, shall have a casting vote.

(6) The procedure in regard to meetings of the Council and the transaction of business at such meetings shall be determined by the Council, including procedures to be followed in regard to the recommendation or approval of persons suitable for any appointment under Article 41B or Article 41C.

(7) Any member of the Council appointed under sub-paragraph (e) of paragraph (1) of Article 41A, who without obtaining prior leave of the Council absents himself from two consecutive meetings of the Council, shall be deemed to have vacated office with effect from the date of the second of such meetings.

**Council to perform other duties.**

**41F.** The Council shall perform and discharge such other duties and functions as may be imposed or assigned to the Council by the Constitution, or by any other law.

**Expenses to be charged on the Consolidated Fund.**

**41G.** The expenses incurred by the Council shall be charged on the Consolidated Fund.

**Finality of decisions of the Council.**

**41H.** Subject to the provisions of paragraphs (1), (2), (4), and (5) of Article 126, no court shall have the power or jurisdiction to entertain, hear or decide or call in question on any ground whatsoever, or in a any manner whatsoever, any decision of the Council or any approval or recommendation made by the Council, which decision, recommendation or approval shall be final and conclusive for all purposes.'.

**Amendment of Article 52 of the Constitution.**

**3.** Article 52 of the Constitution is hereby amended by the repeal of paragraph (7) of that Article, and the substitution therefor of the following paragraph :-

"(7) For the purposes of this Article -

(a) the Office of the Secretary-General of Parliament, the Office of the Parliamentary Commissioner for Administration (Ombudsman), the Constitutional Council, the Public Service Commission, the Election Commission, the National Police Commission and the Office of the Secretary to the Cabinet of Ministers; and

(b) the Department of the Auditor-General,

shall be deemed not to be departments of Government.".

Replacement of Chapter IX of the Constitution.

**4.** Chapter IX of the Constitution is hereby replaced and the following Chapter substituted therefor:

## 'CHAPTER IX - THE EXECUTIVE
### The Public Service

**Public Service Commission**

**54.** (1) There shall be a Public Service Commission (in this Chapter referred to as the Commission") which shall consist of nine members appointed by the President on the recommendation of the Constitutional Council, of whom not less than three members shall be persons who have had over fifteen years experience as a public officer. The President on the recommendation of the Constitutional Council shall appoint one member as its Chairman.

(2) No person shall be appointed as a member of the Commission or continue to hold office as such member if he is or becomes a member of Parliament, a Provincial Council or a local authority.

(3) Every person who immediately before his appointment as a member of the Commission was a public officer in the service of the State or a judicial officer, shall, upon such appointment taking effect cease to hold such office and shall be ineligible for further appointment as a public officer or a judicial officer:

Provided that any such person shall, until he ceases to be a member of the Public Service Commission, or while continuing to be a member, attains the age at which he would, if he were a public officer or a judicial officer, as the case may be, be required to retire, be deemed to be a public officer or a judicial officer and to hold a pensionable office in the service of the State, for the purpose of any provision relating to the grant of pensions, gratuities and other allowances in respect of such service.

(4) Every member of the Commission shall hold office for a period of three years from the date of his appointment, unless he becomes subject to any disqualification under paragraph (2) of this Article or earlier resigns from his office by writing addressed to the President or is removed from office by the President on the recommendation of the Constitutional Council or is convicted by a court of law of any offence involving moral turpitude or if a resolution for the imposition of civic disability upon him has been passed in terms of Article 81 or is deemed to have vacated his office under paragraph (5) of this Article.

(5) A member of the Commission shall be eligible for reappointment as a member, but shall not be eligible for appointment as a public officer or a judicial officer after the expiry of his term of office as a member. No member shall be eligible to hold office as a member of the Commission for more than two terms.

(6) A member of the Commission who without obtaining prior leave of the Commission absents himself from three consecutive meetings of the Commission, shall be deemed to have vacated office with effect from the date of the third of such meetings, and shall not be eligible thereafter to be reappointed as a member of the Commission.

(7) The President may grant a member leave from the performance of his duties relating to the Commission for a period not exceeding two months and shall for the duration of such period on the recommendation of the Constitutional Council, appoint a person qualified to be a member of the Commission to be a temporary member for the period of such leave.

(8) A member of the Commission shall be paid such emoluments as may be determined by Parliament. The emoluments paid to a member of the Commission shall be charged on the Consolidated Fund and shall not be diminished during the term of office of such member.

(9) The Commission shall have the power to act notwithstanding any vacancy in its membership, and no act, proceeding or decision of the Commission shall be or be deemed to be invalid by reason only of such vacancy or any defect in the appointment of a member.

(10) There shall be a Secretary to the Commission who shall be appointed by the Commission.

(11) The members of the Commission shall be deemed to be public servants, within the meaning and for the purposes of Chapter IX of the Penal Code.

**Powers and Functions of Cabinet of Ministers and of the Commission**

**55.** (1) The appointment, promotion, transfer, functions of disciplinary control and dismissal of public officers shall be vested in the Commission.

(2) The Commission shall not derogate from the functions and powers of the Provincial Public Service Commissions established by law.

(3) Notwithstanding the provisions of paragraph (1) of this Article, the appointment, promotion, transfer, disciplinary control and dismissal of all Heads of Departments shall vest in the Cabinet of Ministers, who shall exercise such powers after ascertaining the views of the Commission.

(4) Subject to the provisions of the Constitution, the Cabinet of Ministers shall provide for and determine all matters of policy relating to public officers.

(5) The Commission shall be responsible and answerable to Parliament in accordance with the provisions of the Standing Orders of Parliament for the exercise and discharge of its powers and functions, and shall forward to Parliament in each calendar year, a report of its activities for such year.

**Committees of the Commission**

**56.** (1) The Commission may delegate to a Committee consisting or three persons (not being members of the Commission) appointed by the Commission, the powers of appointment, promotion, transfer, disciplinary control and dismissal of such categories of public officers as are specified by the Commission.

(2) The Commission shall cause the appointment, of any such Committee to be published in the Gazette.

(3) The procedure and quorum for meetings of any such Committee shall be as determined by the Commission by rules made in that behalf. The Commission shall cause such rules to be published in the Gazette.

(4) There shall be a Secretary to each Committee, who shall be appointed by the Commission.

**Delegation of powers to a public officer**

**57.** (1) The Commission may delegate to a f Powers to public officer, subject to such conditions and procedure as may be determined by the Commission, its powers of appointment, promotion, transfer, disciplinary control and dismissal of such category of public officers as are specified by the Commission.

(2) The Commission shall cause any such delegation to be published in the Gazette, including the conditions and procedure determined by the Commission for such purpose.

**Right of Appeal.**

**58.** (1) Any public officer aggrieved by an order relating to a promotion, transfer, dismissal or an order on a disciplinary matter made by a Committee or any public officer under Article 56 or Article 57, in respect of the officer so aggrieved, may appeal to the Commission against such order in accordance with such rules made by the Commission from time to time, relating to the procedure to be followed in the making, hearing and determination of an appeal made to the Commission and the period fixed within which an appeal should he heard and concluded.

(2) The Commission shall have the power upon such appeal to alter, vary, rescind or confirm an order against which an appeal is made, or to give directions in relation thereto, or to order such further or other inquiry as to the Commission shall seem fit.

(3) The Commission shall cause to be published in the Gazette the rules made by it under paragraph (1) of this Article.

**Administrative Appeals Tribunal.**

**59.** (1) There shall be an Administrative Appeals Tribunal appointed by the Judicial Service Commission.

(2) The Administrative Appeals Tribunal shall have the power to alter, vary or rescind any order or decision made by the Commission.

(3) The constitution, powers and procedure of such Tribunal, including the time limits for the preferring of appeals, shall be provided for by law.

**Commission not to exercise power where there is delegation.**

**60.** Upon delegation of any of its powers to a Committee or a public officer appointed under Article 56 or Article 57 as the case may be, the Commission shall not, while such delegation is in force, exercise or perform its functions or duties in regard to the categories of public officers in respect of which such delegation is made, subject to the provisions contained in paragraphs (1) and (2) of Article 58.

**Procedure at meetings.**

**61.** (1) The quorum for a meeting of the Commission shall be five members.

(2) All decisions of the Commission shall be made by a majority of votes of the members present at the meeting. In the event of an equality of votes, the member presiding at the meeting shall have a casting vote.

(3) The Chairman of the Commission shall preside at all meetings of the Commission, and in his absence, a member elected by the members present from amongst themselves, shall preside at such meeting.

**Immunity from legal proceedings.**

**61A.** Subject to the provisions of paragraphs (1), (2), (3), (4) and (5) of Article 126, no court or tribunal shall have power or jurisdiction to inquire into or pronounce upon or in any manner call in question any order or decision made by the Commission, a Committee, or any public officer, in pursuance of any power or duty conferred or imposed on such Commission, or delegated to a Committee or public officer, under this Chapter or under any other law.

**Savings of rules and regulations in force.**

**61B.** Until the Commission otherwise provides, all rules, regulations and procedures relating to the public service as are in force on the date of the coming into operation of this Chapter, shall, *mutatis mutandis*, be deemed to continue in force as rules, regulations and procedures relating to the public service, as if they had been made or provided for under this Chapter.

**Interference with the Commission.**

**61C.** (1) Every person who, otherwise than in the course of such person's lawful duty, directly or indirectly by himself or by or with any other person, in any manner whatsoever influences or attempts to influence or interferes with any decision of the Commission, or a Committee or a public officer to whom the Commission has delegated any power under this Chapter, or to so influence any member of the Commission or a Committee, shall be guilty of an offence and shall on conviction be liable to a fine not exceeding one hundred thousand rupees or to imprisonment for a term not exceeding seven years, or to both such fine and imprisonment.

(2) Every High Court established under Article 154P of the Constitution shall have jurisdiction to hear and determine any matter referred to in paragraph (1) of this Article.

**Oath or affirmation of office.**

**61D.** A person appointed to any office referred to in this Chapter shall not enter upon the duties of his office until he takes and subscribes the oath or makes and subscribes the affirmation set out in the Fourth Schedule to the Constitution.

**Appointments by the President.**

**61E.** The President shall appoint -

(a) the Heads of the Army, the Navy and the Air Force; and

(b) subject to the provisions of Article 41C, the Attorney General and the Inspector General of Police.

**Interpretation.**

**61F.** For the purposes of this Chapter "public officer" does not include a member of the Army, Navy, or Air Force, an officer of the Election Commission appointed by such Commission, a police officer appointed by the National Police Commission or a scheduled public officer appointed by the Judicial Service Commission.?.

Amendment of Article 65 of the Constitution.

**5.** Article 65 of the Constitution is hereby amended as follows:

(1) in paragraph (1) of that Article, by the substitution for the words "shall be appointed by the President", of the words "shall, subject to the provisions of Article 41C, be appointed by the President"; and

(2) in paragraph (6) of that Article, by the substitution for the words "President may appoint a person", of the words "President may, subject to the provisions of Article 41C, appoint a person".

**Amendment of Article 89 of the Constitution.**

**6.** Article 89 of the Constitution is hereby amended in paragraph (j) of that Article, by the substitution for the words and figures? Article 116"of the words and figures "Article 116 or Article 111C, as the case may be?.

**Amendment of Article 91 of the Constitution.**

**7.** Article 91 of the Constitution is hereby amended in paragraph (1) thereof, as follows:

(1) by the insertion immediately after sub-paragraph (d)(iv) of that paragraph, of the following new sub-paragraph:

"(iva) a member of a Provincial Public Service Commission,"

(2) by the substitution for subparagraph (d)(v) of that paragraph, of the following sub-paragraph :-

"(v) the Commissioner-General of Elections,";

(3) by the insertion immediately after sub-paragraph (d)(v) of that paragraph, of the following new sub-paragraphs :-

"(va) a member of the Election Commission,

(vb) a member of the Constitutional Council,

(vc) a member of the National Police Commission," ; and

(4) by the insertion immediately after sub-paragraph (d)(viiia) of that paragraph, of the following new sub-paragraph :-

"(viiia) an officer of a Provincial Public Service holding any office created after February 01,1988, the initial of the salary scale of which is, on the date of the creation of that office, not less than such amount as determined by resolution of Parliament, or such other amount *per annum* as would, under any subsequent revision of such salary scales, correspond to such initial,".

Repeal of Articles 103 and 104 of the Constitution.

**8.** Article 103 and Article 104 of the Constitution are hereby repealed.

**Insertion of Chapter XIVA in the Constitution**

**9.** The following new Chapter is hereby inserted immediately after Article 102 of the Constitution and shall have effect as Chapter XIVA of the Constitution:

## ‘CHAPTER XIVA - ELECTION COMMISSION

### Election Commission

**103.** (1) There shall be an Election Commission (in this Chapter referred to as the “Commission”) consisting of five members appointed by the President on the recommendation of the Constitutional Council, from amongst persons who have distinguished themselves in any profession or in the fields of administration or education. The President shall on the recommendation of the Constitutional Council, appoint one member as its Chairman.

(2) The object of the Commission shall be to conduct free and fair elections and Referenda.

(3) No person shall be appointed as a member of the Commission or continue to hold office as such member if he is or becomes a member of Parliament, a Provincial Council or a local authority, or is or appointed a judicial officer or public officer, or is or enters into the employment of the State in any capacity whatsoever.

(4) The provisions of the Constitution and any other law relating to the removal of judges of the Supreme Court and the Court of Appeal from office shall, *mutatis mutandis*, apply to the removal of a member of the Commission from office.

(5) A member of the Commission who without obtaining prior leave of the Commission, absents from three consecutive meetings of the Commission, shall be deemed to have vacated office with effect from the date of the third of such meetings.

(6) A member of the Commission shall hold office for a period of five years from the date of appointment, unless he becomes subject to any disqualification under paragraph (3) of this Article or earlier resigns from office by writing addressed to the President or is removed from office under paragraph (4) of this Article, or is convicted by a court of law of any offence involving moral turpitude, or if a resolution for the imposition of civic disability upon him has been passed in terms of Article 81 or is deemed to have vacated office under paragraph (5) of this Article.

(7) The President may grant a member leave from the performance of his duties relating to the Commission for a period not exceeding two months and may appoint a person qualified to be a member of the Commission to be a temporary member for the period of such leave. Every such appointment shall be made on the recommendation of the Constitutional Council.

(8) A member of the Commission shall be paid such emoluments as may be determined by Parliament. The emoluments paid to a member of the Commission shall be charged on the Consolidated Fund and shall not be diminished during the term of office of the member.

(9) All members of the Commission shall be deemed to be public servants within the meaning and for the purposes of Chapter IX of the Penal Code.

104. **(1) The quorum for any meeting of the Commission shall be three members**

(2) (a) The Chairman of the Commission shall preside at all meetings of the Commission and, in the absence of the Chairman from any meeting of the Commission, a member elected by the members present from amongst themselves shall preside at such meeting.

(b) Decisions of the Commission shall be by a majority of the members present and voting at the meeting at which the decision is taken, and in the event of an equality of votes, the Chairman or the member presiding at the meeting shall have a casting vote.

(3) The Commission shall have power to act notwithstanding any vacancy in the membership of the Commission, and no act or proceeding or decision of the Commission shall be invalid or be deemed to be invalid by reason only of such vacancy or any defect in the appointment of a member.

**Finality of decisions and immunity from suit.**

**104A.** Subject to the jurisdiction conferred on the Supreme Court under paragraph (1) of Article 126, Article 104H and Article 130, and on the Court of Appeal by Article 144, and the jurisdiction conferred on any court by any law to hear and determine election petitions or Referendum petitions,-

(a) no court shall have the power or jurisdiction to entertain or hear or decide or call in question on any ground and in any manner whatsoever, any decision, direction or act of the Commission, made or done or purported to have been made or done under the Constitution or under any law relating to the holding of an election or the conduct of a Referendum as the case may be, which decisions, directions or acts shall be final and conclusive; and

(b) no suit or prosecution or other proceeding shall lie against any member or officer of the Commission for any act or thing which in good faith is done or purported to be done by him in the performance of his duties or the discharge of his functions under the Constitution or under any law relating to the holding of an election or the conduct of a Referendum as the case may be.

**Powers, functions and duties of the Commission**

**104B.** (1) The Commission shall exercise, perform and discharge all such powers, duties and functions conferred or imposed on or assigned to-

(a) the Commission; or

(b) the Commissioner-General of Elections,

by the Constitution, and by the law for the time being relating to the election of the President, the election of Members of Parliament, the election of members of Provincial Councils, the election of members of local authorities and the conduct of Referenda, including but not limited to all the powers, duties and functions relating to the preparation and revision of registers of electors for the purposes of such elections and Referenda and the conduct of such elections and Referenda.

(2) It shall be the duty of the Commission to secure the enforcement of all laws relating to the holding of any such election or the conduct of Referenda, and it shall be the duty of all authorities of the State charged with the enforcement of such laws, to co-operate with the Commission to secure such enforcement.

(3) The Commission shall be responsible and answerable to Parliament in accordance with the provisions of the Standing Orders of Parliament for the exercise, performance and discharge of its powers, duties and functions, and shall forward to Parliament for each calendar year a report of its activities for such year.

(4) (a) The Commission shall have the power during the period of an election, to prohibit the use of any movable or immovable property belonging to the State or any public corporation -

(i) for the purpose of promoting or preventing the election of any candidate or any political party or independent group contesting at such election ;

(ii) by any candidate or any political party or any independent group contesting at such election.

by a direction in writing by the Chairman of the Commission or of the Commissioner-General of Elections on the instruction of the Commission.

(b) It shall be the duty of every person or officer in whose custody or under whose control such property is for the time being, to comply with and give effect to such direction.

(5) (a) The Commission shall have the power to issue from time to time, in respect of the holding of any election or the conduct of a Referendum, such guidelines as the Commission may consider appropriate to any broadcasting or telecasting operator or any proprietor or publisher of a newspaper as the case may be, as the Commission may consider necessary to ensure a free and fair election.

(b) It shall be the duty of the Chairman of the Sri Lanka Broadcasting Corporation and the Chairman of the Sri Lanka Rupavahini Corporation, to take all necessary steps to ensure compliance with any guidelines as are issued to them under sub-paragraph (a).

(c) Where the Sri Lanka Broadcasting Corporation and the Sri Lanka Rupavahini Corporation as the case may be, contravenes any guidelines issued by the Commission under sub-paragraph (a), the Commission may appoint a Competent Authority by name or by office, who shall, with effect from the date of such appointment, take over the management of such Broadcasting Corporation or Rupavahini Corporation as the case may be, in respect of all political broadcasts or any other broadcast, which in the opinion of the Commission impinge on the election, until the conclusion of the election and the Sri Lanka Broadcasting Corporation and the Sri Lanka Rupavahini Corporation, shall not, during such period, discharge any function connected with or relating to such management which is taken over by the Competent Authority.

(d) Parliament may by law provide for the powers and functions of the Competent Authority appointed under subparagraph (c).

**Deployment of Police by the Commission.**

**104C.** (1) Upon the making of an Order for the holding of an election or the making of a Proclamation requiring the conduct of a Referendum, as the case may be, the Commission shall notify the Inspector-General of Police of the facilities and the number of police officers required by the Commission for the holding or conduct of such election or Referendum, as the case may be.

(2) The Inspector-General of Police shall make available to the Commission the facilities and police officers specified in any notification made under paragraph (1) of this Article.

(3) The Commission may deploy the police officers and facilities made available to the Commission in such manner as is calculated to promote the conduct of a free and fair election or Referendum, as the case may be.

(4) Every police officer made available to the Commission under paragraph (2) of this Article, shall be responsible to and act under the direction and control of the Commission during the period of an election.

(5) No suit, prosecution or other proceeding, shall lie against any police officer made available to the Commission under this Article for any lawful act or thing in good faith done by such police officer, in pursuance of a direction of the Commission or his functioning under the Commission.

**Deployment of Armed Forces.**

**104D.** It shall be lawful for the Commission, upon the making of an Order for the holding of an election or the making of a Proclamation requiring, the conduct of a Referendum, as the case may be, to make recommendations to the President regarding the deployment of the armed forces of the Republic for the prevention or control of any actions or incidents which may be prejudicial to the holding or conducting of a free and fair election or Referendum, as the case may be.

**Commissioner-General of Elections and other officers of the Commission.**

**104E.** (1) There shall be a Commissioner-General of Elections who shall, subject to the approval of the Constitutional Council, be appointed by the Commission on such terms and conditions as shall be determined by the Commission.

(2) The Commissioner-General of Elections shall be entitled to be present at meetings of the Commission, except where any matter relating to him is being considered by the Commission. He shall have no right to vote at such meetings.

(3) The Commission may appoint such other officers to the Commission on such terms and conditions as may be determined by the Commission.

(4) The salaries of the Commissioner-General of Elections and the other officers of the Commission, shall be determined by the Commission and shall be charged on the Consolidated Fund.

(5) The Commissioner-General of Elections shall, subject to the direction and control of the Commission, implement the decisions of the Commission and exercise supervision over the officers of the Commission.

(6) The Commission may delegate to the Commissioner-General of Elections or other officer of the Commission, any power, duty or function of' the Commission, and the Commissioner-General of Elections or such officer shall exercise, perform and discharge such power, duty or function, subject to the direction and control of the Commission.

(7) The office of the Commissioner-General of Elections shall become vacant-

(a) upon his death;

(b) on his resignation in writing addressed to the Commission;

(c) on his attaining the age of sixty five years;

(d) on his removal by the Commission on account of ill health or physical or mental infirmity ; or

(e) on his removal by the Commission on the presentation of an address of Parliament in compliance with the provisions of paragraph (8), for such removal on the ground of proved misbehaviour or incapacity.

(8) (a) The address referred to in sub-paragraph (e) of paragraph (7) of this Article shall be required to be supported by a majority of the total number of Members of Parliament (including those not present) and no resolution for the presentation of such an address shall be entertained by the Speaker or placed on the Order Paper of Parliament, unless notice of such resolution is signed by not less than one-third of the total number of Members of parliament and sets out full particulars of the alleged misbehaviour or incapacity

(b) Parliament shall by law or by Standing Orders, provide for all matters relating to the presentation of such an address, including the procedure for the passing of such resolution, the investigation and proof of the alleged misbehaviour or incapacity and the right of the Commissioner-General of Elections to appear and to be heard in person or by representatives.

**Returning Officers.**

**104F.** (1) The Commission shall from time to time by notice published in the Gazette appoint by name or by office a person to be a Returning Officer to each electoral district, and may appoint by name or by office one or more persons to assist the Returning Officer in the performance of his duties.

(2) Every Officer appointed under paragraph (1) shall in the performance and discharge of such duties and functions as are assigned to him, be subject to such directions as may be issued by the Commission and shall be responsible and answerable to the Commission therefor.

**Public officers.**

**104G.** All public officers performing duties and functions at any election or Referenda shall act in the performance and discharge of such duties and functions under the directions of the Commission, and shall be responsible and answerable to the Commission therefor.

**Power of Supreme Court to issue writs.**

**104H.** (1) The jurisdiction conferred on the Court of Appeal under Article 140 of the Constitution shall, in relation to any matter that may arise in the exercise by the Commission of the powers conferred on it by the Constitution or by any other law, be exercised by the Supreme Court.

(2) Every application invoking the jurisdiction referred to in paragraph (1), shall be made within one month of the date of the commission of the act to which the application relates. The Supreme Court shall hear and finally dispose of the application within two months of the filing of the same.

**Interpretation.**

**104J.** In this Chapter ?during the period of an election" shall mean the period commencing on the making of a Proclamation or Order for the conduct of a Referendum or for the holding of an election, as the case may be, and ending on the date on which the result of poll taken at such Referendum or election, as the case may be, is declared.?.

**Amendment of Article 107 of the Constitution.**

**10.** Article 107of the Constitution is hereby amended in paragraph (1) of that Article, by the substitution for the words "shall be appointed by the President of the Republic by warrant under his hand.", of the words "shall, subject to the provisions of Article 41C, be appointed by the President by warrant under his hand.?.

**Amendment of Article 109 of the Constitution.**

**11.** Article 107 of the Constitution is hereby amended as follows:

(1) in paragraph (1) of that Article, by the substitution for the words "the President shall appoint", of the words ?the President shall, subject to the provisions of Article 41C, appoint? ; and

(2) in paragraph (2) of that Article, by the substitution for the words "the President may appoint", of the words ?the President may, subject to the provisions of Article 41C, appoint?.

**Amendment of Article 111 of the Constitution.**

**12.** Article 111 of the Constitution is hereby amended as follows:

(1) by the repeal of paragraph (2) of that Article and the substitution therefore of the following paragraph :-

"(2) The Judges of the High Court shall ?

(a) on the recommendation of the Judicial Service Commission, be appointed by the President by warrant under his hand and such recommendation shall be made after consultation with the Attorney-General;

(b) be removable and be subject to the disciplinary control of the President on the recommendation of the Judicial Service Commission.? ; and

(2) by the addition immediately after paragraph (3) of that Article, of the following new paragraph :-

"(4) Any Judge of the High Court may resign his office by writing under his hand addressed to the President.".

**Amendment the Article 111A of the Constitution.**

**13.** Article 111A of the Constitution is hereby amended in paragraph (1) of that Article, by the substitution for the words "the President may, by warrant, appoint" of the words "the President may, on the recommendation of the Judicial Service Commission, by warrant, appoint".

**Insertion of new Article 111B of the Constitution.**

**14.** The following Article is hereby inserted immediately after Article 111A of the Constitution, and shall have effect as Article 111B of the Constitution :

**"Fiscal for the whole island.**

**111B.** There shall be a Fiscal, who shall be the Fiscal for the whole Island and who shall exercise supervision and control over Deputy Fiscals attached to all Courts of First Instance."

Re-numbering of Article 116 of the Constitution as Article 111C.

**15.** Article 116 of the Constitution is hereby re-numbered as Article 111C of the Constitution.

**Insertion of Chapter XVA in the Constitution**

**16.** The following new Chapter is hereby inserted immediately after Article 111C of the Constitution, and shall have effect as Chapter XVA of the Constitution :

**'CHAPTER XVA - JUDICIAL SERVICE COMMISSION**

**Constitution of the Judicial Service Commission**

**111D.** (1) There shall be a Judicial Service Commission (in this Chapter referred to as the "Commission") consisting of the Chief Justice and two other Judges of the Supreme Court appointed by the President, subject to the provisions of Article 41C.

(2) The Chief Justice shall be the Chairman of the Commission.

**Meetings of the Commission.**

**111E.** (1) The quorum for any meeting of the Commission shall be two members of the Commission.

(2) A Judge of the Supreme Court appointed as a member of the Commission shall, unless he earlier resigns his office or is removed therefrom as hereinafter provided or ceases to be a Judge of the Supreme Court, hold office for a period of three years from the date of his appointment, but shall be eligible for re-appointment.

(3) All decisions of the Commission shall be made by a majority of the members present, and in the event of an equality of votes, the Chairman of the meeting shall have a casting vote.

(4) The Commission shall have power to act notwithstanding any vacancy in its membership and no act or proceeding of the Commission shall be, or be deemed to be invalid by reason only of such vacancy or any defect in the appointment of a member.

(5) The President may grant to any member of the Commission leave from his duties and may appoint on the recommendation of the Constitutional Council, a person qualified to be a member of the Commission to be a temporary member for the period of such leave.

(6) The President may, on the recommendation of the Constitutional Council, for cause assigned, remove from office any member of the Commission.

**Allowances of members of the Commission**

**111F.** A member of the Commission shall be paid such allowances as may be determined by Parliament. Such allowances shall be charged on the Consolidated Fund and shall not be reduced during the period of office of a member, and shall be in addition to the salary and other allowances attached to, and received from, the substantive appointment:

Provided that until the amount to be paid as allowances is determined under the provisions of this Article, the members of the Commission shall continue to receive as allowances, such amount as they were receiving on the day immediately preceding the date on which this Chapter comes into operation.

**Secretary to the Commission.**

**111G.** There shall be a Secretary to the Commission who shall be appointed by Commission from among senior judicial officers of the Courts of First Instance.

**Powers of the Commission.**

**111H.** (1) The Judicial Service Commission is hereby vested with the power to-

(a) transfer judges of the High Court ;

(b) appoint, promote, transfer, exercise disciplinary control and dismiss judicial officers and scheduled public officers.

(2) The Commission may make -

(a) rules regarding training of Judges of the High Court, the schemes for recruitment and training, appointment, promotion and transfer of judicial offices and scheduled public officers;

(b) provision for such matters as are necessary or expedient for the exercise, performance and discharge of the powers, duties and functions of the Commission.

(3) The Chairman of the Commission or any Judge of the Supreme Court or Judge of the Court of Appeal as the case may be, authorized by the Commission shall have power and authority to inspect any Court of First Instance, or the records, registers and other documents maintained in such Court, or hold such inquiry as may be necessary.

(4) The Commission may by Order published in the Gazette delegate to the Secretary to the Commission the power to make transfers in respect of scheduled public officers, other than transfers involving increase of salary, or to make acting appointments in such cases and subject to such limitations as may be specified in the Order.

**Judicial officers and scheduled public officers may resign.**

**111J.** Any judicial officer or scheduled public officer may resign his office by writing under his hand addressed to the Chairman of the Commission.

**Immunity from legal proceedings.**

**111K.** No suit or proceeding shall lie against the Chairman, member or Secretary or officer of the Commission for any lawful act which in good faith is done in the performance of his duties or functions as such Chairman, member, Secretary, or officer of the Commission.

**Interference with the Commission is an offence.**

**111L.** (1) Every person who otherwise than in the course of such persons lawful duty, directly or indirectly, alone or by or with any other person, in any manner whatsoever, influences or attempts to influence any decision or order made by the Commission or to so influence any member thereof, shall be guilty of an offence and shall on conviction be liable to a fine not exceeding one hundred thousand rupees or to imprisonment for a term not exceeding three years or to both such fine and imprisonment:

Provided however that the giving of a certificate or testimonial to any applicant or candidate for any judicial office or scheduled public office shall not be an offence.

(2) Every High Court established under Article 154P of the Constitution shall have jurisdiction to hear and determine any matter referred to In paragraph (1).

**Interpretation.**

**111M.** (a) In this Chapter

"appointment" includes the appointment to act in any office referred to in this Chapter.

"judicial officer" means any person who holds office as judge, presiding officer or member of any Court of First Instance, tribunal or institution created and established for the administration of justice or for the adjudication of any labour or other dispute, but does not include a Judge of the Supreme Court or of the Court of Appeal or of the High Court or a person who performs arbitral functions, or a public officer whose principal duty is not the performance of functions of a judicial nature; and

"scheduled public officer" means the Registrar of the Supreme Court, the Registrar of the Court of Appeal, the Registrar, Deputy Registrar or Assistant Registrar of the High Court or any Court of First Instance, the Fiscal, the Deputy Fiscal of the Court of Appeal or High Court and any Court of First Instance, any public officer employed in the Registry of the

Supreme Court, Court of Appeal or High Court or any Court of First Instance included in a category specified in the Fifth Schedule or such other categories as may be specified by Order made by the Minister in charge of the subject of Justice and approved by Parliament and Published in the Gazette.

(b) No court, tribunal or institution shall have jurisdiction to entertain or to determine the question whether or not a person is a judicial Officer within the meaning of the Constitution, but such question shall be determined solely by the Commission, whose decision thereon shall be final and conclusive.

(c) No act of such person or Proceeding held before such person, prior to such determination as is referred to in sub-paragraph (b), shall be deemed to be invalid by reason of such determination.?.

**Repeal of Articles 112, 113, 113A, 114, 115 and 117 of the Constitution.**

**17.** Articles 112, 113, 113A, 114, 115 and 117 of the Constitution are hereby repealed.

**Amendment of Article 153 of the Constitution.**

**18.** Article 153 of the Constitution is hereby amended the as follows:

(1) in paragraph (1)of that Article, by the substitution for the words "shall be appointed by the President", of the words "shall, subject to the provisions of Article 41C, be appointed by the President"; and

(2) in paragraph (4)of that article, by the substitution for the words "the President may appoint", of the words "the President may, subject to the provisions of Article 41C, appoint".

**Amendment of Article 154R of the Constitution.**

**19.** Article 154R of the Constitution is hereby amended in sub-paragraph (c) of paragraph (1) of that Article, by the substitution for the words "three other members to represent", of the words "three other members who are appointed by the President on the recommendation of the Constitutional Council, to represent".

**Insertion of new Chapter XVIIIA in the Constitution.**

**20.** The following new Chapter is hereby inserted immediately after Article 155 of the Constitution and shall have effect as Chapter XVIIIA of the Constitution :

**"CHAPTER XVIIIA - NATIONAL POLICE COMMISSION**

**Constitution of the National Police Commission.**

**155A.** (1) There shall be a National Police Commission (in this Chapter referred to as the "Commission") consisting of seven members appointed by the President on the recommendation of the Constitutional

Council. The Constitutional Council may, in making its recommendation, consult the Public Service Commission. The President shall on the recommendation of the Constitutional Council appoint one member as the Chairman.

(2) No person shall be appointed as a member of the Commission or continue to hold office as such member if he is or becomes a member of Parliament, a Provincial Council or a local authority.

(3) Every person who immediately before his appointment as a member of the Commission, was a public officer in the service of the State or a judicial officer, shall upon such appointment taking effect, cease to hold such office, and shall be ineligible for further appointment as a public officer or a judicial officer:

Provided that any such person shall, until he ceases to be a member of the Commission, or while continuing to be a member, attains the age at which he would, if he were a public officer or a judicial officer, as the case may be, be required to retire, be deemed to be a public officer or a judicial officer and to hold a pensionable office in the service of the State, for the purpose of any provision relating to the grant of pensions, gratuities and other allowances in respect of such service.

(4) Every member of the Commission shall hold office for a period of three years from the date of his appointment, unless he becomes subject to any disqualification under paragraph (2) of this Article, or earlier resigns from his office by writing addressed to the President or is removed from office by the President on the recommendation of the Constitutional Council or is convicted by a Court of law of any offence involving moral turpitude or if a resolution for the imposition of civic disability upon him has been passed in terms of Article 81 or is deemed to have vacated his office under paragraph (6) of this Article.

(5) A member of the Commission shall be eligible for reappointment as a member, but shall not be eligible for appointment as a public officer or a judicial officer after the expiry of his term of office as a member. No member shall be eligible to hold office as a member of the Commission for more than two terms.

(6) In the event of the Chairman or a member of the Commission absenting himself from three consecutive meetings of the Commission without the prior leave of the Commission, he shall be deemed to have vacated his office from the date of the third of such meetings and shall not be eligible to be reappointed as a member or as a member or as Chairman of the Commission.

(7) The Chairman and members of the Commission shall be paid such allowances as are determined by Parliament. Such allowances shall be charged on the Consolidated Fund and shall not be diminished during the term of office of the Chairman or member.

(8) The Chairman and members of the Commission shall be deemed to be public servants within the meaning and for the purposes of Chapter IX of the Penal Code.

**Meetings of the Commission.**

**155B.** (1) The quorum for a meeting of the Commission shall be four members.

(2) The Chairman shall preside at all meetings of the Commission and in his absence a member elected by the members present from amongst the members shall preside at such meeting.

(3) Decisions of the Commission shall be by a majority of members present and voting at the meeting at which the decision is taken, and in the event of an equality of votes the Chairman or the person presiding shall have a casting vote.

(4) The Commission shall have power to act notwithstanding any vacancy in its membership, and any act or proceeding or decision of the Commission shall not be invalid or deemed to be invalid by reason only of such vacancy or any defect in the appointment of the Chairman or member.

**Immunity from legal proceedings.**

**155C.** (1) Subject to the jurisdiction conferred on the Supreme Court under paragraph (1) of Article 126, no court or tribunal shall have the power or jurisdiction to inquire into, or pronounce upon or in any manner call in question any order or decision made by the Commission or a Committee, in pursuance of any power or duty, conferred or imposed on such Commission or Committee under this Chapter or under any other law.

**Secretary to the Commission.**

**155D.** There shall be a Secretary to the Commission and such other officers appointed by the Commission on such terms and conditions as may be determined by the Commission.

**Costs and Expenses.**

**155E.** The costs and expenses of the Commission shall be a charge on the Consolidated Fund.

**Interference with the Commission.**

**155F.** (1) Every person who, otherwise than in the course of such person's lawful duty, directly or indirectly by himself or by or with any other person, in any manner whatsoever influences or attempts to influence or interferes with any decision of the Commission or a Committee, or to so influence any member of the Commission or a Committee, shall be guilty of an offence and shall on conviction be liable to a fine not exceeding one hundred thousand rupees or to imprisonment for a term not exceeding seven years, or to both such fine and imprisonment.

(2) A High Court established under Article 154P of the Constitution shall have jurisdiction to hear and determine any matter referred to in paragraph (1).

**Powers of the Commission.**

**155G.** (1) (a) The appointment, promotion, transfer, disciplinary control and dismissal of police officers other than the Inspector-General of Police, shall be vested in the Commission. The Commission shall exercise its powers of promotion, transfer, disciplinary control and dismissal in consultation with the Inspector General of Police.

(b) The Commission shall not in the exercise of its powers under this Article, derogate from the powers and functions assigned to the Provincial Police Service Commissions as and when such Commissions are established under Chapter XVIIA of the Constitution.

(2) The Commission shall establish procedures to entertain and investigate public complaints and complaints of any aggrieved person made against a police officer or the police service, and provide redress in accordance with the provisions of any law enacted by Parliament for such purpose.

(3) The Commission shall provide for and determine all matters regarding police officers, including the formulation of schemes of recruitment and training and the improvement of the efficiency and independence of the police service, the nature and type of the arms, ammunition and other equipment necessary for the use of the National Division and the Provincial Divisions, codes of conduct, and the standards to be followed in making promotions and transfers, as the Commission may from time to time consider necessary or fit.

(4) The Commission shall exercise all such powers and perform all such functions and duties as are vested in it under Appendix I of List I contained in the Ninth Schedule of the Constitution.

**Committees of the Commission.**

**155H.** (1) The Commission may delegate to a Committee (not consisting of members of the Commission) as shall be nominated by the Commission, the powers of appointment, promotion, transfer, disciplinary control and dismissal of such categories of police officers as are specified by the Commission.

(2) The Commission shall cause to be published in the Gazette the appointment of any such Committee.

(3) The procedure and quorum for meetings of such a Committee shall be according to rules made by the Commission. The Commission shall cause such rules to be published in the Gazette.

**Delegation of functions by the Commission.**

**155J.** (1) The Commission may, subject to such conditions and procedures as may be prescribed by the Commission, delegate to the Inspector-General of Police or in consultation with the Inspector-General of Police to any Police Officer, its powers of appointment, promotion, transfer, disciplinary control and dismissal of any category of police officer.

(2) The Commission shall cause any such delegation to be published in the Gazette.

**Right of appeal.**

**155K.** (1) A police officer aggrieved by any order relating to promotion, transfer or any order on a disciplinary matter or dismissal made by the Inspector-General of Police or a Committee or Police Officer referred to in Article 155H and 155J in respect of himself, may appeal to the Commission against such order in accordance with rules made by the Commission from time to time regulating the procedure and the period fixed for the making, and hearing of an appeal by the Commission.

(2) The Commission shall have the power to alter, vary, rescind or confirm such order upon such appeal, or to give directions in relation there to, or to order such further or other inquiry, as to the Commission shall seem fit.

(3) The Commission shall from time to time cause to be published in the Gazelle, rules made by it under paragraph (1) of this Article.

(4) Upon any delegation to the Inspector-General of Police or a Committee or Police Officer under Article 155H and 155J of this Chapter as the case may be, the Commission shall not whilst such delegation of its powers is in force, exercise or perform its functions or duties in respect of the categories of Police Officers in respect of which such delegation is made, subject to the right of appeal hereinbefore provided.

**Appeals to the Administrative Appeals Tribunal.**

**155L.** Any Police Officer aggrieved by any order relating to promotion, transfer, or any order on a disciplinary matter or dismissal made by the Commission, in respect of himself may appeal therefrom to the Administrative Appeals Tribunal established under Article 59, which shall have the power to alter, vary or rescind any order or decision made by the Commission.

**Saving of existing rules and regulations.**

**155M.** Until the Commission otherwise provides, all rules, regulations and procedures relating to the police force as are in force shall continue to be operative and in force.

**Commission answerable to Parliament.**

**155N.** The Commission shall be responsible and answerable to Parliament in accordance with the provisions of the Standing Orders of Parliament for the exercise, performance and discharge of its powers, duties and functions, and shall forward to Parliament in each calendar year a report of its activities in such year.?.

**Amendment Article 156 of the Constitution.**

**21.** Article 156 of the Constitution is hereby amended as follows:

(1) in paragraph (2) of that Article, by the substitution for the words "shall be appointed by the President", of the words "shall, subject to the provisions of Article 41C, be appointed by the President"; and

(2) in paragraph (5) of that Article, by the substitution for the words "the President shall appoint", of the words "the President shall, subject to the provisions of Article 41C, appoint".

**Amendment of Article 170 of the Constitution.**

**22.** Article 170 of the Constitution is hereby amended as follows:

(1) in the definition of the expression "judicial officer", by the substitution for the words "other than in Article 114,", of the words "other than in Article 111M,"; and

(2) in the definition of the expression "public officer", by the insertion immediately after paragraph (c), of the following new paragraphs :

"(ca) a member of the Constitutional Council ;

(cb) a member of the Election Commission ;

(cc) a member of the National Police Commission ;

(cd) the Commissioner-General of Elections ;

(ce) officers appointed to the Election Commission, by the Election Commission ;".

**Amendment of the Ninth Schedule to the Constitution.**

**23.** The Ninth Schedule to the Constitution is hereby amended in Appendix I to List I as follows :-

(1) by the substitution for item 3 of that Appendix of the following :

"3. Recruitment to the National Police Division and promotion of Police Officers in the Provincial Divisions to the National Division, shall be made by the National Police Commission.?;

(2) in item 6 of that Appendix by the substitution for the words "will be referred to the President,", of the words "will be referred to the National Police Commission,";

(3) in item 7 of that Appendix, by the substitution for the words "with the approval of the President,", of the words "with the approval of the National Police Commission."; and

(4) in item 9:2 of that Appendix, by the substitution for the words "The President may, where he considers it necessary provide for alternate training for members of any Provincial Division", of the words "The National Police Commission may, where he considers it necessary provide for alternate training for members of any Provincial Division.".

**Commissions under repealed Articles 56 and 112 of the Constitution to continue.**

**24.** (1) The persons holding office on the date prior to the date of commencement of this Act, as members of the Public Service Commission and the Judicial Service Commission established by Article 56 and Article 112 respectively, of the Constitution, shall continue to hold office as such members continue to exercise the powers vested in those Commissions under the Constitution, prior to the date of commencement of this Act, until the date on which the members of the Public Service Commission and the Judicial Service Commission respectively, are appointed under Article 54 and Article 111D respectively of the Constitution.

(2) The persons holding office on the day prior to the date of commencement of this Act, as the Secretary to the Public Service Commission and as the Secretary to the Judicial Service Commission appointed under paragraph (7) of Article 56 and Article 113 respectively, of the Constitution, shall continue to hold such office under the same terms and conditions.

**Chief Justice, Judges of the Supreme Court, President of the Court of Appeal &c,. to continue to hold office.**

**25.** (a) The Chief Justice and all the Judges of the Supreme Court and the President and all the Judges of the Court of Appeal holding office on the day prior to the date of the commencement of this Act, shall, subject to the provisions of paragraph (3) of Article 41C, continue to hold office.

(b) Every person holding office on the day prior to the date of the commencement of this Act, as the Attorney-General, the Auditor-General, the Inspector-General of Police, the Parliamentary Commissioner for Administration (Ombudsman) and the Secretary-General of Parliament shall, subject to the provisions of paragraph (3) of Article 41C, continue to hold such office under the same terms and conditions.

**Judges of the High Court &c., to continue to hold office.**

**26.** Every person holding office on the day prior to the date of the commencement of this Act ?

(*a*) as a Judge of the High Court;

(*b*) as a judicial officer, a scheduled public officer, a public officer or a police officer,

shall, continue to hold such office under the same terms and conditions.

**Substitution and savings.**

**27.** (1) Unless the context otherwise requires, there shall be substituted for the expressions "Commissioner of Elections" and "Department of the Commissioner of Elections" wherever such expressions occur in the Constitution and in any written law or in any contract, agreement or other document, of the expression "Election Commission".

(2) The person holding office as the Commissioner of Elections on the day immediately preceding the date of the commencement of this Act, shall continue to exercise and perform the powers and functions of the office of Commissioner of Elections as were vested in him immediately prior to the commencement of this Act, and of the Election Commission, until an Election Commission is constituted in terms of Article 103, and shall, from and after the date on which the Election Commission is so constituted, cease to hold office as the Commissioner of Elections.

(3) All suits, actions and other legal proceedings instituted by or against the Commissioner of Elections appointed under Article 103 of the Constitution prior to the amendment of such Article by this Act, and pending on the day immediately prior to the date of commencement of this Act, shall he deemed to be suits, actions and other legal proceedings instituted by or against the Election Commission, and shall be continued and completed in the name of the Election Commission.

(4) Any decision or order made, or ruling, given by the Commissioner of Elections appointed under Article 103 of the Constitution prior to the amendment of that Article, by this Act, and under any written law on or before the date of the commencement of this Act, shall be deemed to be a decision or order made or ruling given, by the Election Commission.

**Pending matters before the Public Service Commission to stand removed to the National Police Commission.**

**28.** All matters pertaining to the appointment, promotion, transfer, disciplinary control and dismissal of any police officer pending before the Public Service Commission, on or before the date of the commencement of this Act, shall stand removed to the National Police Commission established by Chapter XVIIIA of the Constitution and accordingly such matter shall be continued and completed before such National Police Commission.

**Sinhala text to prevail in case of inconsistency.**

**29.** In the event of any inconsistency between the Sinhala and Tamil texts of this Act, the Sinhala text shall prevail.

## Thirteenth Amendment to the Constitution

[Certified on 14th November, 1987]

*An Act to Amend the Constitution of The Democratic Socialist Republic of Sri Lanka*

Be it enacted by the Parliament of the Democratic Socialist Republic of Sri Lanka as follows:-

**Short title and date of operation**

1. This Act may be cited as the Thirteenth Amendment to the Constitution and shall come into operation on such date as the President may, appoint, by Order published in the Gazette.

**Amendment of Article 18 of the Constitution of the Democratic Socialist Republic of Sri Lanka**

2, Article 18 of the Constitution of the Democratic Socialist Republic of Sri Lanka (hereinafter referred to as the "Constitution") is hereby amended as follows:

(a) by the renumbering of that Article as paragraph (1) of that Article;

(b) by the addition immediately after paragraph (1) of that Article of the following paragraphs:

"(2) Tamil shall also be an official language.

(3) English shall be the link language.

(4) Parliament shall by law provide for the implementation of the provisions of this Chapter."

**Amendment of Article 138 of the Constitution**

3. Article 138 of the Constitution is hereby amended in paragraph (1) of that Article as follows:-

(a) by the substitution, for the words "committed by any Court of First Instance", of the words "committed by the High Court, in the exercise of its appellate or original jurisdiction or by any Court of First Instance"; and

(b) by the substitution, for the words "of which such Court of First Instance", of the words " of which such High Court, Court of First Instance".

**Insertion of Chapter XVIIA in the Constitution**

4, The following Chapter and Articles are hereby inserted immediately after Article 154, and shall have effect as Chapter XVIIA and Articles 154A to 154T, of the Constitution:-

## Chapter XVIIA

**Establishment of Provincial Councils**

154A.

(1) Subject to the provisions of the Constitution, a Provincial Council shall be established for every Province specified in the Eighth Schedule with effect from such date or dates as the President may appoint by Order published in the Gazette. different dates may be appointed in respect of different Provinces.

(2) Every Provincial Council established under paragraph (1) shall be constituted upon the election of the members of such Council in accordance with the law relating to Provincial Council elections.

(3) Notwithstanding anything in the preceding provisions of this Article, Parliament may by, or under, any law provide for two or three adjoining Provinces to form one administrative unit with one elected Provincial Council, one Governor, one Chief Minister and one Board of Ministers and for the manner of determining whether such Provinces should continue to be administered as one administrative unit or whether each such Province should constitute a separate administrative unit with its own Provincial Council, and a separate Governor, Chief Minister and Board of Ministers.

**Governor**

154B.

(1) There shall be a Governor for each Province for which a Provincial Council has been established in accordance with Article 154A.

(2) The Governor shall be appointed by the President by warrant under his hand, and shall hold office, in accordance with Article 4(b), during the pleasure of the President.

(3) The Governor may, by writing addressed to the President, resign his office.

(4) (a) The Provincial Council may, subject to sub-paragraph (b) present an address to the President advising the removal of the Governor on the ground that the Governor-

(i) has intentionally violated the provisions of the Constitution;

(ii) is guilty of misconduct or corruption involving the abuse of the powers of his office;

or

(iii) is guilty of bribery of an offence involving moral turpitude, if a resolution for the presentation of such address is passed by not less than two-thirds of the whole number of members of the Council (including those not present).

(b) No resolution for the presentation of an address to the President advising the removal of the Governor on the grounds referred to in sub-paragraph (a) shall be entertained by the Chairman of the Provincial Council or discussed at the Council, unless notice of such resolution is signed by not less than one-half of the whole number of members present.

(5) Subject to the preceding provisions of this Article, the Governor shall hold office for a period of five years from the date he assumes office.

(6) Every person appointed as Governor shall assume office upon taking or subscribing, the oath or making or subscribing the affirmation, set out in the Fourth Schedule, before the President.

(7) Upon such assumption of office a Governor shall cease to hold any other office created or recognized by the Constitution, and if he is a Member of Parliament, shall vacate his seat in Parliament. The Governor shall not hold any other office or place of profit.

(8) (a) The Governor may, from time to time, summon the Provincial Council to meet at such time and place as he thinks fit, but two months shall not intervene between the last sitting in one session and the date appointed for the first sitting in the next session.

(b) The Governor may, from time to time, prorogue the Provincial Council.

(c) The Governor may dissolve the Provincial Council.

(d) The Governor shall exercise his powers under this paragraph in accordance with the advice of the Chief Minister, so long as the Board of Ministers commands, in the opinion of the Governor, the support of the majority of the Provincial Council.

(9) Without prejudice to the powers of the President under Article 34 and subject to his directions the Governor of a Province shall have the power to grant a pardon to every person convicted of an offense against a statute made by the Provincial Council of that Province or a law made by Parliament on a matter in respect of which the Provincial Council has power to make statutes and to grant a respite or remission of punishment imposed by Court on any such person:

Provided that where the Governor does not agree with the advice of the Board of Ministers in any case and he considers it necessary to do so in public interest, he may refer that case to the President for orders.

(10) (a) The Governor may address the Provincial Council and may for that purpose require the attendance of members.

(b) The Governor may also send messages to the Council either with respect to a statute then pending with the Council or otherwise, and when a message is so sent the Council shall with all convenient despatch consider any matter required by the message to be taken into consideration.

(11) It shall be the duty of the Chief Minister of every Province-

(a) to communicate to the Governor of the Province all decisions of the Board of Ministers relating to the administration of the affairs of the Province and the proposals for legislation;

(b) to furnish such information relating to the administration of the affairs of the Province and proposals for legislation as the Governor may call for; and

(c) if the Governor so requires, to submit for consideration of the Board of Ministers any such matter on which a decision has been taken by a Minister but which has not been considered by the Board.

(12) Parliament shall by law or resolution make provision for the salary, allowances, age of retirement and pension entitlement of holders of the office of Governor.

**Exercise of executive powers by the Governor**

154C. Executive power extending to the matters with respect to which a Provincial Council has power to make statutes shall be exercised by the Governor of the Province for which that Provincial Council is established, either directly or through Ministers of the Board of Ministers, or through officers subordinate to him, in accordance with Article 154F.

**Membership of Provincial council**

154D. (1) A Provincial Council shall consist of such number of members as may be determined by or under law, having regard to the area and population of the Province for which that Provincial Council is established.

(2) (a) A Provincial Council may at the commencement of the term of office of its members, decide, by resolution, to grant Members of Parliament elected for electoral districts, the limits of which fall within the Province for which that Provincial Council is established, the right to participate in proceedings of that Council.

(b) So long as a resolution passed under sub-paragraph (a) is in force, a Member of Parliament elected for an electoral district, the limits of which fall within the Province for which that Provincial Council is established, shall have the right, during the term of office of that Council, to speak in and otherwise take part in the proceedings of that Provincial Council and to speak in and otherwise take part in, any committee of the Provincial Council of which he may be named a member but shall be entitled to vote there at only if the resolution passed under sub-paragraph (a) so provides.

(c) The provisions of this paragraph shall cease to operate on the date of dissolution of the First Parliament.

**Term of Office**

154E. A Provincial Council shall unless sooner dissolved, continue for a period of five years from the date appointed for its first meeting and the expiration of the said period of five years shall operate as a dissolution of the Council.

**Board of Ministers**

154F.(1) There shall be a Board of Ministers with the Chief Minister at the head and not more than four other Ministers to aid and advise the Governor of a Province in the exercise of his functions. The Governor shall in the exercise of his functions act in accordance with such advice except in so far as he is by or under the Constitution required to exercise his functions or any of them in his discretion.

(2) If any question arises whether any matter is or is not a matter as respects which the Governor is by or under this Constitution required to act in his discretion, the decision of the Governor in his discretion shall be final, and the validity of anything done by the Governor shall not be called in question in any Court on the ground that he ought or ought not have acted on his discretion. The exercise of the Governor's discretion shall be on the President's directions.

(3) The question whether any, and if so what, advice was tendered by the Ministers to the Governor shall not be inquired into in any Court.

(4) The Governor shall appoint as Chief Minister, the member of the Provincial Council constituted for the Province, who, in his opinion, is best able to command the support of a majority of the members of that Council:

Provided that where more than one-half of the members elected to a Provincial Council are members of one political party, the Governor shall appoint the leader of that political party in the Council as Chief Minister.

(5) The Governor shall, on the advice of the Chief Minister, appoint from among the members of the Provincial Council constituted for that Province, the other Ministers.

(6) The Board of Ministers shall be collectively responsible and answerable to the Provincial Council.

(7) A person appointed to the office of Chief Minister or member of the Board of Ministers shall not enter upon the duties of his office until he takes and subscribes the oath, or makes and subscribes the affirmation, set out in the Fourth Schedule.

**Statutes of Provincial Councils**

154G. (1) Every Provincial Council may, subject to the provisions of the Constitution, make statutes applicable to the Province for which it is established, with respect to any matter set out in List I of the Ninth Schedule (hereinafter referred to as "the Provincial Council List")

(2) No Bill for the amendment or repeal of the provisions of this Chapter or the Ninth Schedule shall become law unless such Bill has been referred by the President after its publication in the Gazette and before it is placed on the Order paper of Parliament, to every Provincial Council for the expression of its views thereon, within such period as may be specified in the reference, and -

(a) where every such Council agrees to the amendment or repeal, such Bill is pas1sed by a majority of the Members of Parliament present and voting ; or

(b) where one or more Councils do not agree to the amendment or repeal such Bill is passed by the special majority required by Article 82.

(3) No Bill in respect of any matter set out in the Provincial Council List shall become law unless such Bill has been referred by the President, after its publication in the Gazette and before it is placed in the Order Paper of Parliament, to every Provincial Council for the expression of its views thereon, within such period as may be specified in the reference, and

(a) where every such Council agrees to the passing of the Bill, such Bill is passed by a majority of the Members of Parliament present and voting ; or

(b) where one or more Councils do not agree to the passing of the Bill, such Bill is passed by the special majority required by Article 82:

Provided that where such references, some but not all the Provincial Councils agree to passing of a Bill, such Bill shall become law applicable only to the Provinces for which the Provincial Councils agreeing to the Bill have been established, upon such Bill being passed by a majority of the Members of Parliament present and voting.

(4) Where one or more Provincial Councils request Parliament by resolution, to make law on any matter set out in the Provincial Council List, Parliament may make law on that matter, applicable only to the Provinces for which these Provincial Councils are established, by a majority of Members of Parliament present and voting.

(5) (a) Parliament may make laws with respect to any matter set out in List III of the Ninth Schedule (hereafter referred to as "the Concurrent List") after such consultation with all Provincial Councils as Parliament may consider appropriate in the circumstances of each case.

(b) Every Provincial Council may, subject to the provisions of the Constitution, make statutes applicable to the Province for which it is established, with respect to any matter on the Concurrent List, after such consultation with Parliament as it may consider appropriate in the circumstances of each case.

(6) If any provision of any statute made by a Provincial Council is inconsistent with the provisions of any law made in accordance with the preceding provisions of the Article, the provisions of such law shall prevail

and the provisions of such statute shall to the extent of such inconsistency, be void.

(7) A Provincial Council shall have no power to make statutes on any matter set out in List II of the Ninth Schedule (hereafter referred to as "the Reserved List").

(8) Where there is a law with respect to any matter on the Provincial Council List in force on the date on which this Chapter comes into force, and a Provincial Council established for a Province subsequently makes a statute on the same matter and which is described in its long title as being inconsistent with that law, then, the provisions of the law shall, with effect from the date on which that statute receives assent and so long only as that statute is in force remain suspended and be inoperative within that Province.

(9) Where there is a law with respect to any matter on the Concurrent List on the date on which this Chapter comes into force, and a Provincial Council established for a Province subsequently makes a statute on the same matter inconsistent with that law, the provisions of the law shall, unless Parliament, by resolution, decides to the contrary, remain suspended and be inoperative within that Province, with effect from the date on which that statute receives assent and so long only as that statute is in force.

(10) Nothing in this Article shall be read or construed as derogating from the powers conferred on Parliament by the Constitution to make laws, in accordance with the Provisions of the Constitution (inclusive of this Chapter), with respect for any matter, for the whole of Sri Lanka or any part thereof.

(11) Notwithstanding anything in paragraph (3) of this Article, Parliament may make laws, otherwise than in accordance with the procedure set out in that paragraph, in respect of any matter set out in the Provincial Council List for implementing any treaty, agreement or convention with any other country or countries or any decisions made at an international conference, association, or other body.

**Assent**

154H. (1) Every statute made by a Provincial Council shall come into force upon such statute receiving assent as hereinafter provided.

(2) Every statute made by a Provincial Council shall be presented to the Governor for his assent, forthwith upon the marking thereof, and the Governor shall either assent to the statute or he may as soon as possible after the statute is presented to him for assent, return it to the Provincial Council together with a message requesting the Council to reconsider the statute or any specified provision thereof and in particular, requesting it to consider the desirability of introducing such amendments as may be recommended in the message.

(3) Where a statute is returned to a Provincial Council by the Governor under paragraph

(2), the Provincial Council shall reconsider the statute having regard to the Governor's message and may pass such statute with or without amendment and present it to the Governor for his assent.

(4) Upon presentation of a statute to the Governor under paragraph (3), the Governor may assent to the statute or reserve it for reference by the President to the Supreme Court, within one month of the passing statute for the second time, for a determination that it is not inconsistent with the provisions of the Constitution. Where upon such reference, the Supreme Court determines that the statute is consistent with the provisions of the Constitution, the Governor shall, on receipt by him of the Court's determination, assent to the statute. Where upon such reference, the Supreme Court determines that the statute is inconsistent with the provisions of the Constitution, the Governor shall withhold assent to the statute.

**Public Security**

154J. (1) Upon the making of a Proclamation under the Public Security Ordinance or the law for the time being relating to public security, bringing the provisions of such Ordinance or law into operation on the ground that the maintenance of essential supplies and services is threatened or that the security of Sri Lanka is threatened by war or external aggression or armed rebellion, the President may give directions to any Governor as to the manner in which the executive power exercisable by the Governor is to be exercised. The direction so given shall be in relation to the grounds specified in such Proclamation for the making thereof.

**Explanation:** A Proclamation under the Public Security Ordinance declaring that the maintenance of essential supplies and services is threatened or that the security of Sri Lanka or any part of the territory thereof is threatened by war, or by external aggression, or by armed rebellion may be made before the actual breakdown of supplies and services, or the actual occurrence or war, of any such aggression or rebellion, if the President is satisfied that there is imminent danger thereof:

Provided that where such Proclamation is in operation only in any part of Sri Lanka, the power of the President to give directions under this Article, shall also extend to any Province other than the Province in which the Proclamation is in operation if, and in so far as it is expedient so to do for ensuring the maintenance of essential supplies and services or the security of Sri Lanka.

(2) A Proclamation under the Public Security Ordinance or the law for the time being relating to public security, shall be conclusive for all purposes and shall not be questioned in any Court, and no Court or Tribunal shall inquire into, or pronounce on, or in any manner call in question, such Proclamation, the grounds for making thereof, or the existence of those grounds or any direction given under this Article.

**Failure to comply with directions**

154K. Where the Governor or any Provincial Council has failed to comply with, or give effect to, any directions given to such Governor or such Council under this Chapter of the Constitution, it shall be lawful for the President to hold that a situation has arisen in which the administration of the Province cannot be carried on in accordance with the provisions of the Constitution.

**Failure of administrative machinery**

154L.(1) If the President, on receipt of a report from the Governor of the Province or otherwise is satisfied that a situation has arisen in which the administration of the Province cannot be carried on in accordance with the provisions of the Constitution, the President may by Proclamation-

(a) assume to himself all or any of the functions of the administration of the Province and all or any of the powers vested in, or exercisable by, the Governor or any body or authority in the Province other than the Provincial Council;

(b) declare that the powers of the Provincial Council shall be exercisable by, or under the authority of Parliament;

(c) make such incidental and consequential provisions as appear to the President to be necessary or desirable for giving effect to the objects of the Proclamation:

Provided that nothing in this paragraph shall authorize the President to assume to himself any of the powers vested in, or exercisable, by any Court.

(2) Any such Proclamation may be revoked or varied by a subsequent Proclamation.

(3) Every Proclamation under this Article shall be laid before Parliament and shall, except where it is a Proclamation revoking a previous Proclamation, cease to operate at the expiration of fourteen days unless before the expiration of that period it has been approved by a resolution of Parliament.

Provided that if any such Proclamation (not being a Proclamation revoking a previous Proclamation) is issued at a time when Parliament is dissolved or the dissolution of Parliament takes place during the period of fourteen days referred to this paragraph but no resolution with respect to such Proclamation has been passed by Parliament before the expiration of that period, the Proclamation shall cease to operate at the expiration of fourteen days from the date on which Parliament first sits after its reconstitution, unless before the expiration of the said period of fourteen days a resolution approving the Proclamation has been passed by Parliament.

(4) A Proclamation so approved shall, unless earlier revoked, cease to operate on the expiration of a period of two months from the date of issue of the Proclamation:

Provided that if and so often as a resolution approving the continuance in force of such a Proclamation is passed by Parliament, the Proclamation shall, unless revoked, continue in force for a further period of two months from the date on which under this paragraph it would otherwise have ceased to operate, but no such Proclamation shall in any case remain in force more than one year:

Provided further that if the dissolution of Parliament takes place during any such period of two months but no resolution with respect to the continuance in force of such Proclamation has been passed by Parliament during the said period, the Proclamation shall cease to operate at the expiration of fourteen days from the date on which Parliament first sits after its reconstitution unless before the expiration of the said period of fourteen days a Proclamation approving the continuance in force of the Proclamation has been passed by Parliament.

(5) Notwithstanding anything in this Article, the President may within fourteen days of his making a Proclamation under paragraph (1) and for the purpose of satisfying himself with regard to any of the matters referred to in that paragraph, appoint a retired Judge of the Supreme Court to inquire into and report upon such matters within a period of sixty days. A Judge so appointed shall in relation to such inquiry have the powers of a Commissioner appointed under the Commission of Inquiry Act. Upon receipt of the report of such Judge, the President may revoke the Proclamation made under paragraph (1).

(6) A Proclamation under this Article shall be conclusive for all purposes and shall not be questioned in any Court, and no Court or Tribunal shall inquire into, or pronounce on, or in any manner call in question, such Proclamation or the grounds for making thereof.

**Parliament to confer powers of Provincial Council to President**

154M. (1) where by a Proclamation issued under paragraph (1) of Article 154L, it has been declared that the powers of the Provincial Council shall be exercised by, or under the authority, of Parliament, it shall be competent-

(a) for Parliament to confer on the President the power of the Provincial Council to make statutes and to authorize the President to delegate, subject to such conditions as he may think fit to impose, the power so conferred, on any other authority specified by him in that behalf;

(b) for the President to authorize, when Parliament is not in session, expenditure from the Provincial Fund of the Province pending sanction of such expenditure by Parliament.

(2) A statute made by Parliament or the President or other authority referred to in subparagraph

(c) of paragraph (1), during the continuance in force of a Proclamation issued under paragraph (1) of Article 154L, shall continue in force until amended or repealed by the Provincial Council.

**Financial instability**

154N.(1) If the President is satisfied that a situation has arisen where the financial stability or credit of Sri Lanka or of any part of the territory thereof is threatened, he may by Proclamation make a declaration to that effect.

(2) A Proclamation issued under paragraph (1)-

(a) may be revoked or varied by a subsequent Proclamation;

(b) shall be laid before Parliament;

(c) shall cease to operate at the expiration of two months, unless before the expiration of that period it has been approved by a resolution of Parliament:

Provided that if any such Proclamation is issued at a time when Parliament has been dissolved or the dissolution of Parliament takes place during the period of two months referred to in sub-paragraph (c), but no resolution has been passed by Parliament before the expiration of that period, the Proclamation shall cease to operate at the expiration of thirty days from the date on which Parliament first sits after its reconstitution, unless before the expiration of the said period of thirty days a resolution approving the Proclamation has been passed by Parliament.

(3) During the period any such Proclamation as is mentioned in paragraph (1) is in operation, the President may give directions to any Governor of a Province to observe such canons of financial propriety as may be specified in the directions, and to give such other directions as the President may deem necessary and adequate for the purpose.

(4) Notwithstanding anything in the Constitution any such direction may include-

(a) a provision requiring the reduction of salaries and allowances of all or any class of persons serving in connection with the affairs of the Province;

(b) a provision requiring all statutes providing for payments into or out of, a Provincial fund to be reserved for the consideration of the President after they are passed by the Provincial Council.

**High Court**

154P. (1) There shall be a High Court for each Province with effect from the date on which this Chapter comes into force. Each such High Court shall be designated as the High Court of the relevant Province.

(2) The Chief Justice shall nominate, from among Judges of the High Court of Sri Lanka, such number of Judges as may be necessary to each

such High Court. Every such Judge shall be transferable by the Chief Justice.

(3) Every such High Court shall-

(a) exercise according to law, the original criminal jurisdiction of the High Court of Sri Lanka in respect of offenses committed with the Province;

(b) notwithstanding anything in Article 138 and subject to any law, exercise, appellate and revisionary jurisdiction in respect of convictions, sentences and orders entered or imposed by Magistrates Courts and Primary Courts within the Province;

(c) exercise such other jurisdiction and powers as Parliament may, by law, provide.

(4) Every such High Court shall have jurisdiction to issue, according to law -

(a) orders in the nature of habeas corpus, in respect of persons illegally detained within the Province; and

(b) order in the nature of writs of certiorari, prohibition, procedendo, mandamus, and quo warranto against any person exercising, within the Province, any power under-

(1) any law; or

(2) any statutes made by the Provincial Council established for that Province in respect of any matter set out in the Provincial Council List.

(5) the Judicial Service Commission may delegate to such High Court, the power to inspect and report on, the administration of any Court of First Instance within the Province.

(6) Subject to the provisions of the Constitution and any law, any person aggrieved by a final order, judgment or sentence of any such Court, in the exercise of its jurisdiction under paragraphs (3)(b) or (3)(c) or (4), may appeal therefrom to the Court of Appeal in accordance with Article 138.

**Functions, powers, election &c. of Provincial Councils**

154Q. Parliament shall by law provide for-

(a) the election of members of Provincial Councils and the qualifications for membership of such Councils;

(b) the procedure for transaction of business by every such Council;

(c) the salaries and allowances of members of Provincial Councils; and

(d) any other matter necessary for the purpose of giving effect to the principles of provisions of this Chapter, and for any matters connected with or incidental to, the provisions of this Chapter.

**Finance Commission**

154R. (1) There shall be a Finance Commission consisting of -

(a) the Governor of the Central Bank of Sri Lanka;

(b) the Secretary to the Treasury; and

(c) three other members to represent the three major communities each of whom shall be a person who has distinguished himself, or held high office, in the field of finance, law, administration, business or learning.

(2) Every member of the Commission shall, unless he earlier dies, resigns or is removed from office, hold office for a period of three years.

(3) The Government shall, on the recommendation of and in consultation with, the Commission, allocate from the Annual Budget, such funds as are adequate for the purpose of meeting the needs of the Provinces.

(4) It shall be the duty of the Commission to make recommendations to the President as to -

(a) the principles on which such funds are granted annually by the Government for the use of Provinces, should be apportioned between various Provinces; and,

(b) any other matter referred to the Commission by the President relating to Provincial finance.

(5) The Commission shall formulate such principles with the objective of achieving balanced regional development in the country, and shall accordingly take into account -

(a) the population of each Province;

(b) the per capita income of each Province;

(c) the need progressively, to reduce social and economic disparities; and

(d) the need, progressively, to reduce the difference between the per capita income of each Province and the highest per capita income among the Provinces.

(6) The Commission shall determine its own procedure and shall have such powers in the performance of its duties as Parliament may, by law, confer on it.

(7) The President shall cause every recommendation made by the Finance Commission under this Article to be laid before the Parliament, and shall notify Parliament as to the action taken thereon.

(8) No Court or Tribunal shall inquire into, or pronounce on, or in any manner entertain, determine or rule upon, any question relating to the adequacy of such funds, or any recommendation made, or principle formulated by the Commission.

**Special provision enabling Provincial Councils not to exercise powers under this Chapter**

154S. (1) A Provincial Council may, by resolution, decide not to exercise its powers under Article 154G with respect to any matter or part thereof set out in the Provincial Council List or the Concurrent List of the Ninth Schedule.

(2) Where a resolution has been passed by a Provincial Council under paragraph (i) and the terms of such resolution have been accepted by Parliament, by resolution, the powers of such Provincial Council under Article 154G shall be deemed not to extend to the matter specified in such resolution and Parliament may make law, with respect to that matter, applicable to the Province for which that Provincial Council is established, otherwise than in accordance with the provisions of Article 154G.

**Transitional measures**

154T. The President may by order published in the Gazette, take such action, or give such directions, not inconsistent with the provisions of the Constitution, as appears to him to be necessary or expedient, for the purpose of giving effect to the provisions of this Chapter, or for the administrative changes necessary therefore, or for the purpose of removing any difficulties.

**Amendment of Article 155 of the Constitution**

5. Article 155 of the Constitution is hereby amended by the insertion, immediately after paragraph (3) of that Article, of the following new paragraph:

"(3A) Nothing in the preceding provisions of this Constitution shall be deemed to prohibit the making of emergency regulations, under the Public Security Ordinance or the law for the time being in force relating to public security, with respect to any matter set out in the Ninth Schedule or having the effect of overriding, amending or suspending the operation of a statute made by the Provincial Council."

**Amendment of Article 170 of the Constitution**

6, Article 170 of the Constitution is hereby amended by the substitution, in the definition "written law", for the words "and includes Orders", of the words "and includes statutes made by a Provincial council, Orders."

**Addition of Eighth and Ninth Schedules in the Constitution**

7. The following Schedules are hereby added immediately after the Seventh Schedule, and shall have effect as the Eighth and Ninth Schedules respectively of the Constitution:-

EIGHTH SCHEDULE

Provinces

Western

North Western

Uva

Sabaragamuwa

Central

Eastern

Southern

North Central

Northern

NINTH SCHEDULE

LIST I

(Provincial Council List)

1. Police and Public Order - Public order and exercise of police powers, to the extent set out in Appendix I, within the Province, but not including National defense, National Security and the use of any armed forces or any other forces under the control of the Government of Sri Lanka in aid of civil power, and not including the city of Colombo, Sri Jayewardenepura Kotte, and their environs the limits of which shall be specified by the President by Order published in the Gazette.

2. Planning - Implementation of provincial economic plans

3. Education and Educational Service - Education to the extent set out in Appendix III

4. Local Government

5. Provincial Housing and Construction

6. Roads and bridges and ferries thereon within the Province, other than -

(a) national highways

(b) bridges and ferries on national highways

7. Social Services and Rehabilitation

8. Regulation of road passenger carriage services and the carriage of goods by motor vehicles within the Province and the provisions of inter-provincial road transport services.

9. Agriculture and Agrarian Services

10. Rural Development

11. Health

12. Indigenous Medicine - Ayurveda, Siddha and Unani -

13.1 Resthouses maintained by local authorities; and

13.2 Circuit bungalows presently administered by Government departments whose functions are exclusively specified in this List.

14. Pawnbrokers

15. Markets fairs

16. Food supply and distribution within the Province

17. Co-operatives

18. Land - Land, that is to say, rights in or over land, land tenure, transfer and alienation of land, land use, land settlement and land improvement, to the extent set out in appendix II.

19. Irrigation

20. Animal Husbandry

21. Subject to the formulation and implementation of National Policy in regard to development and planning, the power to promote, establish and engage in agricultural, industrial, commercial and trading enterprises and other income-generating projects, within the Province without prejudice to the power of the Government and public corporations to have such enterprises and projects

22. Reformatories, Borstal Institutions and other institutions of a like nature and persons detained therein, arrangements with other Provinces for the use of such Institutions

23. Possession, transport, purchase and sale of intoxicating liquors

24. Burials and burial grounds, cremations and cremation grounds, other than those declared by or under law made by Parliament to be national memorial cemeteries

25.1 Libraries, Museums and other similar institutions controlled or financed by a Provincial Council

25.2 Ancient and historical monuments and records other than those declared by or under law made by Parliament to be national importance

26. The regulation of mines and mineral development

27. Incorporation, regulation and judicial winding up of corporations with subjects confined to the Province, excluding trading corporations, banking, insurance and financial corporations

28. Regulation of unincorporated trading, literary, scientific, religious and other societies and associations

29.1 Theaters and dramatic performances, music, cinemas, entertainment's and amusements, excluding the sanctioning of cinematograph films for exhibition and public performance

29.2 Encouragement and development of sports (other than national sports associations)

30. Betting and gambling, other than imposition of license fees and taxes

31. Provincial debt

32. Offences against statutes with respect to any of the matters specified in this list

33. Fees in respect of any of the matters in this List, excluding fees taken in any court

34. Development, conservation and management of sites and facilities in the Province for the generation and promotion of electric

energy (other than hydro-electric power and power generated to feed the national grid)

35. The borrowing of money to the extent permitted by or under any law made by Parliament

36.1 Turnover taxes on wholesale and retail sales within such limits and subject to such exemptions as may be prescribed by law made by Parliament

36.2 Betting Taxes, and taxes on price competitions and lotteries, other than National Lotteries and lotteries organized by the Government of Sri Lanka

36.3 License taxes, arrack, toddy rents, tapping license fees, and liquor license fees

36.4 Motor vehicle license fees within such limits and subject to such exemptions as may be prescribed by law made by Parliament

36.5 Dealership license taxes on drugs and other chemicals

36.6 Stamp duties on transfer of properties, such as lands and motor cars

36.7 Toll collection

36.8 Fines imposed by courts

36.9 Fees charged under the Medical Ordinance

36.10 Fees charged under the Motor Traffic Act

36.11 Departmental fees in respect of any of the matters specified in this List

36.12 Fees under the Fauna and Flora Protection Ordinance

36.13 Fees on lands alienated under the Land Development Ordinance and Crown Lands Ordinance

36.14 Court fees, including stamp fees on documents produced in court

36.15 Regulatory charges under the Weights and Measures Ordinance

36.16 Land revenue, including the assessment and collection of revenue, and survey and maintenance of land records for revenue purposes

36.17 Taxes on lands and buildings, including the property of the State to the extent permitted by law made by Parliament

36.18 Taxes on mineral rights within such limits and subject to such exemptions as may be prescribed by law made by Parliament

36.19 Licensing fees on the possession, transport, purchase and sale of intoxicating liquors

36.20 Other taxation within the Province in order to raise revenue for provincial purposes to the extent permitted by or under any law made by Parliament

37. Protection of environment within the Province to the extent permitted by or under any law made by Parliament

## Apendix I

Law and Order

## Appendix II

Land and Land Settlement

State Land shall continue to vest in the Republic and may be disposed of in accordance with Article 33(d) and written law governing the matter.

Subject as aforesaid, land shall be a Provincial Council Subject, subject to the following special provisions :-

1. State land -

1:1 State land required for the purposes of the Government in a Province, in respect of a reserved or concurrent subject may be utilized by the Government in accordance with the laws governing the matter. The Government shall consult the relevant Provincial Council with regard to the utilization of such land in respect of such subject.

1:2 Government shall make available to every Provincial Council State land within the province required by such Council for a Provincial Council subject. The Provincial Council shall administer, control and utilize such State land, in accordance with the laws and statutes governing the matter.

1:3 Alienation or disposition of the State land within a Province to any citizen or to any organization shall be by President, on the advice of the relevant Provincial Council, in accordance with the laws governing the matter.

2. Inter-Provincial Irrigation and Land Development Projects.

2:1 Such projects would comprise irrigation and land development schemes-

(a) within the Province initiated by the State and which utilize water from rivers following through more than one Province; a Provincial Council however, may also initiate irrigation and land development schemes within its province utilizing water from such rivers;

(b) within the Province which utilize water through diversions from water systems from outside the Province; and

(c) all schemes where the command area falls within two or more Provinces such as the Mahaweli Development Project.

2:2 These projects will be the responsibility of the Government of Sri Lanka.

2:3 The principles and criteria regarding the size of holdings of agricultural and homestead lands arising out of these projects will be determined by the Government of Sri Lanka in consultation with the Provincial Councils.

2:4 The selection of allotees for such land will be determined by the Government of Sri Lanka having regard to settler selection criteria including the degree of landlessness, income level, size of family and agricultural background of the applicants. The actual application of these principles, selection of allottees and other incidental matters connected thereto will be within the powers of Provincial Councils.

2:5 The distribution of all allotments of such land in such projects will be on the basis of national ethnic ratio. In the distribution of allotments according to such ratios, priority will be given to persons who are displaced by the project, landless of the District in which the project is situated and thereafter the landless of the Province.

2:6 Where the members of any community do not, or are unable to take their entitlements of allotments from any such project, they would be entitled to receive an equivalent number of allotments in another inter-provincial irrigation or Land Development Scheme.

This unused quota should be utilized within a given time frame.

2:7 The distribution of allotments in such projects on the basis of the aforesaid principles would be done as far as possible so as not to disturb very significantly the demographic pattern of the Province and in accordance with the principle of ensuring community cohesiveness in human settlements.

2:8 The administration and management of such projects will be done by the Government of Sri Lanka.

3. National Land Commission.

3:1 The Government of Sri Lanka shall establish a National Land Commission which would be responsible for the formulation of national policy with regard to the use of State Land. This Commission will include representatives of all Provincial Councils in the Island.

3:2 The National Land commission will have a Technical Secretariat representing all the relevant disciplines required to evaluate the physical as well as the socioeconomic factors that are relevant to natural resources management.

3:3 National policy on land use will be based on technical aspects (not on political or communal aspects), and the Commission will lay down general norms in regard to the use of land, having regard to soil, climate, rainfall, soil erosion, forest cover, environmental factors, economic viability, &c.

3:4 In the exercise of the powers devolved on them, the powers shall be exercised by the Provincial Councils having due regard to the national policy formulated by the National Land Commission.

## Appendix III

Education

LIST II

(Reserved List)

National Policy on all Subjects and Functions

Defence and National Security: Internal Security; Law and order and prevention and detection of crime except to the extent specified in item 1 of List I

*Foreign affairs*

*Posts and Telecommunications; Broadcasting; Television*

*Justice in so far as it relates to the judiciary and the courts structure*

*Finance in relation to national revenue, monetary policy and external resources; customs*

*Foreign Trade; Inter-Province Trade and Commerce*

*Ports and Harbours*

*Aviation and Airports*

*National Transport*

*Rivers and Waterways; shipping and Navigation; Maritime zones including Historical Waters, Exclusive Economic zone and Continental Shelf and Internal Waters; State Lands and Foreshore, Except to the Extent Specified in Item 18 of List I.*

*Minerals and Mines*

*Immigration and Emigration and Citizenship*

*Elections including Presidential, Parliamentary, Provincial Councils and Local Authorities*

*Census and Statistics*

*Professional Occupations and Training*

*National Archives; Archaeological Activities and sites and Antiquities declared by or under any law made by Parliament to be of National Importance*

All functions not specified in List I or List III

LIST III

(Concurrent List)

1. Planning -
2. and 3. Education and Education Services -
4. Higher Education -
5. National Housing and Construction-
6. Acquisition and requisitioning of Property
7. Social Services and Rehabilitation-
8. Agriculture and Agrarian Services-
9. Health-
10. Registration of births, marriages and deaths
11. Renaming of Towns and Villages
12. Private lotteries within the Province
13. Festival and Exhibitions
14. Rationing of food and maintenance of food stocks
15. Co-operatives, Co-operative Banks

16. Surveys -

17. Irrigation-

18. Social Forestry and protection of wild animals and birds

19. Fisheries-

20. Animal Husbandry-

21. Employment-

22. Tourism-

23. Trade and commerce in, and the production, supply and distribution of-

(a) the products of any industry where the control of such industry by the Government is declared by Parliament by law to be expedient in the public interest, and imported goods of the same kind as such products; and

(b) foodstuffs and cattle fodder

24. Newspapers, books and periodicals and printing presses

25. Offences against statutes with respect to any matters specified in this List

26. Fees in respect of any of the matters in this List, excluding fees taken in any Court

27. Charities and charitable institutions, charitable and religious endowments and religious institutions

28. Price control

29. Inquiries and statistics for the purpose of any matters in this List or in the Provincial Council List

30. Adulteration of foodstuffs and other goods

31. Drugs and Poisons

32. Extension of electrification within the Province and the promotion and regulation of the use of electricity within the Province

33. Protection of the Environment

34. Archaeological sites and remains, other than those declared by or under any law made by Parliament to be of national importance

35. Prevention of the extension from one Province to another of infectious or contagious diseases or pests affecting human beings, animal or plants

36. Pilgrimages

# 25.

## BILATERAL RELATIONS WITH INDIA

### Maritime Boundary between Sri Lanka and India - Island of Kachchativu[1]

September 15, 2008

*The Press Release "Maritime Boundary between Sri Lanka and India Stands Settled", lays down key facts related to the island of Kachchativu. The release highlights the 1974 and the 1976 Agreement, which confirms Sri Lanka's sovereignty over the island. The issue of fishing rights is brought to the fore, which as stated is ruled out. Fishing rights stated in paragraph 1 of the Exchange of Letters between, Mr Kewal Singh and Mr. Wt. Jayasinghe, clearly states that "fishing vessels and fishermen of India shall not exchange in fishing in the historic waters, the territorial sea and the EEZ of Sri Lanka, nor shall the fishing vessels and fishermen of Sri Lanka engage in fishing in the historic waters, the territorial sea and the EEZ of India, without the permission of Sri Lanka or India, as the case may be". This statement is considered as the focal point for settling the dispute between Sri Lanka and India.*

In response to the statement made by Hon. Anura Dissanayake, on 9th September 2008, in the Parliament on the important issue of Kachchcativu, I wish to place before this august assembly the facts from the point of view of the Government of Sri Lanka, for the information of the Hon. Members of the Parliament.

Kachchativu is a barren island that lies about 15 miles North-East of Rameshwaran and approximately 14 miles South-West of Delft Islands. There are no permanent inhabitants or any permanent structures on the Island other than a Roman Catholic Church, administered by the Bishop of Jaffna as part of his Diocese. What makes the island attractive is the richness of the surrounding seabed around Kachchativu with prawns, chank shells, pearl oysters and corals.

---

1. The Statement of Minister Bogollagama on the Maritime Boundary between Sri Lanka and India, September 15, 2008.

Government of Sri Lanka (GOSL) had always maintained a consistent policy founded on historical facts on the issue of the ownership of Kachchativu. Sri Lanka consistently and regularly exercised jurisdiction and control over Kachchativu. In this context, Sri Lanka's claim to Kachchativu was listed in 1924 in a correspondence stating that Survey Officers of the Government of India (GOI) treated the island as a part of then Ceylon as far back as 1876. Moreover Kachchativu Island has been under the jurisdiction of Sri Lanka since the time of Portuguese and later the British rulers of Sri Lanka (then Ceylon).

The issue of Kachchativu first arose in 1921, at the Conference to demarcate fisheries line between India and Sri Lanka and was followed by a series of bilateral discussions, relating to maritime boundary demarcation and related matters. However, the two Parties were able reach an Agreement for the first time in 1974.

The 1974 Agreement regarding historic waters between Sri Lanka and India in the Palk Strait and the Palk Bay formally confirmed Sri Lanka's sovereignty over the Island.

Article 4 of the Agreement stipulates that each State shall have sovereignty and exclusive jurisdiction and control over the waters, the Islands, the Continental Shelf and the sub soil on its side of the Maritime boundary in the Palk Strait and Palk Bay and Kachchativu Island was determined as falling within Sri Lankan waters.

Article 5 of the 1974 Agreement provides that "Subject to the foregoing, Indian fishermen and pilgrims will enjoy access to visit Kachchativu as hitherto, and will not be required by Sri Lanka to obtain travel documents or visas for these purposes."

Article 6 of the Agreement states that, "The vessels of India and Sri Lank will enjoy in each other's waters such rights as they have traditionally enjoyed therein."

By this Article, only navigational rights of the vessels of both Sri Lanka and India over each others waters have been preserved.

The preparatory notes leading to the finalization of the rights of the two Parties, clearly manifests that the rights of pilgrims under Article 5 were restricted to attend the annual feast of the church and the rights of access of fishermen was restricted to dry their nets and catch. Therefore the provisions in Article 5 and 6 taken together do not confer any fishing rights on the Indian fishermen or vessels to engage in fishing in Sri Lankan waters.

As follow up to this process, an Agreement between Sri Lanka and India on the Maritime Boundary between the two countries in the Gulf of Mannar and the Bay of Bengal and related matters was signed in 1976.

This Agreement further clarifies the position established by the 1974 Agreement between Sri Lanka and India.

Article 5, of 1976 Agreement stipulates that;

1. Each Party shall have sovereignty over the historic waters and the territorial sea, as well as the islands falling on its side of the aforesaid boundary.
2. Each Party shall have sovereign rights and exclusive jurisdiction over the Continental Shelf and the Exclusive Economic Zone(EEZ) as well as over their resources, whether living or non-living, falling on its side of the aforesaid boundary.
3. Each Party shall respect rights of navigation through its territorial sea and exclusive economic zone in accordance with its laws and regulations and the rules of international law."

The 1974 and 1976 Agreements taken together with the Exchange of Letters, that was signed between Mr. Kewal Singh, the then Foreign Secretary to the Government of India, and Mr. W.T. Jayasinghe, then Secretary to the Ministry of Defence and Foreign Affairs of Sri Lanka, has put the question of fishing rights beyond doubt. Paragraph 1 of the Exchange of Letters very clearly rules out any fishing rights for the fishermen of the two States in the waters of the other State which reads as follows;

"Fishing vessels and fishermen of India shall not engage in fishing in the historic waters, the territorial sea and the EEZ of Sri Lanka nor shall the fishing vessels and fishermen of Sri Lanka engage in fishing in the historic waters, the territorial sea and the EEZ of India, without the express permission of Sri Lanka or India, as the case may be."

Therefore you would observe that with the signing of the 1976 Agreement and the Exchange of Letters, the maritime boundary between Sri Lanka and India stands settled, and the Letters of Exchange clearly prohibits fishing vessels and fishermen of one country fishing in the others' waters.

Subsequent to the conclusion of the Agreements, the question of fishermen inadvertently straying into each others' waters has been discussed at several bilateral meetings between the officials of the two States.

On several occasions, the Sri Lankan Navy has been accused of involving in alleged attacks on Indian vessels near Kachchativu Island. Sri Lanka Navy has categorically denied any involvement in such activities and as they do not venture out of Sri Lankan territorial waters. In fact contrary to the allegations, the Sri Lanka Navy has on a number of occasions assisted and continues to assist the Indian fishermen in distress.

Meanwhile several personalities in Tamil Nadu State have recently raised the issue of Kachchativu, making proposals based on their own perceptions without any apparent valid legal basis, pertaining to the rights of Indian fishermen. In fact there has been a case filed by the former Chief Minister of Tamil Nadu Ms. Jayalalitha at the Indian Supreme Court.

However, a decision given by a Court of law in a jurisdiction outside Sri Lanka would not be binding on Sri Lanka. Any such Court Order or judgment will not alter or have an impact on a bilateral treaty concluded between two sovereign States.

In conclusion, I would like to reiterate to Hon. Members of Parliament that Kachchativu has always been the territory of the Sri Lankan state according to historical evidence and records of exercise of jurisdiction. And this has been cemented by the Agreements of 1974 and 1976 and the related Exchange of Letters.

(*Source*: http://www.slmfa.gov.lk//index.php?option=com_ content&task= view&id=1396&Itemid=86)

# 26.

## INTERNATIONAL DOCUMENTS

### Need for Collective Efforts to Combat Terrorism[1]

February 8, 2008

*The Sri Lankan President at the SAARC Summit pointed out that the SAARC Charter objective of promoting the welfare and improving the quality of life of the people should remain at the core of all common endeavours. He expressed satisfaction over the economic and social development in South Asian countries, and asserted that South Asia is no more the "poverty trough" of the world. He added that equitable distribution, pro-poor strategies, gender equality and an explicit focus on rural population could help bringing prosperity to the region. He appreciated the establishment of SAARC Food Bank and pointed out that food and energy security concerns remain to be addressed. He also added that regional legal mechanism and intelligence sharing is becoming important as the Asian countries witness the rise of terrorism in the region*

This Colombo Summit takes place amidst a background of significant political events and major international issues, such as food and fuel insecurity and degradation of the environment. It is our responsibility as leaders and representatives of our peoples to give tangible expression to the SAARC Charter objective of promoting the welfare and improving the quality of life of our peoples, which remains at the core of all our common endeavours.

The Delhi Summit launched SAARC as a Partnership for Prosperity, for the Prosperity of Our People, identifying the importance of connectivity as a powerful engine of growth. Continuity, consistency and coordination are all vital to have the desired practical effect towards our goal of regional economic integration.

---

1. Redouble Collective Efforts to Combat Terrorism – President to SAARC, February 8, 2008.

However, we must ensure that SAARC becomes more meaningful to all our people. Therefore, throughout the ensuing year we have to give SAARC a truly people-centred focus through all its programmes and mechanisms. It is then that SAARC can become the robust Partnership for Growth for all our people.

South Asia's continued progress in economic and social development is a matter of great satisfaction to me. Unemployment in our country, as well as in the region, has reached historic low levels leading to declines in overall poverty. South Asia is no more the poverty trough of the world, although we have yet to eradicate poverty from our midst.

Yet, for growth to be sustainable, its benefits must be evenly distributed, pro-poor strategies must be put into place, and the rural populations that make up the vast majorities in all our countries, must be empowered ensuring gender equality.

The SAARC Social Charter and our shared experiences and best practices, already provide a solid foundation to further strengthen empowerment of the rural people. In our own country, the Policy Vision of the Mahinda Chintana, my electoral pledge to the people of Sri Lanka, addresses this issue and seeks to transform current challenges into opportunities for the upliftment of the rural people.

It is a matter of satisfaction that we are progressively inaugurating, in each of our countries, SAARC villages as visible examples of our collective commitment to rural uplift. The most recent such village was opened on 27th July this year in Nawalapitiya, in the central hill region of Sri Lanka.

As we meet today, most countries of our region are faced with the curse of terrorism that threatens the peace and stability that is needed so much for the forward march of our people. No country in the SAARC region has been spared of this plague. We need to redouble our efforts for collective action to combat terrorism in all its forms and manifestations. It is important to remember the element of interdependence which is crucial for a durable peace and the protection of democratic values in the region.

We must ensure strengthening regional legal mechanisms and intensifying intelligence sharing, in order to secure the region's collective prosperity, peace and stability. Further, I would strongly suggest that in-depth studies are carried out to understand the social impact of this menace. Sri Lanka has seen the benefits of such cooperation in combating the terrorism in our midst and hopefully eradicating it sooner, than many once expected.

My gratitude must go to all our regional partners and our many friends from other quarters that have cooperated with us in this matter. In my view it is also necessary that we, as a region, endeavour to set right the many wrong impressions that exist, or are promoted elsewhere, about the actions that are imperative to protect our people and societies from the brutalities of terrorism. Terrorism anywhere is terrorism and there are no good terrorists or bad terrorists.

Asia's economic surge provides our region with manifold opportunities. We are on the threshold of a new age the Age of Asia with South Asia being an important part of it, not only in numbers but also in skills and the strength of growing economies. Today, Asia is the economic power house of the world.

In order to ensure that we in the SAARC provide the necessary thrust for Asia's economic surge, I would once again promote the idea of SAARC intensifying to the maximum possible its regional economic and trade integration. We have to set in motion a process of adopting a single currency in the region. Undoubtedly, full implementation of the SAFTA and other follow up measures will greatly facilitate the realisation of this vision. Our region also should assume a leadership role in the reform of Multilateral Financial Institutions.

Today, as never before we are confronted with the global issues of food and energy insecurity and climate change. Food prices in international markets have increased by 54 percent in the past year alone. World oil prices have increased by 300 percent over the past four years. These are the statistics of near despair. Yet, I believe that we need not despair.

I propose that we seize this challenge and transform it into opportunity, with focus on agriculture, on food security that is largely based on home grown food; that we look at realistic policies on nutrition, at strategies for development that are least dependent on the forces of speculation and markets that have no feel for the people.

We must productively use existing mechanisms such as the SAARC Food Bank and the SAARC Development Fund, for the development of strategic buffer stocks of our staple foods. Food security is vital because of its impact on all sectors of national life. It is today recognised as an essential condition for economic and political stability.

We also need to act fast on meeting the energy crunch. There is the necessity to accelerate our plans for South Asian energy sharing. Knowing that we have to depend on fossil fuels for many more decades to come, we must explore the use of other sources of energy that will take us out of the deadly grip of the oil well. However, pursuit on Bio-fuels must not be at the cost of food crops or arable land.

To take the next leap from fossil fuels to renewable energy, we have to move with speed on harnessing the Sun, the Sea, and the Wind resources that all of our countries have in plenty. South Asia must look at shared research in the areas with potential for local technologies in harnessing renewable energy.

As we grapple with the issues of food and fuel security, we will also need to address as a matter of priority, the looming water deficit in the region. King Parakramabahu, an ancient ruler of Sri Lanka, advised the people not to allow a single drop of water to flow into the sea without first being of use to the people. We must bring a new focus on conservation of water resources to ensure that South Asia would be the best watered region in the world.

Asia's evolution has been founded on ancient traditions of environmental sustainability, integrating environmental responsibility with cultural and religious values. We should go back to the tradition of sharing that sustained our people in the past, shedding the tradition of exploitation of nature that came to us from our former conquerors.

Throughout our region there is increasing movement from the village to the city, resulting in degradation of the environment and human dignity. Let us therefore commit ourselves to upgrade village housing and facilities, through a sound mix of traditional construction methods and material with modern technology, to discourage people from moving out of the villages. In the cities, we need to further evolve models of urban design and housing construction that strengthen the inherited spirit of social community common to all our societies.

The Delhi Summit last year laid stress on connectivity. Today, we find that with the advances of communications technology, good connectivity is not very far from our people. Although the numbers of mobile phone users in South Asia are rapidly increasing yet, our people remain distanced through the barrier of tariffs. I, therefore, propose that we actively promote a reduced tariff for IDD calls within the South Asian region to bring our people much closer, much sooner.

We, in South Asia share a rich and common heritage, a heritage of understanding and of tolerance, a heritage that respects learning and wisdom, and takes pride in sharing the bounties of nature. But for this great heritage that transcends differences and upholds the value of a shared purpose and existence, our diverse cultures, languages and religious traditions could have made us the most divided region in the world. Instead, by and large we see a great harmony among our peoples.

In my own country, the impact of this common heritage is best seen today in what we have achieved in the East, where we have defeated terrorism, restored democracy, elected a Chief Minister from a minority community who was a former child soldier, and, most of all, where the Sinhalese, Tamil and Muslim communities live together, work together, and together seek the common goals of progress and prosperity. This indeed is a unique transformation within a short span of one year. This is my deep desire for the people in the North as well.

In conclusion ay I say that there must be a spirit of large heartedness by all including the stronger and wealthier nations, when some of these crucial issues are addressed. It is my fervent hope that the Colombo Summit will enable our dialogue with the Observer States to broaden into a process for constructive consultations, and project related cooperation in agreed areas. I have no doubt that together we can make our common endeavours, this Partnership, succeed for the benefit of all our peoples.

(*Source*: http://www.president.gov.lk/speech_New.asp?Id=55)

## Global Food Crises-The Sri Lankan View[2]

### September 24, 2008

*President Mahinda Rajapakse, at the 63rd Session of the United Nations General Assembly stressed on combating contemporary challenges. He stated that while Sri Lanka had witnessed an increase in food production, a holistic revitalisation of agricultural sector was needed. He noted the specific importance of SAARC Food Bank in this context. According to the President, transfer of technology to developing countries and addressing the energy crises, ,were issues which needed attention. Addressing the issues of conflict, the President emphasised that the Sri Lankan government was open towards initiating dialogue with democratic leadership of the Tamil community.*

(Speaks in Tamil)

While my mother tongue is Sinhala, let me elaborate a few thoughts in Tamil. Sinhala and Tamil are the two languages of the people of Sri Lanka. Both these have been used through the centuries, are rich in literature, and are widely used in my country, with recognition as Official Languages.

With the widening of democracy in our country, the bonds between the Sinhala and Tamil people of Sri Lanka will grow stronger and remain a major force for its future development. We will march towards a richer freedom and lasting unity that await us as a nation.

(Tamil delivery ends)

The theme for our debate, "The impact of the global food crisis on poverty and hunger in the world, as well as the need to democratize the United Nations" is indeed far sighted. It focuses on one of the critical survival needs of humanity as well as one of the key institutional needs of the world body.

The global food crisis has become a frightening actuality and has the potential to assume even more dangerous proportions if we fail to take urgent and collective action. Similarly, a less democratic United Nations

---

2. President Mahinda Rajapakse Speech at the 63rd UN General Assembly, September 24, 2008.

runs the risk of being less effective and less credible while raising major concerns about its legitimacy.

Through a series of projects with regional impact, Sri Lanka will contribute to the goal of increasing food production, investing more in agriculture and research, and sharing technologies and best practices. This is an integral part of rural empowerment so essential in the developing world, as the vast majority of our people are rural based and depend on agriculture for their livelihood.

Achieving food security would require strengthening and revitalizing the agriculture sector. This calls for the empowerment of small and medium scale farmers through a series of measures. These represent vital collective steps by all of us in the UN system. Sri Lanka sees self-sufficiency as the answer to overcoming the food crisis and giving strength to nations. No longer can we expect farmers in developing countries to be mainly producers for export markets. In this context, implementation of effective social safety nets remains a priority as reassurance and empowerment. This is why we have introduced measures of social security such as the fertilizer and fisheries subsidies. The advice given by some powerful countries and powerful institutions are contrary to this. Yet, it is necessary that we pay no heed to such advice, and determine to do what is best for the innocent people of our countries.

As the current Chair of SAARC, I have the honour to state that at the recent Summit, we affirmed our resolve as a region to make our own contribution to grapple with the food crisis and to make our Region revive its historic critical role in food production, by once again becoming a major granary of the world.

We also decided on the immediate establishment and operationalisation of the SAARC Food Bank. This mechanism, we believe, will help considerably to ensure both food and nutritional security of the people of South Asia. This initiative will contribute to the larger global efforts that we launched in Rome, in June this year, for averting and mitigating the impact of the food crisis.

We also must find solutions to the energy crisis that are both equitable and pragmatic. Energy supplies must be diversified by developing advanced, cleaner, more efficient and cost-effective technologies, for both fossil fuels and renewable energy sources. We need to engage in energy conservation and accept the reality of dependence on fossil fuels for much longer.

Equally obvious is the imperative of transferring new technology to the developing countries. We in our own region will use increasing resources of human and scientific talent to produce our own technologies, making the best use of the natural resources, the sun, wind and ocean that we have in abundance, free of the restrictions of the marketplace. Demands of humanity cannot anymore be allowed to be at the mercy of speculative or captive markets.

To this end, Sri Lanka's own view is that the United Nations and its agencies must take the leadership in developing a framework for international cooperation so that the vulnerable developing countries have access to the energy benefits of the so-called 'nuclear renaissance', at reasonable and affordable rates. This cooperative endeavour will impact positively in such diverse areas as energy, MDGs, climate change and even arms control.

We urge caution in the rush to use bio-fuels to break our dependence of fossil fuels. It is already seen that the rush to bio-fuels has contributed to high food prices. Sri Lanka's policy is that any arable land should not be diverted or directed towards the production of bio-fuels, however profitable it may be in the short-term. It was propitious that Sri Lanka acted with courage and foresight, without being cowed by many pressures, through the last three years, and thus did not face any situation where our people had to face hunger or starvation.

On climate change, the SAARC leaders reiterated the need to redouble efforts within an expanded regional framework for environmental protection, conservation and justice. We stressed that we should contribute to restoring harmony with nature, a part of the heritage of South Asia. We humans have interfered with nature, too much for too long. We must accept that the dangers of Climate Change are manmade, and its solutions too require man's intervention.

With the promulgation of the UN Charter to save succeeding generations from the tragedy of war, at least the major threat of intercontinental war seems to have receded. However, the just struggle of Palestinians for statehood continues. Today, the United Nations and its people are confronted with the fast spreading menace of terrorism that manifests itself in various forms in Asia, Africa and Latin America The United Nations has a grave responsibility to save today's and succeeding generations, from this new and continuing menace. We have been talking for long enough. It is time for clear action in this regard.

Like many other countries, Sri Lanka too has not been spared this global menace. Exploiting perceived ethnic grievances, that must and can be addressed through political means, the vested interests of a well organized terror group, the LTTE indulges in blatant and brutal acts of terrorism, including suicide bombings to seek negotiating leverage, political recognition and legitimacy. What is happening in Pakistan today is the destructive policy of bloody terrorists. I am saddened by the loss of life and destruction caused by the recent terrorist attack there.

Our Government has always been ready to address the causes of these issues and effectively implement political and constitutional solutions to meet the aspirations and rights of all communities. What the Government would not, and could not do is to let an illegal and armed terrorist group, the LTTE, to hold a fraction of our population, a part of the Tamil community, hostage to such terror in the northern part of Sri Lanka and deny those people their democratic rights of dissent and free elections. Through our past actions, we have proved it.

The Government has therefore declared its policy of engaging in dialogue and discussion with the democratic leadership of the Tamil community, a people who have lived in harmony with other Sri Lankans for centuries. Today, there are Tamil leaders holding responsible ministerial posts in my government. A former Attorney General of then Ceylon, Sir Ponnambalam Ramanathan, also a loved Tamil politician, in September 1904, had this to say at a public meeting in Colombo. (I quote) "I have been to many countries in the world. But, no where have I seen such a friendly race as the Sinhalese who also uphold high moral values." (unquote). Such was the harmony between the Tamils and the Sinhalese. But a malicious group has turned all of this upside down.

All successive governments of Sri Lanka have endeavoured to resolve the problem for over twenty five years, including through Norwegian facilitation and international Co-Chairs overseeing a so-called peace process that was treated with contempt by the terrorists. On each occasion that talks were held seeking peace, the terrorists of the LTTE walked out on the flimsiest of excuses and reverted to terrorism of the worst kind, indiscriminately targeting innocent civilians.

Our Government would only be ready to talk to this illegal armed group when it is ready to commit itself to decommissioning of its illicit weapons and dismantling of its military capability, and return to the democratic fold. The Government has also made it clear that the elected Government cannot and will not permit undermining of the territorial integrity of the sovereign UN Member State of Sri Lanka and the division of its territory. We are clear in this message.

The Government's objective is to enable the people to enjoy the benefits of the democratic processes and to speed the development activities in those areas where there is a heavy presence of terrorists. This would be similar to the fast tracking of economic development taking place in the Eastern Province of Sri Lanka, where former terrorists now function as democratically elected Provincial Councilors, and a former child soldier conscripted by the LTTE is now the elected Chief Minister, having abandoned terrorism and embracing democracy. Significantly, the restoration of democracy in the East of Sri Lanka was achieved in less than one year of it being freed from the clutches of terror.

Our Government has also sought and received the cooperation of the United Nations, ICRC and other agencies to help us in providing humanitarian assistance to the Internally Displaced Persons (IDPs) and other affected civilians. The UN Secretary General's special representative on IDP's who visited Sri Lanka some years ago said and I quote: "Sri Lanka represents the unusual situation of a central government providing relief aid to persons under the control of (the) main opposition group. In a world replete with examples of Governments and rebel groups using food as a weapon against civilian populations, the situation in Sri Lanka is one that deserves closer attention if not more publicity as an important precedent. (Unquote)

The Government of Sri Lanka continues this humanitarian policy even today although we know that the terrorists seize a good proportion of these humanitarian supplies. Our supplies are not confined to food; they extend to medicines, and all other essentials as well as schools and hospitals, with teachers, doctors, nurses, and all other essential staff. This is not all, the government also purchases the paddy and other foodstuffs produced in those areas. I do not think there is any country in the world where there is a government that provides such humanitarian assistance to terrorists that attack it. Our government considers the supply of humanitarian relief to its people as its prime responsibility.

The complex situation in Sri Lanka needs to be addressed and resolved through an appropriate process of deterrent law and order action and patient political efforts of consensus building. We have achieved the difficult but essential task of building democracy in the Eastern Province and are confident that it can be done in the North as well.

This session of the Assembly is a good time to take stock of progress made towards MDGs around the globe. As we do so, it is regrettable to note that most are behind schedule. The slowing down of global economic growth, financial turmoil and speculation, rising food and fuel prices and the impacts of climate change are clear and present obstacles. Also, based on their political role, sanctions imposed on the leaders, and the leadership of some countries following some protests, are in fact targeted at the innocent people of those countries.

The steadily growing menace of international terrorism, with related activities such as smuggling of illegal arms, human trafficking, drug trafficking, money laundering, and business empires run by terror groups undoubtedly undermine the fundamentals of humanity and civilization. It appears that steps taken by us to eradicate these illegal activities have not been effective. This further complicates all national and international efforts at moving towards realizing MDGs. Terrorism, as I have emphasized many a time, by its very nature, rolls back even our modest achievements.

Another similar menace is threatening to devour our children, the most valuable asset of any nation. That is the insecurity of the cyber space that has not only helped corrupt the minds of our children but also exposes them to predators such as paedophiles, drug dealers and pornographic sites. Sri Lanka has banned pornographic and similar destructive sites from being available through ISP providers. We are also controlling and restricting the use of mobile telephones for such damaging activities. This is an important area for world leaders to focus on.

It is important that urgent and collective actions, both short and long term, are taken to stem these adverse trends. Only such determined and concerted actions will enable progress towards the realization of the agreed development goals, including the MDGs and frustrate elements which are bent on reversing the gains made. We must deeply commit ourselves as members of the United Nations towards forging a way forward from the limitations not seen by those who laid the foundations for this great institution of humankind. If we fail to do it now, future generations will curse us.

Mr. President, I wish to conclude my address with a stanza from the Dhammapada, words from the Enlightened One.

> Victory breeds hatred
> The defeated live in pain
> Happily the calmed live
> Having set victory and defeat aside
> May the Noble Triple Gem bless you.

(*Source*: http://www.president.gov.lk/speech_New.asp?Id=57)

## The South Asian Economic Summit[3]

August 28, 2008

*Minister of Foreign Affairs, Mr Rohita Bogollagama, in his inaugural address at the First South Asian Economic Summit, spoke on the prospects for economic cooperation in South Asia. He stated that while earlier globalization, liberalization, integration and regionalism were the key themes, connectivity needed to be enhanced in the 21st century. Some of the many points he touched upon for facilitating cooperation were, energy and power, education, food security and intra-regional trade and investment, amongst many others.*

It gives me great pleasure to deliver the inaugural address at the 1st South Asian Economic Summit organised by the Institute of Policy Studies in collaboration with the Federation of Chambers of Commerce and Industry of Sri Lanka.

---

3. Inaugural Address by Minister of Foreign Affairs, Mr Rohitha Bogollagama, on the occasion of the First South Asian Economic Summit, August 28, 2008.

## Introduction

The South Asia is just emerging from the successful conclusion of an extremely significant and momentous regional integration exercise – the 15th SAARC Summit - held in Colombo in the latter half of July and early August. The 1st South Asian Economic Summit, which commences today, will afford us the opportunity to improve, enhance and expand connectivity in the South Asian region, by adhering to the theme of the Colombo SAARC Summit i.e. "Partnership for our People". The theme of the 14th SAARC Summit, which was held in New Delhi, was "Connectivity". The theme of Connectivity was defined as free flow of goods, services, people and ideas between and among the member States of the SAARC. It is understood that Connectivity is crucial and indispensable to the future of the development and advancement of the region of South Asia. Allow me to state that the recent Colombo SAARC Summit chose the theme "SAARC Partnership for our People" in order to have a sense of continuity and extend greater efficacy to the previous theme of "Connectivity". I am happy to be associated with this event as it is a vital platform, bringing together South Asian political leaders, senior government officials, corporate sector, and civil society among others. The Government of Sri Lanka, in the capacity of the Chair of the SAARC, is placed at a vantage point to play a pivotal role with regard to economic integration of South Asia.

As the Chair of SAARC, Sri Lanka endeavours to build on the successes of previous summits in strengthening the SAARC process. Our objective is to ensure that the decisions taken and agreed upon at the Summit are efficaciously implemented and executed, thus delivering tangible economic benefits to the region of South Asia. The 15th SAARC Summit addressed and deliberated some of the pressing and key regional issues such as regional cooperation and trade, trade facilitation, connectivity, energy and power, food security and establishment of food bank, SAARC Development Fund, poverty alleviation, education, tourism, environment, transfer of technology and ICT, South Asian regional standardization and combating of terrorism among others.

## Regional Cooperation and Connectivity

The four key concepts of the era of 1980s and 1990s were globalization, liberalization, integration and regionalism. The Colombo Summit increasingly extended and focussed on enhancing connectivity not only air connectivity but by land and by sea as well. The benefit of greater connectivity between and among the member States, in particular, would make a strong economic impingement in the region with regard to trade, services, food security, tourism, international joint ventures, oil and natural gas and investment as well as foreign direct investments/foreign institutional investments. Connectivity is often described as the common thread or the common denominator of the four concepts of globalization, liberalization, integration and regionalism. The region of South Asia has one of the highest number of people under the poverty line and current economic advancement of the region is far from satisfactory.

The region of South Asia is also one of the less integrated regions in the world. The connectivity, if and when transformed into physical connectivity, it could visibly alleviate poverty from the region of South Asia as well. It may also be reasonable to state that the rapid development and advancement of the EU was due to physical connectivity and it is not alien to many a regions, which have developed, in the world. On the same vein, may I add that the region of South Asia, unfortunately, is not integrated similar to other regional blocs such as ASEAN, the EU, Mercusor, GCC and NAFTA to name a few. As we are well aware that the intra regional trade of the SAARC region is still less than 6% of the total trade. This is despite the fact that the region of South Asia is one of the most endowed regions in natural and human resources. Most of the other established regional blocs have intra regional trade ranging from 20% to over 60%. In order to have greater and deeper economic integration in South Asia, the public and corporate sector as well as the respective governments would have to tenaciously focus on the concepts of regionalism, integration, liberalization and globalization. The share of global trade of the SAARC region, despite being the most populous regional bloc consisting 23% of humanity, is barely 1.45% and the share of global GDP is only 2.8%. Having stated these cogent, yet disturbing, facts of the economic integration of South Asia, the region is well endowed, as stated earlier, and poses increasing economic opportunities, potential and vistas for closer and deeper integration. The region of South Asia possesses a myriad of complementarities, which could be leveraged and mutually exploited through the SAARC as well as through the SAFTA process.

At the Colombo SAARC Summit, the leaders of the member countries were of the conviction that the process of regional cooperation should be people centred since it would strengthen the SAARC as a 'robust' partnership for growth for the peoples of South Asia. I am happy to state as the Chair of the Council of Ministers of SAARC that the SAARC mechanisms did identify and recognize other areas of cooperation, where people centric partnership projects could be initiated. Further, issues such as affordable regional telecommunication is an imperative ingredient of connectivity, thus encouraging growth of people-to-people partnership and augmenting economic integration as well as economic activity. The Colombo SAARC Summit further recognized the indispensability of connectivity in order to realise the objectives of the SAARC. On the same note, I am heartened to state that air connectivity between Colombo and Dhaka has already commenced. The national carrier of Sri Lanka i.e.

SriLankan Airlines is today the largest foreign carrier to India, having over 120 flights per week to 10 cities in India.

### Intra-regional Trade and Investments

The Foreign Direct Investments (FDIs), Foreign Institutional Investments (FIIs) and International Joint Ventures (IJVs) as well as mergers and acquisitions between nations in the region of South Asia are minimal compared to many other developed and developing regions of the world. The intra-regional investment is a key factor for the leaders of the countries of South Asia as well as the corporate sector to focus and address. Sri Lanka has concluded a successful and highly productive Free Trade Agreement (FTA) with India in December 1998 and is about to sign the Comprehensive Economic Partnership Agreement (CEPA) with India. The CEPA would encompass not only the goods which are in the existing FTA, but services as well. In other words, the CEPA would consist of facilitation of investments, extension of services of many a disciplines and trades, and international joint ventures between the two countries. The bilateral trade between India and Sri Lanka is approximately close to USD 3 billion and is envisaged to reach higher, once the CEPA were operational. Further, I wish to add that Sri Lanka has an FTA with Pakistan as well and is poised to be yet another success, similar to the FTA between India and Sri Lanka. The FTAs can be described as a prelude for greater expansion of economic dimensions between the countries. The Partnership Agreements, such as the imminent CEPA between India and Sri Lanka, could make a marked economic impingement on the commercial and trade fabric of the two respective countries. The South Asia Free Trade Agreement would lead to deeper, pro-active and comprehensive economic integration, once it becomes fully operational.

### SAFTA and trade facilitation

In order to evolve greater economic integration, it is necessary for the respective governments of South Asia to address trade facilitation, in all its aspects. At the Colombo Summit, the leaders of the SAARC countries agreed to implement the SAFTA, which would significantly contribute to the SAARC process. Further, it was heartening to note that the leaders of SAARC member countries recognized the necessity to address major and potent impediments, which are hindering trade liberalization between and among the nations in the region. The Colombo Summit deliberated on measures to address the non tariff barriers (NTBs) as well. I wish to broach the importance of the Agreement on South Asian Regional Standards Organization, which was signed at the Colombo Summit. The intrinsic utility of this initiative would be that the standards of the goods and services would be consonant with each of the countries of South Asia, thus increasing bilateral and multilateral trade as well as integration. Also, the standardization would reduce the cost of production, which would particularly be of benefit to small and medium enterprises (SMEs) as well.

**Food Security**

The issue of Food Security was foremost on the agenda of the Colombo Summit highlighting the resolve of member countries to ensure region-wide food security. The adoption of the Colombo Statement on Food Security is a clear depiction of the emphasis placed on this crucial matter. It was agreed that all efforts should be directed towards making South Asia the granary of the world once again. Identifying the uncertainties associated with the emerging global situation of reduced food availability, the member states agreed to convene a meeting of the Minister of Agriculture in November 2008 in New Delhi. The purpose of this Meeting would be to evolve and implement a people-centred short to medium term regional strategy and collaborative projects to address core issues including the increase in food production; Investment in agriculture and agro-based industries; Agriculture research and prevention of soil health degradation; Development and sharing of agricultural technologies; Sharing of best practices in procurement and distribution; and Management of the climatic and disease-related risks in agriculture. Another significant step was the agreement reached to urgently operationalise the SAARC Food Bank and the early drawing up of the SAARC Agriculture Perspective 2020. The leaders also agreed that synergies should be built with the international community to ensure food and nutrition security in South Asia.

**SAARC Development Fund**

The Colombo Summit inked the SAARC Development Fund (SDF). The SDF would be utilised for projects on empowerment of women, maternal and child health care, teachers' training as well as rehabilitation of the infrastructure and poverty alleviation in South Asia. This could be considered as a momentous step towards development of the region since the SAARC Development Fund consists of USD 300 million.

**Energy and Power**

In order to have effective economic integration and advancement in South Asia, it is vital to have access to power and energy at affordable and economical prices. On the same note, Sri Lanka imports approximately 2.6 million barrels of oil per year, which would translate to USD 3.5 billion a year, at the current price of approximately USD 110 per barrel. The progress of the mega tri-lateral gas projects among Iran-Pakistan-India and developing of regional hydro power and grid connectivity could lead to greater economic integration and access to energy. The Colombo Summit unequivocally noted the vitality of energy for growth and development in South Asia. Needless to state at this juncture, the unprecedented rise of oil in the recent past has created an economic disequilibrium not only in South Asia but in the entire world. In order to address this issue, the Colombo Summit focussed on conservation of conventional source of energy and developing renewable alternative energy resources such as hydro power, solar, wind and bio. Further, the Summit discussed and mapped out measures to introduce energy reforms, and trade and sharing of technology and expertise in the realm of energy and power. It was proposed that Sri Lanka would host the Third Meeting of SAARC Energy Ministers next year.

**Education**

The establishment of the South Asian University in New Delhi would benefit all the member countries in enhancing the human resource development and marketable skills and knowledge. It is envisaged that this University would be on par with some of the top universities in the world. For any given country, particularly the member countries of SAARC, the human resource base would be of paramount significance and importance for the development and advancement of the respective countries. The South Asian University is envisaged to commence by year 2010. The Colombo Summit discussed and deliberated increased interaction between and among students and academia as well as to develop youth exchange programmes. I may also add that the Colombo Summit discussed closer regional cooperation in Information and Communication Technology (ICT). It is anticipated that the enhanced digital connectivity and Regional Communication Infrastructure among the States of South Asia too would be enhanced and upgraded. The improvement of ICT and bio-technology could make a positive impact on the quality of life of the peoples of South Asia, thus facilitating to uplift their standards of living.

**Terrorism**

The recent SAARC Summit, succeeded in signing the Agreement on Mutual Assistance on Criminal Matters, which would be beneficial in addressing terrorism and terrorism related activities in the region. It was interesting to note, yet not surprising, that almost all the members of the SAARC as well as some of the Observer States of the Summit vehemently condemned terrorist activities unconditionally. Unfortunately, today terrorism has become ubiquitous and is not alien to any part of South Asia.

**Conclusion**

In conclusion, I listed out the agreements, accomplishments and developments of the Colombo SAARC Summit in the context of the First

South Asia Economic Summit in order to accentuate and impress the manner in which they would contribute to greater economic integration in the region of South Asia. Nevertheless, the South Asia needs to integrate economically, if South Asia were to develop and advance itself similar to her neighbours in South East and Far East Asia, in particular. Historically, nations around the world have developed and advanced in blocs or regions and seldom in isolation. It is also interesting to note that when nations are committed and engaged in dynamics of economics and business to a great extent, they would diminish and dilute any other differences. It is also often stated that economics would not take place in a political vacuum and vice versa. Having stated this premise, the economic integration in South Asia is indispensable not only for advancement but also to establish a sense of stability and predictability. I may also add that given the degree of poverty in the region, the economic integration in South Asia could be a powerful and compelling instrument to lift the underprivileged from the shackles of poverty. Further, the economic integration could integrate a large percentage, which is approximately 64% of the populace who dwell in villages in South Asia, to the economic mainstream, thus extending dividends of economic integration.

I take this opportunity to acknowledge the role played by the Institute of Policy Studies (IPS) and the Federation of Chambers of Commerce and Industry of Sri Lanka (FCCISL), in initiating and hosting this important Summit. Events of this nature and this scale can educate and edify the leaders of South Asia as well as corporate and public sector to extend greater focus and place more importance on economic integration of the region.

(*Source*:http://www.slmfa.gov.lk/index.php?option=com_frontpage&Itemid=1&limit=10&limitstart=50)

## Sri Lanka: Challenges and Opportunities Ahead[4]

March 6, 2008

*President Mahinda Rajapaksa in his address at the Boao Forum for Asia highlighted the importance of working harmoniously with the environment. Emphasizing the economic growth witnessed by Asia, the President noted that the number of people living in absolute poverty had declined from over 920 million in 1990 to about 600 million in 2007. The President pointed out that his development plan for the country would be based on a pro-poor strategy, injecting fresh vitality and dynamism to the existing development programmes and launching new initiatives.*

---

4. President Mahinda Rajapaksa's Address at the Boao Forum for Asia, April 12, 2008.

The world, in the last century, had made remarkable progress in science and technology bringing many positive attributes for human development. These saw the significant improvement of living conditions in so many ways, great advances in health care and education, the expansion of industry, widening of opportunity for travel, and overall brought more comforts to a larger number of people.

We have also seen the emergence of many challenges, These include the fight against terrorism that pervades the world today, the continuing spread of nuclear weapons, the widening gap between the rich and the poor, international trafficking in drugs, women, and children; and in recent years the most alarming problem of the depletion of the earth's natural resources; and the destruction of the environment. With all the wealth that industrial progress has produced, today, we are gravely threatened by global warming and climate change. In the face of these challenges that mock our most determined attempts to solve them within established frameworks, we must fashion our policies to enable continued development while addressing the challenges posed. This Boao Forum has a critical role to play in this regard.

If we journey through to ancient Asia, we find that its evolution has been founded on the cornerstones of environmental sustainability. Our forefathers, who have left their indelible footprints in nurturing our civilizations over centuries ago, integrated environmental responsibility into our cultural values. Our gentle cultures, wherever their roots were from, taught us to respect and live in harmony with nature. The essence of China's ancient wisdom is that we hold the environment in trust, to be handed down to generations to come without damage or destruction. A great king of Sri Lanka when threatened to reveal the storehouse of his wealth, showed the waters of a massive reservoir he had built for irrigation. Another great ruler admonished the people not to allow a single drop of water to drain into the sea, without first having watered the crops. Our history, therefore, should provide us with considerable strength as we face our future challenges, especially in the new challenge of facing up to Climate Change, and seeking consensus of how we should restore harmony with nature and the environment.

Industrialization, the most powerful agent of change that came from the West, saw a marked break with the concept of harmony with nature. We saw the natural environment being defined in terms of man's right to possess and dominate, with the environment being there solely to be exploited for the benefit of man. The social and political philosophies that sprang from industrialization encouraged this selfish approach, for which, we have paid a heavy price since, and will have to do so in the future too.

However in meeting the challenges posed by globalization today, as well as the challenges faced by the environment, we see the need for a new definition of man's relationship with nature and the environment. We need to look back at our traditional values, and also look forward to what today's scientific knowledge can give us to restore our good relations with nature.

As Asia develops at an extraordinary pace, a major transformation is occurring in the distribution of the world's wealth. China and India now contribute over half of the world's GDP and this trend will continue. China's extraordinary economic growth has brought immense benefits to its people; and has been a great inspiration for developing countries. Asia's economic surge, led by these icons of our region, provides us with the opportunity to address some of our global challenges. This brings hope of change to many in our region to whom poverty and deprivation have been the only birthright for centuries. Asia is now firmly a driver of world growth bringing us our century of hope.

This extra-ordinary economic growth has no doubt brought immense benefits to the people of Asia. The number of people living in absolute poverty has declined from over 920 million in 1990 to about 600 million today. The living standards have improved and people have become healthier. This no doubt has become a great inspiration for us to move forward in chartering our course for the future. Despite many challenges, the economy of my country grew by 6.7% last year. To ensure that the benefits of this growth reach all strata of society, my government has pursued a variety of direct initiatives in such fields as gender issues, livelihoods security and rural prosperity.

The Asian resilience could be vividly displayed in terms of the current global economic environment. Although the pace of growth in 2008, could be expected to slow down due to the effects of the new crisis in the US economy, now admittedly approaching a recession, it appears that the slowdown caused by this in emerging Asia will be limited due to strong expansion by China and India. Further, the region has built substantial buffers against external shocks since the 1997 – 1998 financial crises. However, Asia is not totally immune to the potential spillovers. Given these risks, Asia's policy makers need to take the steps necessary to ensure confidence in the global financial markets. They must continue to pursue sound macroeconomic management and improve structural resilience through deeper and more comprehensive reform efforts, as economic growth will still remain one of the prerequisites in the region. But this growth -oriented strategy will also need to be a sustainable, pro-poor and a more inclusive process.

It is necessary to understand that the rapid expansion of Asia's dynamic economies, both large and small, has brought with it the predicament of coping with a serious environmental challenge. Asia's appetite for energy rises steadily, with the need to develop rapidly and further reduce poverty.

As we consume ever increasing quantities of fossil fuels we also emit larger amounts of green house gases. The products that we consume and the waste we create expose our populations to a wider array of potentially harmful consequences than ever before. Significantly, we find that rural eco- systems, which are the bedrock of Asia, coming under enormous pressure.

We are now at a critical juncture. There are deep-seated economic problems and imbalances that need to be fundamentally reversed. It shall give us challenges as well as opportunities. Despite the progress we have made, there are still millions of people living in abject poverty. There is a huge infrastructure gap in the region. Urbanization is putting a serious strain on infrastructure services in Asia's cities. More than half a billion Asian people have no access to safe water and three times as many live without proper sewage and waste disposal, access to paved roads, electricity and other services is uneven.

We owe it to our people, to ensure that our economic development must continue. However, if we are to protect the environment and safeguard nature as we develop, we must focus more on sustainable energy sources, cleaner production processes, sustainable consumption patterns, efficient technologies and agricultural processes. We must ensure investment in improved and eco-friendly infrastructure, including better roads and ports, power and rural electrification, irrigation, renewable energy sources, water supply and sanitation and better health services.

Despite the scale of challenges our region now faces, all is not gloomy. There seems to be a new public awareness building of the dangers of destroying the resources on which our long term health and prosperity depends. Concrete efforts are being taken to address policies and investment that remove barriers and obstacles to the participation of poorer groups in the region. There is a particular focus on creation of sustainable employment livelihoods and investment in improved infrastructure, especially rural infrastructure. More importantly, we are aware that these investments need to be matched by adequate investment in good quality education and training.

An education that focuses on awareness of the current needs for a change in attitude towards development, away from one that lays stress only on the exploitation of nature, but rather on achieving partnership with nature and the environment. This is in keeping with the traditional Asian respect for education, and our strong belief that to ensure the future, we must invest in our future — which is our children.

In this context, I must mention that Sri Lanka has a free education system from kindergarten to university level. We are proud of our achievement in ensuring that the needs of our university students, in terms of maintenance, books and other requirements are provided for by the

State throughout their undergraduate career. 97 percent of our youngsters are enrolled at school. This is our own investment in the future.

We need to take urgent measures to ensure that we leave behind to our children a planet that is livable with the benefits of sustainable progress. This requires measures to mitigate our impact on the environment being pursed simultaneously, with measures to adapt to the sustainable environment that we will progress to. I agree with the view that those who ravaged the environment in their dash to development must bear the brunt of the responsibility for addressing the consequences. They need to assume the main burden for adopting measures that mitigate the harm done and contribute significantly to the new measures that protect nature and favour sustainability. For, it is they who established the signposts of development and progress from which others are still measured. Yet, having witnessed the ravages they have caused, the responsibility can lay not only with them today. With Asia's new important role in driving the world economy, we also share this great responsibility.

We also need to concentrate steadfastly on urban environment improvement. It has become apparent today that the Earth's natural ecosystems will not cope with the style of industrialization and over consumption seen in the world. The destruction of the natural resource base through deforestation, destroying fauna and flora, and disturbing the natural environment for various development activities, that are now questionable, needs re-examination in the light of current knowledge.

You may observe that the world is already locked into significant levels of climate change and its efforts are already visible in the sea level rise, melting glaciers and frequent storms and natural disasters. We are still struggling to mitigate the effects of the unprecedented Tsunami that hit Sri Lanka and many other Asian neighbours in 2004. Similarly the destructions caused in China in the past couple of months due to unexpected severe snow storms are stark realities of the need to pay attention to this global problem.

This calls for the urgent need to take adaptation measures, which is increasingly getting better recognition in our region. However mitigation and adaptation will have to be pursued simultaneously for a synergetic effect. How do we do this in a systematical environment is the question that needs to be answered today by our national efforts being complemented through regional and global procedures.

In Sri Lanka, despite the ravages of brutal terrorism, we have been able to make significant advances in social and economic development. We stand unique with the longest tradition of representative democracy in Asia. As one of the first developing countries to promote universal health and education, gender equality and social mobilization, we have been able to achieve exceptional socio-economic indicators; way ahead of those normally expected of a country in the lower and middle-income range. Today we are moving to achieve or surpass many of the Millennium Development Goals. In recent years we have also seen a welcome rise in the per capita income of our people.

However, a launch pad for a sustainable green Asia remains firmly rooted in the stability of the region. It is in fact a vicious cycle. Without stability, there will not be any sustainability. We in Sri Lanka have been victims of terrorism for over three decades and every single citizen of my country has had to deal with this vicious plague. A terrorist group, recognized as terrorists by most countries, who seek to create a separate state in the north and east of Sri Lanka has been recently named as one of the most ruthless terrorist organizations in the world.

The incidents in New York on 9/11 brought the realization in the world that terrorism is a global phenomenon. The brutal tentacles of terrorism cannot be singled out to any particular locality or region. But are ones which spread far and wide, over a myriad of areas from financing to smuggling be it in humans or narcotics, all contributing in no small measure to bring misery and hardship to thousands, while further handicapping a country on its path to progress and prosperity. My belief is that "terrorism anywhere is terrorism" and there is nothing good in terrorism. Therefore, Sri Lanka has taken an upfront position in the global community's efforts to deal with terrorism.

As a responsible Government, Sri Lanka has faced up to this challenge. We have a cause for satisfaction that the entire Eastern Province has now been cleared of terrorism. My government has already initiated several development measures in the Eastern Province, which is seeing a new awakening with freedom from terror. Release from the shackles of terrorism has brought in its wake, for the people of this long afflicted area, economic opportunity in such fields as agriculture, fisheries, tourism, and small and medium scale industry. The programme attempts to rehabilitate and relocate the people in Eastern Sri Lanka with sustainable livelihood projects in a habitable environment. A measure of our success is the successful holding of local government elections after 14 years in one District of the East. Another measure is the holding of elections for a new Eastern Provincial Council early next month. While my Government will pursue a similar strategy in liberating the North from the tentacles of terrorism, we are not unaware of the need for a political solution to bring a negotiated settlement to the national problem in keeping with the common aspirations of all the people of Sri Lanka. It is our intention to establish in the near future conditions which will enable the implementation of a political solution to fulfill the just aspirations of all communities in our country.

Amongst other problems, Sri Lanka has to deal with her fair share of development perils. While trying to maintain a sustainable economic growth we are determined to reach a more inclusive social development. The Blue Print of my Government introducing the developmental plan for the next decade has clearly emphasized our vision for a growth-centered pro-poor strategy, injecting fresh vitality and dynamism to the existing development programmes and looking forward to new initiatives.

In this connection I am glad to state that Sri Lanka's bio-diversity is part of the world's heritage. At present 13% of land is under biodiversity protection, compared to 8% in the 1950s. Our development efforts and strategies will not let that heritage be lost. They will ensure the protection of our oceanic resources, water, aquatic life, forestry and natural resources. We are implementing the "Haritha Piyasa" (Green Shelter) programme to reforest the hill country mountain slopes and protect watershed areas with species endemic to Sri Lanka. Steps have been taken to promote commercial forestry in view of the growing timber requirements of the nation. Waste management systems are being implemented both in rural and urban areas to produce fertilizer and solve the urban solid waste problem.

Increasing carbon dioxide emissions are of great concern, especially in urban and industrialized areas. Measures have already been taken to address the energy problem in the country with efforts to launch an energy efficient production system. Experiments are being conducted on renewable energy sources. Energy from, solar, wind-power, and mini-hydro projects is being encouraged. In protecting the atmosphere from air pollution, the government has formulated various programmes including vehicle emission reduction, quality improvement in gasoline, combined with tax policies on fuel and vehicles.

Sustainable mobility and harnessing the blue sky and the seas will also be top priority taking due advantage of our strategic location with a vision of Sri Lanka as the center of the Asian Silk Route once more. In this connection the Hambantota integrated development project, being built with Chinese assistance, targeting sustainable rural development will be one of the many projects that would be initiated in Sri Lanka making use of our strategic location in the Asian sea-lanes.

Sri Lanka is only one example of the vast environmentally challenged tapestry of developing countries. While we will take steps to address many of our immediate problems, we will need assistance to adopt measures to mitigate prevailing threats to the environment, and to adapt to demands of the sustainable environment we seek to achieve. The current crises that face the world, and our own country, has made our resource base even more inadequate to achieve all our dreams on behalf of our children.

As energy costs escalate, Sri Lanka has undertaken measures to address the energy problem with efforts to launch an energy efficient production system, as well as explore alternative energy sources.

A key obstacle for creating a broad based vision for eradicating poverty and providing equitable development opportunities is the resource constraints faced by many governments, particularly in Asia. Therefore it is important to particularly to involve the private sector in relevant development programmes and harness its resources and capacity in providing solutions to development challenges. Stakeholder participation in many such programmes allowing them to feel a sense of ownership should be empowered and encouraged. In Sri Lanka such linkages have been successfully created in sustainable energy projects, water conservation & management, bio diversity conservation etc.

We must continue to explore options for developing environment-friendly and cost-effective energy sources. Those who achieved prosperity early at the expense of the environment and our lands must assist those who have been left behind to resort to more efficient energy sources that science has made available today. If not, we will all be condemned to suffer together.

These could be solar energy, wind power or even nuclear energy. All these options must be explored with a view to providing developing countries a better model for development; a model that can be best worked out together with the genius of the Asian region, too.

There is need for a note of caution. The search for alternative fuel sources must not deprive the poor of their food, as we see with the diversion of corn and other food crop lands to produce fuels for motor vehicles. Let us not ignore the hunger pains of the people to fill up the gas guzzlers that brought these threats to our world. Development must be sustainable. It must be conscience driven.

We have watched with admiration the evolution of modern China, its political system, its society and economy to the modern economic giant that China today is. We have closely observed the strategies developed by China's leaders to pursue Chinese national interest with skillful tenacity. In the past five years China has seized remarkably the opportunities presented by the coming Olympics in making necessary institutional innovations and structural fine-tuning and made adjustments in the environment in-line with the requirements of the Scientific Outlook on Development, to make progress in all fronts in building a harmonious society.

It is regrettable, though, that attempts are being made today to disrupt this greatest of all sporting events, to which thousands of sportsmen and sportswomen the world over eagerly look forward to, as well as millions of sports fans from all countries, for the purposes of narrow political gain, using slogans of antagonism that have no place in the world of sport and human understanding. It was not so long ago that we did notice frantic efforts made by some of these same forces that seek to disrupt the Olympics today, stating that it will be a non-starter because of the environmental conditions in Beijing.

We believe that internal problems must be resolved by their own people, if necessary with genuine help from friends outside. I talk with the experience of my own country, where outside forces, often with little understanding of reality or with motives that are not as altruistic as may seem, seek to direct our affairs for us, in the fight against terrorism, which advice they do not give themselves. I believe that contextual factors are of overriding importance. The solutions we propose must be based on our historical experience, our cultural traditions and our economic and social institutions.

China has utilized a major part of its resources for conservation of energy, water, land and material and also in improving the living standards of the people. We have observed the very ambitious plan developed by China to setting targets to bring down the energy consumption, reduce the total discharge of major pollutants and increasing forest cover from 18.2% to 20% by 2010. These environmental targets have been elevated by the Chinese leadership as "key mandatory targets". In simple terms, the GDP in China could no more be used as an excuse to flunk the national investment plan for pollution control, which I presume, is a very ambitious move for a country with the world's largest population. It is also heartening to note that China has the largest area of artificial forests, which is more than 53 million hectares, accounting for 1/3rd of the world total. The latest figures have indicated that the trees planted over the past 25 years have absorbed 5.1 billion tons of carbon dioxide. This explicitly reveals the importance of the forest cover in improving the quality of our environment. In the latest reforms introduced by China and in the creation of an Environment Super Ministry, we see the seriousness of her policy makers to the need for sustainable growth and face up to the Challenges of Climate Change.

Asia's development challenges are of such scale that their solutions require regional co-operation to supplement national efforts. Countries and sub-regions within Asia are already at quite different stages of regional development. If I may turn specifically to South Asia, significant reforms have been made in the SAARC process in trade, investment, industrial and fiscal policies. This has made the growth rates to improve and poverty ratios to decline. In terms of trade flow, today South Asia is progressing well and simultaneously the realization has dawned upon us of the importance of an inclusive growth in harmony with environment. The institutional mechanisms are in place and framework arrangements have been developed within the SAARC process to complement the national policies in giving primacy to attaining a sustainable growth and intensifying regional ties.

The world has taken major strides towards meeting the challenge of climate change, moving on from scientific analysis to public concerns, to develop and implement an international convention on the Protection of the Environment and Climate Change. We have cause for hope in an Asian driven consensus on meeting the challenge to Climate Change. The Nobel Prize for Peace last year saw consensus, with it being shared by an American politician turned visionary on Climate Change and a UN Committee headed by an Indian Scientist that included a Sri Lankan scientist, too. The recent Bali Conference on Climate Change has created the momentum in supporting negotiation of a new pact to succeed the Kyoto Protocols when it expires in 2012, and important world figures who once rejected the Kyoto Protocols are now thinking of going beyond them, even modestly.

It is our firm conviction that the political will be mustered to see through to a successful conclusion of the process that has begun. Sri Lanka has subscribed to around 40 Environment Related International conventions, treaties, protocols and agreements and will continue to undertake further work programmes towards strengthening the process of implementing these accords.

As I thank the Chinese Government and People and the organizers of the "Boao Forum for Asia" for providing this unique opportunity for such a wide range of views and perspectives to be expressed on one of the most pressing problems of today, I wish to draw attention to the necessity to combine the traditional wisdom of Asia, with the leadership that the Asia has, to face the new challenges before Asia and the world.

As I have earlier mentioned, our region is particularly rich in the resource of traditional wisdom. As we gather here today in this intellectual forum, destined to play an important role in the transformation of Asia and the world, I look forward with optimism to the future. We must see the best way to harness this reservoir of wisdom, combine it with the political will to make the much-anticipated change mandatory to reconcile development and the protection of environment. In this respect I suggest that we first achieve an Asian consensus to reach a global climate Agreement by 2009, based on traditional wisdom of Asia, the new knowledge brought to us by science and leadership of those who have helped make this the Asian Century.

The role of history and the influence of Buddhism have conditioned to a great extent the culture and values of Sri Lanka. What I find particularly interesting to note is that Buddhism can provide helpful insights and practices across a wide spectrum of disciplines – and on the protection of the environment too, we discover ancient wisdom in the teachings of Buddhism.

Let me conclude by quoting from this great Wisdom of Asia:

The Buddha had once said:

"A tree is unique. It has unlimited tolerance, patience, and generosity. It provides a congenial atmosphere for many living organisms to survive. It also keeps on providing shade (as long as it stands) even to the man who attempts to destroy the tree with his axe."

(*Source*: http://www.president.gov.lk/speech_New.asp?Id=47)

## President Mahinda Rajapaksa's Address at the UN Food Summit in Rome

March 6, 2008

*President Mahinda Rajapaksa, addressing the global food crises stated that the global community needed to act fast and take short term emergency measures in order to prevent the crises. He noted that total dependence on imported fuel and success in agriculture is dependent on changing weather patterns and problems of storage and distribution were some of the main reasons for addressing the crises. He emphasized the fact that an integrated national drive called 'grow more food towards prosperity' needs to be initiated. The President placed special emphasis on the role of FAO to monitor the crises and emphasized on the creation of a regional buffer stock.*

I greatly value this opportunity to present Sri Lanka's views on the crisis in global food supply that has taken center stage in world affairs. It is a crisis with the potential to have a crippling effect on the smaller, less developed countries with restrictions on the availability of arable land and financial resources. A crisis in food becomes all the more serious as it impacts most severely on the most vulnerable sections of a community, - namely, those living in poverty who constitute around one billion of the world's population. As a global community we need to act fast and take short term emergency measures to ensure that the poorest and most vulnerable sections of our people do not go hungry.

It is regretted that warnings of this crisis, although seen, were largely ignored, until it assumed today's magnitude. It is a crisis that has come from the growing demand for fuel, the failure to act in time on climate change, the ravages of terrorism, and problems of distribution.

Sri Lanka, like many other developing countries, is affected by all of these factors – namely – the total dependence on imported fuel; success in agriculture being dependent on changing weather patterns; and problems of storage and distribution. We are also faced with the fourth factor where food production is made difficult or even hazardous due to the threat of terrorism. Much arable land has been neglected due to land mines being laid by terrorists for over two decades.

While a combination of all these factors, no doubt, has resulted in the present crisis, there is also another set of factors, - socio - political in nature, - to which I would like to direct our attention. Let me explain, Mr. Chairman, by drawing on the experience of my own country, which is not very different from that of many other developing countries of the world.

Before the economy of our country was opened to the play of global market forces, the focus of social and economic development was the rural sector. The granaries of the nation which produced the food for our people, consisting of thousands of villages where 77% of the people live today, were then the main focus of economic development and concern. Rural incomes, rural well being, rural infrastructure, rural transport, rural health, rural education and other rural services constituted the main goals and objectives of social development. Development was focused on enhancing the productivity, well being and dignity of the peasant and small farmer who produced the food for our people.

With advent of the open economy, the focus of development activity shifted - in stages no doubt - from the village to the town. It shifted from that larger part of the country where rural people toiled to produce food for us all, to the urban centres of commerce and industry where goods and services are produced largely for export to high income countries.

The international economic pressures of that time coupled with some domestic political compulsions made us, as a country, shift our focus of development and concern, away from the rural economy and rural society, away from agriculture and food production to manufacture, commerce and services, away from a concern for the dignity and well being of those who produce the food for our people to a concern for those who came to the cities and towns to be engaged in non - farm employment.

We opened our doors so wide to the global market forces, that while we reaped several of the benefits of globalization, we failed at the same time to protect several of our national interests, - in particular, those relating to our food security - from the negative impact of the global market. The earlier development goal of self reliance in food which we had almost reached, and in some years even exceeded, was severely weakened as my country gradually opened even the production and supply of our food requirements to the free play of global and domestic market forces.

The country progressively dismantled its buffer stocks of rice and wheat flour - a then abiding feature of our food security - which cushioned the food supply from the shocks and uncertainties of crop failures on the one side and price fluctuations on the other. As the State for all practical purposes started reneging on its responsibility for providing food to the people at an affordable price, the supply and price of food became more or less a market responsibility.

I will not elaborate too much on the reasons for this crisis. We all know that global food stocks have reached an all time low and prices have escalated to unexpected levels. Sadly the world is conditioned by forces which are beyond the control of poor countries. From a situation of an excess of food supplies, only a few years ago, we have entered an era of shortages.

We needed a change in our policy on development. We have therefore launched an integrated national drive called 'Api Vavamu Rata Nagamu' meaning, 'Grow more food towards prosperity', through which all arable lands in the country are being brought under cultivation. At the same time, during the last two years, we have provided a substantial fertilizer subsidy to rice farmers, at a huge cost to the government, to increase farm productivity. This is continuing despite ever increasing global fertilizer prices and I must say that this bold initiative has paid significant dividends in terms of enhanced production.

We are giving land to farmers who do not have land for cultivation. We have already initiated a number of multi - purpose irrigation schemes to transform otherwise dry land into fertile agricultural settlements. Seed production programmes in the country have been strengthened to ensure that good quality seeds are available to farmers at cheaper prices, as well as to increase overall seed production in the country. We have also strengthened our market network for agricultural produce by re-establishing the Paddy Marketing Board to purchase paddy from farmers at a guaranteed price.

While focusing more specifically on agriculture and food production, we are also implementing a Village Upliftment Programme - 'Gama Neguma'. Through this programme we hope to see all villages of our country emerge as micro centres of growth on modern lines while retaining the impressive strengths and features of rural life. My government seeks to ensure that our country's villages which produce food for our people will have electricity, a common telecommunication system, drinking water, irrigation water for the rice fields, access roads, infrastructure, schools with adequate resources, electronic knowledge centres known as 'Nena Salas' or e-libraries, health centres, market centres, paddy stores, fertilizer stores, rice mills, pre-schools, play grounds, a village forest, and other amenities and factories to generate off farm and non farm employment.

We will continue to give the highest priority to increased agriculture, dairy farming and fisheries to face up to the challenge of ensuring adequate food for our people. Yet, being an island nation, we are faced with the threats to food security from high oil prices and the changing patterns of cultivation abroad – with bio-fuels made more attractive than food crops.

In the prevailing competition between food and fuel, Sri Lanka is firm in the decision that no land that can be used for food will be used for bio-fuel whatever the commercial attraction may be. It is our belief that food for the people should have the highest priority, and not the running of gas-guzzling vehicles.

At national level therefore, even before the issue of global food security had reached a crisis level, my government had already launched an integrated drive towards ensuring our country's food security. But while we act at national level, we need to recognize the fact that in the highly interconnected world of today the causes of the world's food crisis have to be confronted at regional and global levels as well.

While focusing on specific issues relating to the food crisis, we shall welcome the FAO to monitor - systematically and continuously - the production of food in the world. By doing so, FAO will be able to forecast shortfalls and price fluctuations well in advance so that countries and regions can act well in time to mitigate their adverse effects on the people, and a crisis is prevented from suddenly staring them in the face.

It is our considered position that a regional approach to food security within a global framework is essential, since food habits and production are region specific in nature. I would like to request the FAO to initiate a global mechanism for developing regional buffer stocks of staple food. We, in the SAARC region are home to nearly one fifth of the world population. A regional buffer stock of staple food will take pressure off governments in the SAARC enabling them to concentrate on other issues such as reducing poverty and enhancing the quality of life of their peoples.

A regional buffer stock would also cushion individual countries against the fluctuations in food production, caused by the uncertainties of the weather made worse by recent climatic changes. And for regions that may lack adequate financial capacity for such a project, international support will be required. These buffer stocks could be maintained nationally or by regional agencies but be funded internationally. We can explore different options, including through instruments generated by international financial institutions, for funding such mechanisms.

In the midst of all these, I believe there are some countries in the world which have been able to build a surplus of staple foods. These countries are affluent and therefore should move towards helping build the regional buffer stocks by contributing through supply at low cost. That will be a good start and also will help to build a meaningful global cooperation towards reducing the vulnerability of many small developing countries.

Creating a regional buffer stock would be meaningful only if adequate food stocks could be moved to needy countries in a short time. In the past we have witnessed instances where adequate shipping space or other means of transport had been hard to come by. Low freight, minimal handling charges and of course the waiving off of country specific Customs and other duties when such emergency food stocks are being exported is crucially important if we are to make this suggestion workable.

I recognize that buffer stocks became an unpopular concept since the New International Economic Order of the seventies. But the changed global circumstances, in particular the grim fingers of hunger, require changed approaches for the sake of humanity.

As much as we are concerned about food security, attention must also be given towards enhancing productivity in the entire agriculture, fisheries and livestock sector. One impediment experienced by the farmers in my country is the severe shortage of plant seed and other planting material. As this is common to many other developing countries, it must be remedied fast with the help of the international organizations. Establishment of seed banks with state of the art technology is one solution to this problem. In the fisheries sector, there is a serious concern because our ocean's harvest is being poached by foreign fishing vessels thereby reducing the supply for our people.

Most important of all, I strongly commend to the world leaders gathered here to seriously consider the setting up of a Global Food Crisis Fund that will have contributions from all countries and from large business organizations that transcend geographical boundaries, and from financial institutions, arms manufacturers and philanthropists of the world, among others. The mechanics of such a fund will have to be worked out in keeping with the goal of assisting countries faced with serious dangers to food security and also in funding initiatives for greater food production.

We are also of the view that in addition to such a Global Food Crisis Fund or working together with it, there should be Regional Food Security Funds drawing the financial and technology resources within a region to expand food production, improve storage and distribution and also come to the assistance of regional neighbours that may need help in the event of a food crisis as we see emerging today.

In conclusion, let me thank the UN Secretary General and the FAO for bringing this conference together and affording us an opportunity to share our views and experiences across the globe. My country will support you to develop a global action plan to face the crisis in the short run while at the same time to prevent a food crisis of this nature from recurring in the future.

(*Source*: http://www.president.gov.lk/speech_New.asp?Id=53)

# 27.

## MISCELLANEOUS

### Mahinda Rajapaksa talks with Richard Beeston, Foreign Editor of the Times, United Kingdom[1]

June 17, 2008

*Britain stands accused of applying double standards to its counter-terrorism policy because a banned Tamil militant group is being allowed to raise money among expatriates in London.*

President Rajapaksa of Sri Lanka said that supporters of the Liberation Tigers of Tamil Eelam (LTTE) were able to raise millions of pounds each year from the Tamil community in Britain, some of whom were coerced into donating the money.

"You can't have two different attitudes towards terrorism," he told The Times this week during a visit to London for a Commonwealth meeting, where he raised the issue with Gordon Brown. "I don't agree that there are good terrorists and bad terrorists. There is only one kind of terrorist".

There are about 150,000 Tamils living in Britain, mostly in North London. The Sri Lankans estimate that £70million is sent home

These are not voluntary contributions, the money is taken by force, usually a percentage of their income," said Mr. Rajapaksa, who attracted Tamil protesters during his stay. "The money is sent back to buy weapons. London is not the only place; money is also sent from Europe, Canada and other places."

The Sri Lankan leader, who has earned a reputation as a hardliner, came to power nearly three years ago when a fragile ceasefire brokered by Norway was still in place. After a series of clashes — including suicide attacks against the head of the Army and Defence Minister, who is the President's brother — the simmering 25-year old conflict erupted into fresh violence.

Over the past two years government troops have been successful in retaking some rebel-held areas to the east and north of the island, but at a

1. Excerpts from the President's interview with Richard Beeston, Foreign Editor of the Times, UK,June 17, 2008.

heavy cost. Several Sri Lankan sailors and Tamil guerrillas were killed yesterday when the "Sea Tigers", the rebel naval wing, attacked a navy base on the island of Mannar. So far this year an estimated 4,000 Tamil Tigers and 357 government troops have been killed.

Mr. Rajapaksa said that he was taking steps to protect human rights. He blamed his Government's poor international reputation on "clever propaganda" by the Tigers.

"We have failed in the propaganda fight," he said.

Mr. Rajapaksa said he would not resume peace talks with the Tamil Tigers until the organisation agreed to disarm.

"When they are weak they call on the international community to arrange a ceasefire. During this period they train and rearm and then fight back. This time if they want to talk, they should disarm first," he said.

Even if the Tigers were to meet his preconditions it seems unlikely that he would ever be able to conclude a peace deal with [LTTE leader] Velupillai Prabhakaran, "This man and the three or four henchmen around him are blood-thirsty killers," said Mr. Rajapaksa. "They have no feelings. It is very difficult to deal with them."

(*Source*: http://www.president.gov.lk/inter_New.asp?Id=11)

## Mahinda Rajapaksa talks with Raj Chengappa, Managing Editor of India Today[2]

July 2, 2008

*Q*. Do you want to get Prabhakaran dead or alive?

*A*. Alive. For the crimes he has done, he needs to be tried and I would like to send him to India too for he killed a leader who would have changed the face of not just India but the whole region.

*Q*. Why did you decide finally to end the five-year-old Ceasefire Agreement (CFA) between the Government and the LTTE?

*A*. When the CFA was introduced in 2002, I was leader of the Opposition and the first one to speak out against it. When I became the President, I said I will try to negotiate with the LTTE, talk to them and achieve peace to settle the issue. But it did not mean that I approved of the CFA. But they went on a killing spree, not only attacking our army commander, the defence secretary, who is my brother, but also began targeting civilians and children. I wanted the killing to stop. They had violated the CFA so often that it had become a farce. So I decided to end it.

*Q*. What makes you so confident of taking on the LTTE in an all out war now?

2. Excerpts from an Interview of President Mahinda Rajapaksa with Raj Chengappa, the Managing Editor of India Today, July 2, 2008.

*A*. Either the LTTE accept a political solution by giving up arms and terrorist activities or we will have to curtail their moves. The Government can't kneel down to terrorists. Since I came to power we have cleared the eastern and western provinces of LTTE control.

They are now restricted to just one-and-a-half districts. From top to bottom the Government is committed. There is greater coordination between the Government and the defence forces which helps our cause.

*Q*. If the LTTE comes back to the negotiating table, will you talk?

*A*. Yes, only if they give up their weapons. They can't have their cake and eat it too. Ceasefire will give them time again. We don't want them to strengthen themselves and attack us. We want a final solution.

*Q*. If the LTTE doesn't come around, how long will it take to wipe them out?

*A*. We would have cleared them out of the remaining areas long ago but we also had to ensure no civilians were killed. I would say, in a year and a half, we might be able to do it.

*Q*. The LTTE's counter strategy seems to be to attack civilians.

*A*. It is a desperate move in the hope that the international community will put pressure on the Government. They can't achieve anything.

*Q*. Inflation is running high. Do you think people are willing to pay the price of war?

*A*. People will understand. A recent survey done by a rival paper did show that they supported me on the development work that I am doing.

*Q*. So will there be no cut in the defence budget?

*A*. The money we are spending on defence is not high. It is 3.5 per cent of the GDP. I believe no country can afford to compromise on its defence.

*Q*. When you took over as President in 2005 you said that you expected India to do a lot. Has India lived up to your expectations?

*A*. India's approach has been very positive and encouraging. Our relationship is now probably at the best of levels.

*Q*. But India is not willing to sell your Government offensive arms to fight the LTTE.

*A*. We can buy arms from anywhere, but we can't buy a good friend. And that is what we need. India is a power in this region. It is very strong and can do a lot to develop the neighbouring countries. Not just Sri Lanka, but also others. India is with us and they have showed us their support.

*Q*. The EU and other countries have alleged human rights violations by your Government during the conduct of war.

*A*. There are a few allegations in the East. We enquired into all such allegations but no one was even willing to file a complaint to begin action. We have appointed a commission of eminent persons to look into all the allegations but we need a complaint, evidence and witnesses to do justice in such cases. We will take action.

*Q*. Coming to a political solution, the All Party Representative Committee (APRC) to go into a package to solve Tamil grievances has recommended the implementation of the 13th Amendment of the Constitution done in 1987 that wanted power to be devolved to the provinces. Why should the Tamils accept something that was offered to them 20 years earlier?

*A*. Why shouldn't they? It was never implemented because the parties that agreed to it—the LTTE and the then government—fell out soon after that. I believe it is a good way to begin. We should first start something we can implement. I don't need two thirds majority in Parliament to do it. So it's a beginning. The APRC can then give me some new proposals and we can consider them too. But I don't want to waste my time on solutions that are not practical just to satisfy the international community. They may look good on paper but will be burnt in Parliament. There will be riots.

*Q*. How quickly do you see the package implemented?

*A*. I have already appointed an Advisory Cabinet Committee. I am waiting for their report. As soon as I get the report, I will implement it.

*Q*. You had also said that you would give the Tamils more than just the 13th Amendment.

*A*. I am waiting for the proposals to be given to me by the committee to decide. Meanwhile, let us implement something that had the blessings of all—the then government, the LTTE and all other Tamil parties. Something that Rajiv Gandhi had helped get under the Indo-Sri Lanka Accord of 1987. In addition I have already started taking steps to ensure the implementation of the official language policy by promoting the learning and usage of Tamil in administration. I am also recruiting Tamils in the police. Don't think we are only fighting the terrorists.

*Q*. Do you have consensus among the Sinhala parties to implement it?

*A*. How can the UNP oppose this when its own government had passed the 13th Amendment. Only the JVP (Janata Vimukthi Peramuna) is the problem. But let's not forgot that the JVP has asked for more powers for the provinces and even participated in Provincial Councils.

*Q*. Why don't you hold a referendum in the liberated Eastern districts to decide whether they should join the North as envisaged in the Accord?

*A*. Why should I? If you go now to places like Batticalao you would find they oppose it. I will not have this country divided.

*Q*. Why not have a federal system like India?

*A*. Federalism is out—just don't talk about it. Historically the word is suspect and is linked with separatism. Maximum devolution under a unitary government is the mandate that I have got and I am going to implement that.

*Q*. Your party doesn't have a two thirds majority in Parliament. Will you go for elections to implement it?

*A.* I don't need two-thirds majority in Parliament for what has been proposed. When the need arises I certainly will.

(*Source*: http://www.president.gov.lk/inter_New.asp?Id=10)

## Security and Development Concerns in Sri Lanka[3]

May 14, 2008

*President Mahinda Rajapakse stated that empowerment of the rural economy was his government's development strategy as nearly 77 percent of the people in Sri Lanka lived in the rural areas. Giving a historical overview of Sri Lanka and pointing out the progress made by Sri Lanka in various facets of society and polity, he stated that, Sri Lankan military had won over the LTTE in the East, which was one of the gravest internal security threats to the country.*

It is with much pleasure that I address you in these hallowed surroundings tonight. I must thank the Oxford Union and Mr. Dilan Fernando for this opportunity. Many renowned speakers have addressed you from here before me. I do not seek to match them in their eloquence but I do wish to speak to you on a subject of much interest to my country at the present time.

That is the empowerment of rural economy, a central theme of my development strategy for Sri Lanka. Our development strategy towards empowering the rural economy of our country, where majority of our people live, has now become relevant to the global economy itself in the context of the emerging world food crisis and environmental challenges to our own survival. We have an additional burden. We are threatened by the challenge of terrorism and the need to protect the rights of our fellow beings.

Sri Lanka where I was born and bred is a country where our culture is firmly rooted in rural tradition. The Sri Lankan culture has been essentially conditioned by the great religion of Buddhism, but later influenced by Hinduism, Islam and Christianity. The concepts of loving kindness, compassion and tolerance are at the heart of our psychological make up. They nourish and sustain us through the uncertainties of life. Our traditional greeting - 'Ayubowan' means – May you live long.

It is not surprising then that in a world where rulers constructed massive castles and grand palaces to demonstrate their power and wealth, our kings constructed huge reservoirs — Tanks, as we call them — to provide water to sustain food production and ensure sustainable livelihood to the people. The great legacy left behind by our ancient rulers, and which is in use even today scattered across three vast provinces of my island home, is the massive irrigation network.

---

3. President's Speech at Oxford Union May 14, 2008.

This unique hydraulic civilization which sustained an essentially prosperous rural society, was based on a philosophy which has much to offer the modern world. Buddhism taught us that we have no absolute ownership of the forests, the rivers, the oceans and the atmosphere that sustain life; that every generation holds the environment in trust, so that its abuse is prevented; and that our duty was to hand down the environment. to future generations without harm.

Even today, over 77 percent of our people still live in rural areas because of a wide range of attractions in our rural home base. I myself hail from the Deep South, from an agrarian village with a beautiful natural environment. I am extremely proud of that fact. The attraction in our villages is not only the economic resources and greenery, but also the traditional culture, arts, religion and bio-diversity which are incentives to keep our people away from migrating into urban townships. The horrors of poverty and suffering that have engulfed many booming Asian cities have not affected Sri Lanka.

Strengthened by the caring attitude inherited from our ancient rulers, we were able to adapt to modern democracy with great ease. It was in 1931, while still under the British, that Sri Lanka was granted universal franchise. You will recall that Britain achieved this status only in 1926. Since then we have continued to develop and strengthen democratic institutions in Sri Lanka. Political pluralism has always been fundamental to our democracy. We have parties of different political views represented in our parliament. This diversity uniquely enriches Sri Lanka's political canvass.

The government, although elected by a Sinhala Buddhist majority, represents a coalition of Sinhala, Tamil, and Muslim communities and all the religious groups in the country. You will be hard pressed to find a similarly representative government in any of the other democracies of the world. I am proud of our vibrant parliamentary system, the strong judicial establishment, and the independent press. Not a day passes without an attack on me, I must say totally without foundation, from some parts of the media. We have not hesitated to adopt global standards, collaborate with international organizations such as the UN, ILO and the Commonwealth, and participate in efforts to consolidate institutions designed to protect the rights of our fellow humans.

Sri Lanka has contributed with vigour and creativity to the development of the principals incorporated in international conventions, through their work in international organizations and through the International Court of Justice. We have always played our part in global efforts to establish higher standards, and to make our earth a better place for all, because we fundamentally feel that this is the correct thing to do. This is a reflection of our cultural traditions. Sri Lanka's conformity to global environmental standards has been commended time and time again.

Women in Sri Lanka enjoy equal opportunities with men. Over 60 percent of our medical practitioners are women. Over 80 percent of our teachers are women. The nursing profession is dominated by women. The legal profession too is increasingly dominated by women! Women have also entered sections of the work force previously monopolized by men such as, academia, engineering, computing, quantity surveying and architecture. I recall with great delight that Sri Lanka produced world's first elected woman Prime Minister in 1960. Her husband, Mr. SWRD Bandaranaike, whose portrait hangs over there, was also a prime minister of Sri Lanka.

Ladies and gentlemen, for decades we have invested in education and health. My country enjoys one of the highest literacy standards in the world, while still being categorized as a middle income developing country. 97 per cent of our children are enrolled at school. Our infant mortality rate and maternal mortality rate at child birth, is on par with that of many developed countries. The country provides free healthcare to all. Education is free and universal from childhood to university. During the primary and secondary school life of every child the government provides free text books and uniforms. One of my long-lasting joys is the sight of thousands of children in crispy white uniforms heading for school each morning. This is probably a sight that one cannot witness in many other places of the world.

Children are precious to us. I believe they are our future. We have ensured a massive investment in our children. My government firmly believes that no child must be deprived of his or her childhood. We have created a separate ministry to look after the welfare of our children. We do not employ any children in our labour force, and no one below the age of eighteen is recruited to our armed forces; —— unlike the LTTE, which engages thousands in its baby brigades. These children are robbed of their childhood, and brutality is ingrained into their character, making them life-long misfits for society.

Sri Lanka has achieved a very high standard in the United Nations Human Development Index, and we have already, to a large extent, achieved the Millennium Development Goals. It was only last month that a UN Report commended Sri Lanka for being well on its way to eliminating malaria. We have a very low rate of HIV / AIDS infection. I point these things out to you only because of the intense campaign that is being conducted internationally, to describe my country as one that does not care about our fellow human beings and human needs. Facts demonstrate that this is far from the truth.

There are no signs of obvious starvation in any part of the country. In fact for over 25 years, since the beginning of the LTTE's violent challenge to our very existence, to our sovereignty, the government has been sending food, medicine and educational material to the two districts dominated by the LTTE. Every single teacher, nurse, doctor, hospital and government official in the LTTE controlled areas is appointed and paid by the government in Colombo. Very few countries grappling with terrorism have been so accommodating. This itself illustrates the caring nature of our society.

These noteworthy achievements have been possible because of a holistic view of human development to which we have always been firmly committed. We believe that development becomes meaningful to the vast mass of the people only when its fruits are capable of being enjoyed by all segments of the people. That is why we have constantly tried not only to achieve growth and expansion of our national wealth but to ensure that the resources generated by our efforts are distributed among the people, especially, in the rural hinterland, on an equitable basis.

Our development model as presented in my election manifesto, the Mahinda Chinthana, signifies the empowerment of the rural economy. The centre piece of this new strategy will be the development of modern infrastructure throughout the country to provide a basis for development of Agriculture, Industry, Construction, Tourism, SMEs and transport services that will bring about new opportunities to our people in the rural economy. Our strategy has enhanced the public investments over 6 percent of GDP to support 'Randora' – meaning Golden Gate – our infrastructure development initiative — to develop new ports, power generation and distribution networks, and integrated townships to the link rural economy to the global economy and create new space for growth. We have integrated strategies to promote insurance, shipping, aviation, trade, logistic industries and petroleum explorations, and above all, skills and knowledge to position Sri Lanka as an emerging economic hub in south Asia.

Empowering people at grassroots level is equally important in this whole development process. 'Gama Naguma', meaning revival of the village, is an initiative to empower communities, adopting bottom up programmes originating from communities and reflecting their needs. A series of rural development initiatives have been implemented, permitting the community to prioritize their needs and objectives. These initiatives are monitored by community leaders to ensure that a larger volume of resources are productively used for the betterment of the rural community.

The main thrust of this programme is to retain people in rural environments, rather than encouraging them to move into urban areas; which has been the pattern in many developing economies. Why should people move into urban areas and live in slums or sub-standard housing, when they can live in very healthy environments in villages, and enjoy clean air, water and pure and good food. It is my belief that rural people are much healthier than those who live in urban cities.

Our approach to development takes into consideration the dangers of destroying the green environment. Every project that is implemented under

Gama Naguma recognizes the value of green belts and the preservation of the forest cover. The environmental protection programmes that are implemented throughout the island make a serious attempt to ensure that rivers are kept clean, water ways are not dirtied and trees are not destroyed. The bed rock of our development is maintaining and preserving the environment.

Consolidating our achievements in human resource development, we are now working towards a knowledge economy based on productivity, skills, knowledge and technology. Therefore, education and health is being undertaken at grassroots level through multi-faceted government programmes. In particular, I am very keen to ensure that our children are able to become global citizens through the use of Information Technology. In a novel programme called 'Nenasala', a network of 500 rural tele-centers has already been established. I have set a target to increase this up to 1,000 by next year. Three years ago, Sri Lanka's IT literacy stood at a little over 5 percent. Today I feel accomplished that we have been able to enhance this to 20 percent. Which means that more and more people will be able to enter the lucrative IT job market. All this is being done to enhance the employability of rural youth.

The essence of our rural empowerment programme is to ensure that rural infrastructure development takes place at a rapid rate. So far neglected rural roads are being paved today with concrete to make them last the monsoon rains that are common in our part of the world. Rural electricity programmes, community water supply schemes, minor irrigation projects, housing and market facilities are included in our rural infrastructure development drive. In essence our strategy is to level the playing field between the 'urban, organized minority' and the 'rural, unorganized majority', in the national development process. I am encouraged that our development strategy - Mahinda Chinthana – Vision Towards a New Sri Lanka, sustained a near 7 percent economic growth during the last three years, and reached US dollars 1,600 per capita income in 2007. Except in one district, people below the poverty line have declined drastically in 2007.

Unfortunately we are being challenged by "the most brutal terrorist group in the world" as the LTTE has been described by the FBI. Suicide killings using even women and children have become their hallmark. It is this terror group that invented the deadly suicide vest for the suicide killer. Having pioneered the suicide vest, they have freely given this technology to other terror groups in the world. This has now become a global menace.

There have been hundreds of innocents, civilians returning home after work, children going to school and young mothers going to their weekly clinics, being maimed or killed by indiscriminately exploded bombs in crowded centres or being targeted by brain-washed suicide bombers. You need to see the carnage caused by shattered limbs and burning human flesh, to understand the sheer brutality that motivates this group of terrorists. They killed Rajiv Gandhi, the former Prime Minister of India, and Ranasinghe Premadasa, the former President of Sri Lanka. Most recently, a senior Minister of my government, a Tamil speaking Catholic, was brutally murdered by a suicide killer, along with a former Olympic athlete among many others participating in a sporting event.

They also killed our former Foreign Minister Lakshman Kadirgamar, a scholar of distinction, and legal luminary, who once occupied this seat as the President of the Oxford Union with distinction.

Ladies and gentlemen it has become incumbent upon us to confront this group to the extent of our ability, deploying all the resources of the State, to protect the people of Sri Lanka and their democratic way of life. I must add that what I am doing is in no way different to what other democracies have done before, and continue to do, in the face of terrorism. However, I must to state that the LTTE is the most brutal terror outfit the world has ever seen, and defeating them requires global support. What Sri Lanka is doing, in my opinion, is fighting this terror outfit single handed to ensure that democracy and respect for human life prevail in the world. If we fail in our war against the LTTE, the world will fail in its fight against terrorism, and democracy will be the victim. This is the plain truth.

Our development thrust unfortunately has had its own obstacles, the main being the brutal terrorist threat that makes us, a developing country, to take a heavy toll. It is time that the world, raising its united voice, expressed its utter revulsion of the barbaric practice of suicide bombings. It must be made absolutely clear that this form of political expression, if it could be described as such, is utterly unacceptable in the civilized world.

There is a considerable challenge to the security forces of my country, whose goal is simply to protect the innocents and their simple way of life. We need to understand that our security forces do not go out of their way to harass innocents, or to discriminate against a minority. They take great personal risks constantly. The fear psychosis created by the LTTE terror, may cause some lapses in judgment, but by and large, independent observers have always commended the efficiency, politeness and courtesy of the men in uniform.

We must remember that there are no methods or solutions which are universally applicable to situations of this nature. It is the principal duty of a government to assure the public of security of life and limb. It is the terrorist group that decides when to strike: They decide the time, the place and the opportunity. They are in no way constrained by the values and procedures which rightly control the responses of democratic governments. These realities must be taken into account as the basis of a fair and objective assessment of Sri Lanka's situation.

Although many have said that the LTTE is invincible, we have freed our Eastern Province of their terror. Within one year we have restored democracy there after nearly two decades. Only last week we conducted free and fair elections to the first ever Eastern Provincial Council, contested by several political parties.

As our forces seek to defeat and disarm the LTTE, we are firm in our resolve to have a negotiated solution to the crisis in Sri Lanka. I do not believe in a military solution. We have attempted talks with the LTTE on several occasions – thrice since my election as the President – but they have not reciprocated. They have always left the talks with lame excuses. We are still ready to talk, once we are certain of their genuine intent for a political solution… and their readiness to give up arms.

As young leaders, you will take on increasing responsibilities in later life. Destiny will place you in circumstances where you will be called upon to lead and defend your countries. As someone who has been nurtured and strengthened by an ethical and caring culture, I wish to leave with you with some thoughts.

You and I are privileged to be what we are today, but, there are millions of our fellow beings who are not that fortunate, and who need our guidance, leadership and caring. Leadership to these masses of people will have to be given by you. Your leadership must be one that reflects your cultural and religious values, sense of integrity, dedication to the cause of eliminating human suffering, and a sense of generosity.

In conclusion, let me say that our chosen path to development of my country, especially the rural areas, continues to be a challenge for all of us, particularly with threats that are both internal and external. Ladies and gentlemen, the protection and advancement of human rights continues to be a challenge for all of us, not only in Sri Lanka but globally. I only seek to encourage you to think of Sri Lanka as a country that has achieved considerable success in caring for its people, in the face of a most brutal challenge thrown at us by terrorists. We will continue to comply with the highest standards in keeping with values and traditions we hold to be sacrosanct.

(*Source*: http://www.president.gov.lk/speech_New.asp?Id=51)

## The Role of Youth in Sri Lankan Politics[4]

April 27, 2008

*In his address at the Commonwealth Youth Ministers Meeting in Colombo, President Rajapaksa stated that, youth could play a*

4. President Mahinda Rajapaksa's Address at the Seventh Meeting of the Commonwealth Youth Ministers in Colombo, April 27, 2008.

*special role in peace building. He noted that 40 per cent of the nominations of political parties or independent groups contesting local government elections in Sri Lanka were youth between 18 to 35 years of age. Highlighting the potential role played by the youth, he stressed that youth had proved to be a powerful force in the development of democracy and peace building in Sri Lanka. He stated that youth mainstreaming is at the heart of a country's development agenda.*

It is my pleasure to welcome you all to Sri Lanka to participate in this Seventh Meeting of the Commonwealth Youth Ministers. My country one of the oldest members of the Commonwealth is glad to have you in our midst enjoying the renowned hospitality of Sri Lanka.

You will find here a most suitable location to discuss the emerging issues of youth development, specifically, the linkages between peace-building, social development and transformation as you address the theme of this meeting, "Youth and Peace Building".

The unique nature of the Commonwealth spread across the continents with diverse political structures that embrace democracy is well positioned to discuss the issues that affect youth around the world today. Our acceptance of democracy must enable us to identify the problems faced by the youth in our countries linked by so many common causes. Similarly, we are also in a better position to arrive at solutions to these problems based on the traditions and wisdom of our societies and the shared knowledge of modern social structures.

Our government recognizes the importance of youth in national development. We see in our youth the future of our country which leads to a commitment to give the highest priority to ease the concerns of youth and resolve the main problems that face them.

These problems are made worse today by the economic hardships imposed on most of our member countries by external forces largely beyond our control. This situation calls for a common resolve to meet the challenges to the development of our youth.

We see today the importance within the Commonwealth of initiatives directed towards creating greater opportunities for education and employment of youth in a culture of understanding of youth and their aspirations. There is the need for inter-connectivity of youth, where they learn from shared experiences separated as they are, in different cultures but, brought together in the common search for progress.

The theme of this meeting, Youth and Peace Building, can benefit from Sri Lanka's own experience, which can relate very well to other countries of the Commonwealth, too. Sri Lanka has for the past three decades been faced with a threat by the most brutal terrorist organization in the world, a terror outfit that does not hesitate to use our youth as pawns and cannon fodder in its brutal operations to attack the sovereignty and territorial integrity of this country.

Its use of young boys and girls as child soldiers to carry arms for the forces of terror has been condemned by the United Nations and all those who seek peace and democracy in the world, including several members of the Commonwealth. I am aware that Sri Lanka is not alone in facing this brutality of child soldiers.

We know the danger it poses to our children and youth. Among the lasting consequences of the brain washing of child soldiers is such that even in adult life many of them remain committed to violence and terror. Therefore, it is our resolve not to give in to these forces of terror; to save our youth from the clutches of these forces of modern day savagery. Sri Lanka for its part has an extensive rehabilitation programme for children who were involved in armed conflict. However, I believe that these children must be returned to their parents for there can't be anything better than parental love and care.

We trust this meeting will look at this situation for the threat it poses to the youth of the Commonwealth and the world and see how best we could all use the resources of our youth for the cause of peace and reconciliation.

We see today the need for better empowerment of youth to overcome the growing challenge of unemployment that is of increasing concern to youth. This calls for the development of the total personality of the youth through a more balanced education, skills development, sports and recreation, in an environment enriched by culture and religion encouraging life in harmony with nature. All this requires political stability and economic development, matters that are at the very core of interests of the Commonwealth.

In this context Sri Lanka can boast that 40 per cent of the nominations of political parties or independent groups contesting local government elections are from youth between 18 to 35 years of age. Youth thus empowered by the communities they live in, have proved to be a powerful force for development of democracy and peace building in Sri Lanka. Youth main-streaming is at the heart of a country's development agenda. I believe this to be a core element of the Commonwealth Plan of Action for Youth Empowerment.

We must give our youth greater opportunities to develop their own talents which need changes in attitudes towards the role of youth, their aspirations and their search for new challenges to overcome. It's just last Wednesday that my government initiated a programme in partnership with our closest neighbour and fellow Commonwealth member India, to raise the level of English Language teaching in our country and provide access to our youth to the opportunities available by the boom in the IT Industry.

The Commonwealth is today most suited to engage in such participatory development for our youth.

I am happy to state that Sri Lanka's investment in our youth and our future has ensured a free education system from kindergarten to university level which also provides free school text books and uniforms while children are in the primary and secondary schools. It is also a matter of pride and satisfaction that 97 percent of our youngsters are enrolled at school. Our social welfare programmes have consistently placed Sri Lanka high in the United Nations Development Indices.

Also, despite the ravages of terrorism and the enormous strain it places on our economy, we have made significant advances in social and economic development. We are proud to have the longest tradition of representative democracy in Asia and, to be among first developing countries to promote universal health and education, gender equality and social mobilization. We have achieved exceptional socio-economic indicators - way ahead of those normally expected of a country in the lower and middle-income range and we are now on the path to achieve or surpass many of the Millennium Development Goals.

While facing up to the threat of terrorism and the harsh effects of globalization, the Sri Lankan economy grew by 6.8 per cent last year continuing a trend in such growth in recent years indicating progress towards a higher growth path. On employment that is so important to youth, Sri Lanka saw its level of unemployment drop to its lowest rate of 6 per cent last year giving cause for much hope to our youth.

All these successes have helped Sri Lanka to record a significant reduction in poverty among the people with notable achievements in some districts that earlier had high levels. In 2002, 22.7 per cent of our population was below the poverty line and this improved tremendously to 15.7 per cent by December 2007. The percentage drop in poverty over 5 years is the fastest ever. It is also satisfying to note that there has been a substantial increase in the Per Capita Income of our people. It now stands at US dollars one thousand six hundred and seventeen (1,617) a sharp increase from US dollars nine hundred and eighty one (981) in the year 2003.

At the time of our election in November 2005 only 5 per cent of the population had literacy in Information Technology. We are glad to have extended IT literacy to 20 per cent by December 2007 with considerable progress in the rural areas. Our creating a network of 500 rural tele-centres styled, Nenasala has been instrumental in this increase in IT literacy. Our aim is to have 1000 Nenasalas islandwide by January next year with a goal to reach 50 per cent IT literacy by end 2010.

Another aspect concerning the life of youth is morality, the decline of which has given rise to an escalation of the incidence of AIDS throughout the world, particularly among young adults. Here again, religious guidance and spiritual orientation would be the sole remedy to save world's young people from destruction. Coupled with this global menace of AIDS is the use of illegal drugs which has destroyed youth in their prime. Our government having understood this most unfortunate situation has launched a programme "Mathata Thitha" which means a full stop to drugs, tobacco and alcohol. After 2 years of operation the programme has been rated as successful and young people have benefited immensely by it.

There is an interesting observation that youth are used for war but not generally used for peace building. Today, throughout the world it is estimated that over three hundred thousand persons below the age of 18 are involved in armed conflict with non-state actors whilst another five hundred thousand have been recruited to military forces. In many situations youth are seen to be the source and origin of conflict due to perceived grievances and frustrations, both social and economic. Therefore, in all our societies that are affected by conflict it is necessary to build on the hope and goodwill of youth for the cause of peace and understanding.

An important element in regard to youth in conflict is that we must devise ways and means to handle young people in post – conflict situations. What plans have we got for the young people after the conflicts are over? How do we bring back those youth in conflict into normalcy? These are areas still unresolved.

We have in our youth the genuine ambassadors of peace when our societies involve them in peace building and conflict resolution. Youth who are not yet spoilt by the divisions among adults are better able to carry the torch of peace and reconciliation and be the signal of a new order of tolerance and understanding. Therefore I believe that this Colombo meeting will be able to reflect on the manner in which the Commonwealth Youth Programme can involve young people affected by conflict in meaningful and practical programmes, aimed at peace building in areas of conflict throughout the Commonwealth.

It is also important to emphasize, Ladies and Gentlemen, that "youth and peace building" is of relevance not only to war – torn countries and those in the developing world. Even the most economically and socially stable of our member countries are grappling with issues of social breakdown and violence including drug-related crime and terrorism. Peace building has therefore become a vital part of nation building in the widest sense where sustainable peace is secured by building political cultures, institutions and economies that are fully inclusive of young people of all ethnic and social backgrounds. I believe the discussions would focus on the most practical and feasible measures to address these issues.

In this context I am happy that the Commonwealth Heads of Government Meeting's mandate, for Respect and Understanding has been included in your agenda. This report which focuses on the preventive aspect by exploring ways and means to mitigate factors that have a potential fuelling for conflict would provide some important inputs for the Commonwealth Plan of Action for Youth Empowerment.

The Youth of the Commonwealth have every promise of playing a significant role in Peace Building in our world given the opportunity and encouragement for it by greater interaction among societies and cultures. We have sportsmen and sportswomen who can make their own impact for the promotion of peace and understanding.

In this context I propose to this Conference to resume the Commonwealth Youth Exchange Programme to bring about the interaction of youth so important for peace building. Such exchanges of youth are also most useful to strengthen the bonds of friendship within the Commonwealth.

In conclusion I wish to refer to an extract from the Report of Respect and Understanding and I quote "when young people are disenfranchised or humiliated or made to feel that they have little to say and no future, they become drawn into movements or ideologies that appear to guarantee them a place in the work world and give them solid identity (unquote). This reflects the reality of today's society. I leave you Ministers to explore ways and means through your deliberations in arresting this trend.

I wish this conference all success and once again, wish you a very pleasant stay in Sri Lanka.

(*Source*: http://www.president.gov.lk/speech_New.asp?Id=49)

# SAARC and BIMSTEC

# 28.

# SELECT SPEECHES, JOINT STATEMENTS AND DECLARATIONS

## Charter of the South Asian Association for Regional Cooperation

We, the Heads of State or Government of BANGLADESH, BHUTAN, INDIA, MALDIVES, NEPAL, PAKISTAN and SRI LANKA;

1. **Desirous** of promoting peace, stability, amity and progress in the region through strict adherence to the principles of the UNITED NATIONS CHARTER and NON-ALIGNMENT, particularly respect for the principles of sovereign equality, territorial integrity, national independence, non-use of force and non-interference in the internal affairs of other States and peaceful settlement of all disputes;

2. **Conscious** that in an increasingly interdependent world, the objectives of peace, freedom, social justice and economic prosperity are best achieved in the SOUTH ASIAN region by fostering mutual understanding, good neighbourly relations and meaningful cooperation among the Member States which are bound by ties of history and culture;

3. **Aware** of the common problems, interests and aspirations of the peoples of SOUTH ASIA and the need for joint action and enhanced cooperation within their respective political and economic systems and cultural traditions;

4. **Convinced** that regional cooperation among the countries of SOUTH ASIA is mutually beneficial, desirable and necessary for promoting the welfare and improving the quality of life of the peoples of the region;

5. **Convinced** further that economic, social and technical cooperation among the countries of SOUTH ASIA would contribute significantly to national and collective self-reliance;

6. **Recognising** that increased cooperation, contacts and exchanges among the countries of the region will contribute to the promotion of friendship and understanding among their peoples;

7. **Recalling** the DECLARATION signed by their Foreign Ministers in NEW DELHI on August 2, 1983 and noting the progress achieved in regional cooperation;

8. **Reaffirming** their determination to promote such cooperation within an institutional framework;

**DO HEREBY AGREE** to establish an organisation to be known as SOUTH ASIAN ASSOCIATION FOR REGIONAL COOPERATION hereinafter referred to as the ASSOCIATION, with the following objectives, principles, institutional and financial arrangements:

## Article I
## OBJECTIVES

The objectives of the ASSOCIATION shall be:

a) to promote the welfare of the peoples of SOUTH ASIA and to improve their quality of life;
b) to accelerate economic growth, social progress and cultural development in the region and to provide all individuals the opportunity to live in dignity and to realise their full potentials;
c) to promote and strengthen collective self-reliance among the countries of SOUTH ASIA;
d) to contribute to mutual trust, understanding and appreciation of one another's problems;
e) to promote active collaboration and mutual assistance in the economic, social, cultural, technical and scientific fields;
f) to strengthen cooperation with other developing countries;
g) to strengthen cooperation among themselves in international forums on matters of common interests; and
h) to cooperate with international and regional organisations with similar aims and purposes.

## Article II
## PRINCIPLES

1. Cooperation within the framework of the ASSOCIATION shall be based on respect for the principles of sovereign equality, territorial integrity, political independence, non-interference in the internal affairs of other States and mutual benefit.

2. Such cooperation shall not be a substitute for bilateral and multilateral cooperation but shall complement them.

3. Such cooperation shall not be inconsistent with bilateral and multilateral obligations.

## Article III
## MEETINGS OF THE HEADS OF STATE OR GOVERNMENT

The Heads of State or Government shall meet once a year or more often as and when considered necessary by the Member States.

Article IV
COUNCIL OF MINISTERS

1. A Council of Ministers consisting of the Foreign Ministers of the Member States shall be established with the following functions:

a) formulation of the policies of the ASSOCIATION;
b) review of the progress of cooperation under the ASSOCIATION;
c) decision on new areas of cooperation;
d) establishment of additional mechanism under the ASSOCIATION as deemed necessary;
e) decision on other matters of general interest to the ASSOCIATION.

2. The Council of Ministers shall meet twice a year. Extraordinary session of the Council may be held by agreement among the Member States.

Article V
STANDING COMMITTEE

1. The Standing Committee comprising the Foreign Secretaries shall have the following functions:

a) overall monitoring and coordination of programme of cooperation;
b) approval of projects and programmes, and the modalities of their financing;
c) determination of inter-sectoral priorities;
d) mobilisation of regional and external resources;
e) identification of new areas of cooperation based on appropriate studies.

2. The Standing Committee shall meet as often as deemed necessary.

3. The Standing Committee shall submit periodic reports to the Council of Ministers and make reference to it as and when necessary for decisions on policy matters.

Article VI
TECHNICAL COMMITTEES

1. Technical Committees comprising representatives of Member States shall be responsible for the implementation, coordination and monitoring of the programmes in their respective areas of cooperation.

2. They shall have the following terms of reference:

a) determination of the potential and the scope of regional cooperation in agreed areas;
b) formulation of programmes and preparation of projects;
c) determination of financial implications of sectoral programmes;
d) formulation of recommendations regarding apportionment of costs;

e) implementation and coordination of sectoral programmes;
f) monitoring of progress in implementation.

3. The Technical Committees shall submit periodic reports to the Standing Committee.

4. The Chairmanship of the Technical Committees shall normally rotate among Member States in alphabetical order every two years.

5. The Technical Committees may, inter-alia, use the following mechanisms and modalities, if and when considered necessary:

a) meetings of heads of national technical agencies;
b) meetings of experts in specific fields;
c) contact amongst recognised centres of excellence in the region.

Article VII
ACTION COMMITTEES

The Standing Committee may set up Action Committees comprising Member States concerned with implementation of projects involving more than two but not all Member States.

Article VIII
SECRETARIAT

There shall be a Secretariat of the ASSOCIATION.

Article IX
FINANCIAL ARRANGEMENTS

1. The contribution of each Member State towards financing of the activities of the ASSOCIATION shall be voluntary.

2. Each Technical Committee shall make recommendations for the apportionment of costs of implementing the programmes proposed by it.

3. In case sufficient financial resources cannot be mobilised within the region for funding activities of the ASSOCIATION, external financing from appropriate sources may be mobilised with the approval of or by the Standing Committee.

Article X
GENERAL PROVISIONS

1. Decisions at all levels shall be taken on the basis of unanimity.

2. Bilateral and contentious issues shall be excluded from the deliberations.

**IN FAITH WHEREOF** We Have Set Our Hands And Seals Hereunto. **DONE** In **DHAKA, BANGLADESH,** On This The Eighth Day Of December Of The Year One Thousand Nine Hundred Eighty Five.

Hussain Muhammad Ershad
PRESIDENT OF THE PEOPLE'S REPUBLIC OF BANGLADESH

Jigme Singye Wangchuk
KING OF BHUTAN

Rajiv Gandhi
PRIME MINISTER OF THE REPUBLIC OF INDIA

Maumoon Abdul Gayoom
PRESIDENT OF THE REBUPLIC OF MALDIVES

Birendra Bir Bikram Shah Dev
KING OF NEPAL

Muhammad Zia-ul-Haq
PRESIDENT OF THE ISLAMIC REPUBLIC OF PAKISTAN

Junius Richard Jayewardene
PRESIDENT OF DEMOCRATIC SOCIALIST REPUBLIC OF SRI LANKA

## Statement by Mr. Hamid Karzai, President of the Islamic Republic of Afghanistan at the 15th Summit of South Asian Association for Regional Cooperation (SAARC), Colombo, Sri Lanka

August 2, 2008

*Speaking at the 15th SAARC Summit, President Hamid Karzai, called for a greater integrated regional cooperation. Amongst other issues he touched upon was the creation of the SAARC Food Bank. He also highlighted the importance of Afghanistan as an effective conduit between Central and South Asia for meeting energy needs stating that Afghanistan could provide the shortest and the most economical route. The President also mentioned a contract with a Chinese consortium for the exploration of Aynak copper deposits and the construction of railway line which would be connecting Central Asia to South Asia.*

I thank you, Mr Chairman, and the people of Sri Lanka for hosting this important summit of the South Asian Association for Regional Cooperation, and for the very warm reception and hospitality extended to all of us. I also wish to congratulate you, Mr Chairman and the people of Sri Lanka on the 60th Anniversary of Sri Lanka's Independence. I present the warm wishes of the Afghan people to each and all of you in this august gathering.

Addressing, in particular, my friend Prime Minister Manmohan- Singh, I once again share my deep sense of shock and pain for the loss of precious

Indian and Afghan lives at the bombing of Indian Embassy in Kabul on 7 July.

You will agree with me, Your Excellencies, that no amount of outrage and condemnation can suffice to express the anger and frustration we all feel when faced with such mindless brutality and violence. I am sure you realize that these terrorist attacks, callous and destructive as they are, point to a rapidly growing threat that we face, not just in Afghanistan or India, but throughout the entire SAARC region.

As we gather today at the 15th SAARC Summit, we are more cognizant than ever before of the immediate nature of the challenges facing the region we live in. Indeed, over the past twenty three years of SAARC's existence, I cannot think of a period when the need for collective action against challenges that affect us all was more pressing than it is today.

While the region has to deal with a myriad of serious problems such as chronic poverty, food and energy shortages, environmental degradation and the like, terrorism is by far the greatest and most menacing of all. These challenges do not just prevent the realization of our great potentials for growth and prosperity; they put our future gravely at risk.

On terrorism, while the people of Afghanistan today are bearing the brunt of international terrorism on a daily basis, it is with tremendous trepidation that we are watching the wildfire of terrorism spreading across the region. In Pakistan, terrorism and its sanctuaries are gaining a deeper grip, as demonstrated by the tragic assassination of Shaheed Benazir Bhutto. The indiscriminate attacks on civilians in Colombo earlier this year, the recent terrorist bombings in the Indian cities of Bangalore and Ahmedabad, and attacks in Kabul were yet other grim reminders of the growing reach of terrorists across the wider region.

In a region prone to many challenges, terrorism may well prove to be the most destabilizing. Terrorism in our region feeds on a residual tradition of narrow-minded politics, and of pursuing outmoded geopolitical interests. While existing on the absolute fringes of our tolerant and peace-loving societies, terrorists in our region receive institutional nurturing and support. It is this embedded nature of terrorism that makes it a much more sinister threat to our common security, and to the future of our children.

It is for the sake of our common security and for the future of our children that we must counter the spread of terrorism, urgently and decisively. It is time we focus, together, on fighting extremism and terrorism, as the enemies that we have in common. It is time we all realize that the pursuit of narrow geopolitical interests and the use of militant radicalism as an instrument of policy cannot succeed or serve any long term purpose.

I must re-emphasize that the challenge of terrorism must be overcome in order for us to realize the potential of greater regional economic integration. Through greater economic integration, we can work towards shared prosperity and improve the welfare of our people. We must identify what resources, potential and comparative advantages our respective countries offer and work towards the common framework offered by SAARC to maximize these advantages for our people as a whole.

The food crisis in our region is a particularly serious challenge. High food prices are putting reforms, growth strategies, and most importantly, lives at risk. It brings to sharp perspective the urgency for more rapid progress to be made on the establishment of the SAARC Food Bank.

To mitigate future shocks, we must also make rapid progress on the development of a regional food security strategy that includes early warning systems on food vulnerabilities. Preparedness must be the cornerstone of our regional response to food shortages.

Important as it is to be focused on the needs of the people put at risk by the current crisis, it is equally important for us to ensure food security in the longer term. To this end, the SAARC members must dramatically increase investments in agriculture and rural development. My government has identified agriculture, irrigation and energy as priority sectors under Afghanistan's National Development Strategy. We are looking to enhance our agricultural products and productivity by investing across the value chain: land use; water management and irrigation; infrastructures and logistics; and credit for farmers. We warmly welcome opportunities to benefit from our SAARC partners' knowledge, experience, and best practices in agriculture and rural development.

Access to reliable and continued energy sources will define the pace of our economic growth. We believe that Afghanistan can play a critical role in addressing the growing demand for energy in the southern parts of our region and respond to the alarming increase in the price of crude oil by facilitating the transfer of energy from Central to South Asia.

It has been estimated that energy needs of South Asia will increase threefold in the next fifteen to twenty years. Afghanistan can serve as the shortest and least expensive route of transferring energy from Central to South Asia, where the demand for energy is growing constantly. We have already made some progress in the transfer of power from Tajikistan and Kyrgyzstan through Afghanistan to Pakistan. With further support, this process can be expedited.

Afghanistan has the potential to generate a significant amount of hydro electric power. Investing in hydro power plants in Afghanistan and taking action on the transfer of energy from Central Asia, through Afghanistan, to South Asia is one of the most efficient ways of meeting the challenge of energy shortages in the SAARC region. The construction of the pipeline to transfer natural gas from Turkmenistan, through Afghanistan to Pakistan and India is also of vital importance to our region and deserves to be given serious attention and urgency.

Trade, flow of people and ideas will strengthen economic integration and progress in South Asia. Afghanistan is rightly placed to play a key role towards connecting people and expanding markets with and across the wider region.

We have undertaken a number of measures towards strengthening our capacity to serve as an effective route by opening new corridors and improving border facilities. We have liberalized our air transportation policies and simplified transit and custom procedures.

We have also taken concrete measures in building our national highway system towards improving the transport of goods and people in the region and closing the distance between our countries. As part of the contract with a Chinese consortium for the exploration of the Aynak copper deposit, a railway line will be constructed which will connect Central Asia to South Asia, thereby expediting the transport of people and goods within the region and beyond.

In conclusion, I repeat Afghanistan's commitment to regional cooperation, and our conviction that SAARC's success, and our ability to compete globally, will depend on strengthening and integrating our economies and on working collectively to defeat terrorism in the region.

We are at a critical juncture and much hangs in the balance. It is time we open our hearts and minds to the prospects of a new, better and more peaceful future for our countries. This is only possible through peaceful co-existence, recognition of our interdependence and enhanced economic cooperation. I believe, ladies and gentlemen, that we will prevail if we recognize that our common interests are greater than our differences and if we marshal the political will to address the challenges we face as a region through concerted action. This is the way forward. Thank you!!

(*Source*: http://www.president.gov.af/english/speeches/020808_ prespeechatsaarc. mspx)

## Statement by Dr. Fakhruddin Ahmed Honourable Chief Adviser Government of the People's Republic of Bangladesh

August 2, 2008

*Dr. Fakhruddin Ahmed, Honourable Chief Adviser Government of the People's Republic of Bangladesh stated that SAARC had crossed significant milestones in forging closer cooperation between South Asian countries. He pointed out that though poverty alleviation had been an over arching goal for SAARC, South Asian countries were witnessing gross poverty. He stated that global economic slowdown, soaring oil and food prices and growing threats of climate change were further driving people towards poverty. He emphasized that efforts to attain the SAARC Development Goals within the targeted timeline should be undertaken seriously. He pointed that since intra-regional investment flows were very small in South Asia, the Agreement on South Asian Free Trade Area (SAFTA) should be conceived as an instrument for enhancing regional trade leading to greater economic integration. He highlighted that people should be at the centre of the collective efforts and tourism could be an effective means to develop greater "people to people contact".*

I am truly delighted to be here in this charming city of Colombo for the 15th SAARC Summit. I congratulate President Rajapaksa on his election to the Chair. I am confident that his experience and wisdom will enable us to surmount the challenges that we in SAARC are facing today.

I would also like to extend my heartfelt appreciation to the Government and the people of Sri Lanka for the gracious hospitality and warm reception accorded to me, to my wife, and to the members of my delegation.

I take this opportunity to applaud India, in particular to Prime Minister Dr. Manmohan Singh for leading the organisation so skillfully through the past year. His stewardship has infused a new fervour into our organization.

SAARC has crossed significant milestones in forging closer cooperation among our nations. This Summit has rekindled the hope and belief among our peoples regarding the delivery of progress and prosperity that we had collectively promised ourselves some twentyythree years ago. We must not let ourselves down. Let this Summit be the turning point in our endeavours for a more prosperous, peaceful and progressive South Asia.

Poverty Alleviation has been an over arching goal for SAARC. Ironically South Asia is home to almost half of the world's poor. Global economic slowdown, soaring oil and food prices and growing threats of climate change are driving the destitute people of the region even further below the poverty line. We must redouble our efforts to attain the SAARC Development Goals within the targeted timeline. I believe national action on poverty alleviation should be complemented by effective and robust regional initiatives in order to have a penetrative impact on poverty reduction in South Asia. Ensuring self-sufficiency in cereal production and attaining food security would require greater attention to agricultural productivity and should be the critical element in poverty reduction strategy.

Our goal in SAARC is to create new opportunities and to promote linkages for attaining better standards of living for our people. The steady GDP growth seen in all of our countries has led to increase in the purchasing power of our population creating a vast middle class. The Agreement on South Asian Free Trade Area (SAFTA) was conceived as an instrument for enhancing regional trade leading to greater economic integration. We are happy to welcome Afghanistan into SAFTA which will formally take place with the signing of the Protocol of Accession of Afghanistan to SAFTA. This will complete full integration of Afghanistan into SAARC process.

Despite SAFTA, non -tariff and para - tariff barriers, complicated and cumbersome customs procedures stand in the way of greater intra-regional trade. Similarly, long sensitive list closed to preferential tariff and rigidities in other structural and policy framework stand in the way of our desire to have a fully integrated South Asia. Clearly there is a need to remove these hurdles to enhance intra-regional trade. Similarly, intra-regional investment flows are very small in South Asia. Given right kind of environment and confidence, the potential for increased intra-regional investment is huge. I feel that restrictive investment regime is one of the inhibiting factors in attracting foreign direct investment. In this context, it is important that the Draft Agreement on Promotion and Protection of Investments is finalised at the earliest.

The services sector has emerged as most dynamic with an average annual growth rate of over eight percent. The thirteenth SAARC Summit in Dhaka recognised the potential of this sector and had directed for early finalisation of an agreement in this area. I am happy to note that negotiation is about to commence on a Framework Agreement on Trade in Services. This should pave the way for the trade liberalisation. That will be a "win-win" situation for all of us.

A number of inter-governmental mechanisms have been put in place to move forward the agenda of deepening economic cooperation in the region. However, the pace of trade liberalisation has been less than satisfactory. To move the process forward, it may be useful to set-up a consultative mechanism, which could identify the bottlenecks and recommend practical and effective ways to move the process of trade liberalisation towards Customs Union, and finally to Economic Union in a gradual and phased manner.

We are pleased that Charter of the SAARC Development Fund is to be signed at this Summit. The Fund will be an important instrument at our disposal to implement regional projects that would accord visible, tangible and concrete benefits to the member states. Similarly, the establishment of South Asian Regional Standards Organization (SARSO) would be an important step towards trade facilitation and greater economic integration in the region. It is heartening that we are also about to sign the Agreement establishing SARSO during this Summit.

Over the years, SAARC has evolved in many ways. The purpose and success of this regional mechanism largely depend on remaining actively engaged on contemporary issues. Security dimension in the region and beyond has thus taken a centre stage in our deliberations. Organized crimes like smuggling, drug and illegal arms trafficking are matters of great concern for us. The deadly fangs of terrorism are spreading across the region. They threaten to disrupt peace and stability.

We must combat the menace of terrorism across the broadest possible spectrum. I would like to reiterate that Bangladesh stands firm in her resolve to deal with these issues, 1 forcefully and effectively. Let me announce unequivocally that Bangladesh is against terrorism in all its forms and manifestations. Terrorists have perpetrated brutal acts in every part of the world. We condemn the heinous terrorist attacks in Afghanistan, India and Pakistan in recent times which caused unnecessary loss of valuable lives.Bangladesh, as a signatory to international conventions against terrorism, both globally and regionally, is in the process of enacting and modifying relevant domestic laws for their effective implementation at the national level. I am pleased to note the SAARC Convention on Mutual Assistance in Criminal Matters has been finalized and ready for signature at this Summit. I believe this legal instrument would be an important tool at our disposal for effective and meaningful cooperation in our fight against all serious and organized crimes.The recent price hike of food globally creating a situation close to food crisis has led us all to reflect deeply on how to ensure our collective food security. This requires our immediate attention to ensure constant and steady supply of food for our people. We need to develop strategies, not only to address short-term supply-side shocks but also to strengthen cooperation to increase agricultural productivity. This is a must to prevent hunger and malnutrition - one of the key priorities of the Millennium Development Goals. I would stress upon early ratification and operationalization of SMRC Food Bank to address this situation.

Following the path of high growth in the region, we are witnessing tremendous rise in demand for energy. It hardly needs any reiteration that energy plays a vital role in the economic, social and human development, including in poverty alleviation. We must therefore explore all avenues including bilateral, sub-regional and regional cooperation for addressing the supply side-constraints of energy in the region, including capacity building, technology transfer and infrastructure development. The ongoing cooperation in this sector must be intensified. In the wake of sky-rocketing price of fossil fuel, we must harness renewable sources of energy such as hydro-power, solar, bio-fuel and wind to address the energy crisis in the region. We should strive to develop conventional as well as alternate sources of energy to ensure its steady supply at affordable cost. At the same time, we also need to accord greater emphasis on energy conservation and energy efficiency. Achieving energy security is a must if we are to realize our development potentials.

At the core of our efforts is the vision of people's SMRC. People are at the centre of our collective efforts. It is through connecting hearts and minds of South Asians can we hope to build the bridges of trust and confidence that would lead us to a better future. The First SAARC Youth Camp in Dhaka last December was a successful effort in bringing young people from across the region more closer, and affording them a unique opportunity to forge bonds of lasting friendship and amity. Greater interactions among members of civil society, students, teachers, intelligentsia and journalists would create greater standing and sense of togetherness in the region. At the 14th Summit, we had decided to establish the South Asian University in New Delhi. I am told the work on the Main Campus of the University is progressing well. Bangladesh is considering establishment of Dhaka Campus of the South Asian University soon.

Tourism is an effective mean to develop greater "people to people contact". It is important that concerted efforts are taken to implement the comprehensive Plan of Action adopted by the SAARC Tourism Ministers at Cox's Bazaar in 2006. The SAARC Agenda for Culture launched last year is an important step in persevering and protecting the South Asian cultural heritage and buttressing cultural linkages of the region. We must pursue the Agenda whole-heartedly. I believe, these are some of the important elements that will contribute to greater connectivity in the region.

Climate change has become a major cause of concern for us. South Asia is acutely vulnerable to global warming and climate change. The melting of Himalayan glaciers, rising sea level, drought and desertification, increasing salinity in our rivers are most visible manifestations of the changing climate. In South Asia, global warming is rendering natural disasters frequent and more intense, causing greater damages and devastation to lives and livelihood.

I am happy that South Asia is responding to the call of the hour. Last month, Environment Ministers from eight SAARC countries met at Dhaka and adopted an Action Plan on Climate Change. This is the first step in the right direction. It would be important that the Action Plan is implemented and followed through to address climate change issue in the region. We have a long way to go. We must bear in mind that it is our collective responsibility to save our planet for the present and futurity.

At the Council of Minister's Meeting on 31 July 2008, Bangladesh suggested a methodology for structured contacts between our Armed Forces. Already at bilateral levels such links exist. Together we provide a huge majority of the world's peacekeepers. I believe it may be worthwhile to devise such a system that can periodically bring the senior officers of our military forces together to determine how best we can advance our mutual interests. We may also share training facilities under this scheme.

Another point that I wish to raise is with regard to the vast number of workers that SAARC region provides to other parts of the world. We should collaborate to strengthen our capacity to negotiate better terms and conditions of work for them to promote their welfare and to protect their rights.

In this interdependent world, we can only prosper if we act in unison. It is incumbent upon us who have gathered here today to clearly chart out the road map for SAARC for the greater prosperity and welfare of the peoples of South Asia. Our vision is to promote this through accelerated economic growth and social progress across the region. I believe there is a clear political will and commitment to realize this goal. Bangladesh remains deeply committed to making this happen. We shall continue to play our part and take every possible initiative in building the future of our 'South Asian home' as a harmonious abode of peace, progress and prosperity for all our peoples.

(*Source*: http://www.saarc-sec.org/)

## Statement by Mr. Lyonchhen Jigmi Y. Thinley Prime Minister of the Kingdom of Bhutan

August 4, 2008

*Mr Lyonchhen Jigmi Y. Thinley, Prime Minister of Bhutan expressed his appreciation towards the leadership provided by India at the 14th SAARC Summit. He lauded the establishment of SAARC Development Fund, and offered Bhutan as a potential host for the SDF. He emphasized the urgent need for various Asian states to cooperate with each other in order to complete the various regional and sub-regional projects undertaken in the previous SAARC summits. Tourism, he asserted could be an important sector to the region as a whole.*

It is a great honour for me to address the Fifteenth SAARC Summit in Colombo coinciding with the 60th Anniversary Celebrations of Sri Lanka's independence. We are extremely pleased to be able to share this historic moment with the people and government of Sri Lanka. On this joyous occasion, I have the honour to convey the warm felicitations of my King, His Majesty Jigme Khesar Namgyel Wangchuck, and that of the people and government of Bhutan.

Please accept, Mr. Chairman, my congratulations as you and your country assume the important responsibility of guiding the endeavours of our Association at a time when not only the region but globally, human society is faced with serious challenges. These call for greater collaboration through trust and understanding even as doubts, suspicions and fears continue to test our resolve. I am confident that the SAARC process will attain further momentum under your able leadership. To this end, please rest assured Sir, that you will have the full support of my delegation and my government. This, of course, has nothing to do with the extremely warm and gracious hospitality that my delegation and I have received since our arrival here, and for which I would like to convey our deep appreciation to the people and government of Sri Lanka.

His Excellency Prime Minister Manmohan Singh and the Government of India deserve our admiration and appreciation for the outstanding leadership provided to the work of our Association since the Fourteenth Summit. I believe India's commitment to the SAARC process has been well demonstrated both in spirit and through the laudable initiatives undertaken to strengthen regional cooperation.

I congratulate Dr. Sheel Kant Sharma on having assumed office as the new Secretary General of our Association. I have no doubt that he will bring fresh perspectives and dynamism to the Secretariat and build on the progress achieved by his predecessors. Our appreciation also goes to the former Secretary General Lyonpo Chenkyab Dorji for the hard work and commitment with which he carried out his responsibilities. He and his team deserve our highest commendation.

I also wish to acknowledge the presence of the distinguished representatives of Observers at this Summit. We welcome them and look forward to a fruitful and mutually beneficial engagement with the Observers.

Yet again, we might remind ourselves that our gathering symbolizes the hopes and aspirations of one sixth of humanity. It is an expression of our own acceptance that our people do want us to work together. There are immense rewards to be gained by doing so even though we allow ourselves to be deluded ever so often by thoughts and actions that we know are unwise and wrong. In order to make our Summit meaningful we need to open our eyes to the wonders of the great opportunities that we have missed and take stock of the vast potential of South Asia's natural, cultural, scientific and human resources that are the envy of any country or region. We need to generate within ourselves the will and the courage to overcome the inertia that makes us hesitate, falter and dwell in the domain of doubt and suspicion.

Over the last two decades, we have made numerous commitments and created several worthy arrangements to provide enabling frameworks for cooperation in a wide range of areas. What we need now is to act. We need to fulfill the commitments we make each time we come together, implement the declarations we sign and operationalize the instruments we have created. Only then will we be able to make use of our own creations to bring about visible and tangible benefits to our peoples.

In this context, the establishment of the SAARC Development Fund (SDF) is a noteworthy initiative to implement regional and sub-regional projects that can bring about tangible benefits to our people at the grassroots. The signing of the Charter of the Fund at this Summit clearly demonstrates our determination to make the SAARC process result oriented as we endeavour to focus on implementation in the third decade. My delegation attaches high importance to this institution as a means of engendering meaningful cooperation. in many important areas and we are confident that the Fund will evolve into a viable and effective SAARC mechanism. On the question of the domicile of the Permanent Secretariat of the Fund, I wish to reiterate my government's offer to host this important institution in Bhutan. We are willing and ready to shoulder this responsibility and are committed to providing the most conducive operational, tax and legal flexibility for the Permanent Secretariat to function efficiently and effectively. I, therefore, sincerely hope that Bhutan's offer will receive the consideration and valuable support of all Member States.

This Summit is taking place against the backdrop of pressing global challenges, the impacts of which transcend national borders and underscore the interdependence of the economies of the world. Rising oil prices are putting considerable strain on our economies by pushing up the cost of living and fueling inflation. As a short term measure, we hope the oil producing and exporting countries will take steps to stabilize the oil markets by enhancing their capacities and output. But we must explore more sustainable solutions. Our region boasts a tremendous potential and much can be accomplished if we work together and recognize our complementarities. We must make optimal use of our energy resources; identify viable alternative sources of energy; and promote the development and use of renewable energy. Bhutan's experience in this area has been fairly successful. With the support and cooperation of India, we are making rapid progress in harnessing our hydropower potential to generate clean and reliable energy for our mutual benefit.

Likewise, soaring food prices is causing severe hardship, social unrest and suffering to millions all over the world, particularly the poor and vulnerable sections of our societies. This reinforces the need to redouble our efforts to eradicate poverty and hunger, particularly through agricultural and rural development. We need to invest in agriculture and improve agricultural output as the livelihoods of the majority of our people are dependent on it. It is in this regard that I welcome the establishment of the SAARC Food Bank as a very meaningful and timely initiative. My delegation also fully endorses the Colombo Statement on Food Security which clearly demonstrates our collective resolve and solidarity to address the challenges posed by rising food prices.

Since its inception, SAARC has helped build and promote a spirit of camaraderie, mutual trust and understanding which we must consciously endeavour to nurture and foster as they form the bedrock of any meaningful cooperation. During the Fourteenth Summit, we agreed to build a 'Partnership for Prosperity' and underlined the importance of physical, economic and people-to-people connectivity. If we are to achieve a 'Partnership for Growth for our Peoples' as envisaged by this Summit, I believe we must expedite the implementation of the prioritized recommendations of the SAARC Multimodal Transport Study including the sub-regional and regional projects that have been identified.

The imperatives of economic cooperation and free trade in a highly globalized and interdependent world cannot be overemphasized. Recognizing that the furtherance of intra-regional trade is the key to promoting and encouraging an environment of innovation, healthy competition and enterprise that will stimulate economic growth, create gainful employment and generate higher income for our peoples, we have created SAFTA. But for this instrument to be meaningful, the number of items on the negative list must be reduced, non-tariff barriers removed and the trade facilitation measures implemented. At the same time, liberalization of trade in services and investments must also be pursued in earnest.

The tourism sector holds great promise to earn foreign exchange, generate employment and improve the well-being of our people, especially if we put in place policies and opportunities for greater participation of all stakeholders, particularly the rural populations. As a region, we possess unparalleled cultural and natural resources that ought to have made our region the most favoured tourist destination. We must, therefore, commit ourselves more concertedly to seizing the tremendous opportunities that the tourism sector in our region affords.. Furthermore, mutual understanding and goodwill among our peoples is inextricably linked to a better appreciation of each other's cultural and historical heritage. It is in this context that the establishment of the SAARC Cultural Center in Kandy should be seen as an important initiative that can bring about further development and implementation of the SAARC Agenda for Culture.

My delegation notes with appreciation the progress being made towards the establishment of the South Asian University. This Institution will play an important role in nurturing the talent, skills and knowledge of our most precious and abundant resource - the people of South Asia. It will provide a platform for the academia, students, scholars and researchers of our region to interact, learn, share experiences and help foster a spirit of South Asian solidarity.

The primary goal of SAARC to improve the well being of our peoples remains elusive. Millions continue to be mired in inhuman conditions of want and deprivation. We must intensify our efforts so that the poor and destitute have the opportunity to break free from the shackles of poverty and realize their potentials. If we are to make reasonable headway, our national efforts must complement the regional consensus and the Plan of Action on Poverty Alleviation.

As we strive to improve the welfare of our peoples, they continue to suffer the pain of insecurity and fear from terrorism and other transnational crimes. The recent acts of terror in our region are a grim reminder of this menace that continues to haunt and plague our region. My peaceful country too is being afflicted by this scourge and over the last few years has had to grapple with a series of terrorist activities. We unequivocally condemn these senseless and reprehensible acts of violence. Regardless of how sublime, noble or even desperate a cause may be, it can never justify the means that kill and maim innocent men, women and children in the most cowardly and barbaric ways.

Let us renew the commitment we made during the Fourteenth Summit to find the best and the most practical means to implement the provisions of the existing SAARC Conventions on terrorism, drugs, trafficking in women and children and other transnational crimes. The signing of the SAARC Convention on Mutual Legal Assistance in Criminal Matters at this Summit is yet another manifestation of our desire to enhance regional cooperation in fighting crime. We must act decisively and send a clear message to perpetrators, sponsors and supporters alike that we are united in our determination to combat and eradicate these social evils.

As a member of the SAARC family, Bhutan is proud of the SAARC Plan of Action on Environment as well as the recently adopted Dhaka Declaration and Action Plan on Climate Change. Cooperation in Environment and Disaster Management has become extremely vital as globalization and consumerism combine to compromise the interest of mankind's own survival. Climate change is becoming an irreversible phenomenon and its consequences are far too serious to overlook. Bhutan faces considerable risks from Glacial Lake Outburst Floods as a result of global warming despite the fact that we may have contributed the least green house gases. Their impact on life and property in the densely populated lower riparian countries of India and Bangladesh will be most devastating.

We consider the establishment of the SAARC Forestry Center (SFC) in Bhutan as recognition of our success and consistent efforts to preserve and protect our rich bio-diversity and fragile environment. With the support of Member States and the SAARC Secretariat, we hope the Center will add value to regional initiatives to preserve and protect our fragile ecosystems.

The year 2008 marks a very special place in the history of Bhutan and, indeed, in the hearts and minds of the people of Bhutan. Under the wise and able leadership of our fourth King, His Majesty Jigme Singye Wangchuck, Bhutan has undergone profound political changes. Ever since His accession to the throne in 1972, His Majesty has been relentless in His efforts to empower the people through a steady process of democratization. He prevailed over considerable odds and put in place all the institutional arrangements and instruments for a vibrant democracy before he retired in December 2006 at the age of fifty-one.

My country became a Democratic Constitutional Monarchy in March 2008 after the people participated overwhelmingly in the electoral process to elect their first government. This historic transition was successfully accomplished under the able leadership and guidance of His Majesty Jigme Khesar Namgyel Wangchuck, the fifth King of Bhutan, and with the goodwill and support of our well-wishers and friends in the region and beyond.

This year, we will commemorate and pay tribute to the Institution of Monarchy as it completes one hundred years for nurturing, guiding and leading Bhutan from isolation and absolute monarchy to modernization and democracy in a globalized world. Today, Bhutan sees herself as a country that is placed firmly on the path of peace, progress and Gross National Happiness. Our pride in ourselves as a people and our confidence in our future is further enhanced by the good fortune that has blessed us yet again with an extraordinarily wise and compassionate King. The people of Bhutan will, therefore, be rejoicing in the formal coronation of our fifth King, His Majesty Jigme Khesar Namgyel Wangchuck, later this year.

Once again, it is a great honour and pleasure for me to be able to participate in the 15th Summit of our Association. My joy is doubled by the fact that this event is taking place at a time when the friendly people of Sri Lanka are celebrating the 60th year of independence. The other reason for my pride and joy is because this is the first time that Bhutan is participating in a Summit as a full fledged democracy. I wish to pledge here that just as the previous governments had placed their faith and confidence in our regional association, democratic Bhutan will do all it can to make SAARC a powerful and effective mechanism for the realization of the dreams of the people of South Asia.

(*Source*: http://www.lankamission.org/content/view/623/2/ )

## Statement by the Prime Minister of India Dr. Manmohan Singh at the Inaugural Session of the 15th SAARC Summit

August 2, 2008

*Prime Minister Dr Manmohan Singh, welcomed Mauritius as SAARC's new observer and pointed out that a prosperous South*

*Asia would also be a peaceful and stable South Asia. Pointing out that India was an open economy welcoming investment from everywhere, Dr Singh emphasized that South Asian countries should pool resources together in order to create a model of inclusive and sustainable regional development. He stated that economic cooperation, connectivity and integration would be the cornerstone of SAARC in the years ahead. He lauded the efforts made by the SAARC Food Bank in 2007, which he noted was a forward looking decision. He emphasized that the countries of South Asia needed to work towards a collective response which would lead to a quantum leap in agricultural productivity, food grain output and farm incomes so that the food shortages and hunger vanishes from the region. He pointed out that India had recently launched a National Action Plan on Climate Change, and was willing to share experiences with other Asian neighbours.*

I wish to begin by congratulating His Excellency President Mahinda Rajapaksa for his election as Chairperson of SAARC. I also convey my deep appreciation to the Government and people of Sri Lanka for the excellent arrangements made for the 15th Summit, and for the warm and generous hospitality that has been extended to all of us.

I also wish to extend a very warm welcome to our newest Observer, Mauritius, a country with whom South Asia shares enduring historical and cultural ties.

South Asia has travelled a long distance in the twenty three years since SAARC was established. The winds of democracy and political change have swept across our region. Our people's aspirations, particularly of our youth, for a better life and for greater empowerment, are rising and rising very fast. With globalisation, our economies are ever more inter-connected with our neighbours and with the world as a whole.

It is however a fact that South Asia has not moved as fast as we all would have wished. We have only to see the rapid integration within ASEAN and its emergence as an important economic bloc in Asia to understand the opportunities that beckon us all.

The success and prosperity of each one of us provides opportunities to the others to promote their own success and prosperity. This mutuality of interests is the central driving force of regional cooperation everywhere.

Our aim should be to create virtuous cycles of growth in our region. A prosperous South Asia will also be a peaceful and stable South Asia. Realising this vision requires a change in our mindsets, and a new paradigm of creative thinking. We can and must do more to give meaning to the theme of this year's Summit: "Growth through Partnership".

Terrorism continues to rear its ugly head in our region. It remains the single biggest threat to our stability and to our progress. We cannot afford to lose the battle against the ideologies of hatred, fanaticism and against all those who seek to destroy our social fabric.

Terrorists and extremists know no borders. The recent attack on the Indian Embassy in Kabul and the serial blasts in Bangalore and Ahmedabad in the last few days are gruesome reminders of the barbarity that still finds a place here in South Asia. We must act jointly and with determination to fight this scourge. We must defend the values of pluralism, peaceful coexistence and the rule of law.

South Asia clearly has the resources and the skills needed to meet our development challenges. I am happy to say that India has experienced vigorous growth at an average of 8.8% per year for the past four years. India is now an open economy welcoming investment from everywhere. The other countries in our region have also done well. Today, Asia has become the engine of growth of the world economy and South Asia is a part of this resurgence.

This growth must have a multiplier effect in our region. We have rich and varied experience in development, which we must pool together to create a model of inclusive and sustainable regional development. The SAARC Development Fund has made a promising start with the launching of two maternal and child healthcare projects. The development of SAARC Model Villages in each of our countries within the last year is an equally encouraging development. We must build on these innovative programmes.

Economic cooperation, connectivity and integration will be the cornerstone of SAARC in the years ahead. We have already agreed to move towards a South Asian Customs Union and a South Asian Economic Union in a planned and phased manner.

India has granted zero duty access to our markets to LDC members from anuary 1, 2008, one year ahead of the target and also pruned our sensitive list for these countries. India's FTA with Sri Lanka is working satisfactorily bringing benefits to both our economies.

We will go ahead with these initiatives at a pace we are all comfortable with.

All the leaders have emphasized the importance of physical connectivity. On its part, India has upgraded its railway connection to broad gauge at the Raxaul-Birgunj and Jogbani-Biratnagar borders, the Dhaka-Kolkata rail service has begun, and work is underway to upgrade infrastructure along our borders with other neighbours. India looks forward to the finalization of the draft Agreements on Motor Vehicles and Railways.

I have always believed that the people of South Asia know much more about countries of the West than they do about themselves. The fraternity that exists among our students and professionals outside the region must be re-created here in South Asia. The overwhelming response generated by the first SAARC Cultural Festival and the first SAARC Youth Camp reflects the latent desire for such exchanges.

We are excited about the establishment of the South Asian University. The land for the University in New Delhi has been acquired and a Project Office has been set up. When the University becomes operational in 2010, it will cater to 5000 students, and will create a pool of world-class scientists, technologists and thinkers. When they go out into the world, they will represent not just their respective countries but all of South Asia.

To be a dynamic and responsive body, SAARC must identify and address new challenges as they emerge. The unprecedented increase in oil and food prices risks jeopardizing our developmental gains.

SAARC must make its voice heard in the councils of the world to ensure that there is an effective global response that protects the interests of oil consuming countries. We should also pool our resources to tap renewable sources such as solar energy, hydropower and wind energy, all of which South Asia has in abundance.

The establishment of the SAARC Food Bank in 2007 was an extremely forward looking decision. In the context of the global food crisis today, this decision stands out as an example of our foresight and our ability to help ourselves. We should now move forward to an early ratification of the Intergovernmental Agreement by all the Member States.

We in India are acutely conscious that we need a Second Green Revolution. The countries of South Asia need to work towards a collective response that leads to a quantum leap in agricultural productivity, food grain output and farm incomes so that the spectre of food shortages and hunger vanishes from our region.

India will actively work with Member States to realise the several proposals that have been made, including greater exchange of knowledge and experience on breeding livestock, improvement in yields of protein rich pulses and in adoption of modern post-harvest technologies.

We are inheritors and trustees of one of the most vulnerable ecosystems in the world. It is most encouraging that our Ministers have finalised a SAARC Action Plan on Climate Change, which recognizes that rapid development provides the best form of adaptation.

India has recently launched a National Action Plan on Climate Change, and we will be more than willing to share experiences. There are a number of areas in this Plan where we need to cooperate with SAARC member countries such as in our mission on sustaining the Himalayan ecosystem, in our plans for protection of coastal areas, in disaster management strategies and programmes, early warning systems and collaborative research on climate modeling. SAARC already has projects on water harvesting and afforestation but we all need to do much more in these vital areas.

I am confident that under the able leadership of Sri Lanka, we will continue to move these initiatives forward. In recent years we have shifted our focus from declarations to action and implementation, and I am happy to note, this has begun to show results. As we consolidate, prioritize and rationalize our activities, we will bring closer to the doorsteps of our people the benefits of SAARC.

India stands ready to play her part in the evolution of a stable, vibrant, and prosperous South Asia. I am optimistic about our collective future, and I am confident that the best is yet to come.

(*Source:* http://www.saarc-sec.org/)

## Address by Mr. Maumoon Abdul Gayoom President of the Republic of Maldives at the 15th SAARC Summit

August 2, 2008

*Mr. Maumoon Abdul Gayoom, President of the Republic of Maldives stated that global climate change policies are still driven more by economic rationale rather than the important issue of human security. He applauded the efforts made by the SAARC Ministerial Meeting on Climate Change, which he considered as a development in the right direction. He stated that the SAARC Food Bank proposed at the 14th Summit in New Delhi would be a practical instrument that would help meet the challenges of food scarcity .He also touched upon the SAARC Convention on Mutual Assistance in Criminal Matters which he stated would complement the efforts of the law enforcement agencies for greater regional cooperation in the fight against terrorism. He emphasized that introduction of the Social Charter and the SAARC Development Fund, were effective conduits for enhancing people to people ties.*

I thank you, Mr. President, and the government and people of Sri Lanka for the warm welcome and generous hospitality, and the excellent arrangements made for me, my wife and members of my delegation since our arrival in Colombo.

It is of great significance that the Fifteenth SAARC Summit is being held in Sri Lanka to coincide with the proud milestone of the country's sixtieth anniversary of Independence. I, therefore, take this opportunity to extend our best wishes of the occasion to you, Mr. President, and to the Government and people of Sri Lanka.

May I also congratulate you, Mr. Chairman, for your unanimous election to preside over this 15th SAARC Summit. You have taken over the reins of our Association at a time when serious challenges are posed to the progress and prosperity of our region, because of escalating food and energy prices. I am, nevertheless, confident that our collective efforts under your able chairmanship shall be able to overcome these challenges. would also like to express my deep appreciation to the Prime Minister of India, Dr. Manmohan Singh, for the exemplary manner in which he has presided over our Association during the past year. The Maldives extends a warm welcome to observer delegations from China, the European Union, Republic of Korea, Japan, Mauritius and the United States. In addition, today we welcome Myanmar and Australia as new observer states into the SAARC family. Before proceeding further, I would like to extend my congratulations to the new SAARC Secretary-General, Dr. Sheel Kant Sharma, on assuming his important responsibilities.

Over the course of the past twenty three years, we have deliberated, at great length, on how SAARC could be used as a vehicle for ensuring greater peace, progress and prosperity for the people of South Asia. I am pleased that over the last two Summits we embarked on a dedicated mission to make good on our word to make SAARC an effective delivery machine for this purpose. At this Summit, we should resolve to accelerate and expand this process.

Indeed, the theme for this year's Summit, "Partnership for the People of SMRC", could not have been more timely, as the challenges of our times demand an increased focus on the needs and aspirations of our peoples. We should, in short, give consideration to the human dimension of the strategic decisions we make at these forums. Of the many challenges facing us, none is more urgent or has more capacity for calamity than global climate change. One cannot overemphasize the adverse effects that climate change has on fundamental human rights such as the right to life, shelter and a sustainable livelihood.

Science tells us that climate change, if left unmitigated, will have catastrophic consequences for many of us. Paradoxically, global climate change policies are still driven more by economic rationale rather than the all-too important issue of human security. However, I am heartened to note that the recently concluded SAARC Ministerial Meeting on Climate Change is a development in the right direction. The SAARC Environment Ministers recognized that ours is the most vulnerable region in the world to climate change, putting the livelihood of our people at serious risk. I believe, therefore, that our policy decisions must reflect the social and human rights implications of climate change.

Today, the role and capacity of Asian economies have changed considerably. The exponential growth of the region's population, combined with greater purchasing power owed to economic progress has increased pressure on already inflated food prices. Unfortunately, the fact remains that, increased food prices affect the most vulnerable and poor sections of our populations. The SAARC Food Bank proposed at the 14th Summit in New Delhi would be a practical instrument that will help meet the challenges of food scarcity and lay the foundations for greater food security in the region. Early ratification and operationalization of the Food Bank is, therefore, vital for the sustainable supply of essential food items in the region.

Strategies are also required for efficient utilization and allocation of limited natural resources in the regions. Indeed, innovative ideas supported by cutting-edge research will enable us to ensure the welfare of the more than 1.4 billion people living in the region. The other unintended consequence of rapid economic growth in the South Asian region is the high demand for energy, bringing with it a host of challenges, most notably contributing to an unprecedented rise in global oil prices. The question remains as to how we can address the energy crisis without hindering growth and prosperity of Member States. I propose four measures to remedy this problem. First, we need to greatly ease our reliance on fossil fuels and set tangible targets to harness sustainable alternative energy resources.

Second, we need to introduce national policies, including trade reforms, aimed at more sustainable and efficient energy consumption. Third, we should look into developing greater cooperation with other economic partners such as the countries of the ASEAN bloc. Fourth, and most importantly, economic activity must be supported by a desire to protect and sustain the natural environment. SAARC Member States want to live together in harmony and peace. I believe, therefore, it is our most important duty to undertake all efforts to strengthen peace and stability in the region and our collective efforts to combating the scourge of terrorism. The SAARC Convention on Mutual Assistance in Criminal Matters will complement the efforts of the law enforcement agencies for greater regional cooperation in the fight against terrorism.

Since its establishment, the SAARC community has generally been progressing in the right direction with major regional cooperation in economic and trade related activities. Looking back, regional economic integration could have gone faster and further. Even today, we need more urgent action to push economic integration forward; otherwise, our region may not stay abreast of global trends. The way forward IS to make deliberate attempts to include other building blocks for increased regional integration via people-to-people contact and interactions at various levels. Two fine examples are the introduction of the Social Charter and the SAARC Development Fund.

The Social Charter must be used as an effective vehicle in ensuring that the economic, social and political benefits reaped are felt across the full spectrum of our societies. Twenty-three years ago, the nations of South Asia made a promise to themselves. Our dream, based on our common history and geographical proximity, was to build the good society where harmony and progress would prevail. While we have made huge strides in realizing this ideal, there is much that still needs to be done. Our task now is to identify such real terms and building blocks that need to be put in place for the SAARC community to flourish. We must not rest easy with the belief that this process is inevitable; but must strive to ensure that the achievements are irreversible. Our determination, and our effort, must embody the resolve that exists amongst our member countries to realize our common future together.

(*Source*: http://www.saarc-sec.org/)

## Statement by the Mr. Girija Prasad Koirala, Prime Minister of Nepal at the 15th SAARC Summit

August 02, 2008

*Mr Girija Prasad Koirala in his statement at the fifteenth SAARC summit stated that SAARC while focusing on inclusive growth should focus on alleviating poverty and ensuring employment opportunities to the youths throughout the region. He stated that while the price escalation of fuels had created problems to sustain economic growth much needed to promote welfare of the people of South Asia, the rise in food price had put questions on the very livelihood of the people. He stated that since the region suffered from energy deficit, there was a need for increased efficiency in energy use and collective efforts in conservation of energy resources. He emphasized that Nepal was ready to utilize the rich hydropower potentials of the country for equitable benefits in the neighborhood. Mr Koirala welcomed the establishment of the SAARC Development Fund, which, he noted could help initiating the process of regional and sub-regional projects related to social, economic and infrastructure development. Mr Koirala emphasized the need for collective actions to promote collective prosperity.*

It is indeed a privilege for me to be here in the historic city of Colombo to participate in the 15th SAARC Summit. On behalf of the Nepalese delegation and on my own, I would like to extend our sincere gratitude to the Government and the people of Democratic Socialist Republic of Sri Lanka for the warm reception and cordial hospitality.

I would like to congratulate His Excellency Mr. Mahinda Rajpaksa, President of Sri Lanka on his election to the Chair and assure him that my delegation reposes full confidence and trust on his leadership and wisdom to steer the deliberations to a successful conclusion. I would also like to congratulate Sri Lanka on the Diamond Jubilce Celebration of its independence this year. I believe that under the able leadership of the new Chair, SAARC would take further momentum in fulfilling its noble objectives as enshrined in the Charter, while proving its relevance to the people by making them capable to meet the new challenges. I would also like to take this opportunity to express our sincere thanks to India, Immediate Past Chair, for the active leadership role it played during the last year. I would also like to record our appreciation for the committed leadership of the Secretary General and the dedication and hard work of his team.

As we stand here to deliberate on the issues of regional integration and collective action within an Association that covers a quarter of the humanity of the world, we have to do so against the formidable challenges we are confronted with. They are of long term and short term in nature. While promoting an inclusive growth, we should focus ourselves on alleviating poverty, and ensuring employment opportunities to the youths throughout the region. Now, this has to be looked at against the background of an unprecedented rise in the prices of hydrocarbon fuels and food. Whereas the price escalation of fuels has created problems to sustain economic growth needed to promote welfare of the people of South Asia, the rise in food price has put questions on the very livelihood of our people. Our vulnerability to these shocks is more than that of many other countries. These daunting challenges demand that poverty reduction efforts in South Asia should have a comprehensive approach and be focused and result-oriented.

Since our region suffers from energy deficit, we need increased efficiency in our energy use and collective efforts in conservation of energy resources. We must immediately take strategic steps for regional energy connectivity and energy trade for exploitation and use of all energy resources available in the region, while ensuring universal access to commercial fuels. Nepal is ready to utilize the rich hydropower potentials of the country for equitable benefits in the neighborhood. Moreover, we feel that we need to develop a regional strategy for management of waters for all different kinds of uses in the region in view of the increasing problem of water scarcity faced by the people in the region.

The adverse environmental changes induced by climate change is calling on sustainable and judicious use of non-renewable resources and a commitment to an increased use of renewable sources of energy such as hydropower. While there is a larger responsibility of the economically advanced countries to address the problems of global climate change, we must work with a united position to ensure increased resource flow and technology transfer to enhance our capacity in Clean Development Mechanism.

We welcome the preparation for establishment of SMRC Development Fund, which, I believe, will initiate the process of funding regional and sub-regional projects in the areas of social, economic and infrastructure development. From the pilot stage of projects implementation, we need to ensure proper matching of fundingrequirements in our enormous priority areas with the actual availability of funds for their effective implementation. We should make efforts to tap the growing strength of the private sector of the region in getting involved in projects under pUblic-private partnership scheme and the appropriate involvement of the international and regional financial organizations in consonance with the SAARC objectives and principles

Implementation of SAFTA is our first major step towards the arduous course of deeper integration of economies. We must always ask how much benefit our people are getting from this joint effort and how much trade expansion it has fostered. I see more role and responsibility of all of us to make SAFT A an engine of growth in South Asia. At the same time, I request all member countries to be responsive to overcoming the hardships and capacity constraints suffered by LDCs like Nepal in a bid to translate into action the provisions envisaged under SAFTA Agreement. We are in favour of including Trade in Services under SAFT A and implementing all agreements and measures designed to facilitate intra-regional trade as early as possible.

The emphasis on connectivity of the South Asian peoples, places, economies and infrastructure must be reiterated with firmer resolve so that we can implement prioritized projects identified for achievement of these goals. As a landlocked country, we attach importance to improvement of multi-modal transport and transit infrastructure of the region, and proper facilitation of transport and transit in order to lower the cost of doing business and enhancing efficiency and effectiveness of our trade.

Growing disparity between the haves and have-nots is putting enormous stress on social harmony, peace and security in several parts of South Asia. In addressing this problem, we are all aware that we have to make the socio-economic and political development processes more people-centered, inclusive and based on equality and justice. The social sector issues of South Asia are too many as any other issues. But I think the most important ones at hand are combating terrorism in all its forms and manifestations, preventing and controlling the use of narcotic drugs and psychotropic substances, controlling other transnational crimes and addressing the issues of women and children, including the elimination of worst forms of violence against them. The existing conventions in the social sector will prove their worth if they are backed by enabling national legislations and the mechanisms to address these issues. They have to be promoted in a more harmonized way by, among other things, involving the civil society organizations and the private sector in the process.

We in Nepal have made a commitment to bringing all social classes, ethnic groups, and geographic regions into the national mainstream while putting an end to the decade old conflict through the successive consolidation of peace process. Our main priority is how to ensure inclusiveness of the social class, gender and peoples living in various geographic areas in the governance of the country in order to enable them to shape their own destiny. Following the successful Constituent Assembly elections of April 10, 2008, the country is pursuing the path of socio-economic and political transformation process in an attempt to bring the peace process to a logical conclusion and realize the dream of making a new Nepal based on democratic ideals, equality, justice and inclusive progress.

We have built strong bonds of trust and fraternity within SAARC since its establishment 23 years ago. We believe in collective actions to promote collective prosperity. We must consolidate our work to bring this common vision into reality.

This is a propitious time to attain our objectives, and they are indispensable to take our region to a new height. This is the promise that we have made to the people and we must deliver. And looking at the long-term perspectives, we hold the view that we have no other option than to synergize all our efforts, based on the proven complementarities of South Asia, to realize the noble objectives of SAARC.

(*Source*: http://www.saarc-sec.org/)

## Address of the Prime Minister of Pakistan, Syed Yousuf Raza Gilani at the 15th SAARC Summit

August 2, 2008

*The Prime Minister stated that SAARC Charter was a lynchpin to promote the welfare of the people of South Asia. He pointed that the theme of the summit "Partnership for Growth for our People" was a welcome reminder of the joint responsibility of South Asian neighbours to place people at the center of the SAARC process. He emphasized that South Asia must also take steps to ensure full implementation of the SAARC Social Charter and the SAARC Conventions on Women and Children. Pakistan's premier noted that economic development of South Asia was contingent upon assured and inexpensive availability of energy and therefore the region's indigenous energy potential, particularly solar, wind, biomass and hydro energy should be harnessed. He pointed out that there was a need to envisage a network of intra-regional and trans-regional oil and gas pipelines and that project-based cooperation under SAARC should be encouraged. He also noted that SAARC Observers and other international development institutions should be involved in such efforts. The Prime Minister emphasized the need to place people at the center of the SAARC process.*

It is a great honour for me to represent the Islamic Republic of Pakistan at the fifteenth SAARC Summit. I wish to congratulate you, Mr. President, on your assumption of the office of the Chairperson of SAARC. We are confident that under your dynamic leadership, SAARC will move rapidly towards realization of its cherished goals. I assure you of Pakistan's full support to your endeavours in this direction.

We are thankful to the people and the Government of Sri Lanka for the warm welcome and the gracious hospitality extended to us since our arrival in this beautiful city.

I avail myself of this opportunity to express our deep gratitude to His Excellency Dr. Manmohan Singh, the Prime Minister of India, for providing excellent leadership to SAARC during the last one year.

I would also like to thank the Secretary General, His Excellency Dr. Sheel Kant Sharma, and his dedicated team, for their important contribution to the preparatory work of the Summit.

SAARC Charter bestows upon us the onerous responsibility to promote the welfare of the people of South Asia. The theme of the Summit "Partnership for growth for our people" is a welcome reminder of our joint responsibility to place people at the center of the SAARC process. No society can realize its full potential without improving the socio-economic conditions of its people.

We must follow a comprehensive approach, paying urgent attention to poverty alleviation. We must also take steps to ensure full implementation of the SAARC Social Charter and the SAARC Conventions on Women and Children.

Economic development of South Asia is contingent upon assured and inexpensive availability of energy. The contemporary global fossil fuel crisis has exacerbated the need for the South Asia region to look for alternate energy sources. We must harness region's indigenous energy potential, particularly solar, wind, biomass and hydro energy. We should also envisage a net-work of intra-regional and trans-regional oil and gas pipelines, Within SAARC, an enabling environment for regional energy cooperation can be facilitated by concluding a regional framework agreement on energy cooperation.

Humankind lives here. We have a vast pool of talent. We have fertile lands and developed irrigation systems. Our societies are agrarian. We export agro based products to the world. Yet, the region faces food shortages from time to time. Sadly, the region has to look to the outside world for its food security. We must address this issue on priority. We should share and learn from best practices in the region and beyond, modernize our irrigation systems, use appropriate technology, and expand our agricultural research and resource base.

The contemporary global food crisis has underscored the need for SAARC countries to develop a comprehensive regional strategy to ensure food security. This is our common responsibility to the people of South Asia. Together with other Asian countries, we should consider launching a Greater Asia Food Security Programme.

Pakistan supports greater regional economic cooperation. In the last two decades, SAARC has made considerable progress in this area, including SAFTA. We must enable these arrangements to deliver real dividends and create a win-win situation for all. Towards this end, a number of steps can be taken including trade facilitation measures, elimination of non-tariff barriers, reduction of sensitive lists of member states, and strengthening of the existing transportation and communication links across the region.

Closer cooperation in the area of finance and banking is essential to promote economic and commercial cooperation in the region. Under the mechanism of SAARC finance, the Governors of the Central Banks of the Member States can make solid contribution to improve macro-economic policy coordination. The SAARC Development Fund (SDF) could underwrite financial support for important development projects of mutual benefit to SAARC members.

Historically, the arteries of transport and communications have enriched this region. As we attempt to connect our region anew, a people-centered approach can ensure the success of our endeavours.

The rich civilizational and cultural heritage of the people of South Asia is our shared pride. Our arts and craft, cultural traditions, diverse landscape, and magnificent historical monuments are our invaluable assets" We must give priority to promoting tourism, including religious and third country tourism, in our region.

Another pressing issue for SAARC is to enhance cooperation in the field of environment. In this regard, the Dhaka Declaration of the SAARC Environment Ministers is a welcome step. We must take appropriate measures to preserve our environment, including the glaciers of Himalayas and Karakorum, which are the largest source of fresh water in the region.

We must also encourage a move towards project-based cooperation under SAARC. The focus should be on implementing regional and sub-regional projects in the agreed priority areas. Each Member State could take one or two projects as "lead country". We may also involve SAARC Observers and other international development institutions in these efforts. Public-private sector collaboration should also be another venue to achieve our development objectives.

The world is facing today the menace of extremism and terrorism, which has challenged our entire value system and impacted our socio-economic development. Though Pakistan has suffered the most, terrorism afflicts all countries of our region. It is our joint responsibility to rid our region of this scourge. We need to fight terrorism individually as well as collectively. The forthcoming meetings of the SAARC Police Chiefs and Home/Interior Ministers in Islamabad later this year should focus on strengthening regional cooperation against terrorism. We welcome the finalization of the text of the SAARC Convention on Mutual Assistance in Criminal Matters.

In an interdependent, fast globalizing world, no regional grouping can hope to function in isolation. SAARC should develop positive links with the adjoining regions and beyond. We must adopt an inclusive approach. We should be open to mutually beneficial interactions, especially with our larger Asian neighbourhood. Such linkages and interdependencies would create a win-win support system.

I take this opportunity to extend a very warm welcome to the representatives of the SAARC Observers present here in this meeting. We look forward to their valued contribution towards SAARC programmes, activities and projects. We also welcome the interest expressed by Australia and Myanmar to be associated with our organization as Observers.

As we seek to evolve modalities to associate observers with the work of the Organization, we should consider the option of granting "dialogue partnership" status to those Observer states which wish to deepen their relationship with SAARC for mutual benefits.

SAARC has to its credit some notable achievements. We can justifiably take pride in the progress we have made thus far. However, we cannot be complacent. We must recognize in all candidness that the gap between the promise of SAARC and the reality of its accomplishment remains wide. We need concerted efforts to build on areas of convergence. Lets minimize divergences and augment complementarities for the greater good of the people of this region. Pakistan for its part will spare no effort to translate the vision of the SAARC Charter into a reality.

Greater economic integration is inextricably linked to the creation of requisite political climate of peace and stability. SAARC meetings provide a good opportunity not only to deepen trust and understanding but also create the enabling environment for resolution of political disputes and outstanding Issues. We believe that the imperatives of South Asia's socio-economic development demand greater political commitment to build on convergences and resolve our differences.

Pakistan and India are engaged in a peace process. Since the induction of elected government in Pakistan, the peace process has registered noteworthy progress. Success of the process will augur well for the region and SAARC.

It is time to place people at the center of the SAARC processes. Our people are our greatest strength. If SAARC becomes relevant to the lives of our people, we could be assured of our success.

As we look ahead, let the Colombo Summit be remembered as the turning point in SAARC's history. Let this Summit infuse new dynamism in SAARC. Let us pledge to lay a solid foundation of mutual cooperation and trust.

I am confident that the Colombo Summit would provide a fresh impetus to reinvigorating regional cooperation in South Asia.

(*Source*: http://www.saarc-sec.org/)

## Address by His Excellency President Mahinda Rajapaksa at the inaugural Session of the 15th SAARC Summit

August 2, 2008

*The Sri Lankan President in his address at the fifteenth SAARC summit drew attention to the Delhi Summit, which had launched SAARC as a partnership for prosperity of the people. He stated that the importance of connectivity as a powerful engine of growth, needed attention. The President emphasized that South Asia's continued progress in economic and social development was a matter of great satisfaction to Sri Lanka. In context to the rising scourge of terrorism, the President highlighted the importance of intelligence sharing. He also urged the SAARC countries to use existing mechanisms such as the SAARC Food Bank and the SAARC Development Fund persuading them for shared research in the areas with potential for local technologies in harnessing renewable energy.*

I am honoured and privileged to welcome you to Colombo for this fifteenth SAARC Summit.

Your presence in our country adds to the historic importance of this year for us. This year, our nation celebrates the sixtieth Anniversary of our being freed from the yoke of colonial rule. Most of the nations of our region share with us the common heritage of colonial dominance and struggle for freedom to restore our national dignity and honour.

I consider it my duty on this occasion to express on behalf of all Member States of SAARC, our deep appreciation for the dynamic leadership that India has provided to this region and to SAARC since the fourteenth SAARC Summit in New Delhi.

I would also take this opportunity to welcome and extend best wishes to the new Secretary General of SAARC, Dr. Sheel Kant Sharma, while also expressing our appreciation to his predecessor, Mr. Chenkyab Dorji and the SAARC Secretariat for their dedicated and invaluable work in preparation for this Summit.

This Colombo Summit takes place amidst a background of significant political events and major international issues, such as food and fuel insecurity and degradation of the environment. It is our responsibility as leaders and representatives of our peoples to give tangible expression to the SAARC Charter objective of promoting the welfare and improving the quality of life of our peoples, which remains at the core of all our common endeavours.

The Delhi Summit launched SAARC as a Partnership for Prosperity, for the Prosperity of Our People, identifying the importance of connectivity as a powerful engine of growth. Continuity, consistency and coordination are all vital to have the desired practical effect towards our goal of regional economic integration.

However, we must ensure that SAARC becomes more meaningful to all our people. Therefore, throughout the ensuing year we have to give SAARC a truly people-centred focus through all its programmes and mechanisms. It is then that SAARC can become the robust Partnership for Growth for all our people.

South Asia's continued progress in economic and social development is a matter of great satisfaction to me. Unemployment in our country, as well as in the region, has reached historic low levels leading to declines in overall poverty. South Asia is no more the poverty trough of the world, although we have yet to eradicate poverty from our midst.

Yet, for growth to be sustainable, its benefits must be evenly distributed, pro-poor strategies must be put into place, and the rural populations that make up the vast majorities in all our countries, must be empowered ensuring gender equality.

The SAARC Social Charter and our shared experiences and best practices, already provide a solid foundation to further strengthen empowerment of the rural people. In our own country, the Policy Vision of the Mahinda Chintana, my electoral pledge to the people of Sri Lanka, addresses this issue and seeks to transform current challenges into opportunities for the upliftment of the rural people.

It is a matter of satisfaction that we are progressively inaugurating, in each of our countries, SAARC villages as visible examples of our collective commitment to rural uplift. The most recent such village was opened on 27th July this year in Nawalapitiya, in the central hill region of Sri Lanka.

As we meet today, most countries of our region are faced with the curse of terrorism that threatens the peace and stability that is needed so much for the forward march of our people. No country in the SAARC region has been spared of this plague. We need to redouble our efforts for collective action to combat terrorism in all its forms and manifestations. It is important to remember the element of interdependence which is crucial for a durable peace and the protection of democratic values in the region.

We must ensure strengthening regional legal mechanisms and intensifying intelligence sharing, in order to secure the region's collective prosperity, peace and stability. Further, I would strongly suggest that in-depth studies are carried out to understand the social impact of this menace. Sri Lanka has seen the benefits of such cooperation in combating the terrorism in our midst and hopefully eradicating it sooner, than many once expected.

My gratitude must go to all our regional partners and our many friends from other quarters that have cooperated with us in this matter. In my view it is also necessary that we, as a region, endeavour to set right the many wrong impressions that exist, or are promoted elsewhere, about the actions that are imperative to protect our people and societies from the brutalities of terrorism. Terrorism anywhere is terrorism and there are no good terrorists or bad terrorists.

Asia's economic surge provides our region with manifold opportunities. We are on the threshold of a new age the Age of Asia with South Asia being an important part of it, not only in numbers but also in skills and the strength of growing economies. Today, Asia is the economic power house of the world.

In order to ensure that we in the SAARC provide the necessary thrust for Asia's economic surge, I would once again promote the idea of SAARC intensifying to the maximum possible its regional economic and trade integration. We have to set in motion a process of adopting a single currency in the region. Undoubtedly, full implementation of the SAFTA and other follow up measures will greatly facilitate the realisation of this vision. Our region also should assume a leadership role in the reform of Multilateral Financial Institutions.

Today, as never before we are confronted with the global issues of food and energy insecurity and climate change. Food prices in international markets have increased by 54 percent in the past year alone. World oil prices have increased by 300 percent over the past four years. These are the statistics of near despair. Yet, I believe that we need not despair.

I propose that we seize this challenge and transform it into opportunity, with focus on agriculture, on food security that is largely based on home grown food; that we look at realistic policies on nutrition, at strategies for development that are least dependent on the forces of speculation and markets that have no feel for the people.

We must productively use existing mechanisms such as the SAARC Food Bank and the SAARC Development Fund, for the development of strategic buffer stocks of our staple foods. Food security is vital because of its impact on all sectors of national life. It is today recognised as an essential condition for economic and political stability.

We also need to act fast on meeting the energy crunch. There is the necessity to accelerate our plans for South Asian energy sharing. Knowing that we have to depend on fossil fuels for many more decades to come, we must explore the use of other sources of energy that will take us out of the deadly grip of the oil well. However, pursuit on Bio-fuels must not be at the cost of food crops or arable land.

To take the next leap from fossil fuels to renewable energy, we have to move with speed on harnessing the Sun, the Sea, and the Wind resources that all of our countries have in plenty. South Asia must look at shared research in the areas with potential for local technologies in harnessing renewable energy.

As we grapple with the issues of food and fuel security, we will also need to address as a matter of priority, the looming water deficit in the region. King Parakramabahu, an ancient ruler of Sri Lanka, advised the people not to allow a single drop of water to flow into the sea without first being of use to the people. We must bring a new focus on conservation of water resources to ensure that South Asia would be the best watered region in the world.

Asia's evolution has been founded on ancient traditions of environmental sustainability, integrating environmental responsibility with cultural and religious values. We should go back to the tradition of sharing that sustained our people in the past, shedding the tradition of exploitation of nature that came to us from our former conquerors.

Throughout our region there is increasing movement from the village to the city, resulting in degradation of the environment and human dignity. Let us therefore commit ourselves to upgrade village housing and facilities, through a sound mix of traditional construction methods and material with modern technology, to discourage people from moving out of the villages. In the cities, we need to further evolve models of urban design and housing construction that strengthen the inherited spirit of social community common to all our societies.

The Delhi Summit last year laid stress on connectivity. Today, we find that with the advances of communications technology, good connectivity is not very far from our people. Although the numbers of mobile phone users in South Asia are rapidly increasing yet, our people remain distanced through the barrier of tariffs. I, therefore, propose that we actively promote a reduced tariff for IDD calls within the South Asian region to bring our people much closer, much sooner.

We, in South Asia share a rich and common heritage, a heritage of understanding and of tolerance, a heritage that respects learning and wisdom, and takes pride in sharing the bounties of nature. But for this great heritage that transcends differences and upholds the value of a shared purpose and existence, our diverse cultures, languages and religious traditions could have made us the most divided region in the world. Instead, by and large we see a great harmony among our peoples.

In my own country, the impact of this common heritage is best seen today in what we have achieved in the East, where we have defeated terrorism, restored democracy, elected a Chief Minister from a minority community who was a former child soldier, and, most of all, where the Sinhalese, Tamil and Muslim communities live together, work together, and together seek the common goals of progress and prosperity. This indeed is a unique transformation within a short span of one year. This is my deep desire for the people in the North as well.

In conclusion ay I say that there must be a spirit of large heartedness by all including the stronger and wealthier nations, when some of these crucial issues are addressed. It is my fervent hope that the Colombo Summit will enable our dialogue with the Observer States to broaden into a process for constructive consultations, and project related cooperation in agreed areas. I have no doubt that together we can make our common endeavours, this Partnership, succeed for the benefit of all our peoples.

(*Source*: http://www.saarc-sec.org/)

## Bay of Bengal Initiative for Multi-Sectoral Technical and Economic Cooperation, Second BIMSTEC Summit Declaration

November 13, 2008

*The Chief Adviser of the People's Republic of Bangladesh, the Prime Minister of the Kingdom of Bhutan, the Prime Minister of the Republic of India, the Prime Minister of the Union of Myanmar, the Prime Minister of the Republic of Nepal, the President of the Democratic Socialist Republic of Sri Lanka and the Prime Minister of the Kingdom of Thailand met in New Delhi, on November 13, 2008 for the Second BIMSTEC Summit Meeting. The leaders emphasized on the need for developing closer ties between the countries in order to facilitate economic and social development and demanded concerted regional effort to respond to economic, social and environmental challenges. The countries outlined common challenges posed to the BIMSTEC countries like terrorism and transnational crimes and lauded the efforts made on the negotiations of the Agreement on Trade in Goods with agreed General Rules of Origin and Product Specific Rules under the BIMSTEC Free Trade Area. The countries also took note of the establishment of the BIMSTEC Energy Centre in India. Environment, disaster management and connectivity were some other issues raised by the leaders as prospective areas of cooperation.*

We, the Chief Adviser of the People's Republic of Bangladesh, the Prime Minister of the Kingdom of Bhutan, the Prime Minister of the Republic of India,, the Prime Minister of the Union of Myanmar, the Prime Minister of the Republic of Nepal, the President of the Democratic Socialist Republic of Sri Lanka and the Prime Minister of the Kingdom of Thailand met in New Delhi, India on November 13, 2008 for the Second BIMSTEC Summit Meeting;

**Recognising** that with our geographical contiguity, abundant natural and human resources as well as rich historical and cultural heritage, BIMSTEC Member States have great potential for economic and social development which provides a sound basis for mutually beneficial cooperation,

**Acknowledging** that our economies and societies have become increasingly inter-linked and inter-dependent

**Realizing** that globalization has brought about increased opportunity for economic and social development, and that increasing complexity of economic, social and environmental challenges facing the world highlights the need for concerted regional effort to respond to these challenges.

**Noting** the progress made in promoting and strengthening active collaboration and mutual assistance in the economic, social, technical and scientific fields for attaining the purposes and objectives of BIMSTEC,

**Recognizing** that the recent extraordinary volatility in fuel and food prices not only puts our resources and growth prospects under pressure, but also hits hardest the poorest sections of our population calling for timely and effective responses,

**Recognizing** the adverse impact of climate change on the lives and livelihoods of our populations and the serious threat it poses to our region,

**Convinced** that through our close cooperation we can maximize the potential of our capabilities and resource endowments for economic and social development of our states and peoples,

**Recognizing** the threat that terrorism poses to peace, stability and economic progress in the region, emphasize the need for close cooperation in combating all forms of terrorism and transnational crimes,

**Reiterating** our commitment to BIMSTEC as a regional cooperation grouping,

Do hereby:-

**Underscore** our resolve to abide by the founding objectives and principles of BIMSTEC.

Take note with satisfaction of the progress of our cooperation in the energy sector and in the establishment of the BIMSTEC Energy Centre in India.

Take note with satisfaction of the progress and substantive outcome of our cooperation in the environment and disaster management sector and in the establishment of the BIMSTEC Weather and Climate Centre in India. Take note with satisfaction of the progress made in the establishment of the BIMSTEC Cultural Industries Commission and the BIMSTEC Cultural Industries Observatory in Bhutan. Take note with satisfaction of the finalization of the BIMSTEC Convention on Combating International Terrorism, Transnational Organized Crime and Illicit Drug Trafficking.

**Take note** with satisfaction of the progress made on the negotiations of the Agreement on Trade in Goods with agreed General Rules of Origin and Product Specific Rules under the BIMSTEC Free Trade Area.

**Direct** the BIMSTEC Trade Negotiating Committee to conclude the negotiations on Trade in Goods as soon as possible, and to continue its efforts for Agreements on Services and Investments.

**Agree** that improved transportation and communication linkages and greater connectivity between our Member States is an important element for the BIMSTEC process that will lead to direct benefits to our peoples through increased trade and investment, tourism, and people-to-people contacts. In this regard, we acknowledge and note the BIMSTEC Transport Infrastructure and Logistics Study (BTILS) conducted by the ADB in association with the BIMSTEC Member States as an important first step in identifying the bottlenecks and suggesting ways to overcome them.

**Agree** to harness the region's natural, cultural and historical endowments in order to enhance intra-BIMSTEC tourism as well as tourism from other countries.

**Agree** to continue our cooperation in the area of energy and decide to hold the second BIMSTEC Energy Ministers' Conference in Thailand in 2009.

**Agree to** cooperate in expanding the technology base of Member States through collaborations and partnerships targeted towards micro, small and medium scale enterprises and decide to establish a BIMSTEC Technology Transfer/Exchange Facility in Sri Lanka.

**Agree** to continue cooperation for the sustainable use of marine resources through effective conservation and management of resources in the Bay of Bengal and decide to include inland fisheries in the scope of cooperation in this area.

**Agree** to continue and strengthen our cooperation on poverty alleviation in the context of ensuring food security for the vulnerable people in the region and decide to hold the second BIMSTEC Ministerial Conference on Poverty Alleviation in Nepal in 2009 and to establish a BIMSTEC Poverty Alleviation Centre in Bangladesh.

**Agree** to expand cooperation in culture to include cultural values, diversity and heritage and decide to support the establishment of the BIMSTEC Cultural Industries Commission and BIMSTEC Cultural Industries Observatory in Bhutan.

**Agree** to continue cooperation in the field of agriculture and decide to initiate short and long term joint research programmes to increase productivity and yields in our region.

**Agree** to continue our collective efforts to combat public health threats from emerging and re-emerging infectious diseases as well as to cooperate in the area of traditional medicine by setting up a BIMSTEC Network of National Centres of Coordination in Traditional Medicine.

**Agree** to augment our efforts to further promote people-to-people contacts among our States and decide that India will take the lead to establish a

BIMSTEC Network of Policy Think Tanks.

**Agree** to share experience and enhance collaborative efforts to jointly face the current global financial crisis, while taking into account the needs of the vulnerable sections of the society.

**Agree** to intensify our efforts to strengthen cooperation in all areas of activities within the framework of BIMSTEC so as to promote regional cooperation and cohesion.

**Agree** to establish an institutional structure to serve as a focal point for coordination and to follow up on decisions taken by BIMSTEC Summits,

Ministerial Conferences and other official meetings, and decide to establish a Permanent Secretariat for BIMSTEC.

We, the leaders from Bangladesh, Bhutan, Myanmar, Nepal, Sri Lanka and Thailand, express our appreciation to the Government of India for its hospitality and for the arrangements made for the Summit.

(*Source*:http://www.bimstec.org/2ndBimstecSummit_pdf/2nd_BIMSTEC_Summit_Declaration%5B1%5D.pdf)

## Opening Remarks of Hon. Dr. Manmohan Singh, Prime Minister of India at the 2nd BIMSTEC Summit, New Delhi

13 November, 2008

*Dr Manmohan Singh at the 2nd BIMSTEC Summit at New Delhi emphasized the importance of BIMSTEC stating that the combined GDP of the BIMSTEC countries had increased two and a half times and reached 1.7 trillion US dollars in the past ten years. He pointed out that as new transnational challenges had emerged BIMSTEC summit provided an opportunity to provide a new strategic thrust to respond to these growing challenges. The Indian premier pointed out that people to people contacts should be one of the priority overarching goals with an emphasis on areas such as education and tourism.*

"It is my great honour to welcome all of you for the Second BIMSTEC Summit in New Delhi. I would like to thank the Government of Thailand for their efforts in preserving the momentum of our organization.

BIMSTEC is an opportunity we should seize together. Your presence here today is an indication of our political will and commitment to do so. In the past ten years, our combined GDP increased two and a half times to reach 1.7 trillion US dollars. There is much greater connectivity between us, more trade and investment and more people to people exchanges. The winds of democracy have swept across our countries.

Globalisation and economic interdependence offer opportunities for growth and prosperity but also have their downside, as the recent international economic and financial crisis has amply shown. Regional integration has increased dramatically. ASEAN Summits are now held annually.

The East Asian Summit process has begun. SAARC has been revitalized. In this period, new trans-national challenges have emerged. Climate Change, energy and food security threaten our development efforts. Terrorism and threats from the sea continue to challenge the authority of the state. This Summit provides an opportunity for us to give a new strategic thrust to BIMSTEC in the background of these changes.

There are a few cross-cutting issues I wish to place for your consideration on which we should focus so as to strengthen BIMSTEC and make it a viable regional entity.

Firstly, from the experience we have gained, we should undertake a comprehensive review of our activities. We should prepare a blue print for future activities that is focused on a limited number of issues or areas of common priority. These areas should have the maximum potential for producing visible results and strengthen our common vision of the region and of BIMSTEC. We must force the pace of implementation of our projects and ideas.

BIMSTEC is the bridge between South Asia and South East Asia. We all belong to the Bay of Bengal community. Nature and geography have bound us together by land and by water. We should reflect on how best to create opportunities for growth and prosperity centered around the riches of the Bay of Bengal, keeping in mind also the dangers posed by the sea.

Transport infrastructure and logistics would be a key. We need to coordinate on issues of maritime transport such as construction of a deep-water port to service the region, inter-modal connectivity, cooperation among our port authorities and our shipping and logistics networks.We should examine cooperative mechanisms to exploit our marine resources. I am pleased that a BIMSTEC Business Summit was organized yesterday with themes on energy, including hydel power, agri-business including fisheries as well as transportation and connectivity.

The devastating tsunami in 2004 highlighted the imperative need for collective action, and a review of our approach to disaster management.

India has set up a Tsunami Early Warning Centre. We would be happy to extend information exchange and data sharing arrangements to BIMSTEC countries. This could also include training facilities for capacity building.

People to people contacts should certainly be one of our priority overarching goals. The areas of education, tourism and training come to mind. India is already in the process of establishing the Nalanda University as an international university of excellence. We would be happy to have BIMSTEC closely associated with it.

The 300 scholarships that India had offered in 2004 under the ITEC programme for

BIMSTEC countries have had a utilization rate of more than 80%. We would be happy to offer an additional 150 scholarships to encourage greater exchange of technical know-how in areas of mutual benefit.

Each of our countries is an important halt on the tourist map. We already have Buddhist circuits. These can be popularized much more and other innovative packages can be worked out by our tourism boards and jointly promoted.

Lastly, I feel that we should do something visible in the area of trade and economic cooperation as a manifestation of our ability to do something big together. Considerable progress has been made in the negotiations on the BIMSTEC Free Trade Agreement for trade in goods. The early conclusion of such an agreement would be a shining symbol of our cooperation. We also look forward to the next stage of an agreement in the area of investment and services.

The 21st century belongs to Asia. Asia will be the engine of the world economic growth.

BIMSTEC is an important part of the wider Asian community. It has the potential of playing a vital role in the Asian community of nations linked by effective road, rail, air and shipping services across which there would be free movement of people, capital, ideas and goods.

India is firmly committed to the ideals and objectives of BIMSTEC. Our resources are at the disposal of member States.

(*Source*:http://www.bimstec.org/2ndBimstecSummit_pdf/India%20PM%20Opening%20Remarks.pdf)

## Second BIMSTEC Summit, Statement of Dr. Fakhruddin Ahmed, Chief Adviser, Government of the People's Republic of Bangladesh, New Delhi, India,

November 13, 2008

*Dr. Fakhruddin Ahmed, Chief Adviser, Government of the People's Republic of Bangladesh at the second BIMSTEC Summit emphasized that BIMSTEC, was a bridge between the two developing regions of Asia, which epitomized South-South cooperation. He pointed that pertinent challenges like rising food prices, persistent high energy costs, and negative fall-out from climate change were testing the limits of developing countries and that in the coming years poverty alleviation would be prioritized by Bangladesh. He also stated that energy should be another area of priority for BIMSTEC countries and proposed inclusion of climate change as the 14th area of cooperation in BIMSTEC.*

I am truly delighted to be in the historic city of New Delhi for the Second BIMSTEC Summit.

1. We are touched by the warmth of the hospitality accorded to us since our arrival here, for which I would like to thank you in particular and the Government of India in general. I would also like to congratulate you upon your assumption of the Chairmanship of BIMSTEC. I am confident that your experience, wisdom and vision will guide us to a fruitful outcome of this meeting.

2. The Second BIMSTEC Summit is taking place at a defining moment in our history.

BIMSTEC, which bridges the two developing regions of Asia, epitomizes South-South cooperation. We are encouraged by the tremendous opportunities that beckon us today.

Common interests and aspirations of our peoples place us in a unique position to transform the economic and social landscapes of our countries. As a group, we need to be creative and pragmatic in our approach to turn these challenges into tangible opportunities. The 21$^{st}$ century belongs to Asia. But a good deal will depend on how we develop our potential.

3. We are all aware of the growing challenges that our societies are faced with today.

Rising food prices, persistent high energy costs, and negative fall-out from climate change have tested our limits. It is time that we consolidate and forge a stronger alliance to deal with these issues effectively and resolutely.

4. The recent global financial crisis has increased the threat of a deep worldwide recession. A slowdown in foreign direct investment and a

decline in demand for exports from developing countries is a distinct possibility. Concerted and comprehensive global actions are needed to respond to and overcome this crisis. Regionally, increased coordination and consultations amongst our central banks and financial regulators are required. They should continuously monitor and assess the situation and suggest remedial measures.

5. Poverty alleviation is high on our agenda. The development of an Action Plan on Poverty Alleviation as recommended by the First BIMSTEC Poverty Alleviation Ministerial in Dhaka would be a significant step forward in our collective effort in this regard. I am thankful for your support to host the BIMSTEC Poverty Alleviation Centre in Dhaka which will soon be set up. The centre will carry out high-quality research and studies in this vitally important area and provide useful guidance and policy inputs to decision-makers and practitioners.

6. Agricultural Productivity is a critical element in any poverty reduction strategy. The recent rise in food prices has underlined the need for priority attention to food security. While we call for qualitative improvements to the international food trading system based on equity and fair play at the regional level we should also explore ways for increased investment and for the transfer of technology to increase agriculture productivity. We must continue our efforts to address the more systemic challenges to the agriculture sector in the shorter term, we may consider creating an institutional mechanism to maintain a buffer stock of food in the region, similar to a SAARC Food Bank.

7. The high rate of development has enhanced the demand for energy in our countries.

Our developmental efforts will be seriously undermined if we are unable to maintain a steady supply of energy at affordable prices. Cooperation in capacity building, technology transfer and infrastructure development are key in this regard. We must also harness renewable sources of energy such as hydro-power, solar, bio fuel and wind to address the energy needs of the region.

8. The phenomenon of climate change is not a myth but a hard and scientific reality.

Empirical evidence suggests that even a one-metre rise in the sea-level would submerge one fifth of Bangladesh, resulting in an estimated 25 to 30 million people being displaced as “climate refugees”. Other countries in the region would face similar catastrophes. I propose that we include Climate Change as the 14th area of cooperation in BIMSTEC. With your concurrence, Bangladesh would be happy to act as the ‘Lead Shepherd’ in this critical area, if given the task.

9. We have noted that progress has been achieved in the BIMSTEC FTA negotiations, although at a less than ideal pace. I propose that we set

a target date for the BIMSTEC Free Trade Agreement to come into effect. At the same time, tariff reduction and elimination must be accompanied by appropriate measures for the removal of non-tariff barriers to significantly contribute to the growth of intra regional trade.

10. In the one decade of its existence, BIMSTEC has come a long way. Regional cooperation is now expanded to 13 identified areas in economic and social fields. It is time that we make an in-depth review of BIMSTEC. A high-level group of eminent personalities from the region should be constituted to undertake an independent review of the organization and to make specific recommendations to bring greater dynamism to our efforts at regional cooperation.

11. As one of the founding members of BIMSTEC, Bangladesh is deeply committed to its broader objectives and goals. With the growth of the organization, our engagement in BIMSTEC has also increased in depth and dimension over the last one decade. I would like to reiterate Bangladesh's offer to host the Secretariat in Dhaka. It would be our honour to shoulder this responsibility, and I sincerely hope that member states would kindly extend their valuable support to our offer.

12. In this interdependent world, our prosperity and wellbeing depends on our collective and collaborative endeavours. We must chart out a clear roadmap and commit ourselves to effectively follow in through for the 2.2 billion people of this region. A prosperous tomorrow awaits us. The seed of a better future must be sowed today, and nurtured through cooperation and collaboration. Bangladesh remains deeply committed to working collectively to achieve our desired goals of peace and prosperity for our countries and the wellbeing of all our peoples.

(*Source*:http://www.bimstec.org/2ndBimstecSummit_pdf/Bangladesh%20Summit%20Statement.pdf)

## Statement by Nepal's Prime Minister Pushpa Kamal Dahal Prachanda at the Second Summit Meeting of Bay of Bengal Initiative for Multi-Sectoral Technical and Economic Cooperation (BIMSTEC), New Delhi

November 13, 2008

*The Nepalese premier Pushpa Kamal Dahal emphasizing the importance of BIMSTEC stated that aspirations of the people of Nepal for social and economic transformation were logically linked to the promotion of mutually beneficial economic and technical cooperation through regional organizations. He pointed out that as BIMSTEC provides a unique link between South Asia and Southeast Asia, Nepal could get the best of both the regions. He stated that enhanced intra-regional trade would bring about tremendous benefits to the people of the region and that the countries should commit themselves to promote denser economic interactions. The Nepalese premier proposed to host a BIMSTEC Tourism Centre in Nepal.*

It is a great pleasure for me to address the Second Summit of the BIMSTEC in New Delhi. On behalf of the Nepalese Delegation and on my own behalf, may I take this opportunity to convey my deep appreciation to the people and Government of India for making excellent arrangements for the summit.

It is indeed a great honor and privilege for me to address this august Summit as the first Prime Minister of the Republic of Nepal following the historic elections to the Constituent Assembly. You are aware that Nepal has gone through a historic political transformation over the last two and half years. This Government represents the new force for change and the new spirit of the time. It is therefore committed to consolidating peace and institutionalising inclusive democratic polity through a new constitution within the stipulated time frame. We believe that this historic political change in Nepal has also provided us with an opportunity to bring about far reaching and deeper change in the lives of the common people, ensuring equal rights, equal opportunities and inclusive prosperity to all. A logical conclusion of the peace process will therefore herald a new dawn in the country. Our peace process could very well be a reference for others around the world in the days to come.

I believe that following the sweeping political change, the rising hope, expectations and aspirations of the people of Nepal for social and economic transformation, away from the feudalistic structure of the past, is logically linked to the promotion of mutually beneficial economic and technical cooperation through regional organisations. While contributing to compliment the existing bilateral relations, the regional organisations enhance regional synergies through promotion of complementarities. It is in this context that we accord high priority to the principles and activities of BIMSTEC. Its aims and purposes offer us a strong platform where our commonalities and potentials would find a meaningful expression. As BIMSTEC provides a unique link between South Asia and Southeast Asia, we should be able to get the best of both the regions. We should also ensure an optimal use of the vast reservoir of human and natural resources of our vibrant regions. With a dynamic vision and effective program of implementation, we could deepen our cooperation in all the identified areas, while widening the scope of cooperation in the new areas that directly touches on the lives of the people. We must focus our minds on making our organization ever more relevant to the people with innovative thinking in fulfilling their urgent needs and aspirations.

Enhanced intra-regional trade will bring about tremendous benefits to the peoples of our region. Promotion of trade including investment to seize the comparative advantage of various locations of the sub-region is necessary to achieve deeper and wider integration of the BIMSTEC economies. Nepal firmly believes that all Member countries should commit themselves to promote denser economic interactions so that the ongoing negotiations on BIMSTEC- Free Trade Area are concluded and implemented at an early date.

One can hardly overemphasize the importance of the development of all modes of transport and communications in order to promote connectivity and thus create a better synergy and ensure smoother flow of goods, services and people across the region. The BIMSTEC Transport Infrastructure and Logistics Study is one concrete step towards this direction. We need to pursue related projects with due priority.

Persistent and widespread poverty among the masses is one of the major challenges of our region. The rising food prices have further compounded this problem. Given the high potentials of the region, this should not have been the case. The national level endeavors to combat poverty are often constrained by an adverse global environment. The food and energy crises, which are now accompanied by the perils of global financial meltdown, make our task even more daunting. It is therefore imperative to take initiatives at all levels to withstand such crises and implement effective poverty alleviation policies and strategies through mutually beneficial project-based cooperation and other collaboration at the national, regional as well as inter-regional levels. It is with this view in mind that Nepal has offered to host the next ministerial meeting on poverty alleviation in 2009.

Energy has been an issue of intense interest and concern now to every nation as acceleration and sustainability of a higher rate of economic growth largely depends upon its affordable availability. While there is an acute shortage of energy today, the members in the BIMSTEC region possess huge but under utilised natural gas reserves, and similarly huge untapped hydropower. It is therefore high time to focus our attention on the development of hydro-electric projects from regional and sub-regional perspectives. For this, Nepal is ready and eager to invite and encourage investment in its hydro-power projects for regional consumption.

While there is a larger responsibility of the economically advanced countries to redress the problems of global climate change, we could develop a united position to ensure an increased resource and technology flow to enhance our capacity in Clean Development Mechanism. We can initiate cooperation on climate change giving due consideration to the issues of the retreat of the Himalayan glaciers, which is a water tower for so many people living in our region.

Nepal welcomes the finalisation of the text of the BIMSTEC Convention on Combating International Terrorism, Transnational

Organised Crime and Illicit Drug Trafficking and the MOUs to establish three important BIMSTEC centres to give further impetus to our cooperative endeavours. Similarly to enhance people to people contacts within the region and beyond, we propose to host a BIMSTEC Tourism Centre in Nepal. These are concrete steps to deal with the urgent issues affecting all of us in the region.

I feel that in a globalised world the external linkages also play an important role in promoting our common interests. For this purpose, BIMSTEC could give appropriate priority to establish close cooperative ties with other economic blocs and relevant international organisations.

In conclusion, let me reiterate here that South Asia and South East Asia are not only geographically contagious; we share historic connections, common cultural heritage and growing interactions. They are indeed strong foundations upon which we can move ahead resolutely. Looking around the world, we see that regional cooperation has a great future, if it is pursued with a common vision backed up by concrete action. We must make the best use of our potentials with vigor and commitment. Nepal stands ready to play its part for the evolution of a stable, vibrant, and prosperous BIMSTEC region. I am optimistic about our common future and I am confident that the best is yet to come. I take this opportunity to express once again Nepal's solemn commitment to the objectives of BIMSTEC and our earnest desire to see concrete achievements in the days ahead.

(*Source*: http://www.mofa.gov.np/uploads/news/20081116133305.doc)

## Statement by Mr. Mahinda Rajapaksa, President of Sri Lanka at the 2nd BIMSTEC Summit, New Delhi

November 13, 2008

*The Sri Lankan President, Mr Mahinda Rajapakse at the 2nd BIMSTEC Summit, New Delhi stated that Poverty Alleviation should be the key aim of the BIMSTEC countries. He pointed out that as the lead country for BIMSTEC cooperation in technology, Sri Lanka accords highest priority to the BIMSTEC initiatives for the establishment of the Energy Centre and the Trans Power Exchange and Development Project. He also emphasized that the operationalization of the BIMSTEC Free Trade Agreement should be expedited. The President supported the BIMSTEC Convention on Cooperation in Combating International Terrorism, Organized Crime and Illicit Drug trafficking as an important and vital milestone for BIMSTEC countries on counter terrorism.*

On this landmark occasion of the Second BIMSTEC Summit in New Delhi, I express my deep appreciation to His Excellency Dr. Manmohan Singh,

Prime Minister of India and the Government of India for the warm and gracious hospitality extended to me and my delegation and for the excellent Summit arrangements. I felicitate His Excellency the Prime Minister of India on his unanimous election as Chairperson of BIMSTEC.

May I also take this opportunity to congratulate Your Excellency Dr Manmohan Singh, the Government and the people of India on your great achievement of launching the "Chandrayaan". We, as South Asians take pride in this achievement.

I also take this opportunity to acknowledge the continuous and remarkable contribution made by the Government of Thailand, and for having played the role of sheet anchoring the absence of a permanent secretariat during all these years.

This is the first BIMSTEC Summit that I am attending as the President of Sri Lanka. I wish to reiterate my commitment to furthering the objectives of the Grouping. I propose that we meet bi-annually as originally envisaged.

Our Summit is taking place at a time when an international financial crisis, originating in Western capital markets, is sweeping across the world. While the BIMSTEC nations have constructively and prudently engaged in the process of globalization, nevertheless the economic challenges faced by many of our major trading partners, will inevitably have some impact on our own pace of growth.

The situation has therefore made all of us very much aware of the protection that regional self-reliance can afford, against global economic uncertainties. Our host India, with its vast capacity and economic potential can indeed serve as an engine, driving and guiding us to withstand the fallout of the global crisis while ushering prosperity for our region.

Poverty is an issue for not just some countries of our Group, but for a significant part of the world population. The recently concluded Ministerial Meeting on Cooperation in Poverty Alleviation manifests the importance that BIMSTEC attaches to this subject. In addition, the fisheries and agriculture sectors which have great potential for poverty alleviation merit the strongest possible focus by BIMSTEC. The alleviation of poverty forms one of the core objectives of my government. After three years of active implementation, a majority of the proposals contained in the' Mahinda Chintana' which is my election manifesto, have delivered many benefits to my people. A number of poverty alleviation programmes, both direct and indirect, indeed have proved to be success stories, and have empowered the rural people. Sri Lanka will continue to share her experiences in this field with the other Member States, while contributing whole-heartedly to the collective effort against poverty.

Achieving energy security has come to the forefront of the global agenda and has posed a tremendous challenge, particularly to developing countries. Oil prices have increased significantly since 2002, although there has been a decline in the prices in recent weeks.

Our efforts at developing alternate forms of energy such as solar, wind and bio-fuels for domestic consumption and for use by industry must remain paramount. However, we do not support the use of arable land to produce bio fuels to drive cars. As the lead country for BIMSTEC cooperation in Technology, Sri Lanka urges that the highest priority should be assigned to the BIMSTEC initiatives for the establishment of the Energy Centre and the Trans Power Exchange and Development Project.

The promotion of trade among us is an important means for regional development and growth. The operationalization of the BIMSTEC Free Trade Agreement has despite our best efforts been delayed. Nevertheless, we are all looking forward to the timely finalization of an Agreement that provides for all Members equitable benefits. We are pleased that Sri Lanka had been unanimously elected to continue as the Chair of the Trade Negotiating Committee.

It is in our collective interest to pursue initiatives to promote inter and intra-regional tourism. The move to establish a Tourism Information Centre and very importantly, a Tourism Fund is commendable. We should also seriously consider the joint marketing of the BIMSTEC region as one destination.

In this regard, I am pleased to announce that Sri Lanka looks forward to contributing to regional familiarization tour programmes, conducted with the collaboration of fellow Member States. Furthermore, the Sri Lanka Hotel School is ready to extend opportunities for nationals of member states to follow its internationally acclaimed training programmes.

The establishment of the Cultural Industries Observatory in Bhutan is a significant development. I am confident that such measures will contribute immensely to the development of the tourism industry in the region including in pilgrimage tourism.

Sri Lanka wholeheartedly supports the BIMSTEC Convention on Cooperation in Combating International Terrorism, Organized Crime and Illicit Drug Trafficking as an important and vital milestone in our efforts on counter terrorism.

Terrorist groups are able to sustain themselves by illegal fundraising, narcotics and people trafficking, money laundering using international networks, and arms and ammunition smuggling including through the sea routes in the Bay of Bengal. I urge you to consider setting up a mechanism to effectively police the seas of the Bay of Bengal, to deny these terrorists mobility and connectivity.

For over two decades, Sri Lanka has been facing a tremendous challenge to our democratic way of life through the barbaric actions of a terrorist group, the LTTE. There is no doubt that such groups have to be dealt with militarily. At the same time Sri Lanka believes that any underlying causes, exploited by the terrorists in an attempt to seek legitimacy for their operations, should be dealt with politically. I wish to assure this august gathering that we are firmly on the path to apolitical solution. We welcome the consensus on establishing a Secretariat. This will give the necessary institutional strength. Sri Lanka is ready, in a spirit of commitment to the success of the BIMSTEC process, to host the Secretariat in Colombo.

By founding this grouping, we have united in a community of littoral and hinterland states of the Bay of Bengal. Through our efforts in BIMSTEC, we must resolutely ensure that our peoples would be the beneficiaries of a number of freedoms, including most importantly, freedom from the fear of terrorism and freedom from hunger and poverty.

(*Source*: http://www.bimstec.org/2ndBimstecSummit_pdf/Sri%20Lanka%20President%20Statement.pdf)

## Joint Statement of the Tenth BIMSTEC Ministerial Meeting, New Delhi

August 29, 2008

*In the Tenth BIMSTEC Ministerial Meeting held in New Delhi on 29 August 2008, the delegates representing BIMSTEC countries identified thirteen issue areas for mutual cooperation. These included trade and investment, transport and communication, tourism, energy cooperation, technology, fisheries, poverty alleviation, culture, agriculture, counter-terrorism & trans national crimes, environment & disaster management, public health and people–to-people contacts.*

The Tenth BIMSTEC Ministerial Meeting was held in New Delhi, India on 29 August, 2008. The meeting was attended by H.E. Dr. Iftekhar Ahmed Chowdhury, Adviser for Foreign Affairs of the People's Republic of Bangladesh, H.E Lyonpo Ugyen Tshering, Minister for Foreign Affairs, of the Kingdom of Bhutan, H.E. Mr. Pranab Mukherjee, External Affairs Minister of the Republic of India, H.E. U Nyan Win, Minister for Foreign Affairs of the Union of Myanmar, H.E. Mr. Upendra Yadav, Minister for Foreign Affairs of Federal Democratic Republic of Nepal, H.E. Mr. Rohitha Bogollagama, Minister of Foreign Affairs of the Democratic Socialist Republic of Sri Lanka and H.E. Mr. Tej Bunnag, Minister of Foreign Affairs of the Kingdom of Thailand. H.E. Mr. Pranab Mukherjee, External Affairs Minister of India chaired the Meeting. The Meeting approved the Report of the Twelfth Meeting of the Senior Officials held on 28 August 2008.At the conclusion of the Meeting; the Heads of Delegation issued the following Joint Statement.

We, the Heads of Delegation of the Tenth BIMSTEC Ministerial Meeting, having gathered in New Delhi on 29th August, 2008 reiterated our commitment to the founding objectives and principles of BIMSTEC to accelerate economic and social growth in the region and noted with satisfaction the progress made since our last Meeting in New Delhi in August 2006.

We considered it opportune to review activities in the regional cooperation grouping, with BIMSTEC having crossed the landmark of its 10th Anniversary last year. We reviewed the progress made in the various sectors and noted with satisfaction the achievements since the last Meeting.

We reiterated our agreement to pursue cooperation in the following 13 areas identified under the BIMSTEC framework:

**Trade and Investment**

We reaffirmed the importance of realizing a BIMSTEC Free Trade Area for increasing trade and investment, enhancing competitiveness and promoting socio-economic development of BIMSTEC countries. We noted with satisfaction the progress made at meetings of the Trade Negotiating Committee. We reiterated our resolve to conclude the negotiations on trade in goods under the proposed FTA at an early date, preferably before the next BIMSTEC Summit. We noted the progress made at the Experts Group meetings on the BIMSTEC Business Visa Scheme as well as the BIMSTEC Business & Economic Forum during the last two years since the 9th Ministerial Meeting.

**Transport and Communication**

We reaffirmed that optimal transport linkages are necessary for achieving efficient levels in connectivity amongst member countries to promote movement of goods and people.

Accordingly, we recognized the need for development of key infrastructure, including transportation and communication linkages. In this context, we noted with satisfaction the progress made since our last meeting. We complimented the Asian Development Bank which has concluded the mandated study on BIMSTEC Transport Infrastructure and Logistics (BTILS). We noted BTILS including the proposed institutional mechanisms and the terms of reference which are being examined by BIMSTEC member countries.

**Tourism**

We recalled our earlier decision that tourism should be actively encouraged, both intra-BIMSTEC cooperation among member countries as well as from outside the BIMSTEC region. In this context, we expressed satisfaction that considerable progress had been made since our last meeting. We welcomed the 2nd Round Table and Workshop of Tourism

Ministers held in Kathmandu in August 2006 and endorsed the Kathmandu Declaration and the Plan of Action for taking forward tourism related activities in the BIMSTEC framework. We decided to constitute a Tourism Working Group to implement tourism programmes and follow up on the Plan of Action. We welcomed the establishment of the BIMSTEC Information Centre in New Delhi for promoting tourism.

**Energy Cooperation**

We reemphasized the importance of sharing experiences and strengthening cooperation amongst member countries in the fields of grid connectivity, gas pipelines, hydro power, renewable sources of energy, energy efficiency and energy sector reforms, restructuring, regulations and best practices with a view to promoting energy security in the BIMSTEC region. In this context, we welcomed the BIMSTEC meetings and activities during the last two years, and particularly the progress made in realizing the BIMSTEC Energy Centre in India. We approved the Memorandum of Association (MoA) for setting up the BIMSTEC Energy Centre in India and recommended the MoA for signing during the forthcoming BIMSTEC Summit. We expressed the hope that the Energy Centre would be operational as soon as possible.

**Technology**

We reiterated the need to enhance cooperation in advanced areas of fundamental and applied scientific and technological research. We welcomed the progress made since our last meeting including regarding the BIMSTEC Technology Transfer Exchange Facility and expressed the hope that the facility would be realized as soon as possible. We appreciated the progress in the sector including the decision to establish the BIMSTEC Centre for Weather and Climate. We approved the Memorandum of Association (MoA) for setting up a BIMSTEC Centre for Weather and Climate in India and recommended the MOA for signing during the next BIMSTEC Summit.

**Fisheries**

Marine resources through effective conservation and management of the resources in the Bay of Bengal in close coordination with existing frameworks. We welcomed the progress in terms of the Workshop and Joint Survey undertaken during 2007.We reiterated our commitment to continue our efforts to promote the sustainable use of Poverty Alleviation

We welcomed the progress made particularly at the first Ministerial Meeting on Poverty Alleviation held in Dhaka in July 2008 and noted the observations of the Ministerial meeting. We focused on poverty alleviation in the context of ensuring food security in the BIMSTEC region. We noted the proposal of Nepal to prepare a Plan of Action on Poverty Alleviation to be submitted to the second BIMSTEC Ministerial Meeting on Poverty Alleviation to be held in Nepal in 2009. We noted with appreciation the proposal of Bangladesh to host BIMSTEC Poverty Alleviation Centre in Dhaka.

**Culture**

We recalled the Paro Initiative and Plan of Action adopted at the First BIMSTEC Ministerial Meeting on Cultural Cooperation held in Bhutan in May 2006. We welcomed the finalization of the Memorandum of Understanding (MoU) for the establishment of the BIMSTEC Cultural Industries Observatory (BCIO) and BIMSTEC Cultural Industries Commission (BCIC) as the institutional mechanisms to facilitate cooperation in the area of culture. We recommended that the approved MoU be signed during the Second BIMSTEC Summit.

**Agriculture**

We welcomed the progress made during meetings held in the last two years and the wide array of cooperation activities and projects identified at the Expert Group meetings along with lead coordinating country for each. We expressed the hope that these concrete activities and projects would be implemented expeditiously. We felt the need to address the issues relating to agricultural productivity in this regard.

**Counter-Terrorism & Trans National Crimes**

We welcomed and accepted the offer of India to be the lead country. We reiterated the significance of the work done in the Joint Working Group on Counter Terrorism & Transnational Crimes and its four sub-groups covering Intelligence Sharing; Legal and Law Enforcement Issues; Combating the Financing of Terrorism and Prevention of Illicit Trafficking in Narcotic Drugs, Psychotropic Substances and Precursor Chemicals. We expressed the hope that the draft BIMSTEC Convention be finalized as soon as possible for signing during the next BIMSTEC Summit.

**Environment & Disaster Management**

We welcomed the Workshops organised since our last meeting and endorsed the Agenda for Action for effective regional cooperation among BIMSTEC countries prepared by the Workshop on Disaster Risk Reduction and Management in October 2006.

**Public Health**

We welcomed initiatives to host the BIMSTEC meeting on Traditional Medicine and Generic Drugs for the poor and to organise a study visit regarding Avian Influenza Pandemic. We appreciated India's ongoing programme offering 30 'Ayush' scholarships to BIMSTEC students to study traditional medicine.

**People–to-People Contacts**

We expressed appreciation for initiatives to organise various events and activities including to mark the 10th Anniversary of BIMSTEC in Thailand last year to promote people to people contacts and interaction amongst member countries.

al Meeting, on the

We the Heads of Delegation of the BIMSTEC tenth Ministerial Meeting on the recommendation of the 12th BIMSTEC Senior Officials Meeting approved the following.

(a) The Memorandum of Association of BIMSTEC Energy Center in India.
(b) The Memorandum of Understanding of BIMSTEC cultural industries and BIMSTEC Cultural Industries Observatory.
(c) The setting up tourism working group and its terms of references and

The setting up of joint working group to consider all aspects including organizational structure, financing mechanism and staffing of BIMSTEC centers.

Further, We the Heads of Delegation of the tenth BIMSTEC Ministerial Meeting agreed to the following:

**BIMSTEC Centre**

We also thanked Thailand for its continued contribution to the BIMSTEC Centre Particularly its decision to extend the contract of the BIMSTEC Centre for another year.

**BIMSTEC Official Website**

We expressed satisfaction on the improvements made to the BIMSTEC website

www.bimstec.org maintained by Sri Lanka in coordination with BIMSTEC Centre in Bangkok and BWG.

**BIMSTEC Summit**

We noted with satisfaction BIMSTEC achievements thus far and reaffirmed our commitments to further deepening our partnership within the BIMSTEC framework. We expressed confidence that the 2nd BIMSTEC Summit to be hosted by India in November 2008 will carry forward our cooperation activities with renewed dynamism. The 2nd

BIMSTEC Summit will also provide an opportunity to review the achievements since the establishment of BIMSTEC which as a regional cooperation and integration grouping celebrated its 10th Anniversary last year. It will also provide further impetus to BIMSTEC cooperation activities and projects.

(*Source*:http://www.bimstec.org/downloads/mm/Joint%20Statement%20of%20the%2010th%20Ministerial%20statement,%2029%20August%202008,%20New%20Delhi.pdf)

# LIST OF DOCUMENTS

## Afghanistan

**Pakistan**

## SAARC and BIMSTEC